# THE
# ONTARIO GOVERNMENT
## STRUCTURE AND FUNCTIONS

GEORGE G. BELL AND ANDREW D. PASCOE
YORK UNIVERSITY

**WALL & THOMPSON**
TORONTO

Copyright © 1988 by Wall & Thompson, Inc.,
Six O'Connor Drive, Toronto, Ontario, Canada M4K 2K1

**Canadian Cataloguing in Publication Data**

Bell, George G., 1920-
The Ontario government

Includes index.
ISBN 0-921332-00-9

1. Ontario - Politics and government. I. Pascoe,
Andrew D., 1962-    . II. Title.

JL270.B45 1988      320.4713      C88-093555-3

ISBN  0-921332-00-9
Printed in Canada  by John Deyell Company
1  2  3  4  5    92  91  90  89  88

# TABLE OF CONTENTS

**Section 2**
**POLICY DEVELOPMENT AND BUDGETING / 27**

**Section 3**
**THE PUBLIC SERVICE IN ONTARIO / 35**

**ANNEXES / 44**

## PART TWO
## THE MINISTRIES

### Section 4
### ECONOMIC POLICY MINISTRIES / 59

### Section 6
### SOCIAL POLICY MINISTRIES / 235

## Section 7
## GENERAL GOVERNMENT MINISTRIES / 319

# PREFACE

## Introduction

This first edition of *The Ontario Government: Structure and Functions* is intended to fill a major gap in the literature on the structure and functions of government in Ontario. It reflects the significant changes in the structure of the provincial government over the relatively recent past. Its purpose is:

1. To make the structure and functions of the many ministries, agencies, boards, and commissions, etc., more clearly understood and perceived by those with a general, professional or academic interest in the subject; and

2. To provide a ready reference tool for those individuals and institutions, both within and outside the provincial government, where such a reference source would be of functional value to their vocation, field of interest or staff training responsibility.

Although a considerable amount of publicity and program information is available from the various ministries, most officials and academics have had little of a comprehensive nature available to them, except such summary information as is contained in the Government of Ontario *Telephone Directory* and the *KWIC Index to Services*. Recently some scholars have devoted more attention to the study of government and politics in Ontario, but most have focused on areas of special interest and none has produced a basic text on the organization of the Government of Ontario.

## The Organization of this Book

*The Ontario Government: Structure and Functions* is divided into two major parts:

Part One provides an overall description of the system of government in Ontario. It is divided into three sections. The first section describes parliamentary government in Ontario, including the structure and functions of the Executive and Cabinet Committees; the Legislative Assembly, Legislative Committees, Legislative Offices; and the Judiciary. The second section describes the process of public policy development and budgeting. The third section describes the Ontario Public Service, which encompasses the Central Agencies, Central Ministries, and Line Ministries; and the Agencies, Boards, Commissions, and Special Purpose Bodies.

Part Two provides a succinct description of the roles and functions; background history; organization; programs; budget; agencies, boards, and commissions; legislation administered; and selected innovations of each ministry and central agency. This part is divided into four major sections: Economic Policy; Justice; Social Policy; and General Government. Each section groups the ministries and/or central agencies which follow logically with each category, as demonstrated by the structure of the Cabinet Policy Committees. The reader should be aware that this method of sub-dividing the provincial government organization should not be taken as absolute; political emphasis or expediency may cause some changes in groupings and ministry structure related to a change of government or the legislative life of a particular government.

## General Format

All of the chapters in Part Two have been standardized, and available information is presented in the following manner:

1. Legal name of the ministry, agency, secretariat, etc;

2. Description of overall responsibilities;

3. Historical background of department (including name changes);

4. A description of the way in which the department is organized;

5. A description of the programs administered;

6. Most recent expenditure budget;

7. Description of agencies, boards, and commissions reporting through the ministry or agency;

8. List of statutes administered with a brief description of purpose; and,

9. Innovations (where appropriate).

## Acknowledgements

It would not have been possible to assemble the necessary information and to coordinate and produce this first edition of *The Ontario Government: Structure and Functions* without the fullest cooperation of all ministries and central agencies (particularly the staff of the Communications Branches), which is greatly appreciated. Special acknowledgement and thanks go to the Management Policy Division of Management Board Secretariat for their support in the development and publication of this book, and especially to Barry Gardiner, Director of the Policy Development and Administration Branch, for his direction and guidance and for his efforts in coordinating the information gathering and assembly process. Special thanks as well to Shirley Lobraico for her assistance in creating the ministry organization charts and for her efforts in monitoring the inflow of material from each ministry.

Acknowledgement also goes to the Faculty of Administrative Studies, York University, for their provision of resources for research assistance and computing, and most especially to Gisela Birmingham, whose personal contributions to the assembly, word processing, and administrative management of this project ensured its effective completion. Finally, special thanks to Byron Wall and Keith Thompson, for their creative input, technical expertise and tireless efforts in the final editing and production of this book.

## Communications

The currency and accuracy of annual revisions and future editions will depend on an effective two-way process. Therefore, all suggestions and comments as to how to improve *The Ontario Government: Structure and Functions* will be welcomed by: Professor George G. Bell, Faculty of Administrative Studies, York University, 4700 Keele Street, North York, Ontario M3J 1P3.

GGB
ADP

# Part One
# THE SYSTEM OF GOVERNMENT IN ONTARIO

# Section 1
# PARLIAMENT IN ONTARIO

Ontario has enjoyed responsible government for over one hundred and fifty years. Today, parliamentary government in the province encompasses three major areas of responsibility: Executive, Legislative, and Judicial.

"Parliament" in Ontario refers to the "formal" executive (the Lieutenant Governor), the "political" executive (the Premier and Cabinet Ministers), the Legislative Assembly and its offices, and the system of judicial courts which exist to settle legal disputes.

In Canada, the distribution of legislative powers between the federal and provincial governments is set out in Sections 91 and 92 of the *British North America Act, 1867,* and the *Constitution Act, 1982.* The limitations and restrictions on the powers of the federal government and the provinces are set out in judicial decisions of the United Kingdom Privy Council prior to 1949 and the Supreme Court of Canada since 1949. (A detailed discussion of the latter may be found in J.R. Mallory, *The Structure of Canadian Government,* 1984, chapters nine and ten.) The Meech Lake agreement between the federal and provincial governments and subsequent constitutional discussions will result in further definition of their respective powers.

This Section of the book describes the structure and functions of the three divisions of Parliament in Ontario: the Executive, which formulates government policy and oversees the public service in the administration of government programs; the Legislature, which enacts, amends, and repeals legislation, authorizes the collection and expenditure of funds, and debates the policies put forth by the Government; and the Judiciary, which adjudicates civil and criminal disputes in the province.

# THE LIEUTENANT GOVERNOR AND THE EXECUTIVE

## THE LIEUTENANT GOVERNOR

The Queen of Canada is the official Head of State. The Lieutenant Governor is the nominal Head of State at the provincial level, empowered with the responsibility of representing the Sovereign in the province. The real power of governing, however, resides with the Premier and the Executive Council, the elected Members of Provincial Parliament who are appointed as Ministers of the Crown by the Lieutenant Governor on the recommendation of the Premier.

The Lieutenant Governor of Ontario is appointed by the Queen on the recommendation of the Prime Minister of Canada. The document of appointment is signed by the Governor General on behalf of the Queen. The appointment, by tradition, is for a period of five years—or "at the pleasure of the Crown"—and carries the title of "The Honourable" for life. In conversation and correspondence the Lieutenant Governor is addressed as "Your Honour," as is his or her spouse.

The Lieutenant Governor serves in a dual capacity; first as representative of the Sovereign for all purposes of the provincial Government, and second, as a federal officer in discharging certain functions of the Sovereign. The Lieutenant Governor, as Head of State, opens, prorogues (closes), and can dissolve the Legislature. The Lieutenant Governor is responsible for swearing in the Premier and Cabinet Ministers and must ensure that a Government is in office at all times.

The Lieutenant Governor also has the discretionary authority: to select the Premier, for example in the event of the death of the holder of that office; to refuse a request by the Premier for dissolution of the Legislature; or to ignore the advice of the incumbent Premier and Cabinet. The Lieutenant Governor also has the authority to dismiss a Government. Given that much of the Lieutenant Governor's authority is symbolic and ceremonial in nature, such occurrences are rare. The Chief Justice of Ontario acts for the Lieutenant Governor when the latter is unable to do so. One or the other must be in the province at all times.

The Lieutenant Governor must sign (give "Royal Assent" to) all Bills passed by the Legislature before they can become law. The Lieutenant Governor also signs proclamations and appointments of persons to government posts, including provincial judges, crown attorneys, justices of the peace, and commissioners. A major responsibility of the Lieutenant Governor is to deliver the Speech from the Throne at the opening of a new session of Legislature, which outlines proposed legislation to be introduced in the forthcoming session.

In addition to formal duties, the Lieutenant Governor engages in a large number of discretionary, but traditional, activities, such as becoming honorary patron to volunteer organizations, sponsoring awards, receiving dignitaries, sending messages of congratulations or condolence, presenting citations, and participating in investitures, dedications, and other major events. The Lieutenant Governor holds receptions, luncheons, and dinners for guests of various occupations, organizations, and professions; receives members of the Royal Family, heads of state, ambassadors, consuls, and other representations of foreign countries; attends religious, cultural, educational, and recreational events; and visits hospitals, senior citizens homes, centres for the disabled, and other public institutions. The Lieutenant Governor is supported in his role by a staff of five in the Office of the Lieutenant Governor.

### 1987–88 Expenditure Estimate:

Office of the Lieutenant Governor: $416,000.00

## THE PREMIER AND OFFICE OF THE PREMIER

*The Premier of Ontario* is the leader of the governing political party. He or she is the First Minister of Cabinet and President of the Executive Council, the chief Government spokesperson in the Legislative Assembly, and an elected representative of a specific constituency. The Premier makes formal recommendations to the Lieutenant Governor on the appointment of Cabinet ministers, approves the appointment of deputy ministers, and initiates the "Order-in-Council" appointment (Cabinet approval on behalf of the Lieutenant Governor) of approximately one-third of the members of the governing bodies of provincial Crown corporations, agencies, boards, and commissions. The Premier determines the portfolio structure of the Government and the organization of the Cabinet. He or she is the ultimate authority on government policy and the principal advisor to the Lieutenant Governor.

*The Office of the Premier* is primarily concerned with supporting the Premier as the leader of the Government and as the elected representative of his or her constituents. A functional relationship is maintained between the Premier's Office and Cabinet Office, which supports the Premier as head of the Cabinet. The Premier is supported by two senior staff members of deputy minister rank: a Principal Secretary, who heads up the functions associated with the development and communication of government policy, and an Executive Director, who provides leadership in administrative and appointment matters. Under Premier William Davis, the Premier's Office was headed by a Deputy Minister, Office of the Premier, assisted by an Executive Director. Dr. Edward Stewart, the Deputy Minister, was also "double-hatted" as Secretary of Cabinet. Under Premier David Peterson, the position of Secretary of Cabinet has been separated from the Premier's Office. The staff of the Office of the Premier, numbering approximately forty, are hired on personal service contracts to provide partisan political advice and administrative support.

*Figure 1*
**CABINET OFFICE**

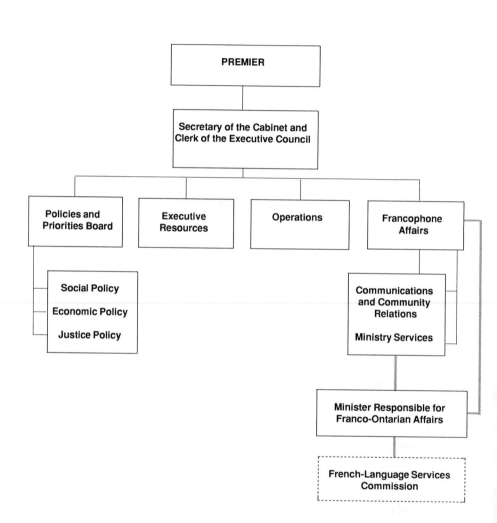

They are not public servants.

The principal *advisory* functions of the Office of the Premier are: to provide the political policy link between the Premier, all Ministers and ministries, and the major policy committees of Cabinet; to coordinate Government processes consequent to the establishment of policy; to provide input to the Government's legislative program, long-term strategy, and priorities; and, to coordinate the political processes of the Office, and develop the Lieutenant Governor's Speech from the Throne.

The principal *service* functions of the Office of the Premier are: to budget the Premier's time, schedule and complete travelling arrangements; to maintain relations with the communications media, write speeches and statements; to brief the Premier daily on legislative matters; to receive, record, and reply to correspondence; to handle invitations and appointment requests; to assist with constituency matters; to maintain liaison with caucus members; to deal with inquiries from the public and from special interest groups; and to receive delegations and unscheduled visitors.

### 1987–88 Expenditure Estimate:

Office of the Premier:                    $1,977,731.00

## CABINET AND CABINET OFFICE

*Cabinet* is the focal point for decision-making in the Ontario Government, in that it is responsible for initiating, approving, and executing Government policy. Cabinet exists in law as the Executive Council of the Province of Ontario. All ministers are members of Cabinet. The Premier or a designated Minister may serve as chairman of Cabinet. Currently, Cabinet meetings are held every Wednesday.

Cabinet is based on long-standing constitutional convention. As the executive decision-making authority of the Government, Cabinet reflects the notion of responsible government. That is, its members are ultimately accountable to the Legislature and the people of Ontario for the policy, programs, and administration of Government. Cabinet decision-making is by consensus and its documents and deliberations are secret. Ideally, Cabinet membership is structured to reflect the cultural and demographic makeup and regional nature of Ontario society.

Cabinet attempts to set the broad direction and priorities of the Government, decide the content of the Speech from the Throne, and coordinate the Government's legislative program for each session. It also makes decisions on budget and manpower allocations each fiscal year. By its very nature, Cabinet is linked to all ministries and central agencies of Government. Cabinet is supported in its administrative role by several standing and special purpose committees, which bring together matters of policy and administrative concerns at the highest level of decision-making in the Government.

Cabinet size has fluctuated in recent years. For example, one of the major changes to the structure of Cabinet made by Premier Frank Miller in 1985 was to increase its size from 28 under Premier William Davis to 33 members, with the appointment of seven ministers "without portfolio." This position, much like a federal Minister of State, is designed to fill a special political need, serve as a training ground for future Ministers, or to give extra support to a Minister with major administrative responsibilities and a heavy work load. Conversely, in 1985, Premier David Peterson contracted the size of Cabinet to 21 members by eliminating the Provincial Secretariats for Resource Development, Justice, and Social Development, which had headed the three policy fields from 1972 to 1985, and assigning the responsibilities for chairing the Cabinet Committees for Economic Policy, Justice, and Social Policy to three line ministers in addition to their assigned ministerial responsibilities. He also combined several portfolios under selected ministers. After winning a large electoral majority in the 1987 election, Premier Peterson increased the size of Cabinet to 30 members, but continued the practice of "double-hatting" in filling the chair positions for the three Cabinet policy committees.

*Cabinet Office* is the central agency which provides administrative services and policy analysis for Cabinet and its Committees. Cabinet Office is headed by the Secretary of the Cabinet, who also carries the title of Clerk of the Executive Council. The Office has two main divisions (see *Figure 1*): a Policy Section, under the Secretary of the Policy and Priorities Board, and an Operations Section under the Associate Secretary of Cabinet for Operations. In addition, the Associate Secretary of Cabinet for Executive Resources (who reports to the Premier) and the Executive Director for Francophone Affairs (who reports to the Minister Responsible for Francophone Affairs) are situated within Cabinet Office. Cabinet Office personnel, numbering approximately 100, are all public servants.

The *policy* functions of Cabinet Office are: to undertake expenditure reviews, coordinate the allocation process, and assist the Ministry of Treasury and Economics and Management Board of Cabinet in developing the annual expenditure allocations among the ministries; to review legislative proposals and decisions and draft the Government's legislative program in consultation with the Government House Leader and individual ministers; to assist in the preparation of the Speech from the Throne and the Prorogation Speech; to make briefing arrangements for the Premier, for Cabinet, and Policy and Priorities Board meetings; to analyze submissions, brief Cabinet committee chairmen, prepare the agenda for each committee meeting, and prepare committee reports and recommendations to full Cabinet for policy and ad hoc committees; to coordinate and manage the Government's policy priorities process and large cross-Cabinet issues; and to provide staff support to the Policy and Priorities Board and the Cabinet Committees on Economic Policy, Justice, and Social Policy.

The *operational* functions of Cabinet Office are: to arrange Cabinet and Cabinet committee meetings, to prepare agenda, record discussions and prepare and distribute minutes of meetings, to provide document service for Cabinet, to research and retrieve information for ministries, to monitor implementation of political commitments, to make arrangements for delegations to Cabinet, to organize ceremonial activities such as swearing-in procedures for change of Government or minister(s), and to provide liaison with the Lieutenant Governor, the Speaker, the Clerk of the

House, the Government House Leader, the Board of Internal Economy, Management Board of Cabinet, and the Ministry of Treasury and Economics.

### 1987–1988 Expenditure Estimates:

Cabinet Office: $8,657,400.00

## Cabinet Committees

The Ontario Cabinet system has evolved from a plenary-style, decision-making body to one where the focus of policy development rests with a number of powerful Cabinet committees. (See *Figure 2*.) This development can be traced to the recommendations of the Committee on Government Productivity (COGP) report of 1972, a watershed review of the structure and operations of the Government of Ontario. COGP foresaw that the growing volume and complexity of policy issues would become unmanageable for any single body of Ministers. A more specialized and accountable system of issues management was considered necessary for the future. It therefore recommended a restructuring of Cabinet and the establishment of several Cabinet Committees. Formally, a Cabinet committee does not make final decisions on policy issues. Instead, it makes recommendations to full Cabinet. Nonetheless, the role of the latter has become, essentially, one of ratification of these recommendations with a minimum of debate, and with the occasional need to resolve policy disputes that cannot be settled at the committee level. This evolution reflects the COGP's perceived need to improve the efficiency of the decision-making process within the political executive.

Cabinet submissions normally originate within the staff of a ministry in response to a public concern or a policy initiative of the Government, and are placed before Cabinet by the responsible minister after scrutinization and deliberation by any number of committees (see "The Public Policy Development Process" below). There are two types of Cabinet committees: standing and ad hoc. The former meet regularly and have an ongoing mandate to examine a well-defined set of policy issues. The latter meet periodically to deal with special or unique issues and are disbanded when the problem is resolved.

The standing Cabinet committees include: the Policy and Priorities Board; the Management Board of Cabinet; the Legislation Committee; the Regulations Committee; the Cabinet Committees of Economic Policy, Justice, and Social Policy; as well as other standing committees with more specific mandates.

### Policy and Priorities Board

The Policy and Priorities Board is the powerful "inner Cabinet." This committee's purpose is to develop, review, coordinate, and advise on policy and priorities relating to the social and economic needs of the province as reflected by the Government's short- and long-term goals. The "P & P Board" also studies general budgetary and fiscal policy and priorities, including expenditure and transfer payment programs and recommendations submitted by the Cabinet policy com-

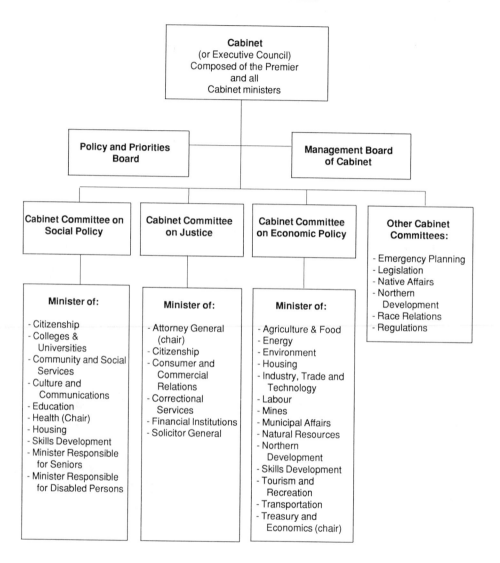

**Figure 2**
**CABINET AND ITS COMMITTEES**

**Cabinet**
(or Executive Council)
Composed of the Premier
and all
Cabinet ministers

**Policy and Priorities Board**

**Management Board of Cabinet**

**Cabinet Committee on Social Policy**

**Cabinet Committee on Justice**

**Cabinet Committee on Economic Policy**

**Other Cabinet Committees:**

- Emergency Planning
- Legislation
- Native Affairs
- Northern Development
- Race Relations
- Regulations

**Minister of:**

- Citizenship
- Colleges & Universities
- Community and Social Services
- Culture and Communications
- Education
- Health (Chair)
- Housing
- Skills Development
- Minister Responsible for Seniors
- Minister Responsible for Disabled Persons

**Minister of:**

- Attorney General (chair)
- Citizenship
- Consumer and Commercial Relations
- Correctional Services
- Financial Institutions
- Solicitor General

**Minister of:**

- Agriculture & Food
- Energy
- Environment
- Housing
- Industry, Trade and Technology
- Labour
- Mines
- Municipal Affairs
- Natural Resources
- Northern Development
- Skills Development
- Tourism and Recreation
- Transportation
- Treasury and Economics (chair)

mittees. The P & P Board oversees the coordination of government-wide issues and projects and attempts to resolve issues that cross governmental, ministerial, or policy committee boundaries. Like other Cabinet committees, with the exception of Management Board of Cabinet, the P & P Board does not make decisions on policy, but recommends courses of action to full Cabinet.

The Board is chaired by the Premier; other members traditionally include the Deputy Premier (if applicable), the Chairman of Management Board of Cabinet, the Treasurer, and four or five other influential ministers. In the Government of Premier William Davis, the Provincial Secretaries of the Resource Development, Justice, and Social Development policy fields, and the Minister of Intergovernmental Affairs, also sat on the P & P Board. Premier Frank Miller increased the size of the P & P Board to eleven, but excluded the Provincial Secretaries. The composition of the P & P Board under Premier David Peterson includes eight portfolios (see *Annex F* below): the three Chairmen of the Cabinet policy committees—the Deputy Premier (who is also the Minister of Treasury and Economics and the Minister of Financial Institutions), the Minister of Health, and the Attorney General—along with the Chairman of Management Board, the Government House Leader (who is also the Minister of Mines), the Minister of the Environment, the Minister of Housing, and the Minister of Northern Development. The P & P Board usually meets once a week.

The P & P Board, through its membership, links all the central agencies that have responsibilities for policy development and administration. The Board is a final policy review body for most major policy issues prior to full Cabinet consideration. The Board often refers items to Management Board for consideration of financial, manpower, and administrative implications. The P & P Board is served by the Committee of Advisors (consisting of the Deputy Ministers of the member ministries) and a small secretariat of senior civil servants in Cabinet Office. The Committee of Advisors meets before each Board meeting to review and discuss agenda items and to review ministry submissions to be presented at the meeting.

### Management Board of Cabinet

Management Board of Cabinet is a key standing committee of Cabinet, concerned with the efficient and effective utilization of public resources. It performs the overall general management function for the Ontario Government on behalf of Cabinet. "Management Board" has four main duties:

1. Managing expenditures by participating in the Government's annual resource allocation exercise;

2. Ensuring probity, prudence, efficiency, and integrity in the conduct of Government business;

3. Establishing overall management, technological, and administrative policies; and

4. Fulfilling the role of "employer" for the Government in collective bargaining with its employees.

Membership on Management Board varies. It usually consists of a Chairman (a Cabinet minister responsible for Management Board), a Vice-Chairman (currently the Deputy Premier, who is also the Minister of Treasury and Economics and the Minister of Financial Institutions), and several other ministers (currently the Ministers of Citizenship, Energy, Environment, and Government Services, the Solicitor General, and the Minister without Portfolio for Senior Citizens'Affairs). The Chairman is traditionally a member of the Policy and Priorities Board. Unlike other Cabinet committees, Management Board can make decisions on resource allocations without approval by full Cabinet, although it may be vetoed.  As a rule, Management Board meets once a week, on Tuesday.

The activities of Management Board are supported by two central agencies and a regulatory body: Management Board Secretariat, the Human Resources Secretariat, and the Civil Service Commission (see "Public Service," below).

### Legislation Committee

Before receiving final approval from full Cabinet for introduction in the Legislature, Government bills are examined by the Legislation Committee to ensure internal consistency and conformity with Government policy. This Committee also considers the relative priority of bills in terms of the Government's overall legislative program, and reviews private members' bills, motions, and petitions to Cabinet. This Committee currently has seven members: The Attorney General (Chairman); the Government House Leader (who is also the Minister of Mines); the Ministers of Community and Social Services; Industry, Trade and Technology; Municipal Affairs; and Transportation; and the Minister without Portfolio for Disabled Persons. The Committee meets approximately every two weeks.

### Regulations Committee

The Regulations Committee reviews all regulations which require the approval of the Lieutenant Governor in Council prior to concurrence by Cabinet and submission to the Lieutenant Governor for signature. The composition of this Committee has varied over time to include only Cabinet ministers, or only parliamentary assistants, or a combination of ministers and parliamentary assistants, or a combination of Cabinet ministers and Members of Provincial Parliament. Currently chaired by the Minister of Labour, it includes the Minister of Consumer and Commercial Relations and seven MPPs. The Committee meets most Mondays.

### Cabinet Committees on Economic Policy, Justice, and Social Policy

These committees are responsible for the review and consideration of policy issues and proposals before they are submitted to the Policy and Priorities Board, full

Cabinet or other Cabinet committees. They identify policy issues and coordinate inter-ministerial and intergovernmental activity to ensure appropriate policy and program development within their areas of responsibility. The policy committees meet approximately every other week. They are supported by small secretariats in Cabinet Office which assist with policy development and coordination and liaison within and among the three committees. Although matters before the policy committees can be referred to key central agencies for evaluation, senior representatives from the Ministry of Treasury and Economics, Ministry of Intergovernmental Affairs and Management Board Secretariat attend the meetings of these committees, in order to monitor policy development and offer assessments of intra-provincial or federal-provincial policy ramifications, budgetary or taxation implications, and administrative issues.

*Other Standing Committees*

Other standing committees are concerned with specific issues, and are established by the Premier and Cabinet in order to address an emerging policy issue. They oversee policy development in areas that may not be covered in the mandate of a particular ministry, or which transcend either ministerial boundaries or the boundaries of federal and provincial governments. These include the Committee on Emergency Planning, the Committee on Native Affairs, the Committee on Northern Development, and the Committee on Race Relations.

*Committee on Emergency Planning:* Attempts to coordinate governmental efforts in dealing with emergency situations (e.g. a provincial security problem). It is chaired by the Solicitor General, whose ministry is responsible for emergency planning in the province. The Committee includes 12 ministers. In 1985, Ontario signed a memorandum of understanding with the federal government that ensures federal assistance, when requested by the province, during peacetime emergencies.

*Committee on Native Affairs:* Coordinates the Government's position for all matters involving native people in Ontario and for all dealings with other governments and organizations in this area. The Committee is chaired by the Attorney General and includes 14 ministers. A Secretariat for Native Affairs is attached to the Ministry of the Attorney General.

*Committee on Northern Development:* Coordinates the Government's position on all matters involving Northern Ontario, and reviews the impact of Government policies and programs that affect Northern Ontario. The Committee is chaired by the Minister of Northern Development and includes 13 ministers.

*Committee on Race Relations:* Coordinates the Government's policies on all matters involving race relations, and receives reports from the race relations program commissioner in the Ontario Human Rights Commission. The Committee is chaired by the Minister of Citizenship and includes 11 ministers.

*Ad Hoc Committees*

Ad hoc Cabinet committees are created to deal with special issues, and are dissolved when the solution to a problem is reached. There are no ad hoc Cabinet committees at present, but recent examples include the committees on Municipal Assessment Taxation and Grants, on Manpower, and the Ontario Bicentennial Commission.

# THE LEGISLATURE: ASSEMBLY, COMMITTEES AND OFFICES

## Legislative Assembly

In a parliamentary system, the general role of the legislative branch is to refine and legitimize major government policies and proposals for expenditure and taxation, to audit and critique government actions and hold the government accountable, to constitute a representation of the province's political, economic, and social interests, and to form a focal point for debate of society's major issues. In contrast with the federal bicameral system (House of Commons and Senate), Ontario and the other provinces have unicameral parliaments. The Legislative Assembly in Ontario (see *Figure 3*) consists of 130 Members of Provincial Parliament("MPPs"), elected from 130 electoral districts, for a period of no longer than five years. The Speaker of the Assembly, an MPP from the Government party, who is appointed by the Legislature, is the presiding officer, and is responsible for the policy and operations of the Legislature.

### Structure

The "Government" is formed by the political party able to elect or obtain the support of a majority of the representatives to the Assembly. By custom and tradition, the leader of the majority party normally becomes Premier.

In certain circumstances where the party winning the election does not have a clear majority, the opposition parties may combine to form a coalition government or develop through collusion an "accord" whereby one of the opposition parties agrees under a set of negotiated conditions to support a minority government formed by the other opposition party, rather than allowing the party which gained the most seats in the election to govern. This rare phenomenon occurred in 1985, allowing the Liberal party under David Peterson to form the Government.

The Premier selects Cabinet ministers, the most influential group of MPPs, from his or her "caucus" (those party members elected to the Legislative Assembly). The Lieutenant Governor formally appoints Ministers to the Cabinet. The next tier in the Government hierarchy comprises the members who act as "Parliamentary Assistants" to cabinet ministers. As these members fill in when their Cabinet ministers are absent from the House, they must be able to answer for the policies and programs of their ministry. The remaining members of the Government caucus are the "Backbenchers." These members have less direct influence. Nonetheless,

**Figure 3**
**THE ONTARIO LEGISLATURE**

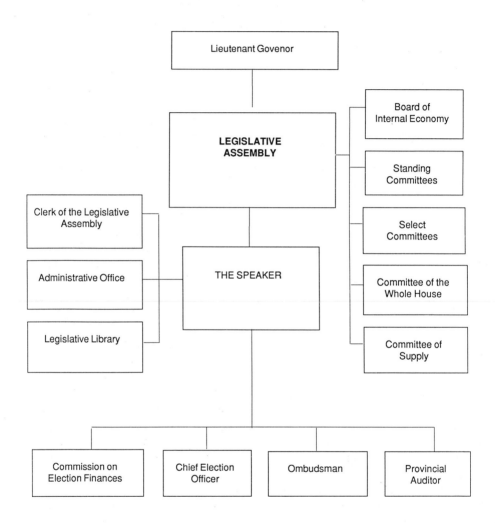

through chairmanships of and participation in Legislative committees, these individuals can have a significant impact on Government legislation and resolutions. They also can make input to Government deliberations through discussion in caucus.

The Opposition side is made up of the "Official Opposition" (the party with the second highest number of seats), and the third party in the Ontario political system. At the top of the hierarchy within each of these two groups is the party leader; then a "Shadow Cabinet," consisting of critics of various Government portfolios; then the backbenchers. Opposition MPPs are primarily responsible for ensuring accountability of the Government, exercised through participation in House debate, written questions, Question Period, and Legislative committees.

House leaders and party whips are members of each of the three caucuses—Government, Opposition, and third party. They are responsible for coordinating and executing the strategy and tactics of their party with respect to passage of bills, legislative agenda, and debate in the Legislature. When the House is in session, the three House leaders and three party whips meet weekly to determine the agenda for the next week. This coordinating activity is based on the legislative program reflected in a report from the meetings of the Legislative Committee of Cabinet and is led by the Government House Leader.

*Sessions*

Each annual session of the Legislature is opened by the Lieutenant Governor, who reads the Speech from the Throne, which is a document prepared by Cabinet Office within the parameters identified by the Premier and Cabinet. The Throne Speech states the Government's political philosophy, policy proposals, and legislative program for the new session. There are times when sessions of the Legislature, generally scheduled for March to June and October to December, run longer than scheduled. This is particularly true at Budget time or during debates on major policy issues, when discussion may spill over into periods when the House is normally in recess. Each session of the Legislature is closed by the Lieutenant Governor's Prorogation Speech.

*Legislative Process*

There are several steps involved in passing a bill into law. At "first reading" there is no debate or vote: the Minister introducing the bill makes an explanatory statement, and background information is distributed. At "second reading" the general principles of the bill are debated in the House. A vote may be taken at second reading to pass or kill a piece of legislation, or it may be passed on to the "Committee of the Whole House" (see below) or to a standing committee for refinement. In the former, minor amendments to the bill may be made during a clause-by-clause examination, without direct public input. In contrast, Legislative committees allow for appearances by public interest groups and concerned citizens. On average, forty percent of Government bills are sent to a Legislative committee for refining after second reading. Finally, after either a second reading vote or examination by the Committee of the Whole House and/or a standing committee, the bill gets "third reading," and may then be passed on to the Lieutenant Governor for signing. Such "Royal Assent" commonly takes place immediately after third reading, but in some cases proclamation may be delayed. Upon "Royal Assent", the bill becomes law. (See *Figure 5*, the Policy Implementation Approval Process flow chart.)

The Legislature deals with three types of legislation. The most important are Government or public bills, which encompass major Government policy proposals, spending or tax measures, and routine governing items, and are introduced by a Cabinet minister. Secondly, the Legislature may examine certain "private members' public bills." These are usually proposals to amend public statutes, put forth by a private member, not a minister. As they have not received Cabinet sanction, such bills cannot involve the spending or taxing of money. They are rarely introduced and even more infrequently passed; many never make it to first reading. Of those that do, most get left on the order paper when a session dissolves, because they do not carry enough priority to become Government policy. The best private members' bills usually become Government bills, and are therefore more likely to pass into law. The final type of legislation is the private bill, which can be introduced by any MPP. These bills concern the activities and interests of a particular group, corporation, profession, or municipality. They are generally considered to be non-controversial, and almost always pass into law.

## Legislative Committees

Legislative Committees are an important feature of the legislative process, and are essential to the conduct of business in the Legislature. In Ontario, there are several types of Legislative Committees which review legislation, scrutinize budget estimates, and undertake special studies or investigations: The Board of Internal Economy, Standing Committees of the Legislature, and Select Committees. Two other Legislative "Committees") refer to the whole Legislative Assembly when it is engaged in certain committee-like functions. These are the Committee of the Whole House and the Committee of Supply.

*The Board of Internal Economy:* A permanent committee, the Board was created under the *Legislative Assembly Act*. The Board is responsible for the approval and management of the budgets of the Legislative Assembly and its Committees and Offices, as well as approval for the organization and staff establishment of the Offices of the Legislature. The Board is composed of seven members: a Chairman (The Speaker of the House), three Cabinet ministers, and one member each from the Government, the Opposition, and the third party. The Board meets approximately every three weeks when the House is in session.

*Standing Committees of the Legislature:* These are bodies crucial to the performance of the Legislature's policy development and accountability roles. These Committees, composed of Members drawn from each political party and chaired by a Government MPP (except Public Accounts), are created and given areas of jurisdiction at the beginning of each Session. Standing committees meet according to a set schedule, from one to three times a week, as long as the Legislature is in session, and report to the House on matters referred to them. Standing committees are automatically terminated at the end of each Session. At present there are four major standing committees in the Legislature: Administration of Justice, Resources Development, Social Development, and General Government. Other minor standing committees include Public Accounts, Legislative Assembly, Government Agencies, Finance and Economic Affairs, Regulations and Private Bills, and Ombudsman.

*Select Committees:* These are non-permanent, ad hoc bodies set up to examine or investigate particular issues. Once the task is complete, select committees report to the House, and are dissolved. Recent examples include the Select Committee on Retail Store Hours and the Select Committee on Constitutional Reform.

*Committee of the Whole House:* This is the term used to refer to the Legislative Assembly when it sits in the Legislative Chamber to debate certain issues, such as a clause-by-clause examination of a piece of legislation after second reading, or bills arising out of the Budget. All MPPs are members of the "Committee of the Whole." The Deputy Speaker takes the chair when the Committee of the Whole House is in session, and, generally, the rules of procedure are more relaxed.

*Committee of Supply:* This is the term used to refer to the Committee of the Whole House when it is considering the "Estimates"--the annual expenditure budgets of the ministries and central agencies of the government.

Membership in standing and select committees is, ideally, proportional to party standings in the Legislature. Ministers are never members of Legislative committees. Meetings of Legislative committees are generally informal; they are open to the public and the press, and presence of MPPs from all parties is an implicit requirement for any meeting. This can create problems when the composition of the House is in imbalance, as minority parties may find it difficult to contribute adequately to all committee meetings. Under these circumstances, parties with a limited number of MPPs usually find it necessary to assign a member to more than one committee, and to provide for alternates.

## Offices of the Legislative Assembly

There are a number of offices and positions unique to the legislative branch of the government that are crucial to its operation. The offices of the Legislative Assembly (see *Figure 3*) include: Speaker of the Legislative Assembly, Clerk of the Legislative Assembly, Legislative Assembly Administration Office, Office of the Chief Election Officer, Commission on Election Finances, Legislative Library, Office of the Ombudsman, and Office of the Provincial Auditor.

## Speaker of the Legislative Assembly

A member of the Government caucus, the Speaker is elected by the Assembly in its first meeting after a general election to preside over its meetings, adjudicate, and enforce parliamentary procedures and rules ("standing orders"). The Speaker, in essence a Minister responsible for the policy and operations of the Legislature, is responsible under the *Legislative Assembly Act, 1974* for the Office of the Clerk of the Legislative Assembly, the Legislative Assembly Administration Office, and the other major offices of the Legislature listed below. The Speaker has traditionally been nominated and acclaimed by the Legislative Assembly through an understanding between the Premier and the Leader of the Opposition.

## Clerk of the Legislative Assembly

A public servant of deputy minister status, the Clerk advises the Speaker and members of the Legislature on questions of procedure and interpretation of rules and practices of the House. The Clerk is supported by the Office of the Clerk of the Legislative Assembly, which coordinates daily publication of the Orders and Notices, Votes and Proceedings, and Daily Business papers. These documents contain matters before the House, and are the official records of the activities of the Legislature. The Office of the Clerk provides record-keeping services for the Legislature and for Legislative committees, ensures the safekeeping of such papers and records, and handles public enquiries concerning the status of legislation, parliamentary procedure, and issues pertaining to standing and select committees.

## Legislative Assembly Administration Office

The Administration Office provides personnel and associated administrative services for each MPP and his or her staff, the three party caucus offices, MPP constituency offices, and other offices of the Legislative Assembly. Branches of the Administration Office include:

*Finance Branch* provides administrative support, purchasing, supply management, printing, accounting, payroll, and the coordination of constituency offices.

*Human Resources Branch* provides personnel services for the Legislative Assembly, Legislative offices, and MPPs. The 276 staff of the Legislature are employees of the Legislative Assembly. They are not public servants, nor are they unionized.

*Information Services Branch* coordinates the Members Office Automation/Networking System, the Parliamentary Public Relations Office (which provides public tours, information, and interpretation services), and the Ontario Legislative Television Service.

*Hansard Reporting Service* covers the sittings of the Legislative Assembly and committees, and publishes an official report, *Hansard*, which is distributed to all MPPs and most libraries.

*Office of the Chief Election Officer*

This Office conducts provincial elections under the *Ontario Election Act*. The Office coordinates the appointment, training, and payment of Returning Officers and other election officials, reports election returns, and arranges the rental, equipment, and supply of the polling stations in the 130 electoral districts during an election. The Office maintains an index of provincial election districts by street name and number, and publishes historical information on elections, Legislatures, Cabinets, and political candidates.

*Commission on Election Finances*

This Commission administers the *Election Finances Act, 1986*, which provides for registration of political parties, riding associations, and candidates for elections, by-elections, and leadership conventions. The Commission supervises limits on campaign expenses, political contributions to registered parties, constituency associations, and candidates, and imposes a time limit on political advertising during an election campaign. The Commission provides subsidies for campaign expenses to eligible candidates and political parties, and collects audited financial statements of parties, riding associations, and candidates.

*Legislative Library*

The Library provides reference and information services to Members of Provincial Parliament and their staff, officers of the Legislative Assembly, research officers of the three parties, and members of the Legislative Press Gallery. It also provides research services exclusively for MPPs. The Library has an extensive collection of Ontario, Canadian, other provincial, and American government publications, as well as major daily and weekly newspapers and a press clipping service.

*Office of the Ombudsman*

The Ombudsman administers the *Ombudsman Act*. An officer of the Legislature of Ontario, the Ombudsman is appointed by the Lieutenant Governor in Council on the advice of the Assembly for a period of 10 years. His or her function is to investigate any decision, recommendation, act, or omission made in the administration of any ministry, agency, board, commission, or tribunal of the Government of Ontario. The Ombudsman reports annually to the Speaker. Concerns can be raised, in writing, by any Ontario resident, through any one of eight regional offices. The staff is multilingual. The *Ombudsman Act* does not apply to municipalities, hospitals, school boards, the judiciary, or to the Executive Council.

*Office of the Provincial Auditor*

Appointed under the *Audit Act*, the Provincial Auditor's major responsibility is to audit the financial statements of the Province, all government ministries, and a number of provincial agencies, boards, and commissions. The Auditor's primary goal can be described as helping the Legislature hold the Government accountable for the management of the province's resources. This goal is achieved through the presentation of the Auditor's Report to the Legislature each year. This report is reviewed by the Legislature's Public Accounts Committee, which summons ministers and senior officials to discuss issues raised by the report. The Auditor's secondary goal is to help deputy ministers and heads of Crown agencies by reporting on the quality of the management of funds in their organizations. The Office of the Provincial Auditor is divided into several branches: Economic Policy, Justice, Social Policy, General Government, Reporting and Standards, Electronic Data Processing and Resources, and Administration. The Office employs approximately 110 staff, the majority of which are professional accountants.

### 1987–88 Expenditure Estimates:

| | | |
|---|---|---|
| Legislative Assembly | | $68,081,000 |
| *which includes:.* | | |
| Office of the Speaker: | $ 689,100 | |
| Clerk of the Assembly: | 4,535,000 | |
| Commission on Election Finances: | 1,220,000 | |
| Legislative Library: | 4,440,000 | |
| Chief Election Officer: | | $ 551,600 |
| Office of the Ombudsman: | | 6,546,700 |
| Provincial Auditor: | | 6,699,800 |

*For further information on legislative support services and the remuneration of MPPs, see Annex A and Annex B.*

# THE JUDICIARY

The Judiciary is the system of courts which the state provides to settle legal disputes arising between individuals, between individuals and the state, and between different levels of government. The primary role of the Judiciary is to provide a forum for the impartial interpretation and application of legal rules and principles, derived from statutes, custom and precedent. Under the Canadian Constitution, the administration of justice is designated as a provincial responsibility which encompasses the constitution, maintenance, and organization of both civil and criminal courts at the provincial level, with jurisdiction over matters arising under provincial and federal laws.

The appointment of judges, however, is a divided responsibility. The Governor General of Canada, on the advice of the Privy Council, appoints judges for the Superior and District Courts in the province, while the Lieutenant Governor, on the advice of the Attorney General and Cabinet, appoints the judges for the Small Claims, Surrogate, and Provincial Courts. The organization of the Ontario court system is governed by the *Courts of Justice Act*, which establishes the province's courts and regulates their proceedings. As the senior law officer in the province, the Attorney General is responsible for the administration of the court system in Ontario. Advice to the Attorney General can be provided by the Ontario Courts Advisory Council, the Judicial Council of Ontario, and the Inspector of Legal Offices. In general, all court hearings are open to the public. The judicial system in Ontario for both civil and criminal matters is structured hierarchically (see *Figure 4*):

## The Supreme Court of Ontario

The Supreme Court of Ontario is the superior court, in the sense that it is not subject to supervisory control by any other court except by due process of appeal. The Supreme Court is divided into two sections:

1. *The Court of Appeal:* The highest court of final resort in the province, it generally hears civil and criminal appeals from the lower courts, or questions referred to it by the provincial government. It is comprised of the Chief Justice of Ontario, his Associate Chief Justice, and 14 other Justices of Appeal. Proceedings take place primarily in Toronto, are generally heard by three judges, who decide cases by majority.

2. *The High Court of Justice:* This is the trial division of the Supreme Court, comprised of the Chief Justice of the High Court, his Associate Chief Justice, and 60 judges. With certain exceptions, such as family matters, parties

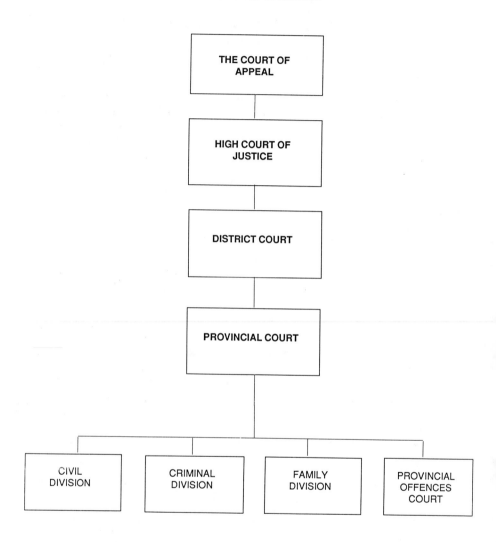

**Figure 4**
**THE JUDICIARY IN ONTARIO**

THE COURT OF APPEAL

HIGH COURT OF JUSTICE

DISTRICT COURT

PROVINCIAL COURT

CIVIL DIVISION

CRIMINAL DIVISION

FAMILY DIVISION

PROVINCIAL OFFENCES COURT

before the High Court of Justice may be granted trial by judge and jury. The Divisional Court is a division of the High Court with jurisdiction to hear appeals from provincial administrative tribunals and from Provincial Small Claims Court. The Family Law Division of the High Court handles divorce trials and motions for child custody and support. There is a local office of the Supreme Court in every county and district in the province.

## The District Court of Ontario

The District Court has civil and criminal jurisdiction, and is subject to review by the Superior Court. The District Court consists of the Chief Justice of the District Court, the Associate Chief Justice, and 163 judges, including a senior judge for most counties, districts, and judicial districts in the province. In civil cases, any amount of damages may be claimed, but the action may be moved from the District Court to the Supreme Court for an amount over $25,000. District Court hears appeals of decisions of the Provincial Court (Family Division), Provincial Court (Criminal Division), Provincial Offences Court, and Youth Court. It can also try persons charged with an indictable offence. Sheriffs serve documents, summon jurors, and administer the court houses in the 12 Judicial Districts, 11 Districts and 26 Judicial Counties in the province. District Court judges also serve as judges of the Surrogate Court in their district or county. The Surrogate Court considers matters relating to the validity of wills and the administration of the estates of persons who die intestate.

## The Provincial Court of Ontario

The Provincial Court is divided into four sections:

1. *Provincial Court (Civil Division):* also known as Small Claims Court, adjudicates damage actions, disputes over goods and services, or claims for outstanding debts, where the amount claimed or the value of property does not exceed $3,000 in Metropolitan Toronto, or $1,000 elsewhere in the province. Procedures in Small Claims Court are generally informal; representation by a lawyer is not required. Referees of the Small Claims Court are available to counsel individuals on their claims.

2. *Provincial Court (Criminal Division):* deals with persons charged with offences under the Criminal Code of Canada, in a trial setting. This court also sits preliminary hearings to determine sufficiency of evidence, bail hearings, and appeals from Provincial Offences Court. Under the federal *Young Offenders Act,* this Provincial Court may sit as Youth Court to try young offenders, 16 or 17 years of age, charged with criminal offences. There are approximately 160 judges in the Criminal Division.

3. *Provincial Court (Family Division):* has jurisdiction over family law matters such as spousal and child support, child custody and access, criminal restraining orders, guardianship, child protection, and adoption. When a young offender (aged 12 to 15) is involved, this division may also sit as

Youth Court, though matters may be referred to the Criminal Division. There are approximately 60 judges in the Family Division.

4. *Provincial Offences Court:* tries persons charged with offences under the Statutes of Ontario, particularly the *Highway Traffic Act.* Proceedings are usually heard by a Justice of the Peace, who is a judicial officer supervised by a provincial judge.

Beyond the provincial court system, a resident of Ontario may have recourse to the federal court system in certain matters, for example, appeals to the Supreme Court of Canada.

# Section 2
# POLICY DEVELOPMENT AND BUDGETING

The processes by which Government policies are developed and approved, and the collection and allocation of the resources necessary for the implementation of Government programs, are the subjects of this Section.

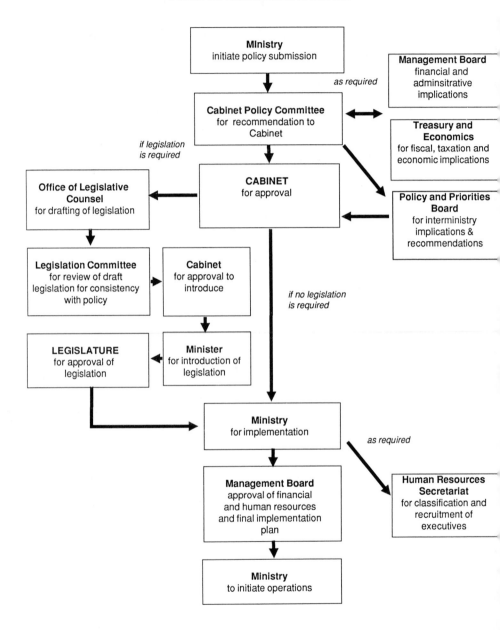

**Figure 5**
**POLICY IMPLEMENTATION APPROVAL**

# THE PUBLIC POLICY DEVELOPMENT PROCESS IN THE GOVERNMENT OF ONTARIO

A policy is a definite course of action developed to meet identified needs and to address existing and emerging issues. Policies are developed at many levels in the public sector, and may be divided into three general categories:

1. *Public policy* has a direct impact on the public through provincial government program delivery.
2. *Strategic or tactical policy* is designed to deal with a specific situation.
3. *Management policy* comprises operational and administrative directives designed to improve effectiveness of management of the government.

Although public policy-making is ultimately a Cabinet responsibility carried out by elected representatives, the policy development process involves both ministers and senior public servants. The staff support Cabinet decision-making by supplying the best available information, advising ministers, implementing policies, and administering programs.

### Sources of public policy ideas

The most common source of public policy ideas in Ontario is the public service, which among its other duties, is responsible for offering policy advice to the Government. Each ministry has a management committee comprised of the Deputy Minister, Assistant Deputy Ministers, and key branch Directors. The management committee meets on a regular basis and recommends the development of policy papers in response to a perceived inadequacy of a particular government program or policy. The research, analysis, and development of public policy issues is usually delegated to the Policy Branch within each ministry. Often government program and policy development is initiated within the public service as a result of contact between senior public servants and outside public interest groups.

Cabinet Ministers and Cabinet Committees often initiate policy development and debate at the Executive level. One of the primary functions of the Cabinet Committees of Economic Policy, Social Policy, and Justice, is to anticipate emerging public policy issues and to initiate the study of these issues by Cabinet Office and by individual ministries. This is particularly important when a public policy issues crosses the jurisdiction of more than one ministry. Inter-ministry committees are often

created to study a problem or policy issue that involves several ministries, reporting
back to the appropriate Cabinet policy committee. For example, development of
provincial policy on industrial waste disposal might involve the Ministries of the
Environment, Municipal Affairs, Natural Resources, and Industry, Trade and Technology.

Public policy initiatives can also originate with the policy advisors to the Premier
and to Cabinet ministers in response to the influence of interest groups. Often, these
issues are a reflection of the governing political party's policy platform. Within the
Government caucus, a private member's bill or a caucus committee report may
prompt the Government to develop a policy proposal. Royal Commissions or Task
Forces often recommend public policy which the Government incorporates into its
program. The Opposition may suggest a policy that the Government considers
popular or pragmatic. The Press may advocate public policies through the expression of opinions, editorials, and letters to the editor. Finally, a Government may act
upon the urging and suggestions of public interest groups.

### Analysis and discussion of public policy proposals

Once the public policy initiative has been researched, analyzed, examined,
debated, and developed into a proposal, the management committee of the ministry
responsible for the issue will approve or reject the submission of the policy to the
appropriate Cabinet policy committee for analysis and discussion. As demonstrated
by *Figure 5,* the policy submission may be referred by the Cabinet policy committee to Management Board Secretariat, for an assessment of financial and/or administrative implications, or to the Ministry of Treasury and Economics for an
assessment of fiscal and taxation implications. Once approved by the policy committee, the proposal is forwarded to the Policy and Priorities Board for discussion.
As the most powerful Cabinet committee and the centre of public policy debate in
the Cabinet, the P & P Board decides whether or not to proceed with a policy issue,
and makes its recommendation to full Cabinet.

### Policy implementation

Once approved by Cabinet, a policy will be implemented by the appropriate ministry on the basis of an Order-in-Council, a Cabinet directive signed by the Premier
and the Chairman of Cabinet. If enabling legislation is required, it will be drafted
and submitted to the Cabinet Legislation Committee for review, to ensure consistency with already existing Government policy and programs. The Legislation Committee makes its recommendations to full Cabinet, which must approve the
legislation for introduction into the Legislative Assembly by the Cabinet Minister
responsible for the policy. The Legislature will then debate the legislation (see
*Legislative Process,* above), which must pass it by majority before it can be
proclaimed law and passed on to the responsible ministry for implementation.

Before a public policy issue can become a government program, the responsible
ministry may have to submit it to the Human Resources Secretariat for approval of

staffing, and must submit it to Management Board for final approval of financial and human resources. Only then can the ministry initiate operations. This process may take as long as several months, even years, depending on the perceived urgency and political ramifications of the policy issue. Debate may delay passage at the Cabinet committee level, in the central agencies and ministries, or in the Legislative Assembly.

The policy development and approval process is most effective when it assists in resolving identified issues, satisfies established policy objectives and meets public needs, when it supports and responds to the political decision-making system in a democratic, responsible system of government, when it respects approved administrative procedures designed to assign specific responsibilities to ministries and central agencies, and when it ensures participation of all appropriate individuals within and beyond government.

# BUDGETING IN THE ONTARIO GOVERNMENT

## The Budget Process

The annual revenue and expenditure (or "estimates") budgeting process in Ontario can take up to 18 months from initial planning in the Ministry of Treasury and Economics to final approval by the Legislative Assembly. The Policy and Priorities Board of Cabinet examines documents placed before it by Treasury and Economics, which outline provincial fiscal strategies based on current economic data, and sends its recommendations to full Cabinet for discussion. Following Cabinet approval, Treasury and Economics, Management Board Secretariat, and Cabinet Office produce a summary document, which sets out specific targets for government expenditure, revenue, and cash requirements, taking into consideration decisions on spending and transfer payments by the federal government. This process is usually completed by August each year so that the estimates process can begin by September.

The estimates process involves the approval of the allocation of funds among ministries, by Cabinet, and of the allocation of money for specific programs by each ministry, in consultation with Management Board Secretariat and Treasury and Economics. By January, detailed estimates are submitted to Management Board of Cabinet. The Estimates are tabled in the Legislative Assembly in May and are debated by the Committee of the Whole House (as the Committee of Supply) and other relevant Legislative committees, ministry by ministry, throughout the year.

The revenue Budget, by contrast, is centred on the Provincial Treasurer and the Ministry of Treasury and Economics, in consultation with the Premier and with private sector financial advisors and special interest groups. The Treasurer generally "brings down" a Budget—a speech in the Legislative Assembly on provincial economic policy and tax changes—in April or May each year, after four to six months of research and preparation. The Budget statement is generally a reflection of Government policies presented in the Speech from the Throne at the beginning of the Legislative session, and outlines the Government's fiscal and economic priorities.

## Sources of Revenue

Taxation raises approximately 66 percent of the $34.2 billion of revenue the government will collect in the 1987–88 fiscal year. Half of the taxation revenue, approximately $11 billion, is raised through personal income tax, collected on behalf of the province by the federal Department of National Revenue. The rest of the province's tax revenue is collected by the Ministry of Revenue through the retail sales tax, corporation tax, gasoline and diesel tax, and other taxes. Federal government transfer payments of approximately $5 billion account for a further 15 percent of provincial revenue in Ontario, while miscellaneous revenue such as OHIP premiums, provincial fees, licenses and permits, LCBO profits, and interest on investments account for a further 14 percent of revenue. The final 5 percent of provincial revenue comes from trust revenues and repayment of provincial loans.

## Expenditures

Social policy ministries account for approximately 65 percent of provincial government spending, with Health accounting for half this amount, approximately $11 billion of the government's $35.2 billion expenditure budget in 1987–88. Education and Colleges and Universities account for a further one-third of social policy spending, while Community and Social Services and the other Social policy ministries round out the 65 percent share. Spending on Economic policy ministries accounts for 17 percent of the provincial expenditure budget, while General Government ministries and Justice ministries account for 4 percent and 3 percent of expenditures respectively. The final 11 percent of the expenditure budget, close to $4 billion annually, goes to "service," or pay interest on, the provincial public debt of $37 billion. For 1987–88, the provincial budget deficit, or "net cash requirement" stands at approximately $1 billion.

Transfers account for 70 percent of provincial expenditures, with 27 percent going to hospital and medical services, 11 percent to municipalities, 11 percent to school boards, 9 percent to universities and community colleges. Income support such as Welfare and Family Benefits, and other transfers account for the final 12 percent of government transfer expenditures. The salaries and operating expenses of the public service account for 19 percent of expenditures. The final 11 percent of expenditures goes to the public debt.

For a detailed breakdown of the 1987–88 Expenditure Estimates, refer to the individual ministries listed in Part Two of this book.

# Section 3
# THE PUBLIC SERVICE
# IN ONTARIO

The policies developed and monitored by the Executive, Legislative, and Judicial divisions of Parliament in Ontario are *implemented* by the much larger Ontario Public Service. This Section describes the institutions of government and those created by government which implement government policy. The public service includes the central agencies and the central and line ministries of the government. Other government policies are implemented by agencies, boards, commissions, inquiries, and other special purpose bodies created by government.

# THE PUBLIC SERVICE

The general role of the public service in the province of Ontario is to provide policy advice to the Premier, Cabinet, and individual ministries, and to administer policies approved by the Legislature. The provincial public service includes approximately 68,000 "classified" staff who are employed on a full-time basis, and a further 15,000 unclassified staff, who are appointed for a defined term (contract) on a part-time or full-time basis.

The labour rights of non-managerial public servants are guaranteed by the *Crown Employees Collective Bargaining Act* and the collective agreements negotiated between the Human Resources Secretariat and such large unions as the Ontario Public Service Employees Union. Ontario public servants are not permitted to engage in certain political activities; they must also take an oath of allegiance to the Crown and an oath of secrecy. Government employees are not permitted to strike. They rely, instead, on a two-stage process of mediation and binding arbitration. The public service in Ontario is structured into central agencies, central ministries, and line ministries.

## CENTRAL AGENCIES

For the purposes of this book, the central agencies of the government are those offices which coordinate and manage government activity, each working within its own sphere of responsibility with a common purpose of supporting Cabinet and the line ministries. Although they account for only one percent of the population of the public service, Cabinet Office and Management Board of Cabinet play a role in coordinating and managing Government decision-making disproportionate to their size.

### Cabinet Office

Perhaps the most important of all central agencies, Cabinet Office provides staff support to Cabinet and Cabinet committees. For a more detailed description of Cabinet Office, see "Cabinet," above. The duties of Cabinet Office include: arranging Cabinet meetings, preparing the agendas, recording discussion and preparing minutes, analyzing ministry submissions, briefing committee chairman, preparing Throne Speech and Prorogation Speech, and coordinating the annual expenditure budget. The planning and research capabilities of the once-independent Provincial Secretariats, which were dissolved in 1985, have been incorporated into Cabinet Office by the Government of Premier David Peterson.

## Management Board of Cabinet

"Management Board" performs the overall general management function for the Ontario Government on behalf of Cabinet (see "Cabinet Committees," above). Its activities are supported by:

1. *Management Board Secretariat:* The Secretariat supports Management Board by developing guidelines for government-wide management and administrative practices, administering the annual estimates (budgeting) process, coordinating program implementation, monitoring expenditures and program results, and providing advice to Cabinet and its committees on a range of financial, program, and administrative matters. Management Board is structured into three divisions: Management Policy, Programs and Estimates, and Information Technology.

2. *Human Resources Secretariat:* The Secretariat is the corporate advocate for promoting and ensuring that systems are maintained to support the best practices in human resources management by: developing policies, programs, and initiatives in consultation with ministries, providing advice to Management Board, and acting on behalf of the Government in collective bargaining and employee relations matters. The Human Resources Secretariat is organized into three divisions: Employee Relations and Compensation, Corporate Services, and Planning and Development.

3. *Civil Service Commission:* The Commission monitors the performance of the Government as an employer, with particular emphasis on protecting the merit principle and developing corporate values on matters such as conflict of interest and employee ethics. The Civil Service Commission consists of a full-time chairman and four commissioners.

### 1987–88 Expenditure Estimates:

Cabinet Office: $ 8,657,000.00
Management Board: 208,654,338.00
*including the Management Board Secretariat, Human Resources Secretariat, and the Civil Service Commission.*

## CENTRAL MINISTRIES

Central ministries are those which perform functions and provide advice on policy development, coordination, and implementation on an overall government basis. These include the Ministries of Treasury and Economics; Intergovernmental Affairs; Revenue; Government Services; and the Attorney General.

*Ministry of Treasury and Economics:* This Ministry evolved from the Ministry of Treasury, Economics, and Intergovernmental Affairs (TEIGA), which operated from 1972 to 1978. The Ministry of Treasury and Economics advises the Government on general fiscal, economic, and regional policies, and provides advice to ensure consistency among these policies and other government programs. The Ministry plays a strategic role in the development of the provincial Budget and economic policy, coordinates regional economic development, and controls provincial borrowing and the management of cash resources, statistical information and the provincial public debt. The Treasurer influences government policy as a member of the Cabinet's Policy and Priorities and Management Board, and as Chairman of the Cabinet Committee on Economic Policy.

*Ministry of Intergovernmental Affairs:* Created in 1978 as a central ministry, MIGA concentrates on the relationship between the Government of Ontario and governments outside provincial jurisdiction (primarily the federal government, other provincial governments, and governments beyond Canada). The Ministry is also responsible for the Office of Protocol. MIGA provides advice and assistance on various areas of intergovernmental policy to all Ontario government ministries. Given the nature of intergovernmental affairs, the Premier typically plays a more active role in MIGA than in other ministries. Since 1985, the Minister of Intergovernmental Affairs has been the Premier.

*Ministry of Revenue:* The chief function of the Ministry of Revenue is to collect the revenue necessary for the continued operation of the government by administering the major taxing statutes of Ontario (such as the *Retail Sales Tax Act, Corporations Tax Act, Tobacco Tax Act,* and *Gasoline Tax Act*). The Ministry also conducts property value assessments to provide the tax base for Ontario municipalities, and administers several income redistribution progams, a small business development program, and the Province of Ontario Savings Office.

*Ministry of Government Services:* This Ministry is concerned with virtually every aspect of the working environment of the government, and provides central support services to the Government as a whole. Its functions include the provision of services to Government ministries (payroll and employee benefits, computing services, human resource planning, purchasing, government mail, and information technology), administration of government real estate holdings (acquisition, construction, renovation, repair, maintenance, leasing, and disposal), coordinating government contracts, and delivering customer services to the public.

*Ministry of the Attorney General:* This Ministry is responsible for the administration of justice in Ontario, and ensures the effective operation of the courts system across the province. The Ministry conducts and regulates all civil litigation and criminal prosecutions for and against the Government. Staff lawyers, on secondment to the Legal Branches of the line ministries, advise heads of ministries and agencies in their legal matters. The Attorney General is the law officer of the Executive Council, and advises the Government and attends to all matters of a legislative nature.

## 1987–88 Expenditure Estimates:

| | |
|---|---|
| Treasury and Economics: | $4,347,933,132 |
| Intergovernmental Affairs: | 7,471,000 |
| Revenue: | 736,148,606 |
| Government Services: | 520,498,138 |
| Attorney General: | 346,682,638 |

For additional information concerning the background, roles and functions, organization, programs, budget, agencies, boards, commissions, and legislation covered by each central agency and central ministry, consult Part Two.

## LINE MINISTRIES

These are ministries which deliver services to the residents of the province. The Committee on Government Productivity (COGP) Report of 1972 recommended reorganization of many line ministries. It also introduced the title of Ministry (to replace that of Department), in recognition of a Minister's responsibility not only for a line department but also for the agencies, boards, and commissions associated with that department. The chief administrative officer of a ministry is the deputy minister, who is appointed by the Premier. While the number and organization of the ministries has been modified since 1972, the basic structure of government continues to be based on the principles and structural concepts established at that time. Typically, line ministries are structured hierarchically into divisions (under assistant deputy ministers, executive directors, or executive co-ordinators, depending on the size and the role of the division), branches (under directors), and sections (under managers or section heads).

The legal basis of a ministry is defined by an "organic" statute, which establishes the ministry (e.g. *Ministry of Revenue Act*), and a set of "programmatic" statues (e.g. *Topsoil Preservation Act*), which delineate the general scope of the Ministry's policy responsibilities. A list of line ministries, by policy area, with a brief description of their general function, follows.

## LINE MINISTRIES BY POLICY AREA

### Economic Policy

*Agriculture and Food:* Administers programs supporting food production and marketing.

*Energy:* Responsible for the development and administration of provincial energy policy.

*Environment:* Responsible for promotion of environmental quality (air, land, water) in the province.

*Housing:* Responsible for provision, conservation of affordable housing, and administration of rent legislation.

*Industry, Trade and Technology:* Encourages domestic and international trade, and the development and application of technology.

*Labour:* Promotes industrial relations, occupational health and safety, equality of treatment, and opportunity in employment.

*Municipal Affairs:* Responsible for supporting the administration of local government and for community planning.

*Natural Resources:* Promotes resource development and conservation and protection from natural hazards.

*Northern Development and Mines:* Stimulates economic and social growth in Northern Ontario and encourages development of province's mineral resources.

*Tourism and Recreation:* Promotes tourism, recreation, sports, and fitness in the province.

*Transportation:* Responsible for roads and highways, driver licensing, motor vehicle licensing, and safety.

## Justice

*Attorney General:* Responsible for administration of justice in the province; acts as government's legal advisor.

*Consumer and Commercial Relations:* Regulates business practices and ensures protection of consumers.

*Correctional Services:* Provides custody and supervision of offenders, as directed by the courts; also responsible for offender rehabilitation and for crime prevention.

*Financial Institutions:* Regulates activities of businesses in the financial sector.

*Solicitor General:* Responsible for law enforcement and for public safety.

## Social Policy

*Citizenship:* Promotes racial harmony and participation of all citizens in Ontario society.

*Colleges and Universities:* Administers financial support of post-secondary educational ins'itutions and students.

*Community and Social Services:* Administers a wide variety of public welfare programs.

*Culture and Communications:* Promotes multiculturism, cultural expression, cultural preservation, and coordinates provincial communications policy.

*Education:* Ensures provision of elementary and secondary school education in the province.

*Health:* Oversees administration of the province's public hospitals and public health programs.

*Skills Development:* Promotes skills development and training programs to stimulate employment.

For additional information concerning the background, roles and functions, organization, programs, budget, agencies, boards, commissions, and legislation covered by each line ministry, consult Part Two.

For more information on the composition of the Public Service, see *Annex B, Annex C* and *Annex D.* For a detailed list of the Ministers, Deputy Ministers, and Principal Officers of these Ministries and Agencies, as of March 1988, see *Annex E.*

# AGENCIES, BOARDS, COMMISSIONS, AND SPECIAL PURPOSE BODIES

There are several categories of agencies, boards, commissions (ABCs), and special purpose bodies in the Government of Ontario:

## Agencies, Boards, and Commissions

Agencies, Boards, Commissions, Institutes, Foundations, Tribunals, Councils, or Crown corporations are created under specific Acts, and are administered by and/or report to an appropriate Government ministry. Although Ontario lacks a formal legal definition of an agency comparable to that in the federal *Financial Administration Act,* the Committee on Government Productivity (COGP) report of 1972 laid the groundwork for a system of classifying and administering agencies, boards, and commissions in order to ensure appropriate accountability to the Government, the Legislature, and the people of Ontario. At present, there are 248 ABCs in the Ontario government. The 203 "Schedule I," agencies are those which are financially supported by the Government, and to which the Cabinet appoints some or all directors or members through an Order-in-Council. The 20 "Schedule II" agencies are self-supporting, fully operational Crown corporations, such as Ontario Hydro and the Ontario Lottery Corporation, which operate at arm's length from the the government. The 25 "Schedule III" agencies are social/cultural or research enterprises, such as the Royal Ontario Museum or the Ontario Cancer Institute, which are funded in part by the government and in part through their own public fundraising initiatives. Agencies, Boards, and Commissions perform three basic functions: Advisory (85 ABCs, including the Advisory Council on Women's Issues and the Advisory Council on Occupational Health and Safety), Regulatory (90 ABCs, including the Liquor Licence Board of Ontario and the Ontario Securities Commission), and Operational (73 ABCs, including GO Transit, and Ontario Place Corporation). Agencies vary in size and activity. They are generally created to improve administrative or operational flexibility, to deliver programs or services which cross jurisdictional boundaries of government ministries, to respond quickly to a political issue, or to secure independence from day-to-day government control.

A more detailed description of the functions of each of the major agencies, boards, and commissions in the Government of Ontario may be found in Part Two of this book, under the ministry through which they report.

## Royal Commissions

Royal Commissions are investigatory bodies appointed by an Order-in-Council under the *Public Inquiries Act* to investigate a specific public concern, such as a sudden or catastrophic event (e.g. Royal Commission on Grand River Flood or Royal Commission on High Rise Fires), the conduct and activities of public service employees (e.g. Royal Commission concerning Police Activities), areas of government policy (e.g. Royal Commission on Freedom of Information and Individual Privacy or Royal Commission on Confidentiality of Health Records), or a public safety issue (e.g. Royal Commission on Health and Safety of Asbestos Workers in Ontario). The *Public Inquiries Act* is administered by the Attorney General, who governs the methods and procedures used by a Royal Commission, such as subpoena powers and hearings. Royal Commissions report to Cabinet; over 30 different Commissions have been appointed since 1973.

## Judicial Inquiries

A final category of special purpose body is comprised of Judicial Inquiries, or tribunals, which are short term appointments under the *Court of Justice Act*, designed to examine complaints arising from the conduct of a provincial judge. In such circumstances, a judicial council (a panel of judges) examines the complaint or allegations, and makes a recommendation to the Attorney General concerning the appointment of a Supreme Court judge to lead a public Judicial Inquiry.

## ANNEXES

### Annex A:
### Legislative Support Services

- One office per member; the Legislative Assembly provides equipment and supplies.

- $98,883 per annum salary allowance for staff; members do their own hiring, with no restriction on the number of staff.

- Unlimited volume of mail service; unlimited local and long distance telephone service.

- $15,400 per annum allowance for constituency (riding) office rental, renovation, postage, operation and maintenance, advertising, staff travel, and miscellaneous expenses.

- $11,450 Toronto accommodation allowance for out-of-town MPPs.

- Staff in the constituency offices are hired under same staff allowance as those in the Legislative office. Partisan political activity is not permitted in the constituency offices.

- Caucus Offices: each party has a caucus office to provide services to the elected party members and to field inquiries from the public. Caucus office funding levels are established by the Board of Internal Economy, based on party standings (i.e. number of seats held in the Legislative Assembly).

- Research services:

    a. Legislative Library: 84 employees (15 researchers): non-partisan research for MPPs, committees.
    b. Each member may hire a personal research assistant.
    c. Caucus research staff:
    
    | | |
    |---|---|
    | Government: | 15 |
    | Opposition: | 10 |
    | Third party: | 10 |

- *Hansard* Reporting Service: provides final printed version of Assembly proceedings within 48 hours; 10 days for committee proceedings.

- Computerization of members' offices: Members Office Automation/Networking System, located in all members offices, caucus offices, all offices and departments of the Legislative Assembly, and constituency offices. Word processing, electronic mail, customized correspondence, data processing, interface with *Hansard*. Assembly business papers and bills available.

# Annex B:

## Remuneration for Members of the Legislative Assembly

Basic Salary for all Members: $52,400 ($33,229 sessional indemnity plus $12,616 tax free allowance)

Additional indemnities:

| | |
|---|---|
| Premier: | $48,367 |
| Minister: | 28,743 |
| Minister without Portfolio: | 14,433 |
| Parliamentary Assistant: | 8,880 |
| Opposition Leader: | 33,684 |
| Third Party Leader: | 16,902 |
| Speaker: | 21,217 |
| Deputy Speaker: | 8,880 |
| Standing Committee Chairman | 4,810 |

Members also receive per diems and allowances for committee work, travel, and accommodation.

*Source:* Legislative Assembly Administration Office

## Remuneration Ranges for Senior Public Servants

| | |
|---|---|
| Deputy Ministers | $79,000 – 113,000 |
| Assistant Deputy Ministers | $68,800 – 86,000 |
| Executive Directors | $63,700 – 79,600 |
| Executive Co-ordinators | $57,500 – 71,800 |
| Branch Directors | $48,800 – 60,900 |

*Source:* Human Resources Secretariat

## Annex C:
## Classified Civil Servants and 1987-88 Expenditure Estimates by Ministry and Central Agency

| | | |
|---|---|---|
| Agriculture and Food | 1,711 | $ 559,203,838 |
| Attorney General | 3,410 | 346,682,638 |
| Cabinet Office | 89 | 8,657,400 |
| Citizenship | 260 | 40,218,833 |
| Colleges and Universities | 241 | 2,394,402,800 |
| Community and Social Services | 8,873 | 3,496,461,138 |
| Consumer and Commercial Relations | 1,667 | 126,611,938 |
| Correctional Services | 5,856 | 363,842,000 |
| Culture and Communications | 401 | 221,294,499 |
| Disabled Persons | 27 | 4,432,825 |
| Education | 1,472 | 4,366,894,238 |
| Energy | 221 | 44,092,000 |
| Environment | 1,714 | 412,020,638 |
| Financial Institutions | 297 | 37,564,700 |
| Government Services | 2,903 | 520,498,138 |
| Health | 10,381 | 11,231,672,638 |
| Housing | 885 | 366,293,538 |
| Industry, Trade and Technology | 640 | 253,994,738 |
| Intergovernmental Affairs | 69 | 7,471,100 |
| Labour | 1,549 | 104,081,138 |
| Management Board of Cabinet | 341 | 208,654,338 |
| Municipal Affairs | 419 | 928,875,038 |
| Native Affairs | 13 | 4,379,800 |
| Natural Resources | 3,660 | 531,171,938 |
| Northern Development and Mines | 439 | 243,406,406 |
| Revenue | 3,902 | 736,148,606 |
| Senior Citizen's Affairs | 19 | 4,591,825 |
| Skills Development | 479 | 446,247,938 |
| Solicitor General (including O.P.P.) | 6,165 | 393,569,638 |
| Tourism and Recreation | 654 | 185,100,938 |
| Transportation | 8,466 | 1,832,730,038 |
| Treasury and Economics | 391 | 4,347,933,132 |
| Women's Issues | 53 | 17,942,800 |
| **Totals:** | **67,667** | **$34,787,143,210** |

*Note:* The staff total does not include the Provincial Auditor, Office of the Ombudsman, the Legislative Assembly, or the Office of the Premier, as they do not employ public servants.

*Source:* Human Resources Secretariat, March 1988.

## Annex D:
## Classified Service by Age and Salary

| Salary in $ | under 25 | 25–34 | 35–44 | 45–54 | 55–64 | 65+ | Total | % |
|---|---|---|---|---|---|---|---|---|
| under 15,000 | 59 | 120 | 147 | 150 | 371 | 9 | 856 | 1.2 |
| 15,000–19,999 | 769 | 1,853 | 1,378 | 944 | 1,066 | 25 | 6,035 | 8.8 |
| 20,000–24,999 | 1,295 | 7,311 | 6,461 | 4,202 | 3,566 | 54 | 22,899 | 33.2 |
| 25,000–29,999 | 482 | 3,304 | 3,561 | 2,290 | 1,745 | 22 | 11,404 | 16.6 |
| 30,000–34,999 | 81 | 3,019 | 3,892 | 2,541 | 1,619 | 22 | 11,174 | 16.3 |
| 35,000–39,999 | 22 | 1,774 | 3,135 | 1,829 | 846 | 14 | 7,620 | 11.1 |
| 40,000–44,999 | 0 | 494 | 1,377 | 936 | 483 | 3 | 3,293 | 4.8 |
| 45,000 + | 0 | 298 | 2,261 | 1,790 | 1,174 | 35 | 5,558 | 8.1 |
| Total | 2,708 | 18,173 | 22,212 | 14,682 | 10,870 | 184 | 68,829 | 100.0 |
| percentage | 3.9 | 26.4 | 32.2 | 21.3 | 15.8 | 0.3 | 100.0 | |

There are 39,024 males (56.7%) and 29,805 females (43.3%) in the Ontario public service. Average salary for males is $32,170, while the average salary for females is $24,921.

Source: Civil Service Commission, Annual Report, 1985–86.

# Annex E:
## Ministers, Deputy Ministers and Principal Officers
### *(as of March, 1988)*

**Office of the Premier:**

Room 281
Queen's Park
Toronto, Ontario
M7A 1A1    (416) 965-1941

Premier: *Honourable David Peterson*
Executive Director: *Gordon Ashworth*
Principal Secretary: *Hershel Ezrin*

**Cabinet Office:**

Room 381
Queen's Park
Toronto, Ontario
M7A 1A1    (416) 965-1945

Chairman of Cabinet: *Honourable Murray Elston*
Secretary of Cabinet and Clerk of the Executive
   Council: *Robert Carman*
Government House Leader: *Honourable Sean Conway*

## ECONOMIC POLICY MINISTRIES:

**1. Ministry of Agriculture and Food:**

11th Floor
801 Bay Street
Toronto, Ontario
M7A 1A2    (416) 965-1041

Minister: *Honourable Jack Riddell*
Deputy Minister: *Dr. Clayton Switzer*
Parliamentary Assistant: *Gordon Miller*

**2. Ministry of Energy:**

12th Floor
56 Wellesley Street West
Toronto, Ontario
M7A 2B7    (416) 965-4286

Minister: *Honourable Robert Wong*
Deputy Minister: *Donald Crosbie*
Parliamentary Assistant: *none*

**3. Ministry of Environment:**

15th Floor
135 St. Clair Avenue West
Toronto, Ontario
M4V 1P5    (416) 323-4359

Minister: *Honourable James Bradley*
Deputy Minister: *Gary Posen*
Parliamentary Assistant: *Christine Hart*

**4. Ministry of Housing:**

10th Floor
777 Bay Street
Toronto, Ontario
M5G 2E5    (416) 585-7111

Minister: *Honourable Chaviva Hosek*
Deputy Minister: *Gardner Church*
Parliamentary Assistant: *Maurice Bossy*

**5. Ministry of Industry, Trade and Technology:**

Minister: *Honourable Monte Kwinter*
Deputy Minister: *Patrick Lavelle*
Parliamentary Assistant and Small Business
Advocate: *Rick Ferraro*

8th Floor
900 Bay Street
Toronto, Ontario
M7A 2E1    (416) 965-1617

**6. Ministry of Labour:**

Minister: *Honourable Gregory Sorbara*
Deputy Minister: *Glenn Thompson*
Parliamentary Assistant: *Shirley Collins*

14th Floor
400 University Avenue
Toronto, Ontario
M7A 1T7    (416) 965-4101

**7. Ministry of Municipal Affairs:**

Minister: *Honourable John Eakins*
Deputy Minister: *Donald Obonsawin*
Parliamentary Assistant: *Dave Neumann*

17th Floor
777 Bay Street
Toronto, Ontario
M5G 2E5    (416) 585-7000

**8. Ministry of Natural Resources:**

Minister: *Honourable Vincent Kerrio*
Deputy Minister: *George Tough*
Parliamentary Assistant: *James McGuigan*

6th Floor
99 Wellesley Street West
Toronto, Ontario
M7A 1W3    (416) 965-1301

**9. Ministry of Northern Development and Mines:**

Minister of Northern Development:
*Honourable Rene Fontaine*
Minister of Mines: *Honourable Sean Conway*
Deputy Minister: *Brock Smith*
Parliamentary Assistants:
*Taras Kozyra* (Northern Development)
*Sterling Campbell* (Mines)

10th Floor
10 Wellesley Street East
Toronto, Ontario
M4Y 1G2    (416) 965-1417

**10. Ministry of Tourism and Recreation:**

Minister: *Honourable Hugh O'Neil*
Deputy Minister: *James Keenan*
Parliamentary Assistant: *Harry Pelissero*

7th Floor
77 Bloor Street West
Toronto, Ontario
M7A 2R9    (416) 963-1401

**11. Ministry of Transportation:**

Minister: *Honourable Edward Fulton*
Deputy Minister: *David Hobbs*
Parliamentary Assistant: *Tony Lupusella*

Main Floor East
1201 Wilson Avenue
Downsview, Ontario
M3M 1J8    (416) 235-4449

## JUSTICE MINISTRIES:

**1. Ministry of the Attorney General**

Attorney General: *Honourable Ian Scott*
Deputy Attorney General: *Richard Chaloner*
Parliamentary Assistant: *Steven Offer*

18th Floor
18 King Street East
Toronto, Ontario
M5C 1C5    (416) 965-1664

**2. Ministry of Consumer and Commercial Relations**

Minister: *Honourable William Wrye*
Deputy Minister: *Valerie Gibbons*
Parliamentary Assistant: *Ray Haggerty*

9th Floor
555 Yonge Street
Toronto, Ontario
M7A 2H6    (416) 963-0311

**3. Ministry of Correctional Services**

Minister: *Honourable David Ramsay*
Deputy Minister: *Robert McDonald*
Parliamentary Assistant: *none*

2001 Eglinton Avenue East
Scarborough, Ontario
M1L 4P1    (416) 750-3301

**4. Ministry of Financial Institutions**

Minister: *Honourable Robert Nixon*
Deputy Minister: *Bryan Davies*
Parliamentary Assistant: *Brad Nixon*

8th Floor
555 Yonge Street
Toronto, Ontario
M7A 2H6    (416) 963-6361

**5. Ministry of the Solicitor General**

Solicitor General: *Honourable Joan Smith*
Deputy Solicitor General: *John Takach*
Parliamentary Assistant: *Ron Kanter*

11th Floor
25 Grosvenor Street
Toronto, Ontario
M7A 1Y6    (416) 965-6063

## SOCIAL POLICY MINISTRIES:

**1. Ministry of Citizenship:**

Minister: *Honourable Gerry Phillips*
Deputy Minister: *Maureen O'Neil*
Parliamentary Assistant: *Tony Ruprecht*

6th Floor
77 Bloor Street West
Toronto, Ontario
M7A 2R9    (416) 965-6202

**2. Ministry of Colleges and Universities:**

Minister: *Honourable Lyn McLeod*
Deputy Minister: *Tom Brzustowski*
Parliamentary Assistant: *Monika Turner*

13th Floor
101 Bloor Street West
Toronto, Ontario
M5S 1P7    (416) 965-6423

**3. Ministry of Community and Social Services:**

Minister: *Honourable John Sweeney*
Deputy Minister: *Peter Barnes*
Parliamentary Assistant: *Gilles Morin*

6th Floor
80 Grosvenor Street
Toronto, Ontario
M7A 1E9    (416) 965-2341

**4. Ministry of Culture and Communications:**

Minister: *Honourable Lily Munro*
Deputy Minister: *David Silcox*
Parliamentary Assistant: *none*

6th Floor
77 Bloor Street West
Toronto, Ontario
M7A 2R9    (416) 965-8098

**5. Ministry of Education:**

Minister: *Honourable Christopher Ward*
Deputy Minister: *Bernard Shapiro*
Parliamentary Assistant: *Yvonne O'Neill*

22nd Floor
900 Bay Street
Toronto, Ontario
M7A 1L2    (416) 965-5277

**6. Ministry of Health:**

Minister: *Honourable Elinor Caplan*
Deputy Minister: *Dr. Martin Barkin*
Parliamentary Assistant: *Ken Keyes*

10th Floor
80 Grosvenor Street
Toronto, Ontario
M7A 2C4    (416) 965-2421

**7. Ministry of Skills Development:**

Minister: *Honourable Alvin Curling*
Deputy Minister: *Glenna Carr*
Parliamentary Assistant: *none*

13th Floor
101 Bloor Street West
Toronto, Ontario
M5S 1P7    (416) 965-8282

**8. Office for Disabled Persons:**

Minister Responsible for Disabled
Persons: *Honourable Remo Mancini*
Senior Adviser: *Clement Sauve*

3rd Floor
700 Bay Street
Toronto, Ontario
M5G 1Z5    (416) 965-3165

**9. Office for Senior Citizens' Affairs:**

Minister (without portfolio) for Senior
Citizens' Affairs: *Honourable Mavis Wilson*
Special Advisor to the Minister: *Glen Heagle*

6th Floor
76 College Street
Toronto, Ontario
M7A 1N3    (416) 965-5106

## GENERAL GOVERNMENT MINISTRIES:

**1. Management Board of Cabinet:**

Chairman: *Honourable Murray Elston*

7th Floor
7 Queen's Park Crescent
Toronto, Ontario
M7A 1Z6 (416) 586-2020

Members:  *Honourable Robert Nixon*
Treasurer and Minister of Financial Institutions
(Vice-Chairman)

*Honourable James Bradley*
Minister of Environment

*Honourable Richard Patton*
Minister of Government Services

*Honourable Gerry Phillips*
Minister of Citizenship

*Honourable Joan Smith*
Solicitor General

*Honourable Robert Wong*
Minister of Energy

*Honourable Mavis Wilson*
Minister (without Portfolio) for Senior Citizen's Affairs

Senior Officials:

Secretary of Management Board: *John Sloan*

Deputy Minister, Human Resources Secretariat: *Elaine Todres*

Chairman, Civil Service Commission: *Gerard Raymond*

**2. Ministry of Government Services:**

Minister: *Honourable Richard Patten*
Deputy Minister: *Dennis Caplice*
Parliamentary Assistant: *none*

12th Floor
77 Wellesley Street West
Toronto, Ontario
M7A 1N3     (416) 965-1101

**3. Ministry of Intergovernmental Affairs:**

Minister: *Honourable David Peterson*
Deputy Minister: *David Cameron*
Parliamentary Assistant (to the Premier
and to the Minister of Intergovernmental
Affairs): *Joseph Cordiano*

6th Floor
900 Bay Street
Toronto, Ontario
M7A 1C2 (416) 965-1941

**4. Ministry of Revenue:**

Minister: *Honourable Bernard Grandmaitre*
Deputy Minister: *Dr. Terry Russell*
Parliamentary Assistant: *none*

33 King Street West
Oshawa, Ontario
L1H 8H7     (416) 433-0870

**5. Ministry of Treasury and Economics:**

Minister: *Honourable Robert Nixon*
(Treasurer and Minister of Economics)
Deputy Minister: *Mary Mogford (Deputy*
*Treasurer and Deputy Minister of Economics)*
Parliamentary Assistant: *Claudio Polsinelli*

7th Floor
7 Queen's Park Crescent
Toronto, Ontario
M7A 1Y7     (416) 965-6361

**6. Office of Francophone Affairs:**

Minister Responsible for Francophone Affairs:
*Honourable Bernard Grandmaitre*
Minister of Revenue
Executive Director: *Remy Beauregard*

6th Floor
900 Bay Street
Toronto, Ontario
M7A 1C2     (416) 965-3865

**7. Office Responsible for Native Affairs:**
(Ontario Native Affairs Directorate)

Minister Responsible for Native Affairs:
*Honourable Ian Scott*, Attorney General
Executive Director: *Mark Krasnick*

3rd Floor
18 King Street East
Toronto, Ontario
M5C 1C5     (416) 965-4826

**8. Office Responsible for Women's Issues:**
(Ontario Women's Directorate)

Minister Responsible for Women's Issues:
*Honourable Gregory Sorbara,*, Minister of Labour
Assistant Deputy Minister: *Naomi Alboim*

2nd Floor
480 University Avenue
Toronto, Ontario
M5G 1V2     (416) 597-4500

## Annex F:
## Membership on Committees of Cabinet

| PORTFOLIO MINISTER | Policy & Priorities Board | Management Board | Economic Policy | Social Policy | Justice | Regulations | Legislation | Northern Development | Native Affairs | Race Relations | Emergency Planning | |
|---|---|---|---|---|---|---|---|---|---|---|---|---|
| Premier | C | | | | | | | | | | | David Peterson |
| Deputy Premier | * | V | C | * | | | | | | | | Robert Nixon |
| Government House Leader | * | | * | | | | * | * | | | | Sean Conway |
| Chairman of Cabinet | * | C | | | | | | | | * | * | Murray Elston |
| **ECONOMIC POLICY** | | | | | | | | | | | | |
| Agriculture and Food | | | * | | | | | * | | | | Jack Riddell |
| Energy | | * | * | | | | | | | | * | Robert Wong |
| Environment | * | * | * | | | | | * | | | * | James Bradley |
| Housing | * | | * | * | | | | * | | | * | Chaviva Hosek |
| Industry, Trade and Technology | | | * | | | | V | * | | * | | Monte Kwinter |
| Labour | | | * | | C | | | * | | * | * | Gregory Sorbara |
| Mines | * | | * | | | | | * | * | | | Sean Conway |
| Municipal Affairs | | | * | | | | | * | * | | * | John Eakins |
| Natural Resources | | | * | | | | | * | * | | * | Vincent Kerrio |
| Northern Development | * | | * | | | | | C | * | | | Rene Fontaine |
| Tourism and Recreation | | | * | | | | | * | * | | | Hugh O'Neil |
| Transportation | | | * | | | | | * | | | | Edward Fulton |
| **JUSTICE** | | | | | | | | | | | | |
| Attorney General | * | | | | C | | C | | C | * | * | Ian Scott |
| Consumer & Comm. Relations | | | | | * | * | | | | * | | William Wrye |
| Correctional Services | | | | | * | | | * | * | * | | David Ramsay |
| Financial Institutions | * | V | C | | * | | | | | | | Robert Nixon |
| Solicitor General | | * | | | * | | | | * | * | C | Joan Smi |
| **SOCIAL POLICY** | | | | | | | | | | | | |
| Community and Social Services | | | | * | | | V | | * | * | * | John Sweeney |
| Citizenship | | * | | * | * | | | | * | * | C | Gerry Phillips |
| Culture and Communications | | | | * | | | | | | * | | Lily Munro |
| Colleges and Universities | | | | * | | | | * | * | * | | Lynn McLeod |
| Education | | | | * | | | | | * | * | | Christopher Ward |
| Health | * | | | C | | | | | * | | * | Elinor Caplan |
| Skills Development | | | * | * | | | | | * | * | | Alvin Curling |
| Senior Citizen's Affairs | | | * | * | | | | | | | | Mavis Wilson |
| Disabled Persons | | | | * | | | * | | | | | Remo Mancini |
| **GENERAL GOVERNMENT** | | | | | | | | | | | | |
| Chairman of Management Board | * | C | | | | | | | | * | * | Murray Elston |
| Government Services | * | * | | | | | | | | | | Richard Patton |
| Intergovernmental Affairs | C | | | | | | | | | | | David Peterson |
| Revenue | | | * | | | | | * | | | | Bernard Grandmaitre |
| Treasury and Economics | * | V | C | * | | | | | | | | Robert Nixon |
| Francophone Affairs | | | * | | | | | * | | | | Bernard Grandmaitre |
| Native Affairs | * | | | | C | | C | | C | * | * | Ian Scott |
| Women's Issues | | | | * | | C | | * | | * | * | Gregory Sorbara |

* = Committee member
C = Chairman
V = Vice Chairman

## Annex G:
## Premiers of Ontario 1867 – 1988

| | |
|---|---|
| 1867 – 1871 | John Sandfield Macdonald (Conservative) |
| 1871 – 1872 | Edward Blake (Liberal) |
| 1872 – 1896 | Sir Oliver Mowat (Liberal) |
| 1896 – 1899 | Arthur S. Hardy (Liberal) |
| 1899 – 1904 | George W. Ross (Liberal) |
| 1904 – 1914 | James P. Whitney (Conservative) |
| 1914 – 1919 | William H. Hearst (Conservative) |
| 1920 – 1923 | E.C. Drury (UFO) |
| 1923 – 1930 | George H. Ferguson (Conservative) |
| 1930 – 1934 | George S. Henry (Conservative) |
| 1934 – 1942 | Mitchell F. Hepburn (Liberal) |
| 1942 – 1943 | Gordon D. Conant (Liberal) |
| 1943 – 1944 | Harry C. Nixon (Liberal) |
| 1944 – 1948 | George A. Drew (Conservative) |
| 1948 – 1949 | Thomas L. Kennedy (Conservative) |
| 1949 – 1961 | Leslie M. Frost (Conservative) |
| 1961 – 1971 | John P. Robarts (Conservative) |
| 1971 – 1985 | William Davis (Conservative) |
| 1985 | Frank Miller (Conservative) |
| 1985 – | David Peterson (Liberal) |

## Annex H
## References

Fleming, Robert J., ed. *Canadian Legislatures: The 1986 Comparative Study.* Toronto: Office of the Assembly, Queen's Printer for Ontario, 1986.

MacDonald, Donald C. ed. *The Government and Politics of Ontario.* Scarborough: Nelson Canada, 1985. See especially Chapter 2, "The Structure of the Ontario Political System," by Richard A. Loreto; Chapter 4, "The Evolving Ontario Cabinet: Shaping the Structure to Suit the Times," by Hugh Segal; and Chapter 5, "Government by Other Means: Agencies, Boards and Commissions," by John Eichmanis and Graham White.

Mallory, J.R. *The Structure of Canadian Government.*Toronto: Gage, 1984.

Ontario. Civil Service Commission. *Annual Report, 1986.* Toronto, 1986.

Ontario. Committee on Government Productivity. *Report Number Ten: A Summary.* Toronto, 1973.

Ontario. Management Board of Cabinet. *The Cabinet and Central Agencies: Roles and Responsibilities.* Toronto, 1987.

Ontario. Ministry of Government Services. *KWIC Index to Services.* Toronto, 1987.

Ontario. Ministry of Treasury and Economics. *Expenditure Estimates, 1987–1988.* Toronto, 1987.

Ontario. Ministry of Treasury and Economics. *Ontario Budget, 1987.* Toronto, 1987.

Schindeler, Frederick *Responsible Government in Ontario.* Toronto: University of Toronto Press, 1969.

# PART TWO
# THE MINISTRIES

# Section 4
# ECONOMIC POLICY MINISTRIES

The Economic Policy Ministries promote and support economic growth and development and coordinate economic policy in the key sectors of the Ontario economy: agriculture, energy, manufacturing, natural resource development, and tourism. The Economic Policy Ministries are the Ministries of Agriculture and Food; Energy; the Environment; Housing; Industry, Trade and Technology; Labour; Municipal Affairs; Natural Resources; Northern Development and Mines; Tourism and Recreation; and Transportation.

# MINISTRY OF AGRICULTURE AND FOOD

## ROLES AND FUNCTIONS

The Ministry of Agriculture and Food is responsible for encouraging an efficient and competitive agriculture and food sector and for enhancing the natural and human resources of this sector for the well being of all the people of Ontario. The Ministry administers farm assistance, foodland preservation, crop insurance, marketing, technology development, and educational and research programs. The Ministry also operates a Consumer Information Centre, which responds to agriculture, horticulture, and food information requests from consumers.

## BACKGROUND HISTORY

The Ministry of Agriculture and Food is one of the oldest ministries in the Ontario Government. Prior to the formation of the Ontario Department of Agriculture in 1888, agricultural administration in Upper Canada was handled by a Board of Agriculture, which was concerned for the most part with colonization and immigration.

The period from 1867 to 1900 saw an increase in demand for farm produce and a corresponding specialization in government activity, as the new Department expanded its operations. From 1900 to 1940 was a tremendous growth period for the Ministry, with the enacting of over one hundred pieces of legislation designed to assist the agricultural sector. This period saw the development of an Agriculture and Horticulture Societies Branch, a Crop Branch, Dairy Branch, Livestock Branch, Fruit Branch, Markets Branch, and the Agriculture Development Board, Ontario Marketing Board, and Milk Control Board, all reflecting the rapid growth of population in the province and the expansion of the agriculture sector.

During World War II, agricultural production was expanded to meet the needs of the war effort, which led to a period of agricultural overproduction in the province during the 1950s and 1960s. In 1965 the Department of Agriculture became the Department of Agriculture and Food (later, in 1972,the Ministry of Agriculture and Food) to reflect more accurately the responsible role the government has taken in the food production chain.

In 1982, the Ministry was restructured into the current three divisions—Finance and Administration, Marketing and Standards, and Technology and Field Services—to better reflect the range of services offered by the Ministry. Branches with advisory services to the rural community were relocated from Toronto to Guelph, to facilitate closer liaison with the agricultural sector, the University of Guelph, and the Ontario Veterinary College. These advisory services are administered from the Guelph Agriculture Centre.

## ORGANIZATION

The Ministry of Agriculture and Food is organized into three major divisions (see organization chart):

1. *Finance and Administration:* Responsible for support services, such as Audit and Personnel, and for the delivery of foodland preservation and financial assistance programs. Branches include Foodland Preservation, Crop Insurance and Stabilization, Management Systems, and the Farm Assistance Programs Branch.

2. *Marketing and Standards:* Responsible for agriculture and food marketing activities, livestock and food quality programs, and for inspection standards. Branches include Farm Products Marketing, Market Development and Food Processing in the Marketing area, Livestock Inspection, Fruit and Vegetable Inspection, and Dairy Inspection in the Quality and Standards area.

3. *Technology and Field Services:* Responsible for advisory and technical services and for administration of education and research facilities. Branches include Agricultural Representatives, Animal Industry, Plant Industry, Agricultural Laboratory Services, Veterinary Laboratory Services, and Soil and Water Management on the Advisory and Technical side, and Rural Organizations and Services, and Horticultural Research on the Education and Research side.

In addition, twenty six agencies, boards, and commissions, including the Agricultural Council of Ontario, the Ontario Food Terminal Board, and the Agricultural Research Institute of Ontario, report to the Legislative Assembly through the Minister of Agriculture and Food (see Agencies, Boards, and Commissions).

The head office of the Ministry of Agriculture and Food is presently located in Toronto, but will be moving to Guelph by 1990. The Ministry also staffs 54 county and district field offices with Agricultural Representatives, and operates the Guelph Agriculture Centre, numerous agricultural and veterinary laboratories, 5 colleges of agriculture and food technology, the Ontario Agricultural College at the University of Guelph, and the Ontario Agricultural Museum. The Ministry employs approximately 1,700 public servants.

MINISTRY OF AGRICULTURE AND FOOD

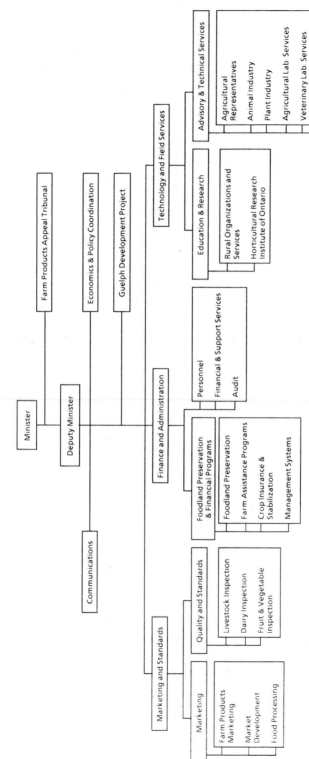

# PROGRAMS

## Consumption Tax Benefits Programs

The Ministry of Agriculture and Food makes available to farmers the following programs administered by the Ministry of Revenue:

*Fuel Tax Exemptions:* On coloured middle distillate fuel, at purchase; farmers can apply for a refund on non-taxable use of clear fuel.

*Retail Sales Tax Exemptions:* Available on items readily identified as goods used exclusively in a farming operation, and on items which may not be used in a farming operation but are exempt from tax when purchased for use by a person engaged in farming.

*Retail Sales Tax Refunds:* Available on materials or components purchased to construct grain bins or dryers, farm fencing materials including lumber for fences, and irrigation systems.

*Tax Refund Program on Gasoline:* Provides refunds on gasoline purchases within the farm operation.

## Credit Programs

The Ministry of Agriculture and Food administers the following credit programs:

*Beginning Farmer Assistance Program:* Provides interest rebates to beginning farmers to assist in their entry into the agricultural industry.

*Farmers in Transition Program:* Comprised of five social and economic initiatives designed to assist farm families who are trying to remain on their farms, and those who are re-establishing themselves outside of the industry. The program includes an immediate temporary deferral of action against farmers enrolled in Ministry financial assistance programs, a help-line, an independent farm family advisor service, re-establishment assistance, and a campaign to increase awareness of farmers' rights under existing programs.

*Ontario Family Farm Interest Rate Reduction:* Designed to ease the financing burden on those Ontario farmers who have accumulated high debt by providing a direct interest-reduction grant on up to $260,000 of short-term, intermediate and long-term debt. Assistance is targeted to viable operations which would under normal circumstances provide a family living for the owner/operators.

*Ontario Farm Adjustment Assistance Program:* Provides continuing assistance in the financial restructuring, reorganization, and consolidation of those farm enterprises which have loan guarantees and are experiencing financial difficulties, but which could be viable.

*Ontario Young Farmer Credit Program:* Provides a source of credit for young farmers (18–35 years of age) who are beginning or expanding their farm operation, when lenders are unwilling to advance normal loans because of the individual's lack of experience in managing a farm operation and in borrowing money.

*Operating Loan Guarantee Program:* Provides an improved cash flow and access to operating credit on an annual basis for up to three years for farm enterprises which are experiencing financial difficulties.

## Fruit and Vegetable Programs

*Fruit and Vegetable Quality Improvement Program:* Provides assistance to improve Ontario's ability to supply domestic and export markets with high quality produce, by encouraging the use of the latest storage and post-harvest treatment technology.

*Ontario Tender Fruit for Processing and Tree Planting Assistance:* Provides a rebate on the cost of new plantings of clingstone peaches.

## Land Improvement/Development Programs

*AgriNorth:* A six-part program which provides incentive grants for land development, new technology demonstrations, market development activities, and grain production development to improve and expand the Northern Ontario agricultural land base.

*Community Pastures Program:* Helps improve the income of livestock farmers by demonstrating proven pasture management techniques and providing off-farm pasture land, to enable livestock producers to increase the carrying capacity of their operation.

*Drainage Program:* Improves the productivity of agricultural land through construction or improvement of drainage works. Two or more landowners must identify a drainage problem on their property in order to qualify. The province pays one-third of the cost of the work assessed against agricultural lands in counties, two-thirds in territorial districts, and 80 percent of the cost in unorganized territories.

*Installation of Agricultural Tile Drainage:* Provides loans through municipal councils for installation of tile drainage. Upon approval, the municipality sells a debenture to the province to cover 75 percent of the cost of the work, or $20,000 per farmer, whichever is less.

*Northern Ontario Agricultural Development Program:* Provides funds to thirteen committees of district farmers to encourage agricultural development in Northern Ontario. Funding is provided through the Ministry of Agriculture and Food and the Ministry of Northern Development and Mines.

*Ontario Soil Conservation and Environmental Protection Assistance:* Provides assistance to producers for soil erosion control, sustaining crop productivity, and protecting water resources. Incentive grants are given for erosion control devices and manure storage projects.

*Soil and Water Environmental Enhancement Program:* Aimed at reducing phosphorus loadings from non-point agricultural cropland sources in the Lake Erie basin by 200 tonnes per year by 1990. This federal-provincial program includes demonstrations, technical assistance to farmers on soil and water conservation management, evaluation and development of new technology.

## Livestock Programs

*Artificial Insemination of Livestock Program:* Provides grants to cattle owners in Northern Ontario to promote the use of artificial insemination.

*Bear Damage to Livestock Compensation Program:* Provides compensation to owners whose livestock or poultry are killed or injured by bears.

*Canadian Western "Agribition" Livestock Transportation Assistance:* Provides assistance, jointly with the federal government, to transport livestock for show from Ontario to the Canadian Western Agribition, held annually in Regina, Saskatchewan.

*Dog Licensing and Livestock and Poultry Protection:* Provides for payment or compensation for loss or damage to livestock or poultry injured or killed by wolves or dogs. Under the terms of the Act of the same name, each municipality pays the compensation for both wolf and dog damage. The Ministry reimburses municipalities only for wolf damage claims paid out. In unorganized municipalities, compensation is provided by the Ministry directly to the producers for wolf damage. Compensation is also provided for loss or damage to honey bee colonies caused by bears.

*Hunter Damage Compensation Program:* Compensates farmers for loss or damage to livestock, farm machinery or equipment as a result of actions by careless hunters.

*Livestock Improvement Program for Northern Ontario:* Provides grants to assist farmers in Northern Ontario to improve production. The program is designed to reduce the cost differential of cattle prices between Northern and Southern Ontario.

*Northern Ontario Livestock Transportation Assistance Program:* Enables farmers in Northern Ontario to obtain livestock for herd improvement at delivered prices comparable to similar livestock purchased by southern Ontario farmers.

*Ontario Pork Industry Improvement Plan:* Provides incentive grants to improve the productivity, profitability, and competitive position of Ontario producers. The program is not intended to increase the number of pork producers or increase pork production, but to improve the efficiency of existing producers.

*Poultry Shows Assistance Program:* Assists local poultry associations in their efforts to promote, protect, and develop purebred poultry.

*Purebred Dairy Cattle, Beef, Sheep and Swine Sales Assistance:* Promotes the distribution of superior quality livestock within Ontario, through grants to breeders' clubs to defray the costs of conducting consignment sales.

*Rabies Indemnification Program:* Compensates owners for livestock that die as a result of rabies. This joint program of the federal and provincial government was established to encourage livestock production in Ontario.

*Red Meat Plan:* Provides a series of incentive grants to improve the efficiency and ensure the long-term viability of the red meat industry. Grants are directed at herd health improvement, handling facilities, feed testing, management practices, and research.

*Special Livestock Shows Assistance Program:* Encourages the improvement of livestock breeds raised for commercial purposes by providing grants for prize money at special shows of breeding stock. Shows must be sponsored by an Ontario breeders' association or club.

*Transportation of Livestock Exhibits Assistance Program:* Assists purebred livestock associations in assisting members to defray expenses incurred shipping livestock exhibits to national or international shows or exhibitions outside Ontario.

## Stabilization Programs

*Ontario Stabilization Programs:* The Ministry of Agriculture and Food administers nine programs to stabilize the incomes of Ontario farmers in periods of low market prices. Programs are in place for corn, soybeans, white beans, winter wheat, barley, apples, canola, potatoes, and oats.

*Tripartite Stabilization Programs:* Reduce income loss to producers from market risks by stabilizing prices. Producers receive a payout when prices fall below a pre-determined price formula. Cost of the program is shared equally by the province, the federal government, and participating producers. The program covers feeder calves, slaughter cattle, hogs, and sheep.

## Other Programs

*Beef Cattle Protection Program:* Protects producers and other sellers of beef cattle when a buyer defaults on payment, by assuring compensation for all cattle sold to packing plants, country dealers, slaughterhouses, or on consignment through community sale operators or commission agents. The program is self-financing: dealers, packing plant operators, slaughterhouse operators, and community sales operators are required to pay a license fee; buyers and sellers contribute to the compensation fund through deductions on sales of cattle for slaughter or further feeding (including calves).

*Cream Quality Assistance Program:* Grants are provided to assist producers in the purchase of new mechanical coolers, cream separators, and equipment used to wash utensils. Assistance is also available for construction or alteration of facilities required for the proper handling of farm-separated cream.

*Crop Introduction and Expansion Program:* Provides financial assistance to stimulate co-operation between private and public research and development efforts to accelerate the development of expanded crop opportunities for Ontario farmers. An expanded number of crop alternatives will offer producers greater flexibility in deciding their production mix and help improve their economic viability.

*Farm Assessment Procedures and Property Tax Program:* Farm assessment is based on the market value of the property as used for farming purposes (determined by examining farmer-to-farmer sales). This is generally lower than non-farm assessment, especially in those areas abutting urban municipalities. Farms are exempt from business tax except if a farmer carries on a separate business on the farm property. The province introduced the Farm Tax Reduction Program in 1970, which provides a 60 percent rebate of property taxes paid on eligible farm assessment.

*Grain Dryer Retrofit Assistance:* This program provides grants to retrofit existing commercial grain dryers with fully automatic control systems, to reduce the energy used in grain drying by an estimated 10 percent. The program is a co-operative venture of the Ministry of Agriculture and Food and the Ministry of Energy.

*Grain Financial Protection Program:* Provides compensation to grain corn and soybean producers if a licensed dealer defaults on payment, or if there is a shortfall in grain corn or soybeans held by a storage operator licensed under the *Grain Elevator Storage Act.* The program is self-financing, as dealers submit an annual fee and producers pay into the compensation fund through deductions on all producer-to-dealer sales of grain corn and soybeans.

*Greenhouse Energy Efficiency Incentive Program:* Funds are available to upgrade greenhouses to conserve energy, lower production costs, and make Ontario-grown greenhouse products more competitive in the marketplace.

*Marketing Assistance Program for Pork:* Assists the Ontario pork industry by providing incentive grants for upgrading pork packing and processing, developing new products, supporting export initiatives, and conducting consumer attitude studies.

*Produce Vegetables Financial Protection Program:* Protects growers of processing vegetables by providing compensation, should a processor default on payment. The program is self-financing, as processors pay an annual license fee, while producers contribute to the plan through payments deducted by the processor at the time of sale.

*Seasonal Housing Assistance Program:* Assists fruit, field-grown vegetable, and tobacco producers with construction or renovation costs of housing for seasonal workers. The program is funded jointly by the Ministry of Agriculture and Food and the federal government's Canada Employment and Immigration Commission.

*Small Food Processors Assistance Program:* Encourages expansion of small food processors by improving their access to market information, strengthening business planning capabilities, and providing financial assistance for capital projects.

## EXPENDITURE ESTIMATES

*Estimated Expenditures 1987–88:*

| | |
|---|---|
| Ministry Administration | $ 18,965,438 |
| Agricultural Marketing and Standards | 34,847,100 |
| Agricultural Technology Development and Field Services | 184,423,700 |
| Financial Assistance to Agriculture | 320,967,600 |
| **Ministry Total:** | **$559,203,838** |

## AGENCIES, BOARDS, AND COMMISSIONS

The following ABCs report to the Legislative Assembly through the Minister of Agriculture and Food:

*Advisory Committee on Diploma Education:* Acts in an advisory capacity regarding diploma education at the five colleges of agricultural technology. The committee may assess the changing educational requirements of those people involved in farming, agribusiness, and the agricultural industry in the future, and make recommendations about future educational programs.

*Agricultural Council of Ontario:* Provides a regular and independent channel of information and advice to the Minister from senior persons with expertise in the practical aspects of agribusiness and consumerism; functions as a knowledgeable and authoritative resource to which issues of longer-term impact can be referred for research and comment.

*Agricultural Licensing and Registration Review Board:* Hears appeals under the following Acts: *Agricultural Tile and Drainage Installation Act, Animals for Research Act, Artificial Insemination of Livestock Act, Dead Animal Disposal Act, Farm Products Grades and Sales Act, Grain Elevator Storage Act, Livestock and Livestock Products Act, Livestock Community Sales Act, Livestock Medicines Act, Meat Inspection Act, Plant Diseases Act, Provincial Auctioneers Act,* and *Riding Horse Establishments Act.*

*Agricultural Rehabilitation and Development Directorate:* Enables the Province to jointly undertake programs with the federal government for the more efficient use and economic development of rural lands, the development of income and employment opportunities in rural areas, and the improvement of the standard of living in those areas.

*Agricultural Research Institute of Ontario:* Reviews Ministry-funded research programs at the Ministry's colleges of agricultural technology, the University of Guelph, and horticultural research and experimental stations, and makes recommendations to the Minister to ensure that these programs meet the needs of Ontario agriculture.

*Beginning Farmer Assistance Program Review Committee:* Provides an avenue of appeal for applicants denied assistance under the Beginning Farmer Assistance Program.

*Cooperative Loans Board of Ontario:* Administers existing loans of cooperative associations under the *Cooperative Loans Act.*

*Crop Insurance Commission of Ontario:* Provides farmers with an insurance program against loss due to natural perils for the major crops grown in Ontario; conducts surveys and research programs relating to crop insurance; and obtains statistics for Commission use.

*Farm Income Stabilization Commission of Ontario:* Provides for surveys and research relating to farm income stabilization, and obtains statistics for Commission use.

*Farm Products Marketing Board:* Provides an independent, accessible avenue of appeal in matters relating to the *Ontario Farm Products Marketing Act* and the *Milk Act.* Serves as a License Review Board under the *Milk Act,* the *Farm Products Marketing Act,* the *Edible Oil Products Act,* and the *Oleomargarine Act.*

*Farm Products Payment Board:* Administers the fund established under the *Farm Products Payments Act* to protect producers from non-payment by dealers; investigates claims; grants or refuses payment of claims; and determines the amount and manner of payment.

*Farm Tax Rebate Appeal Board:* Provides an owner of farm property with an independent avenue of appeal when denied a rebate under the Farm Tax Reduction Program.

*Grain Financial Protection Board:* Collects fees, administers the fund, and approves claims made against the fund set up under the Grain Financial Protection Program, to protect producers in the event of default on payment by a licensed dealer.

*Livestock Financial Protection Board:* Collects fees, administers the fund, and approves claims made against the fund set up under the Ontario Beef Cattle Financial Protection Program, to protect producers and other sellers of beef cattle in the event of default on payment by a licensed buyer.

*Livestock Medicines Advisory Committee:* Reviews all legislation and regulations pertaining to livestock medicines, and advises the Minister on matters relating to the control and regulation of livestock medicines.

*Milk Commission of Ontario:* Supervises the Ontario Milk Marketing Board and Cream Producers Marketing Board; develops and implements policy;

provides producer and consumer education about marketing; and evaluates markets and market research priorities.

*Ontario Agriculture Museum Advisory Board:* Advises the Minister on matters relating to the museum and those concerned with achieving the museum's mandate.

*Ontario Agricultural Museum Artifacts Valuation Committee:* Performs appraisal services of artifacts and structures in which the Ontario Agricultural Museum has a interest, either as a purchaser, borrower, lender, recipient of a donation, or for any other purpose.

*Ontario Crop Insurance Arbitration Board:* Hears appeals on administration of the Crop Insurance Plan.

*Ontario Drainage Tribunal:* Provides a readily accessible forum for appeals under the *Drainage Act*; establishes rules of practice and procedure; deliberates on evidence of hearings; and makes decisions independent of the Ministry. The Tribunal may recommend to the Minister any changes in legislation that it considers advisable.

*Ontario Farm Machinery Board:* Encourages the resolution of problems encountered by farmers and the farm machinery industry arising out of the sale of farm machinery, its repair, maintenance, and use.

*Ontario Grain Corn Council:* Studies, advises, and makes recommendations on all matters relating to the production and marketing of Ontario grain corn, to any or all segments of the grain corn industry, and to any level of government.

*Ontario Junior Farmers Establishment Loan Corporation:* Ensures the repayment of outstanding loans of mortgagor and repayment to the Treasurer of Ontario of any indebtedness.

*Processing Vegetable Financial Protection Board:* Arbitrates payment disputes between fruit and vegetable producers and the dealers to whom they have sold their produce.

*Produce Arbitration Board:* Arbitrates payment disputes between fruit and vegetable producers and the dealers to whom they have sold their products.

*Wolf Damage Assessment Board:* Makes binding decisions in situations where the Livestock Commissioner feels there is insufficient evidence to conclude that wolves were responsible for any claim.

## LEGISLATION

The Ministry of Agriculture and Food is responsible for the following Acts:

*Abandoned Orchards Act:* Provides for action against neglected orchards by commercial fruit growers to prevent spread of disease and insect infestation.

*Agricultural Associations Act:* Provides for incorporation of agricultural producer groups by Order-in-Council, and regulates their operation.

*Agricultural Committees Act:* Provides for committees to be formed to cooperate with the local agricultural representative for the improvement of agriculture, the encouragement of farm youth activities, and the coordination of agricultural groups.

*Agricultural Rehabilitation and Development Act:* Provides for federal-provincial cost sharing and cooperation in programs concerning rural land use, rural employment, conservation, and related matters.

*Agricultural Representatives Act:* Provides for the appointment and remuneration of agricultural representatives.

*Agricultural Research Institute of Ontario Act:* Provides for the appointment of persons to the Agricultural Research Institute, which has the responsibility for research in all matters relating to agriculture.

*Agricultural Societies Act:* Provides for the formation and regulation of agricultural societies to study, hold fairs, exhibitions, public meetings, horse racing meets, and other related activities.

*Agricultural Tile Drainage Installation Act:* Provides for the regulation and licensing of tile drainage installation operators.

*Animals for Research Act:* Provides for the care and provision of animals for research and teaching, and regulates research and supply facilities.

*Artificial Insemination of Livestock Act:* Provides for the regulation and licensing by the Livestock Commissioner of those engaged in the business of providing artificial insemination services for livestock.

*Beef Cattle Marketing Act:* Provides for the establishment and standardization of procedures affecting the sale of cattle or carcasses and for the designation and financing of the Ontario Cattlemen's Association.

*Bees Act:* Provides for the registration and regulation of beekeepers.

*Bull Owners' Liability Act:* Provides for civil and quasi-criminal liability of persons who allow a bull to escape their property.

*Commodity Boards and Marketing Agencies Act:* Authorizes the imposition and collection of levies by commodity boards or marketing agencies.

*Commodity Board Members Act:* Prohibits a person from becoming or continuing to be a member of a commodity marketing board while in contravention of the *Farm Products Marketing Act.*

*Cooperative Loans Act:* Provides for first mortgage loans of up to $100,000 to be made to agricultural cooperative associations by the Treasurer of Ontario.

*Crop Insurance Act:* Provides for insurance of agriculture crops to be written in cooperation with the Government of Canada on a cost-sharing basis.

*Dead Animal Disposal Act:* Provides for the regulation of the disposal of the carcasses of animals dying for reasons other than slaughter and for the licensing of those engaged in this service.

*Dog Licensing and Livestock and Poultry Protection Act:* Permits municipalities to levy taxes on owners of dogs and provides for the payment of awards to owners of livestock killed by dogs or wolves, or aviaries destroyed by bears.

*Drainage Act:* Provides for municipally constructed drainage works paid for by the municipality which collects back the cost by levy against all benefitting owners.

*Edible Oil Products Act:* Regulates the marketing of non-butterfat dairy substitutes and provides for licensing of manufacturers and wholesalers.

*Farm Income Stabilization Act:* Provides for the establishment of an Income Stabilization Commission with powers to collect premiums and make payments to producers enrolled in a plan with respect to marketed farm products in times of low prices.

*Farm Products Containers Act:* Provides funding for the Ontario Fruit and Vegetable Growers' Association by means of licensing fees imposed on farm product containers.

*Farm Products Grades and Sales Act:* Provides for the inspection, grading, packing, and marketing of farm products.

*Farm Products Payments Act:* Provides for funds to be set up for payment of compensation to unpaid producers of farm products.

*Fur Farms Act:* Provides for the licensing and regulation of fur farms.

*Grain Elevator Storage Act:* Provides for the licensing and regulation of grain storage facilities.

*Horticultural Societies Act:* Provides for the incorporation of societies interested in horticultural pursuits and regulates their procedures.

*Hunter Damage Compensation Act:* Provides for compensation to farmers who suffer injury to animals and certain classes of equipment by hunters.

*Junior Farmer Establishment Act:* Provides for loans to be made to "Junior Farmers" as defined in the Act, to be secured by mortgage.

*Livestock and Livestock Products Act:* Provides for the licensing and regulation of livestock dealers and for the grading of livestock and livestock products, including eggs.

*Livestock Branding Act:* Provides for the recording of livestock brands.

*Livestock Community Sales Act:* Provides for regulation of livestock community sales and licensing of operators of such sales.

*Livestock Medicines Act:* Provides for regulation and licensing of persons other than pharmacists or veterinarians selling livestock medicines to owners of livestock for the treatment of livestock.

*Meat Inspection Act:* Provides for inspection of animals and carcasses in slaughtering plants and regulates plant conditions and methods of operations.

*Milk Act:* Provides for regulation of marketing of milk and milk products and regulates the conditions under which milk is produced and distributed, except the grading of milk and its products.

*Ministry of Agriculture and Food Act:* Vests control of the Ministry in the Minister of Agriculture and Food and provides for the establishment of programs to encourage agriculture.

*Non-Resident Agricultural Land Interest Registration Act:* Provides for the registration of non-residents who purchase agricultural land.

*Oleomargarine Act:* Regulates the marketing of oleomargarine and provides for licensing of manufacturers and wholesalers.

*Ontario Agricultural Museum Act:* Provides for the establishment of the Ontario Agricultural Museum.

*Ontario Food Terminal Act:* Establishes the Ontario Food Terminal and provides for its direction and management.

*Plant Diseases Act:* Provides for the control or eradication of diseases that affect plants, for the power of inspectors, and for the licensing of nursery operators.

*Pounds Act:* Provides for the impounding of livestock animals running at large and fixes responsibility.

*Provincial Auctioneers Act:* Provides for the licensing of auctioneers of pure-bred livestock, which eliminates the necessity for municipal licensing.

*Riding Horse Establishments Act:* Provides for the licensing of riding horse establishment operators and provides for regulations respecting care of horses in such establishments.

*Seed Potatoes Act:* Provides for the establishment of "seed potato restricted areas," provides controls over movement of potatoes into, out of, or within such areas, and provides for restrictions on the type of potatoes planted in such areas.

*Sheep and Wool Marketing Act:* Provides for payments of licence fees to the Ontario Sheep Association on sales of sheep and wool.

*Stock Yards Act:* Establishes the Ontario Stock Yards Board and defines its powers and duties.

*Tile Drainage Act:* Provides for loans to farmers from municipalities to construct tile drains. Loans are repaid by a rate levied on the property and financed in the interim by municipal debentures sold to the Treasurer of Ontario.

*Topsoil Preservation Act:* Provides authority for municipalities to enact by-laws regulating or prohibiting the removal of topsoil and for the issuing of permits.

*Veterinarians Act:* Provides for the registration and governance of veterinarians in Ontario.

*Weed Control Act:* Provides for destruction of weeds, appointment of inspectors, and collecting costs from landowners.

MINISTRY OF ENERGY

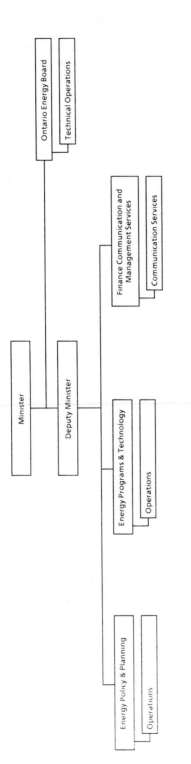

Minister

Ontario Energy Board

Technical Operations

Deputy Minister

Finance Communication and Management Services

Communication Services

Energy Programs & Technology

Operations

Energy Policy & Planning

Operations

# MINISTRY OF ENERGY

## ROLES AND FUNCTIONS

The Ministry of Energy ensures that Ontario has an adequate and secure supply of energy that meets the needs of Ontario residents and industry, at reasonable prices, in a manner consistent with the protection of the environment. To fulfill this responsibility the Ministry works with other ministries and agencies of the government and with the private energy sector. Major functions include reviewing and advising on energy matters and policy; maintaining liaison between the government and Ontario Hydro; applying policy by coordinating the government's energy-related activities that support research, development, and demonstration of energy technologies; promoting effective and efficient use of energy; and intervening on energy matters before federal and provincial tribunals.

## BACKGROUND HISTORY

An Advisory Committee on Energy, appointed by an Order-in-Council in August 1971, recommended that a separate Ministry for Energy be established to develop a comprehensive and coordinated energy policy for Ontario. At that time, energy matters in Ontario were affected by 39 major acts, and nine ministries were involved to varying degrees. This recommendation was accepted and a new ministry was established in 1973 under the *Ministry of Energy Act*.

## ORGANIZATION

The Ministry of Energy is organized into three major divisions (see organization chart):

1. *Energy Policy and Planning:* Responsible for the development, review, and presentation of policies and priorities related to the supply, demand, and pricing of all forms of energy. It is also responsible for the analysis and collection of available energy information to provide a framework for policy and program initiatives. The five Sections in this Division include Economics and Forecasts, Electricity, Energy Contingency, Finance, Rates and Utilization, and Oil and Gas.

2. *Programs and Technology:* Responsible for programs and activities to encourage the development and use of conservation, demand management, and

alternative energy options. The Division maintains expertise and awareness of energy technologies, products, and services and provides assistance to government, municipalities, industry, and the general public. The four Sections in this Division include Conservation and Community Programs, Industry and Transportation Programs, Energy Technology Development, and Energy Technology Research.

3. *Communications and Management Services:* Provides a communications function for the Ministry.

In addition, Ontario Hydro, the Ontario Energy Board, and the Ontario Energy Corporation report to the Legislative Assembly through the Minister of Energy (see Agencies, Boards, and Commissions).

The head office of the Ministry of Energy is located in Toronto. The Ministry employs approximately 220 public servants.

## PROGRAMS

### Energy Policy and Planning Division

*Economics and Forecasts Section*

The Economics and Forecasts Section collects and disseminates statistical information on Ontario's energy situation. It gives advice and prepares analyses on economic developments internationally and within Canada, and on the impact of energy environment changes on the national and provincial economies. The Section assists in developing policies on revenue sharing, taxation, deregulation, and pricing of all energy forms. It forecasts energy prices and primary and secondary energy demand in Ontario.

*Electricity Section*

The Electricity Section provides analysis and policy advice on the means of generating electricity and its distribution by Ontario Hydro, municipal utilities, and the private sector. It advocates Ontario's position to the federal government and other jurisdictions, including representing Ontario's interest before regulatory hearings. It encourages the economic development and utilization of indigenous hydraulic resources and provides policy advice and analysis on the role of alternative electrical generation.

*Energy Contingency Planning Section*

The Energy Contingency Planning Section provides analysis, policy advice, and coordination of the development, maintenance, and implementation of an effective provincial contingency plan for a possible future oil shortage. It advocates Ontario's position to the federal government, other provincial governments, and municipal governments.

*Finance, Rates, and Utilization Section*

The Finance, Rates, and Utilization Section provides advice and analysis on the financial impact of changes in the energy environment and energy policy on the energy industry, government, and the private sector. This section examines the impact on the energy sector of changes in the business and financial environment, tax policy, and program financing. Policy advice and analysis is given on rates, tolls, and tariffs for the sale, transportation, distribution, and the efficient use of energy by business, industry, and individuals.

*Oil and Gas Section*

The Oil and Gas Section provides analysis and policy advice on issues relating to the supply, distribution, and pricing of crude oil, petroleum products, petrochemical feedstocks, and natural gas. It advocates Ontario's position to the federal government and other jurisdictions, and represents Ontario's interest before regulatory hearings. It provides policy advice and analysis on the role, supply, and pricing of alternative fuels.

**Programs and Technology Division**

*Conservation and Community Programs Section*

The Conservation and Community Programs Section develops and implements programs for consumers, homeowners, public and secondary schools, religious and commercial buildings, and public, institutional, and municipal buildings. The Ministry provides grants for energy management for government or public institutional and municipal buildings. Programs include:

*Consumer/Residential Conservation Programs:*

1. *Association of Municipalities of Ontario Joint Program:* Provides information to promote energy efficiency in all municipalities through a newsletter, seminars, and conference presentations.

2. *Draftproof Ontario:* Teams are trained and supervised by local contractors to caulk and weatherstrip the homes of low-income people and senior residents, at no cost. In this ongoing program, eligible homes include Ontario Housing Corporation subsidized units, and the homes of people receiving Welfare and Family Benefits from the Ministry of Community and Social Services.

3. *Residential Advisory Program:* Technical advisory (HeatSave) clinics and related services are available in selected Ontario cities and northern communities each heating season. To improve homeowners' energy awareness, technical publications and demonstrations are provided. The program is delivered through regional and local municipal governments.

4. *Retail Sector Training Program:* Provides support to industry and retail groups which are in direct contact with the public in supplying energy-effi-

cient products and services. Support includes training and upgrading of skills in home renovation. Retail Sector Training is administered through a cost-sharing agreement with the federal government.

5. *Small Business Advisory:* Features technical advice on cost-saving measures to small business, as well as professional and retail services, that are based in residential-type premises. Regional and local municipal governments are responsible for delivery of the program, and energy audits are emphasized.

6. *Training and Technical Assistance:* Funds training programs, case studies, and provides technical information on an ongoing basis.

*Energy Education Programs:*

1. *Children's Outreach:* Drama, puppets, and film are used to illustrate to young children the importance of energy and why they should use energy wisely; features the Ministry's energy conservation play, "The Conserving Kingdom."

2. *Curriculum, Documents and Teaching Aids:* Production of curriculum materials in cooperation with the Ministry of Education to help teachers with energy topics in the classroom. Includes teaching aids referred to in the professional development program.

3. *Teacher Professional Development:* Workshops, seminars, and an annual conference assist educators in upgrading their energy knowledge and teaching skills. This program funds the Energy Educators of Ontario, a teacher organization, to provide networking in education through regional meetings, computer data, and a news magazine called *Energy Alert,* published three times a year.

*Municipal Oil Conversion and Energy Conservation Programs:*

1. *Cities Energy Forum:* Involves voluntary support from the private business community at an executive level, and public sector support at the municipal level, for the development, maintenance, and monitoring of energy conservation in buildings. It applies to municipalities across Ontario.

2. *Downtown Energy Forum:* This program is similar to the Cities Energy Forum. This ongoing program began in Toronto, in 1978, and in Ottawa, in 1982.

3. *Municipal Energy Audit Program:* Cost-sharing salary subsidies are provided to municipalities to offset the cost of hiring an assigned energy auditor.

*Public/Institutional Energy Programs:*

1. *Government Oil and Energy Management Program:* Stimulates the use of cost-effective technical and operating measures to improve energy efficiency and fuel use in government facilities through advice, financial assistance,

and operation training.

2. *Institutional Oil and Energy Management Program:* Stimulates the use of cost-effective technical and operating measures to improve energy efficiency and fuel use through advice, financial assistance, and operation training for: medical buildings, homes for children, educational institutions, tourism, and recreational facilities.

3. *Religious Buildings and Private Schools Energy Management:* A low-cost, self-help voluntary program designed to encourage cost-effective energy-saving measures in religious buildings and private schools through technical and management advice.

*Industry and Transportation Programs Section*

The Industry and Transportation Programs Section develops and implements programs for energy management and energy efficiency measures designed for the private sector. Programs include:

*Agriculture Energy Services Programs* (in cooperation with the Ministry of Agriculture and Food):

1. *Grain Dryer Retrofit Assistance Program:* Aims to reduce energy use in the commercial grain drying sector and to increase product revenue by reducing shrinkage and improving dried grain quality.

2. *Greenhouse Energy Efficiency Program:* Aims to improve energy use in existing greenhouses.

*Small Hydro Encouragement Programs:*

1. *Industry Development:* Offers Ontario's small hydro industry assistance in improving small hydro technology and expanding export markets.

2. *Northern Small Hydro:* Provides assistance to commercial and industrial businesses in remote areas of Northern Ontario not connected to the provincial electricity grid system.

3. *Site Assessment:* Provides assistance to prospective site developers in the initial engineering assessment of small hydro sites, and in the financial and legal evaluation of development options.

*Transportation Energy Programs:*

1. *DriveSave:* Working with representatives of private sector clients, the aim of this program is to improve the energy efficiency and fuel mix of light vehicle fleets, to improve energy efficiency in new drivers, and to transfer information to the general public.

2. *Municipal Transport:* Working with urban planners, municipal engineers, and fleet managers, the aim of this program is to improve the efficiency of urban travel through systems management and infrastructure improvements, and to improve the efficiency and fuel mix of municipal fleets.

3. *Government Programs:* applies DriveSave, TruckSave, and fuel substitutions information to the Government of Ontario fleet.

4. *TruckSave:* Working with the trucking industry, the aim of this program is to improve the energy efficiency of heavy vehicles through engineering, maintenance, management, and driver training.

*Energy Technology Development Section*

The Energy Technology Development Section develops and manages energy technology activities to assist the private sector to develop technologies for energy conservation and energy supply options. Assistance is available through the provision of advice and information and through financial assistance to share the risk of specific energy technology development. Section activities deal with alternative transportation fuels including propane, natural gas for vehicles, diesel substitution, and methanol blends; the demonstration of energy from waste and the management of a municipal solid waste program; and the development of remote electrical power. In addition, the Section is involved with energy efficient processes concerning gas and residential and building technologies. Programs include:

*Energy from Waste Program:* EFW provides technical and capital assistance to municipalities and private interests to encourage them to develop energy from waste projects.

*EnerSearch:* In 1986, the Ministry introduced EnerSearch, an incentive program to assist the private sector in research, development, testing, and initial demonstration activities of innovative energy technologies in Ontario.

*Northern Ontario Wood Energy Program:* Financial assistance is available to promote energy recovery from wood residue.

*Energy Technology Research Section*

The Energy Technology Research Section develops and manages energy activities to assist industry and the research community to increase energy supply options and improve efficiency. Services include technical advice, information, co-ordination, and matching of diverse research activities and industry interest. Funding assistance is available to share the risk of specific energy research. Current activities deal with electrotechnology projects including plasma applications in metallurgy and waste destruction, high temperature heat pumps, microwaves, and other forms of radiant heat; fuels research, fossil fuels, and natural gas research related to industrial applications, and alternative transportation fuels; advanced energy systems, including conversion of biomass to fuels and chemicals, anaerobic digestion of industrial waste, hydrogen fuel cells, batteries, and fusion technologies. Federal funding is allocated to a number of the above projects.

## Communications Services Group

The Communications Services Group provides public information on energy. The group is also responsible for the development of programs for public relations and community events, including display shows, conferences, seminars, media events, and openings. The group co-ordinates and directs production of information materials such as audio-visuals, publications, and exhibits. A key function of the section is to offer advice to the Ministry on its various programs dealing with effective communication strategies, promotion, distribution planning, and marketing.

## EXPENDITURE ESTIMATES

*Estimated Expenditures 1987–88:*

| | |
|---|---|
| Administration | $ 10,092,600 |
| Policy and Planning | 4,837,000 |
| Energy Management and Technology | 24,193,800 |
| Ontario Energy Board | 4,968,600 |
| **Ministry total:** | **$ 44,092,000** |

## AGENCIES, BOARDS, AND COMMISSIONS

The following ABCs report to the Legislative Assembly through the Minister of Energy:

*Ontario Energy Board:* Jurisdiction over energy-related matters including: regulation of natural gas rates; municipal franchise approvals; hydrocarbon pipeline construction and related environmental concerns; expropriations for utility access; and control of utility accounting procedures. No natural gas utility operating in Ontario under the Board's jurisdiction can change its rates, construct certain facilities or enter into franchise agreements with municipalities without first obtaining the approval of the Board through the public hearing process. Upon reference being made to it, the Board also acts in an advisory role to the Minister of Energy with regard to Ontario Hydro, to the Minister of Natural Resources respecting certain oil and gas production concerns, and to the Lieutenant Governor in Council on other energy matters.

*Ontario Energy Corporation:* Established by the Government of Ontario in 1975 to implement government policies through investment in energy ventures. The Corporation invests in new energy technologies and in energy exploration, primarily with private sector companies. The OEC has established four subsidiary companies through which most of its investments are managed:

1. *Ontario Energy Ventures Limited:* A participant in commercially attractive projects which explore creative alternatives to conventional sources of energy or involve new energy technologies.

2. *Ontario Energy Resources Limited:* A holding company for the Corporation's 25 percent interest in Suncor Inc.

3. *Onexco Oil & Gas Limited:* Invests in ventures which explore for and develop oil and natural gas throughout Ontario and Canada. In addition, Onexco Oil and Gas Ltd. is two-thirds owner of Trillium Exploration Corporation, which explores for oil and gas on frontier prospects.

4. *Onexco Minerals Limited:* Involved in energy minerals exploration.

*Ontario Hydro:* Supplies electrical energy to the people of Ontario indirectly through 316 associated municipal utilities, and directly to more than 779,000 rural customers. The Ontario Hydro Electrical Inspection Program provides technical guidance to consultants, contractors, architects, manufacturers, and customers on problems concerning installation of electrical equipment and adherence to the Electrical Safety Code Book. The Rural Electrical Service and Billing Inquiry Program answers inquiries on policy and practices from rural services. Hydro also operates Nuclear Communication Centres in Pickering, Bruce, and Darlington to provide educational information to the public on nuclear power.

## LEGISLATION

The Ministry of Energy is responsible for the following Acts:

*Ministry of Energy Act:* This Act defines the Ministry's objectives and responsibilities for reviewing energy matters and coordinating the energy-related activities of the government.

*Ontario Energy Board Act:* This Act defines the structure and powers of the Ontario Energy Board. The Board regulates natural gas utilities in Ontario.

*Ontario Energy Corporation Act:* This Act defines the structure and powers of the Ontario Energy Corporation. The Corporation participates in energy projects.

*Power Corporation Act:* This Act governs Ontario Hydro, which is a publicly-owned utility supplying electric power at cost to municipal utilities, rural, and large industrial customers.

# MINISTRY OF THE ENVIRONMENT

## ROLES AND FUNCTIONS

The goal of the Ministry of the Environment is to protect human health and the ecosystem of Ontario by ensuring that acceptable environmental standards of air, water, and land are maintained. The Ministry of the Environment is primarily concerned with the regulation, implementation, and enforcement of the environmental standards and guidelines set out in such Acts as the *Ontario Water Resources Act* and the *Environmental Assessment Act*, through its Operations Division. Although the Ministry develops policy, standards, and guidelines and provides laboratory services, the majority of its activity is in the field, where Ministry staff enforce policy and ensure that industry, institutions, local governments, and other potential polluters are meeting environmental requirements.

## BACKGROUND HISTORY

In the mid 1950s, responding to general concern about water and its purity, the Ontario Legislature passed the *Ontario Water Resources Act*. This created the Ontario Water Resources Commission (OWRC) and gave it responsibility in areas of water quality, water supply, and purification. The OWRC made rapid strides toward solving water supply problems throughout the province by creating water treatment facilities to combat pollution. During its 15 years of operation, the OWRC established a world-wide reputation as one of the leading authorities in this field. With the water-related programs underway, attention began to shift to other forms of environmental pollution. The Department of Health established branches in the mid-1960s to investigate air pollution and pollution of the environment by waste disposal. The Pesticides Control Service of the Department of Health became more involved with environmental matters as the broader ecological implications of pesticide use were questioned in the late 1960s.

The passage of the *Environmental Protection Act* in 1971, acknowledged to be one of the strictest documents of its type in North America, resulted in the creation of the Department of the Environment. This Department was comprised of the Air and Waste Management and Pesticides Control Sections from the Department of Health plus a branch that dealt with Ontario's conservation authorities. Ontario then had two major agencies dealing with the protection of the environment, the OWRC and the Department of the Environment. Subsequently, it was felt that a more cohesive and coordinated effort toward preserving the environmental quality of the

MINISTRY OF THE ENVIRONMENT

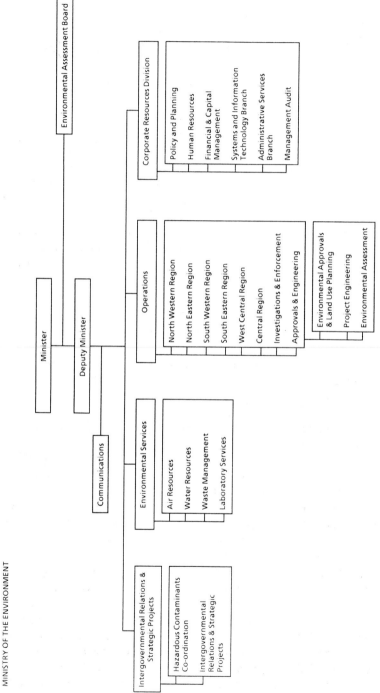

Minister

Environmental Assessment Board

Deputy Minister

Communications

Intergovernmental Relations & Strategic Projects

- Hazardous Contaminants Co-ordination
- Intergovernmental Relations & Strategic Projects

Environmental Services

- Air Resources
- Water Resources
- Waste Management
- Laboratory Services

Operations

- North Western Region
- North Eastern Region
- South Western Region
- South Eastern Region
- West Central Region
- Central Region
- Investigations & Enforcement
- Approvals & Engineering

- Environmental Approvals & Land Use Planning
- Project Engineering
- Environmental Assessment

Corporate Resources Division

- Policy and Planning
- Human Resources
- Financial & Capital Management
- Systems and Information Technology Branch
- Administrative Services Branch
- Management Audit

province could be made by one organization. With this in mind, the Ontario Ministry of the Environment was created in April 1972, combining the OWRC, and the Air Management and Waste Management Branches and Pesticides Control Service of the Department of the Environment. The legislative mandate of the Ministry was extended in 1973 through the passing of the *Pesticides Act.*

In April 1974, the Ministry underwent a major reorganization, which had two basic objectives. One of these was to regroup the staff of the Ministry so as to facilitate the achievement of four defined goals:

1. Control over contaminant emission;

2. Establishment of environmental safeguards in planning;

3. Improved management of waste and water; and

4. Maintenance of restorative and enhancement measures.

A further objective was to transfer the "delivery" of programs from Toronto to local communities throughout the province, bringing service and control functions closer to the people they affect. To this end, regional offices have been established in Kingston, Toronto, Hamilton, Thunder Bay, London, and Sudbury; and a number of district offices have been opened, to deliver more local service within each region. This has brought the services the Ministry delivers into closer contact with the people needing them, thus allowing the Ministry to better fulfill its role.

In 1975, the *Environmental Assessment Act* was put in place. This Act requires that proposed major undertakings, whether governmental, municipal, or private, be assessed at the earliest stage for their environmental consequences and may require that an undertaking be altered or even cancelled.

## ORGANIZATION

The Ministry of the Environment is organized into four divisions (see organization chart):

1. *Environmental Services:* Includes the Air Resources, Laboratory Services, Waste Management, and Water Resources Branches.

2. *Intergovernmental Relations and Strategic Projects:* Includes the Hazardous Contaminants Coordination, Acid Precipitation Coordination, and Intergovernmental Relations and Strategic Projects Branches.

3. *Operations:* Includes the Approvals and Engineering, Environmental Approvals and Land Use Planning, Environmental Assessment, Investigations and Enforcement, and Projects Engineering Branches, and the Spills Action Centre, plus six regional operations branches.

4. *Corporate Resources:* Provides administrative support to the Ministry, such as Policy and Planning, Human Resources, and Management Audit.

In addition, ten agencies, boards, and commissions, including the Ontario Waste Management Corporation (OWMC) and the Environmental Assessment Board, report to the Legislative Assembly through the Minister of the Environment (see Agencies, Boards, and Commissions).

The head office of the Ministry of the Environment is located in Toronto. The Ministry also operates 30 regional and district offices throughout the province, and employs approximately 1700 public servants.

## PROGRAMS

### Environmental Services Division

The role of the Environmental Services Division is: to provide specialized technical, scientific, and engineering support services in the delivery of Ministry programs designed to protect air quality, protect surface and groundwater quality and quantity, manage wastes, and ensure an adequate quality and quantity of drinking water; and to research, plan, develop and modify programs necessary to implement the legislative responsibilities of the Ministry. The Division consists of four branches: Air Resources, Laboratory Services, Waste Management, and Water Resources.

*The Air Resources Branch:* Develops and monitors the results of plans and programs designed to protect air quality. Branch activities include assessing the presence and transport of airborne substances and determining their effects; developing regulatory mechanisms to protect air quality; formulating policy recommendations concerning all matters of air pollution in the province and working as directed on similar policy formulation exercises at the federal and intergovernmental level; and providing expertise on a pollution control technology and processes.

*Laboratory Services Branch:* Provides analytical laboratory services to the Ministry, including sample testing support for Ministry programs, developing analytical methods for measuring pollutants, and provision of expertise in data interpretation and in planning and implementing Ministry programs.

*Waste Management Branch:* Develops plans and programs designed to monitor and manage the generation, reuse, collection, transportation, treatment, and disposal of domestic, commercial, and industrial wastes. Branch activities include the development of regulatory mechanisms for the control of treatment and disposal systems for hazardous wastes, hauled liquid industrial wastes, and other wastes requiring special treatment in order to protect public health and the environment; the development of regulatory mechanisms for the control of waste management sites in order to confine or reduce their detrimental effects; and the promotion of recovery and utilization of material and energy resources from waste through the provision of market information, financial assistance, and the development of technology.

*Water Resources Branch:* Strives to protect and upgrade water quality in lakes, rivers, streams, and groundwater; to develop water resources and provide for the fair sharing and conservation of available resources for multiple uses; and to protect the public from contaminants in water and fish. Branch activities include assessing the presence of waterborne pollutants and determining their pathways and effects on water quality and aquatic ecosystems; developing regulatory mechanisms and management techniques to protect the quality of drinking water, surface water, and ground water and their uses; evaluating conditions in the Great Lakes and determining plans for the protection and enhancement of water quality; and providing expertise on drinking-water control technology and on drinking-water treatment processes.

### Intergovernmental Relations and Strategic Projects Division

The role of the Intergovernmental Relations and Strategic Projects Division is to coordinate the approach of the Ministry to designated critical issues, to coordinate its intergovernmental activities, and to assess the significance of hazardous contaminants and coordinate Ministry activities for their control. The Division consists of the Acid Precipitation Coordination Office, the Hazardous Contaminants Coordination Branch, and the Intergovenmental Relations and Strategic Projects Branch.

*Acid Precipitation Coordination Office:* Coordinates all activities in the Ministry associated with acid precipitation. Branch activities include providing resources for Ministry branches involved in scientific, socio-economic, legal, and public relations aspects of the acid precipitation issue and providing support for interprovincial and international initiatives concerning acid precipitation.

*Hazardous Contaminants Coordination Branch:* Assesses the significance of hazardous contaminants and coordinates Ministry activities for their control, and establishes standards for the protection of public health and the environment. Branch activities include identifying hazardous contaminants and their potential effects on the environment; assigning priorities to hazardous contaminants requiring control strategies; coordinating the development of plans and programs for the control of hazardous contaminants and pesticides; identifying and assigning priorities regarding the need for the Ministry to establish environmental standards and to coordinate their development; and providing technical expertise and support to other branches and regions on hazardous contaminants, including pesticides.

*Intergovernmental Relations and Strategic Projects Branch:* Coordinates the intergovernmental activities of the Ministry and the implementation of strategic projects. Branch activities include providing advice and assistance in the development of Ministry positions for the resolution of pollution problems shared with other jurisdictions; fostering and maintaining links with key staff of other jurisdictions so that information on matters of concern to Ontario in the environmental area is readily available to the Ministry; and developing and negotiating bilateral and multilateral agreements with other jurisdictions in support of the ongoing control strategies of the Ministry. Current strategic projects include:

1. *Niagara River Improvement:* Coordinates the improvement of environmental quality in the Niagara River by identifying and recommending areas where enhanced abatement action or court intervention is necessary. Project activities include assisting in the development of proposals to reduce pollution in the Niagara River; undertaking special studies or monitoring activities designed to enhance the effectiveness of Ministry programs in the Niagara River; assessing and monitoring the impact and effectiveness of pollution control strategies and programs applied in the State of New York as they relate to the Niagara River; and maintaining liaison with officials of Environment Canada, the U.S. Environmental Protection Agency, and the State of New York, in the development and implementation of joint objectives and actions for pollution abatement in the Niagara River.

2. *Detroit/St. Clair/St.Mary's River Improvement:* Coordinates the assessment of environmental quality in the Detroit, St. Clair, and St. Mary's Rivers, recommends future monitoring and control measures, and initiates the implementation of these monitoring and control programs. Project activities include assisting in the development of proposals to resolve pollution problems in the Detroit/St. Clair Rivers corridor and the St. Mary's River; initiating special monitoring programs for these rivers and their associated inputs; assessing and monitoring the impact of pollution control strategies and programs applied in the State of Michigan as they relate to these rivers; and maintaining liaison with officials of Environment Canada, U.S. Environmental Protection Agency, and the State of Michigan, in the development of joint objectives and actions for pollution abatement in the Detroit/St. Clair Rivers corridor and the St. Mary's River.

**Operations Division**

This Division is the compliance and delivery arm of the Ministry. Its job is to enforce regulations, control emissions, and deliver abatement programs in accordance with plans and policies developed by the Environmental Services Division. The role of the Operations Division is to deliver programs to ensure compliance with environmental requirements; to protect air quality; to protect surface and ground water quality and quantity; to manage the disposal of wastes; to ensure an adequate quality of drinking water; to control the use of pesticides; to assist in the funding of municipal water and sewage servicing projects; and to coordinate the environmental assessment process.

Activities in this division include administering programs for the regulation of pollution sources; administering regulations for the proper construction and operation of water wells; administering plans and policies for the proper development, operation, and closure of waste disposal sites and the proper operation of waste management systems; administering regulatory mechanisms for the storage and use of pesticides; managing and operating Ministry water and sewage plants and systems; monitoring the quality of the natural environment; responding to public complaints and environmental emergencies; and reviewing development proposals in order to encourage environmental safeguards in land development.

Further, this division evaluates environmental assessments of proposed undertakings and monitors environmental assessment recommendations; administers regulatory programs for water use to provide for a fair sharing of available resources and the maintenance of water supplies; monitors and investigates discharges to the environment; contributes to water management plans; administers programs for the control of noise; investigates and enforces actions to achieve compliance with Ministry regulations; develops environmental planning guidelines and policies; and administers grant programs for municipal water and sewage works. This division is comprised of the Approvals and Engineering Branch, the Investigations and Enforcement Branch, and six regional operations branches.

*Approvals and Engineering Branch*

The Approvals and Engineering Branch sets overall policy and administrative direction for major program areas; reports to and maintains liaison with the Assistant Deputy Minister--Operations Division—and senior management on the program areas identified; oversees the coordination of identified program areas with other divisions and other government agencies; and promotes overall financial management and accountability in Approvals and Engineering. The Approvals and Engineering Branch is made up of:

*Environmental Approvals and Land Use Planning Branch:* Reviews and processes applications required under the *Environmental Protection Act*, the *Ontario Water Resources Act*, and the *Pesticides Act*, and promotes the consideration of the environment in land use policies and programs. This branch reviews applications for the approval of air emissions, noise, and waste water discharges, for the approval of proposed municipal water treatment systems, and for the approval of proposed municipal and industrial waste management sites and systems; administers licensing and permit-issuing functions relating to pesticides and water use; coordinates environmental comments on land-use planning activities and land-use policies; and assesses the impact of noise on the environment to develop regulatory mechanisms for its control.

*Environmental Assessment Branch:* Promotes the consideration and inclusion of environmental, social, and economic alternatives in the planning and development of undertakings, and coordinates the review and evaluation of environmental assessments of proposed undertakings.

*Project Engineering Branch:* Encourages the development of a water supply and sewage treatment infrastructure through the provision of engineering and construction assistance to municipalities; establishes priorities and eligibility in allocating grant funds for water supply and sewage treatment infrastructure; develops and revises standards and guidelines related to the design, tendering, and construction of sewage and water works; provides project management and engineering services where appropriate; and reviews applications for funding from municipalities for the support of water and sewage works.

*Spills Action Centre* (SAC): Receives and responds to notification of spills and other urgent environmental concerns on a 24-hour-per-day basis; manages the Spills Contingency Planning Program for Ontario and encourages the development of industrial and municipal spill plans; and serves as a focal point within the Ministry on policy matters with respect to spill response. This Branch coordinates and facilitates a consistent province-wide Ministry approach for dealing with environmental spills and other urgent matters; provides spill statistics and a uniform reporting approach for all incidents reported to SAC; critically reviews drafts of industrial and municipal spill contingency plans and related field exercises; participates in the development of spill response training material and in the delivery of training programs; coordinates environmental comments on matters relating to the programs under the federal *Transportation of Dangerous Goods Act*; and represents the interests of the Ministry on various inter-agency spill response teams established pursuant to the Canada-U.S. Great Lakes Water Quality Agreement, and other commitments.

## Investigations and Enforcement Branch

The Investigations and Enforcement Branch ensures compliance with environmental legislation and regulations through investigation and initiation of legal action for non-compliance. Branch activities include: enforcement and investigation on a province-wide basis, and investigation of specific cases and monitoring for evidence at a regional level.

### Financial Assistance Programs

*Construction of Water and Sewage Infrastructure:* Assistance is provided to municipalities for the construction of water and sewage facilities. This is achieved through the following programs:

1. *Canada/Ontario Agreement Sewage Program:* A federally funded program administered by the Ministry that provides grants for sewage treatment projects under the Canada-Ontario Agreement to improve water quality in the Great Lakes Basin.

2. *Direct Disbursements:* The Ministry builds facilities on its own or jointly with a municipality. No new projects have been approved under this program since 1978.

3. *Regional Priorities:* The Ministry of Northern Development and Mines authorizes expenditures by the Ministry on its behalf for the construction of water and sewage services in Northern Ontario municipalities.

4. *Up-Front Grants:* Direct "up-front" grants are provided by the Ministry to municipalities for 15 to 85 percent of the total capital costs depending on the size of the population served. This is the major ongoing infrastructure program of the Ministry.

*Grants for Agreements under the Environmental Protection Act:* Provided to municipalities and health units to assist them in the administration of the Act.

*Grants for Compensation under the Environmental Protection Act:* Provides financial compensation for loss or damages resulting from accidental spills.

*Grants for Orders under the Environmental Protection Act:* Provides financial compensation to persons carrying out clean-up orders.

*Grants to Environmental Organizations:* Grants are provided to non-profit environmental organizations to fund specific activities that advance Ministry programs.

*Health Related Environmental Research:* Grants are provided in advance to consultants and university researchers to conduct scientific research that will build a sound scientific basis for policy and decision making on environmental issues and for the solution of pollution problems.

*Pesticide Research Grants:* Provided to universities and other organizations to conduct research on pesticides.

*Household Special Waste Collection Grants:* Provided to municipalities for the collection of household special wastes.

*Recycling Grants:* Provided to private companies starting recycling ventures.

*Security Fund for Environmental Contingencies:* Provides funds to study and clean-up contaminated areas where environmental damage or risk to health is known or expected, to provide alternative water supplies on an interim basis when communal or private local supplies have been contaminated, and to take action to remove or reduce potential long-term hazards.

*Source Separation Grants:* Provided to municipalities and non-profit organizations to assist in the development or expansion of multi-material source separation projects.

*Termite Control Grants:* Provided to municipalities with termite infestations for distribution to owners of single family homes for the control of termites.

*Waste Disposal Site Improvement Grants:* Provided to municipalities to assist in the upgrading and closure of municipal waste disposal sites.

*Waste Management Master Plans Assistance:* Provides subsidies to municipalities undertaking waste management master plans.

## EXPENDITURE ESTIMATES

*Estimated Expenditures 1987–88*:

| | |
|---|---|
| Ministry Administration | $ 24,189,838 |
| Environmental Services | 62,480,800 |
| Environmental Control | 171,190,100 |
| Utility Planning and Operations | 254,159,900 |
| **Ministry total:** | **$412,020,638** |

## AGENCIES, BOARDS, AND COMMISSIONS

The following ABCs report to the Legislative Assembly through the Minister of the Environment:

*Board of Negotiation:* Acts as the final authority within the Ministry for settling claims. The Board has implicit influence in securing settlements of damage to vegetation and livestock caused by contaminants. Board activities include assessing claims of pollution damage to vegetation and livestock causing economic loss, and negotiating a settlement between the person responsible for the damage and the claimant.

*Environmental Appeal Board:* Provides citizens with a mechanism for appealing decisions that are made by the Ministry of the Environment and local health authorities under provisions of the *Environmental Protection Act*, the *Ontario Water Resources Act*, and the *Pesticides Act*. Board activities include conducting hearings in response to appeals of Ministry decisions made under the *Environmental Protection Act* regarding plans, specifications, and certificates of approval; and conducting hearings in response to appeals of Ministry decisions made under the *Ontario Water Resources Act* and the *Pesticides Act* regarding licenses and permits.

*Environmental Assessment Advisory Committee:* Committee activities include providing advice on matters relating to requests for exemptions from the provisions of the *Environmental Assessment Act*, as well as requests or proposals to designate undertakings subject to the Act; and advising and commenting on reasons provided by the proponent for exempting an undertaking with particular reference to public health and safety, economic necessity, and environmental effects.

*Environmental Assessment Board:* Strives to further the consideration of environmental factors, both natural and human, in the decision-making processes of the proponents of major projects. Board activities include facilitating public input prior to decisions being made on projects with a significant environmental impact; conducting public hearings on undertakings and on environmental assessments related to them, to determine if they should be accepted, amended and accepted, or rejected; and conducting public hearings on proposed sewage works, waste disposal sites, waste management systems, and other matters with environmental implications at the request of the government.

*Environmental Compensation Corporation:* Administers part of the provincial financial assistance system for support to those with duties or losses associated with spills. Activities of the Corporation include assessing applications for compensation or payment and authorizing payments accordingly; and recovering, on behalf of the beneficiary of compensation or a payment, the amount of the payment.

*Farm Pollution Advisory Committee:* Advises the Ministry on specific odour, water pollution, and farm noise problems in specific instances and determines whether they are in accordance with normal or acceptable farming practices. Committee activities include investigating specific complaints and thereby advising the Ministry as to whether animal waste is handled and disposed of in accordance with normal farming practices; investigating complaints and advising the Ministry on situations involving water and noise pollution associated with farming activities; and making recommendations to assist in the resolution of specific problems regarding odour, water pollution, and noise.

*Hazardous Waste Listing Advisory Committee:* Solicits the public's view on interim decisions of the Ministry to list or "de-list" a waste substance as a hazardous waste. Activities of the Committee include receiving written public comment at the request of the Minister on decisions by the Ministry to list or de-list hazardous wastes; advising the Minister on the acceptability of interim listing or de-listing decisions; and undertaking such associated tasks or projects relating to the overall implementation of regulations that the Minister may wish to request.

*Ontario Waste Management Corporation* (OWMC): Established to design, construct, and operate a management system for liquid industrial waste and hazardous waste. Objectives of the Corporation include finding a suitable and safe site or sites in Ontario for facilities for the treatment and disposal of waste; participating in any hearings that may be required for the siting and establishment of facilities. Establishing facilities which may include a secure landfill site, secure storage facilities for waste, physical-chemical treatment, solidification, and incineration, together with transfer stations as are necessary for the collection of waste. In September 1985, the OWMC announced its selection of a preferred site in the Township of West Lincoln, Region of Niagara. A suitability study commenced in November, 1985.

*Pesticides Advisory Committee:* Advises the Ministry on all matters pertaining to the use of pesticides in Ontario. Committee activities include undertaking an annual review of the content and operation of the *Pesticides Act* and recommending changes or amendments; inquiring into and considering any matter the committee considers advisable concerning pesticides and the control of pests; managing a pesticides research program with the objective of finding alternative pesticides for those deemed environmentally hazardous; reviewing all publications of the Ontario Government respecting pesticides and the control of pests; and reviewing and recommending the classification of all new pesticides prior to sale and use in Ontario.

*Recycling Advisory Committee:* Advises the Ministry on measures to promote the establishment of multi-material source separation programs, and advises the Ministry on matters related to the regulation of carbonated soft drink containers. Committee activities include advising the Minister on methods of measuring recycling rates, on recycling rates that have been achieved, on recycling targets, and on sanctions for the failure to meet the requirements of the regulations; establishing and administering a fund supported by private contributions for the purpose of promoting recycling in the Province; and advising the Minister on activities to improve recycling.

## LEGISLATION

The Ministry of Environment is responsible for the following Acts:

*Consolidated Hearings Act, 1981:* This legislation provides a streamlined approval process for municipal, private, and provincial projects or proposed activities which may otherwise require hearings by more than one tribunal. The agencies that conduct hearings covered by the Act include the Ontario Municipal Board, the Environmental Assessment Board, Committees of Adjustment, and Inquiry Officers under the *Expropriations Act.*

*Environmental Assessment Act, 1975:* This Act provides for the assessment of any proposed major undertaking—governmental, municipal, or private—at the very earliest stage, to permit alteration or even cancellation of the undertaking should it be environmentally unacceptable. It also provides for full public participation in the decision-making process. The Act is being implemented in stages. It applies to major provincial undertakings and to certain municipal undertakings. Preliminary discussions are under way concerning its extension to the private sector.

*Environmental Protection Act, 1971:* This Act covers all types of pollution, forbidding the discharge of any contaminant to the natural environment in amounts or concentrations exceeding those prescribed by regulation. Contaminant definition includes solids, gases, liquids, odours, sounds, vibrations, radiation, or the combination of any of these which results directly or indirectly from activities of man, and which may cause injury to humans, flora, or fauna. In addition to regulation limits, the Act prohibits any discharge that is likely to impair the natural environment, or to injure or damage plant or animal life, cause harm or discomfort to any person, affect the health or safety of any person or render any property, plant, or animal life unfit for use by man.

*Fisheries Act, 1970 (Federal):* The Ministry administers Section 33 of the Federal *Fisheries Act* in Ontario on behalf of the Government of Canada. Section 33 prohibits the deposition of deleterious substances of any type in water frequented by fish or in water that may enter any such water. Specific regulations have been established under the Act by industrial sector. They include pulp and paper, petroleum refining, metal finishing, metal mining, potato processing, chlor-alkali plants, and meat and poultry product plants.

*Ministry of the Environment Act:* Provides for the establishment of the Ministry of the Environment to regulate, implement, and enforce environmental standards and guidelines.

*Ontario Waste Management Corporation Act, 1981:* Provides for the establishment of the Ontario Waste Management Corporation (OWMC) to develop and implement a long-term, province-wide program for the treatment and storage of liquid industrial and hazardous wastes.

*Ontario Water Resources Act, 1956:* This Act gives the Ministry of the Environment extensive powers to regulate water supply, sewage disposal, and the control of water pollution. It authorizes the Ministry to supervise and examine all surface waters and groundwater in Ontario, to determine the extent, nature, and causes of contamination in these waters. The Ministry can construct and operate water and waste treatment facilities, or it can require an industry or municipality to construct and operate approved facilities.

*Pesticides Act, 1973:* This legislation restricts the storage, distribution, sale, and use of pesticides. The Ministry examines and licenses professional exterminators and maintains a classification system to ensure that hazardous chemical pesticides are not handled or used by unqualified persons.

## INNOVATIONS

The following innovations have had a positive impact on the operations of the Ministry of Environment:

### Administrative Procedures

1. The development and implementation of a Management-By-Results Reporting System which provides management with information to assess Ministry performance in relation to objectives.

2. The enhancement of data processing and management systems through increased automation, which has expanded the scope of monitoring networks and provided readily available information to enhance decision making at both the field and management levels. These improvements include an Air Quality Telemetry System, automated laboratory analytical procedure, and integrated data processing systems.

3. The establishment of the Investigations and Enforcement Branch to enhance environmental protection efforts.

4. The foundation of the Spills Action Centre to provide 24-hour-a-day responses to spills, other contingencies, and off-hour complaints.

5. The regulation of all waste generators within the province under Regulation 309 of the *Environmental Protection Act*.

6. The raising and tightening of fines for regulatory and pollution offences.

7. The establishment of the Security Fund for Environmental Contingencies to finance the investigation and clean-up of spills, waste sites, and the

provision of emergency water supplies.

8. The development and operation of a comprehensive drinking water surveillance program to ensure good quality water to the people of Ontario.

## Policies

1. The establishment of the Ontario Waste Management Corporation to design, build, and operate a facility for the treatment and disposal of toxic and hazardous wastes on behalf of the people of Ontario.

2. The initiation of the Municipal/Industrial Strategy for Abatement to establish a technology-based control strategy to limit the discharge of pollutants to waterways.

3. The proclamation of Part IX of the *Environmental Protection Act*, which provides the Ministry with added powers to ensure the clean-up of spills and the prompt compensation of spill victims.

# MINISTRY OF HOUSING

## ROLES AND FUNCTIONS

The Ministry of Housing is responsible for strategies to help meet the need for affordable rental housing. While encouraging the conservation of existing accommodation, it provides rent-geared-to-income housing for qualified low- and moderate-income households through the Ontario Housing Corporation and helps support municipal, private, and cooperative non-profit housing. The Ministry also administers rent review legislation; helps ensure that all structures in Ontario are built safely and efficiently by developing and maintaining the Ontario Building and Plumbing Code; and is responsible for strategies to strengthen Ontario's building industry through the Building Industry Strategy Board.

## BACKGROUND HISTORY

Provincial housing legislation passed in the 1860s made municipalities responsible for housing the poor. Those committed to the care of the state were given manual labour employment and were expected to try not to be a burden to society. As late as 1897, when Ontario passed "An Act Respecting Provincial Aid Toward the Establishment of Houses of Refuge," conditions for the homeless had improved only marginally. Under the new legislation, the province agreed to provide a measure of financial assistance to municipalities for their social housing, but, for the most part, shelter for the homeless was not considered a major provincial priority in the nineteenth century.

The federal government first entered the housing market in 1918 to deal with a general scarcity of housing across the nation. Ottawa provided some $25 million to the provinces, which loaned funds to municipalities for construction of modest housing. Throughout the 1920s, housing construction boomed in Ontario, stimulated by an expanding economy. As the economy collapsed in the Depression, so did the housing market. In 1935, attempting to stimulate the economy, the federal government passed the *Dominion Housing Act*, which established a $10 million fund for loans for housing construction.

Under the federal *Municipal Housing Act* of 1938, municipalities could borrow funds from the federal government for the provision of housing and the creation of employment in housing construction. A federal Crown corporation, Wartime Housing Limited, built some 25,000 small homes in Canada during the war years. In 1944, with World War II drawing to a close, the *National Housing Act* was amended to help returning servicemen find employment in the housing industry and to avert a serious housing shortage. Ottawa created the Central (later Canada) Mortgage and Housing Corporation to distribute housing program funds.

In 1948, Ontario passed the *Housing Development Act*, which acknowledged that the province was primarily responsible for the housing needs of its citizens In 1949, the federal government entered into agreements with the provinces to provide public housing at shared cost. This led to the development of a system of local housing authorities in Ontario in the 1950s. These were comprised of local citizens who served without remuneration on the housing authority in their community, selecting tenants, collecting rents, preparing budgets, and ensuring that social housing in their community was administered fairly and responsibly.

By the early 1960s, social housing policy had become more decentralized, as control moved from Ottawa to the provinces. In 1964, an amendment to the *National Housing Act* made it possible for each province to administer its own portfolio of public housing. In that same year, the Ontario Housing Corporation (OHC) was created as a Crown corporation of the provincial Department of Economics and Development. The OHC was headed by a Board of Directors.

The OHC was given responsibility for the 38 local housing authorities and their portfolio of 6,200 federal/provincial social housing units. The Housing Branch of the Department of Economics and Development was then dissolved. Throughout the 1960s, the OHC was involved in a variety of housing acquisition and construction programs. By the late 1960s, OHC was the largest social housing landlord in Canada, including a portfolio giving it responsibility for the production of student housing as part of the expansion of the provincial university system.

This growth continued through the 1970s, with programs such as HOME--Home Ownership Made Easy—which supported the development of new subdivisions in urban areas. In 1972, in a major reorganization of the provincial public service, the Ministry of Treasury, Economics and Intergovernmental Affairs (TEIGA) was formed, merging, among other functions, the activities associated with housing and community planning. Subsequently, in 1974, in response to a perceived need for special and concentrated action in the housing and development field, those functions were transferred from TEIGA to the new Ministry of Housing, which incorporated the Ontario Housing Corporation. In 1981, after three years of planning and discussion following the 1978 reorganization of TEIGA, the Municipal Affairs function of the government was merged with Housing to form the Ministry of Municipal Affairs and Housing. This latter Ministry was again divided in 1985 to form the current Ministry of Municipal Affairs and the Ministry of Housing.

## ORGANIZATION

The Ministry of Housing is organized into four divisions (see organization chart):

1. *Building Programs:* Coordinates the Ministry's Building Industry Policy and administers the Ontario Building Code.

2. *Corporate Resources:* Provides administrative support to the Ministry, including planning, human resources, financial services, audit, and legal services.

3. *Housing Policy:* Responsible for developing the Ministry's rental policies, and for administering the Ontario Rent Registry and the rent review process.

4. *Social Housing:* Responsible for developing and delivering the Ministry's housing policies and program and for managing the Ontario Housing Corporation's rental housing portfolio.

In addition, four agencies, boards, and commissions, including the Residential Tenancy Commission, the Ontario Housing Corporation, and the Building Industry Strategy Board, report to the Legislative Assembly through the Minister of Housing (see Agencies, Boards, and Commissions).

The head office of the Ministry of Housing is located in Toronto. The Ministry also delivers its programs through six regional offices and 58 local housing authorities. The Ministry employs approximately 900 public servants.

## PROGRAMS

*Convert to Rent:* The Ministry of Housing offers interest-free loans of between $5,000 and $7,000 per unit to help produce some 10,000 moderate-cost rental housing units, primarily through conversions of non-residential buildings under the Convert-to-Rent program. Loan assistance is also available for the production of hostel-type accommodation for single people, as well as new rental housing within single-family homes. Additional loans of $2,000 are available for units that are accessible to physically-handicapped persons. Factories, schools, warehouses, and space over retail stores are eligible for conversion into apartments. New rental housing can be constructed on existing non-residential properties or through a combination of conversion and construction on non-residential sites. In keeping with the program's intent of making better use of existing facilities, space in residential complexes—such as garage and storage areas—that is not used for shelter may be converted. The interest-free loans are also available for building new rental units onto existing housing projects and adding new rental units on residential sites.

*Federal-Provincial Rural Housing Program:* Mortgage payments are geared to the household's income under this home-purchase program administered by the federal government. Assistance is provided for the acquisition and rehabilitation of existing family units, or for the construction of new family units in rural communities with populations of less than 2,500. Canada Mortgage and Housing Corporation, the federal agency, provides 75 percent of the funds of this mortgage payment-geared-to income program, and Ontario Housing Corporation provides

MINISTRY OF HOUSING

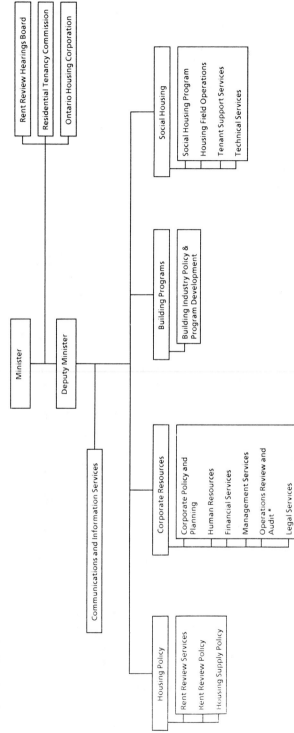

Minister

Rent Review Hearings Board
Residential Tenancy Commission
Ontario Housing Corporation

Deputy Minister

Communications and Information Services

Housing Policy
- Rent Review Services
- Rent Review Policy
- Housing Supply Policy

Corporate Resources
- Corporate Policy and Planning
- Human Resources
- Financial Services
- Management Services
- Operations Review and Audit *
- Legal Services

Building Programs
- Building Industry Policy & Program Development

Social Housing
- Social Housing Program
- Housing Field Operations
- Tenant Support Services
- Technical Services

25 percent.

*Federal-Provincial Senior Citizen Rural Housing Program:* Where a need has been determined, a limited number of senior citizen rent-geared-to-income projects may be built in communities with populations of less than 2,500. Capital funding is shared by the federal and provincial governments on a 75:25 ratio. In both organized and unorganized communities, operating deficits are shared on the same 75:25 basis. Projects developed by the province are managed by local housing authorities.

*High-Rise Rehabilitation Program:* This demonstration project is designed to assess the magnitude of rehabilitation work required in Ontario's high-rise buildings and to determine the government's level of involvement in assisting this activity. High-rise buildings account for about 430,000 apartments--more than 40 percent of rental housing in the province. By 1990, about half of the buildings will be more than 20 years old, and signs of physical deterioration are becoming apparent. The project will also involve experimenting with different technologies that can be used in upgrading work. The results of the research and development will be made available to companies and organizations involved in high-rise properties, so that problems associated with aging housing stock can be tackled effectively. The first phase of this four-year project involves consultation with special interest groups such as landlords, property managers, and the Association of Municipalities of Ontario.

*Home Sharing:* The Ministry is promoting the concept of sharing housing, a living arrangement often practised by younger people and recently shown to be an excellent housing alternative for the elderly. Each person has his or her own private space and shares some common areas such as the living room and kitchen. With the advantages of company, shared housekeeping, and lower costs, this approach can provide the kind of supportive environment many elderly need in order to live independently in the community. The Ministry has co-sponsored three match-and-share projects in Ottawa-Carleton and Metro Toronto; over the next four years, this assistance will be extended to ten new home sharing projects. The sharing concept will be supported and promoted through matching agencies which provide safe introductions and follow-up counselling. Municipalities wishing to share the cost of counselling services may apply for grants of up to $20,000 per year for two years, to cover up to 50 percent of the operating costs. The municipality must demonstrate the way in which the service would become integrated with area community and social services networks and must have a policy commitment to alternative housing for seniors. The service need not be confined to seniors, but must be sensitive to seniors' needs. It must also serve both homeowners and renters. Other eligibility requirements include a local administering board or committee comprising representatives of local housing, health, and social services networks.

*Low-Rise Rehabilitation Program:* This program offers landlords forgivable loans of up to $5,000 per unit to help them upgrade some 17,000 older low-rise apartments in Ontario over the next four years. The apartments must be in buildings of less than five storeys and must have been built prior to 1960. Administered by municipalities, the program is designed to improve the physical condition of low-rise rental housing while retaining its suitability for low- and moderate-income tenants. About 30 percent of Ontario's rental housing is in low-rise apartment buildings, duplexes, and triplexes. At least three out of every five of these units are more than 25 years old. Many of these buildings are now in need of upgrading and essential services such as plumbing, wiring, and heating. Municipalities wishing to take part in the program must have property maintenance and occupancy standards by-laws. They must also have experience in administering housing rehabilitation programs. Only essential repairs required to bring the building up to minimum standards, set out in the by-law, will be eligible. Landlords with buildings of ten or more units may be asked to offer ten percent of the units to the Rent Supplement Program, under which tenants pay rent based strictly on household income, rather than the size or type of accommodation provided. A forgivable loan of up to two-thirds of the cost of rehabilitating a unit is available. No repayments will be made for the first five years of the loan. After that, forgiveness will be earned at the rate of ten percent per year, subject to certain conditions which include the units remaining as rental housing.

*Municipal Building Profile Program:* The program is designed to help municipalities define the characteristics of their rental housing by age, location, and type of projects. Grants of up to $20,000 are being made to urban municipalities in which rental stock makes up a fair proportion of their total housing. Aided by comprehensive profiles of the rental accommodation within their boundaries, municipalities will be able to make plans for the future of their rental housing and to benefit from any available government assistance such as support for the upgrading of older rental stock. The first phase of the four-year Municipal Building Profile Program involves extensive liaison with municipal representatives, including planning and building officials, in order to encourage project proposals.

*Municipal Housing Statement Program:* The Ministry offers study grants or technical assistance to help municipalities prepare or update their housing statements. A municipal housing statement defines a municipality's housing requirements and policy directions. It consists of two major components—a housing market analysis and the basis of a housing strategy. Housing statements also examine issues affecting maintenance of housing, such as housing renewal, quality of housing, energy efficiency, and the conversion of vacant core area space to rental housing. When endorsed by a municipal council and approved by the Ministry, a housing statement can form the basis for a municipality's request for federal and provincial assistance for housing programs.

*Non-Profit Housing Program:* Under this program, non-profit housing corporations owned by municipalities, private or co-operative community groups build and manage rental housing with assistance from the federal and provincial governments. A minimum of 40 percent of the units in each municipal and private non-profit project are allocated to the most needy households in the community, which pay rents based on their household income rather than on the size or type of accommodation. Rules are slightly different for co-operative non-profit projects. A total of 6,700 units were committed in 1986, with an equal number anticipated for each of the next four years. The remaining 60 percent of the units may be made available to those with eligible household incomes, or to households that can afford market rents, or to a combination of the two groups. Eligible households qualify for rent-geared-to-income assistance if they cannot afford market rents in the project without paying more than 25 percent of their incomes in rent. Tenants eligible for rent-geared-to-income assistance under the program include families, senior citizens, and physically, developmentally- and psychiatrically-handicapped people. Some units may be built for people requiring some form of support care, and innovative demonstration projects for low-income single people are also considered. The exact mix of income groups housed in each project is set by the individual housing corporation, reflecting program criteria based on the particular needs of the local community. The federal and provincial governments share, on a 60:40 basis, the cost of subsidies to cover the difference between the actual cost of operating the building and the rents paid by those tenants who are in what is referred to as "core need." These are defined as people who would have to pay more than 30 percent of their incomes to rent suitable accommodation in their community. Subsidies for tenants who do not fall into this category are paid by the province alone. Development grants and interest-free loans are available to corporations developing their projects.

*Ontario Community Housing Assistance Program:* Ontario provides subsidies for private non-profit and cooperative housing developments. Private non-profit and cooperative programs administered by the federal government call for some units to be allocated to persons eligible for rent-geared-to-income housing. In certain projects offering special support care services, up to 100 percent of the units may be allocated on a geared-to-income basis. The province pays 100 percent of the difference between geared-to-income charges and the established monthly payments for the units that are being subsidized under the program.

*Ontario Home Renewal Program:* Administered by municipalities in many areas of the province, this program assists homeowners in upgrading their homes, with an emphasis on faulty structural and sanitary conditions, and on plumbing, insulation, heating, and electrical systems. Loans of up to $7,500 are made to eligible owner-occupants who wish to bring their homes up to standard. A portion of a loan may be forgiven, depending on the recipient's income. Physically-handicapped homeowners, or home-owners with physically-handicapped relatives residing permanently with them, may qualify for loans of up to $9,500 to cover extra costs involved in alterations that make homes more appropriate for their needs. For applicants, the maximum annual qualifying family income, after allowable deductions are made, is $20,000, effective August 1, 1986.

*Portable Living Units for Seniors:* An innovative approach to seniors' housing that originated in Australia, the so-called "granny flat" is a detached housing unit which can be placed in the yard of an existing family home. Intended solely for occupancy by an elderly parent or parents of the owner of the main house and property, the self-contained units are designed to be temporary and portable, so that they can be removed and relocated when no longer required. The term "granny flat" originated because of the proportionately higher number of women in the 65-plus age group. Indeed, in Ontario for every 100 males in this age category, there are 140 females. However, the "granny flat" option is by no means exclusively for women. To test the applicability of this housing approach, the Ministry is constructing and placing a small number of these units through its Portable Living Units for Seniors (PLUS) demonstration project. A total of 12 units are being produced during the demonstration, four each in three municipalities: the Regional Municipalities of Ottawa-Carleton and Sudbury and the City of Waterloo. During the three-year demonstration, the units, owned and operated by the province, are rented to occupants at a rent equivalent to that of the nearest market alternative. Based on an evaluation of the demonstration project, a decision will be made regarding the longer-term implications and opportunities of the concept as a private market housing alternative.

*Property Management Support Program:* This program encourages the use of education and training programs for landlords through the joint development of seminars, courses, visual aids, and information packages. Wherever possible, these programs make use of existing resources. Studies have shown that a high proportion of rental housing units are operated as small businesses; these landlords have indicated a desire for better information and training in important operational areas. These include finance, accounting, rent review procedures, landlord and tenant legislation, and maintenance and modernization strategies. The Ministry is working with landlord representatives in defining their priorities, developing appropriate training packages and ensuring a workable delivery system.

*Rent Supply Program:* Ontario Housing Corporation acquires the use of rental units in properties now owned by the corporation, with qualified families, senior citizens, and handicapped persons paying rents based solely on their incomes. OHC has agreements covering some 11,000 rent supplement units across Ontario. The federal and provincial governments subsidize the difference between the rent paid by tenants and the full rental rate, as negotiated between the Ministry and participating landlords. Generally, no more than 25 percent of the units in a complex or building are leased under the program. The landlord chooses prospective tenants from the local housing authority priority list for rent-geared-to-income housing.

*Seniors Co-ownership Demonstration Project:* Many senior citizens have indicated they would like to move out of their large homes and buy a smaller, easy-to-maintain type of housing. The Ministry is combining this need with its own objective of improving the use of our older, larger housing stock. Through the Seniors Co-ownership Demonstration Project, the Ministry is encouraging the conversion of existing single-family houses into multiple units that will be sold as condominium or cooperative units. This concept can work especially well in rural and smaller communities with houses too large for the needs of their owners. With the help of municipalities, local sponsors, and senior citizens' housing groups, the Ministry will work through the legal, economic, and practical issues involved in conversion of these single-family houses to co-ownership. Groups participating in this demonstration project are eligible for the following grants: $3,000 for organizational assistance; $10,000 for planning, legal, and architectural assistance ("soft costs"); and up to $5,000 per unit (to a maximum of $30,000 per project) for renovation costs. Although not the primary goal of the demonstration, there are cases in which grants for organizational and "soft" costs can be made available for unique, new construction of seniors' housing.

*Seniors Retirement Communities Project:* Retirement communities are planned residential areas designed for adults 50 years or older. They can range from groups of mobile homes to detached, single-family houses. More retirement communities consist of two elements; a number of housing units and a community-shared, non-residential facility. The senior citizen retirement community is one of several housing options for seniors being explored by the Ministry. The planning period associated with the development of seniors' ownership retirement communities is often lengthy. This not only increases costs, but also discourages others from developing such communities. In addition, it is not clear how well projects being developed are integrated with the social service networks in the community. The Ministry is offering municipalities incentive grants to encourage them to accelerate the approval process of planned retirement communities. A grant of $2,000 for each unit sold in a planned seniors' retirement community is being offered to municipalities. The grant can be used by the municipalities to cover costs associated with the impact the retirement community may have on physical or social services, such as sewers and water, fire protection, health care, and visiting homemakers. Alternatively, the municipalities may choose other uses for the grants.

*Starter Homes:* This is a small-scale project to demonstrate the long-term potential for creating low-cost, yet attractive, starter homes for families. Modest financial incentives are being offered to municipalities to work with builders to produce eligible units. The project is designed to develop expertise on the part of municipalities and builders in reducing construction and development costs without lowering quality standards, and to provide renters with a reasonable-cost housing alternative and the chance to become homeowners. Significant savings can be made in housing production costs by changing engineering and site planning standards. The changes could apply to sewage and utilities connections, road allowances, lot and unit sizes. Grants of $2,500 for each unit produced are offered to municipalities. A total of 1,000 detached and semi-detached houses and townhouses, as well as condominiums, will qualify for the incentive grants. In order to be eligible, a municipality must have a rental stock that accounts for at least 30 percent of its total residential accommodation. Communities near major metropolitan areas that attract potential homeowners from outside their jurisdictions may take part in the project, even if they do not meet the 30 percent requirement. Participating communities must have an Official Plan.

## Other Ministry of Housing Initiatives

*The Building Industry Strategy*

The building industry is a major force in Ontario's economy. It is twice the size of the automotive industry and three times that of the agricultural sector. It employs close to 400,000 men, women, and young people in some 80,000 firms across the province. Yet the industry faces many challenges. Construction activity in Ontario has declined by 27 percent over the last ten years as a share of gross provincial product. It suffers nearly 20 percent unemployment; it is heavily burdened by regulations; and, because of fragmentation, it cannot act as a cohesive group to overcome its problems. In addition, education and training programs to support skills development and career growth are not meeting industry needs.

After extensive consultations with representatives from all sectors of the industry, the Ministry of Housing has created a building strategy to revitalize Ontario's building industry. As part of the Ministry of Housing's Assured Housing for Ontario strategy, the building industry strategy has five goals:

1. Streamline building regulations;
2. Expand production for both export and domestic markets;
3. Improve productivity;
4. Increase co-operation and awareness within the industry;
5. Promote the establishment of a world-class building centre.

Several initiatives have been launched to achieve these goals. The Building Action Program offers financial assistance to municipalities to promote more efficient administrative practices in their building departments, and enhance the skills of their building staff. Financial assistance available under the Building Administration Fund encourages municipalities to make changes to improve the processing of building permits, to refine inspection procedures, to upgrade building records maintenance and/or to share services with neighboring municipalities. The Building Officials Training Grant helps building officials acquire the new technical information and expertise they need to do the best possible job in the face of rapid changes in their field.

Several initiatives are helping to develop both new and existing markets for Ontario's building products and services. Programs are also underway to provide information on new export market opportunities; to identify import replacement opportunities; to expose foreign and domestic buyers to Ontario products and services;

to improve government programs related to export development and import replacement; and to ensure that the necessary support structure is in place to capitalize on identified opportunities. To help raise productivity within the industry, programs are being developed to ensure effective skills training, management improvement, and career development. In addition, initiatives are underway to promote research, development, and technology transfer among all industry sectors.

## EXPENDITURE ESTIMATES

*Estimated Expenditures 1987–88*:

| | |
|---|---|
| Ministry Administration | $ 17,996,338 |
| Building Industry and Housing Supply | 17,953,400 |
| Social Housing | 305,067,100 |
| Rent Review | 25,276,700 |
| **Ministry total:** | **$366,293,538** |

## AGENCIES, BOARDS, AND COMMISSIONS

The following ABCs report to the Legislative Assembly through the Minister of Housing:

*Building Industry Strategy Board:* Created to implement the Ministry's Building Industry Strategy, the Board is comprised of representatives from industry, labour, and government. The strategy is intended to increase employment opportunities, expand production, and foster growth in the industry. With respect to regulatory reform, the Board has a comprehensive program to streamline the hundreds of provincial rules and regulations governing building. Simpler and clearer regulations will result in a speedier and more efficient building process and will encourage industry application of innovative technologies. The Assistant Deputy Minister, Building Programs, is Vice-Chairman of the Building Industry Strategy Board.

*Ontario Housing Corporation* (OHC): The Corporation owns a portfolio of 84,500 subsidized units for qualified residents who pay rent based solely on income rather than the size or type of housing provided. Family housing is for parent(s) with at least one dependent child under 18 years of age. Those attending learning institutions on a full-time basis are considered dependents even if they are over 18 years. Senior citizen housing is for couples with at least one spouse aged 60 years or more, and for individuals aged 60 or more. Physically handicapped adults are also eligible to apply for subsidized housing, if they are able to live independently. As well, developmentally-handicapped adults are eligible for subsidized housing. Such persons must be capable of independent living based on the assessment of a professional agency. Tenants pay about 25 percent of gross household income on rent. Day-to-day management of the rental units is the responsibility of 58 local housing authorities throughout the province (e.g. Metro Toronto Housing Authority administers six district offices in Toronto). The OHC was created in 1964, and is administered by a Board of Directors. The Assistant Deputy Minister, Social Housing Division is Vice-Chairman of the OHC.

*Residential Tenancy Commission:* Ontario's *Residential Tenancies Act* limits the amount and frequency of rent increases in certain rental accommodation to one per year. Increases are limited to 4.7 percent in 1988 unless the landlord/landlady has obtained approval from the Commission for a large increase. Rent review applies to rental houses, apartments, townhouses, rooming houses, and mobile homes. Commission offices are located in 21 communities throughout Ontario to provide information and advice on all landlord and tenant matters, and to handle rent review cases in local areas.

*Task Force on Roomers, Boarders, and Lodgers:* The Ministry has commissioned a provincial task force to address the need for improved regulations to protect roomers, boarders, and lodgers, and to recommend ways to increase the supply of affordable housing for low-income single individuals. This task force stems from the government's recognition of the acute housing problems faced by roomers, boarders, and lodgers. The chairman of the task force is assisted in his review by an advisory committee of tenants, landlords, and municipal representatives. The mandate of the task force is to develop recommendations with respect to adequate supply of affordable, accessible accommodation for low-income single individuals; protection for occupants of single-room accommodation; and recognition of the rights and requirements of landlords of this form of housing.

## LEGISLATION

The Ministry of Housing is responsible for the following Acts:

*Building Code Act:* The Building Code consists of building requirements to minimize the risk of injury and property damage from structural failure, fire and health hazards.

*Elderly Persons' Housing Aid Act:* The Act outlines grants that may be made by the Minister of Housing to corporations to assist in the constructing and equipping of low rental housing units for the elderly.

*Housing Development Act:* This Act outlines all powers of provincial and municipal governments in undertaking the development of housing in Ontario.

*Ministry of Municipal Affairs and Housing Act, 1981:* Establishes and continues the Ministry of Housing.

*North Pickering Development Corporation Act, 1974:*

*Ontario Housing Corporation Act:* This Act incorporated Ontario Housing Corporation, a Crown agency.

*Ontario Water Resources Act* (subsections 44(2)a,b, and c, and sections 45 to 48 inclusive): These sections deal with the regulation and control of the location, construction, and repair of water works, service pipes, and sewage systems on public property; and the procedure for municipal or local plumbing inspections and subsequent repairs.

*Rental Housing Protection Act:* The Act is designed to preserve the existing supply of rental housing in Ontario. The Act, which took effect on July 10, 1986, restricts for a period of two years certain activities which serve to reduce the stock of rental housing.

*Residential Tenancies Act:* This Act regulates rent increases in residential housing, and outlines the responsibilities of the Residential Tenancies Commission.

*Residential Complexes Financing Costs Restraint Act:* This Act limits the rent increase for a residential complex caused by a landlord's increased financing costs resulting from the purchase of the building.

*Rural Housing Assistance Act:* This Act incorporates the Rural Housing Finance Corporation, with the power to lend and invest money on mortgage or real estate to provide financial assistance in the building of houses in rural areas.

*Residential Rent Regulation Act:* The Act extends rent review to cover all private rental units in Ontario; creates a process for rent review; establishes a rent review guideline, adjusted annually; creates a province- wide rent registry; and provides for a residential rental standards board to ensure proper maintenance of all rental properties.

MINISTRY OF INDUSTRY, TRADE AND TECHNOLOGY

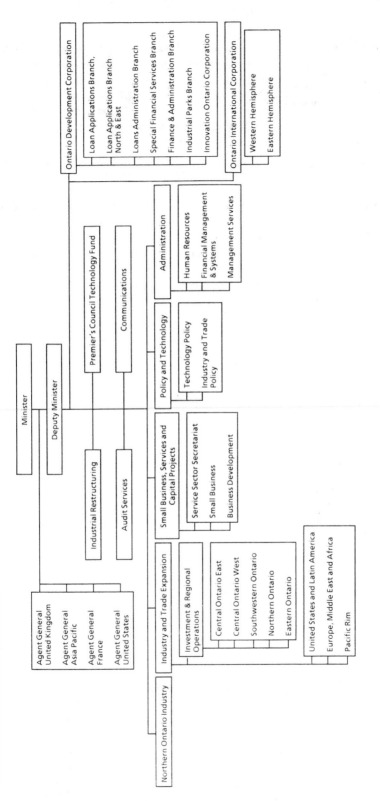

# MINISTRY OF INDUSTRY, TRADE AND TECHNOLOGY

## ROLES AND FUNCTIONS

The Ministry of Industry, Trade and Technology (MITT) encourages accelerated introduction and application of new manufacturing technology; assists in product innovation and commercialization of new products and processes; promotes investment, both domestic and foreign; encourages companies to export; supports trade through international offices, trade shows, and missions; promotes and assists the formation of small businesses; and, encourages expansion of the domestic market by identifying domestic sources of supply. In all its activities, the Ministry supports the growth of productive and stable employment in consultation and partnership with the private sector.

## BACKGROUND HISTORY

In 1972 the Department of Trade and Development and the Department of Tourism and Information were merged to form the Ministry of Industry and Tourism. In 1982 the Tourism Division left the Ministry to form the Ministry of Tourism and Recreation. At the same time, a division of Trade and a division of Technology were created to form the Ministry of Industry and Trade. In 1985, the Ministry's mandate was expanded to promote aggressively the adaptation of manufacturing technology; the Ministry's name was changed to the Ministry of Industry, Trade and Technology.

## ORGANIZATION

The Ontario Ministry of Industry, Trade and Technology is organized into five divisions (see organization chart):

1. *Industry and Trade Expansion:* Formulates Ministry policies and programs directed at the growth of employment by expanding domestic and international trade and by encouraging investment and strengthening the province's industrial base.

2. *Policy and Technology:* Encourages the development of new manufacturing processes and new industrial technology. Branches include Technology

Policy, and Industry and Trade Policy.

3. *Small Business, Services and Capital Projects:* Supports growth in the small business and service industry sectors.

4. *Northern Ontario Industry:* Develops policies and programs designed to encourage the growth of employment in Northern Ontario. This division operates offices in five Northern Ontario communities.

5. *Administration:* Provides corporate services to the Ministry, including planning, human resources and management services.

The Ministry of Industry, Trade and Technology operates an international network of Ontario government offices in conjunction with the Ministry of Tourism and Recreation and the Ministry of Intergovernmental Affairs. Senior Representatives of MITT abroad are located in the following cities and countries:

| *Government of Ontario Offices* | *Ontario Houses* *(headed by an Agent-General)* |
|---|---|
| Atlanta, Georgia, U.S.A. | London, U.K. |
| Boston, Massachusetts, U.S.A. | Paris, France |
| Chicago, Illinois, U.S.A. | Tokyo, Japan |
| Los Angeles, California, U.S.A | |
| New York, New York, U.S.A. | |
| Dallas, Texas, U.S.A. | |
| Frankfurt, West Germany | |
| Hong Kong | |
| Singapore | |
| Seoul, South Korea | |

*Plus:* The Ontario-Jiangsu Science and Technology Centre in Nanjing, China

In addition, the Ontario Research Foundation, Ontario International Corporation, three Ontario Development Corporations, and seven Technology Centres report to the Legislative Assembly through the Minister of Industry, Trade and Technology (see Agencies, Boards, and Commissions).

The head office of the Ministry of Industry, Trade and Technology is located in Toronto. Many of the Ministry's programs are delivered to business through the Ministry's 18 domestic field offices. The Ministry employs approximately 640 public servants.

# PROGRAMS

## Industry and Trade Expansion Division

The Industry and Trade Expansion Division seeks to motivate, coach and financially assist non-exporting companies to export. Its programs also help existing exporters secure and expand their markets, promote the export of services in education and capital projects, and to research and address trade-related issues. The Division also promotes Ontario as an investment location and directs the development and implementation of international marketing in order to expand international trade and increase employment in Ontario. The division maintains a network of offices in Europe, the United States, China and the Pacific Rim (see list of Government of Ontario Offices and Ontario Houses above) to promote Ontario. Division programs include:

*Export consultants:* Develop marketing plans and provide advice on strategy to encourage Ontario companies to increase exports.

*Export Success Fund:* Provides financial assistance for market research, market evaluation, product modification, package design, merchandising and promotion, to help Ontario firms break into the export business or into new foreign markets. Contributions are made up to $35,000 toward qualifying marketing expenses.

*Group missions:* Visit foreign markets or exhibit at international trade fairs. Arranged with the trade mission program.

*Incoming Buyers Program:* Brings in key agents, distributors, and buyers to visit specific Ontario industries.

*International Marketing Intern Program:* Provides financial assistance to hire recent graduates for two years to learn about export marketing and provide Ontario exporters with in-house expertise. Contributions of 50% of salary (maximum $15,000 annually) are available for two years.

*Export Managers For Hire Program:* Helps Ontario exporters hire experienced export managers. Contributions include shared cost of the export manager's salary (maximum $2,000 per month) for up to six months.

*Capital Projects Abroad Program:* Locates projects for Ontario engineering and construction companies in overseas markets.

### Domestic Offices Branch

The Domestic Offices Branch delivers programs and services related to product development, manufacturing, financing and marketing through 13 field offices located throughout Southern Ontario.

*Investment Branch*

The Investment Branch attempts to market Ontario as an attractive location for new increased investment and offers a consulting service to new industries considering the establishment of new or expanded manufacturing facilities. Branch programs include:

*Site Location Program Information:* Available for plant sites, buildings, local services, taxes, utilities, labour availability and rates, transport services and introductions to municipal development commissioners.

*Foreign Investment Review:* Provides information and advice to help investors obtain approvals through Investment Canada.

*Selective Placement Program:* Helps locate and arrange entry for skilled trades not available in Canada.

*Mergers and Acquisitions Program:* Provides information on businesses for sale and investors looking for investment opportunities.

*Immigrant Entrepreneur Assistance Program:* Helps foreign business investors to get established in Ontario. Its recommendations are taken into consideration by the Canada Employment and Immigration Commission when the entrepreneur applies for permanent residency.

*Licensing and Joint Ventures Program:* Provides information on manufacturing opportunities available from abroad.

## Policy and Technology Division

The Policy and Technology Division was created to promote increased competitiveness in Ontario industry by supporting the development and implementation of modern industrial technologies. Its programs provide technology policy advice directly to the *Premier's Council*, which is in charge of a $1 billion special technology fund to support science-and-technology research in the private sector and post-secondary institutions. As well, the Division aims to support technology training of private sector management; develop a policy framework for community economic development programs; strengthen inter-ministry and intergovernmental policy coordination; and focus Ontario's role in the Canada-U.S. free trade negotiations.

The Ministry's seven technology and innovation centres are agencies of this Division. Their role is to develop awareness and provide information application and technologies to Ontario industry (see Agencies, Boards, and Commissions).

## Small Business, Services, and Capital Projects Division

The Small Business, Services, and Capital Projects Division is comprised of the Service Sector, Small Business, and Business Development branches.

*Service Sector Branch*

The purpose of the Service Sector Branch is to improve the calibre of management skills in small service operations and to encourage the creation of new service enterprises in the province—particularly through the New Ventures Program, which provides up to $15,000 in start-up capital at prime plus one percent through major chartered banks and financial institutions.

*Small Business Branch*

The Small Business Branch offers seminars on starting a business, marketing, finance and other subjects in an effort to enhance management skills in small businesses. The University Small Business Consulting Service provides funds to the business schools of 12 Ontario universities, permitting commerce and MBA students to offer small business consulting services. This Branch acts as the voice of the province's small business community within the government, and handles inquiries concerning financing, legislation and regulation. The Parliamentary Assistant to the Minister of Industry, Trade and Technology also carries the title of Small Business Advocate.

*Business Development Branch*

The Business Development Branch helps private sector companies identify market opportunities related to new technology, government procurement, global product mandating and changing customer requirements. It assists in the development of joint ventures, to enable to the manufacturing sector to recognize new business opportunities and to enable multinationals to increase domestic sourcing. Three important directories are produced by this branch: The "Made in Ontario Directory" lists products and services available form Ontario manufacturers. "Computer System Sources" lists manufacturers of hardware, software, and computer peripherals in the province. "Public Sector Buyers," lists the buying officers in all Ontario government ministries and agencies.

## EXPENDITURE ESTIMATES

*Estimated Expenditures 1987–88*:

| | |
|---|---|
| Ministry Administration | $11,213,438 |
| Policy and Technology | 34,032,000 |
| Industry and Trade | 35,758,900 |
| Small Business, Services & | |
|     Industrial Assistance | 89,025,800 |
| Ontario Development Corporations | 76,933,800 |
| Northern Industry | 7,030,800 |
| **Ministry total:** | **$253,994,738** |

## AGENCIES, BOARDS, AND COMMISSIONS

The following ABCs report to the Legislative Assembly through the Minister of Industry, Trade and Technology:

*Ontario Development Corporation (ODC), Northern Ontario Development Corporation (NODC) and Eastern Ontario Development Corporation (EODC):* Encourage employment and the development and diversification of Ontario industry by providing selective financial assistance to business and industry. Financial assistance is directed primarily towards the development and expansion of secondary manufacturing industries, tourist operations and international trade. Financial assistance, and technical and business information is available for establishing new operations, expanding existing operations, export financing, production of high-tech products, and buying pollution control and energy saving equipment. The programs generally fall into three categories: term loans, bank guarantees, and export support lines of credit. The head office of the Development Corporations is located in Toronto. The ODC operates six regional offices, in Toronto, Mississauga, Orillia, Kitchener, Hamilton and London. The EODC has offices in Peterborough, Kingston, and Ottawa. The NODC has offices in Sudbury, Timmins and Thunder Bay.

*Ontario International Corporation* (OIC): Assists the private sector in Ontario to sell consulting expertise and capital goods in the world market for capital projects. It promotes and supports the marketing of Ontario public sector expertise and systems internationally. It also provides intergovernmental contact and an Ontario government presence, in support of exports of services and capital goods for international capital projects. More recently the OIC has focused its attention on selling skills developed by the province in areas such as policing, public transportation and health care.

*Ontario Research Foundation* (ORF): An independent, not-for-profit industrial research organization, working for more than 2,000 industrial, governmental and consultative clients annually. ORF handles applied industrial research with its activities in three broad categories: idea development, problem solving, and evaluations. It has specific expertise in five technical areas: energy, environment, materials, products and processes, and resources. ORF works on a contract or fee basis with charges based on straight cost recovery. Initial consultations are free.

*Technology Centres:* Seven centres across Ontario develop awareness and provide information application and assistance, demonstration and training to Ontario industries. Three—the Ontario Centre for Microelectronics (Ottawa), the Ontario Computer-Aided Design/Computer-Aided Manufacturing (CAD/CAM) Centre (Cambridge) and the Ontario Robotics Centre (Peterborough)—are technology-specific centres. Four—the Ontario Centre for Automotive Parts Technology (St. Catharines), the Ontario Centre for Resource Machinery Technology (Sudbury), the Ontario Centre for Farm Machinery and Food Processing Technology (Chatham), and the joint Canada-Ontario Centre for Advanced Manufacturing (Windsor)—are industry specific.

## LEGISLATION

The Ministry of Industry, Trade and Technology is responsible for the following Acts:

*Development Corporations Act:* Establishes and continues the Ontario Development Corporations.

*Ministry of Industry and Trade Act:* Establishes and continues the Ministry of Industry, Trade and Technology.

*Ontario Research Foundation Act:* Establishes and continues the Ontario Research Foundation in Mississauga.

*Technology Centres Act:* Establishes and continues the Ministry's Technology Centres.

# MINISTRY OF LABOUR

## ROLES AND FUNCTIONS

The responsibility of the Ministry of Labour is to promote sound industrial relations, safe working conditions, and equality of treatment and opportunity in employment. Programs and services are concerned with the rights and responsibilities of the individual worker, and the rights and obligations of management and labour in ensuring health and safety in the workplace.

## BACKGROUND HISTORY

The Ontario Ministry of Labour had its origin in 1882, when the Ontario Government established the Bureau of Industries, under the then Department of Agriculture, to "institute inquiries and collect useful facts related to the agricultural, mechanical and manufacturing interests of the Province."

By 1900, Ontario's work force included more than half the industrial workers of the Dominion of Canada. In that year, the government expanded the province's labour service by establishing the Bureau of Labour and transferring labour affairs from the Department of Agriculture to the Department of Public Works.

The principal function of the Bureau of Labour was similar to that of the erstwhile Bureau of Industries: "to collect, sort, systemize and publish information and statistics." But, in addition, its responsibilities were broadened to encompass dealing with labour-management disputes, cooperating with trade unions and labour organizations, encouraging harmonious relations between "labour and capital," and involving itself in other areas of interest to Ontario workers.

In 1916 the Bureau of Labour was replaced by the Trades and Labour Branch, still under the Department of Public Works, and was given charge of the administration of various safety and training-standards laws that had come into effect over the years. There was an ever-increasing interest within the labour offices of the government in addressing working conditions and participating in safety, health, job-finding, welfare, and training, as well as in setting minimum standards for the protection of the public. Consequently, in April 1919, the Ontario legislature passed Bill 169 to establish the Department of Labour and bring all labour matters under a single ministry. With the new name and structure came the responsibility for the administration of five acts: The *Factory Act, Department of Labour Act, Steam Boiler Act, Stationary and Hoisting Engineers Act*, and the *Building Trades Protection Act*.

One of the first tasks of the new Department of Labour was the establishment of a Minimum Wage Board with the power to regulate, in certain cases, the minimum wages of women and girls. In 1923, after two years of inquiry by the board, the Department of Labour set the minimum wage for women at $12.50 per week in Toronto and $12.00 per week elsewhere in the province. Farm help and domestics were not included.

In 1922 the department established the Provincial Employment Service Council, but this service, with other placement services in the various provinces, was later assumed by the federal government. Between 1923 and 1930 the Ontario Government enacted many law reforms and the Minimum Wage Board Regulations were amended to include women working in theatres.

The spirit of reform carried through the mid-1920s and into the Depression era. During this period, some people worked 16 hours a day in sweatshops for nine dollars a week; bread truck drivers earned as little as five dollars a week; and, in Ottawa, lumberjacks earned $5.50 a month after charges for lodging.

In 1935 the Ontario Government passed the *Industrial Standards Act* in an attempt to bring some order to the wage structure. The first industries covered by the new Act were men's and boys' clothing, ladies' cloak and suit, millinery, barbering, and 28 building trades. In 1937 the government established a new Industry and Labour Board to administer both the new Act and minimum wage regulations for women. Thirty-nine minimum wage schedules were drawn up, including a minimum of $12.50 a week for women, and $16 a week for men, in the textile industry. Trade schools, other than those under the Department of Education, were brought under the Department of Labour by a revised *Apprenticeship Act*. The Workmen's Compensation Board was transferred from the Department of the Attorney General to the Department of Labour. Conciliation services were expanded.

With the advent of the Second World War, the apprenticeship system was enlarged to meet the need of weapons production. In 1941 the Ontario Regional War Labour Board was established to administer the basic scale of wages in line with the federal wage control orders. Realizing that labour harmony was essential to the war effort, a select committee of the legislature began an intensive study of the collective bargaining process. In April 1943, the legislature passed the *Collective Bargaining Act*, which gave employees the right to the union of their choice. Once a union had been certified by the newly established Labour Court, the Act obliged employers to bargain with the union. In 1944 the Labour Court was replaced by the Ontario Labour Relations Board.

On July 1, 1944, the *Hours of Work and Vacations with Pay Act* was passed. This was administered by the Industry and Labour Board. Additional areas of jurisdiction for this board included the *Industrial Standards Act*, the *Apprenticeship Act*, and the *Minimum Wage Act*.

In the late 1940s and through most of the 1950s the Department of Labour continued to expand and to assume the beginnings of its present day structure. It surpassed its own traditional role as a regulatory body in the labour relations and working conditions areas to become a multifaceted agency helping people to meet,

MINISTRY OF LABOUR

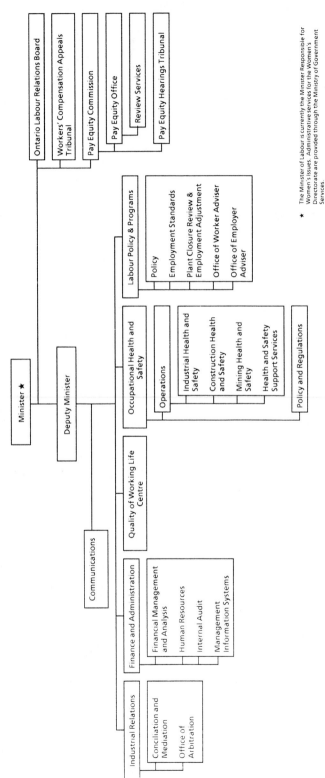

Minister ★

Ontario Labour Relations Board

Workers' Compensation Appeals Tribunal

Pay Equity Commission
- Pay Equity Office
  - Review Services
- Pay Equity Hearings Tribunal

Deputy Minister

Communications

Industrial Relations
- Conciliation and Mediation
- Office of Arbitration

Finance and Administration
- Financial Management and Analysis
- Human Resources
- Internal Audit
- Management Information Systems

Quality of Working Life Centre

Occupational Health and Safety
- Operations
  - Industrial Health and Safety
  - Construction Health and Safety
  - Mining Health and Safety
  - Health and Safety Support Services
- Policy and Regulations

Labour Policy & Programs
- Policy
- Employment Standards
- Plant Closure Review & Employment Adjustment
- Office of Worker Adviser
- Office of Employer Adviser

★ The Minister of Labour is currently the Minister Responsible for Women's Issues. Administrative services for the Women's Directorate are provided through the Ministry of Government Services.

and benefit from, social change, which included the complex field of interracial and interfaith understanding. In 1951 the department entered into a new era in human relations with the *Fair Employment Practices Act* and the *Female Fair Remuneration Act*. Four years later, the *Fair Accommodation Practices Act* was passed.

Throughout the 1960s the department became engaged in a structural reorganization reflecting significant changes in policy, priorities, and techniques of discharging its responsibilities. Legislation was thoroughly revised and updated. Up to 1962 all the different pieces of legislation covering human rights were administered by various branches of the Department of Labour. In 1962 all these laws were incorporated into one law when the *Ontario Human Rights Code* was enacted. The Ontario Human Rights Commission was created by statute that same year to administer and enforce the new Code. A new *Employment Standards Act*, which came into effect January 1, 1969, consolidated several pieces of legislation into one act that provided a basic framework outlining for employees and employers their rights and obligations regarding working conditions. In 1971, the Department of Labour was renamed the Ministry of Labour under the *Ministry of Labour Act*.

From the beginning, the Ministry's role has been shaped by major societal forces and events. The two world wars, the Oshawa General Motors Strike in 1937, the Great Depression, and the tremendous permanent influx of women into the work force in recent years, have been but a few of the influences that have contributed to government participation in the labour field and moulded Ministry policy.

## ORGANIZATION

The Ministry of Labour is organized into four major divisions (see organization chart):

1. *Finance and Administration:* Responsible for corporate services to the Ministry. Branches include Financial Management and Analysis, Administrative Operations, Communications, Internal Audit, Human Resources, and Library and Information Services.

2. *Industrial Relations:* Responsible for the Conciliation and Mediation Services Branch and the Office of Arbitration.

3. *Labour Policy and Programs:* Responsible for the development and enforcement of employment standards. Branches include Employment Standards, Legal Services, and the Handicapped Employment Program.

4. *Occupational Health and Safety:* Responsible for Branches for Industrial, Construction and Mining Health and Safety; and Occupational Health.

In addition, twenty agencies, boards, and commissions, including the new Pay Equity Commission, the Workers' Compensation Board, and the Ontario Labour Relations Board report to the Legislative Assembly through the Minister of Labour (see Agencies, Boards, and Commissions).

The Head Office of the Ministry of Labour is located in Toronto. The Ministry also delivers programs through 20 regional, district, and field offices, 7 mine rescue stations, and a number of clinics and laboratories. The Ministry of Labour employs approximately 1,500 public servants.

## PROGRAMS

*Handicapped Employment Program:* This program promotes equal opportunity by developing strategies to increase the hiring, retention, and career advancement of people who have disabilities.

*Industrial Relations Program:* This program consists of activities designed to assist in the development and maintenance of harmonious relations between employers and employees, in order to help ensure a stable labour relations climate in the province. This objective is pursued through three activities: program administration, the Ontario Conciliation and Mediation Services, and the Office of Arbitration.

*Labour Policy Program:* This program encompasses the Ministry's policy development activities and new legislative initiatives, and monitors existing programs and policies to determine their effectiveness. This includes overseeing the Ministry's Policy Branch, which has a mandate to initiate, develop, and coordinate policy activities as well as to coordinate and prepare ministerial correspondence and maintain liaison with other ministries. This program is responsible for employment standards, plant closure review, employment adjustment, the Handicapped Employment Program, the Office of the Employer Adviser, and the Office of the Worker Adviser.

*Occupational Health and Safety Program:* This program promotes and assists in securing a healthful and safe work environment by administering the *Occupational Health and Safety Act* and regulations, by encouraging employers and workers to cooperate in identifying and controlling health and safety hazards, and by developing appropriate legislation and programs to accomplish this. The program is responsible for construction health and safety, industrial health and safety, mining health and safety, occupational health, and special studies.

*Quality of Working Life:* This program's mandate is to promote and support the enhancement of the quality of working life of people in Ontario. This has been developed through three major areas of activity: the initiation, implementation, monitoring, and evaluation of quality of working life projects in joint union-management settings, the education and training of individuals and organizations in quality of working life approaches, and the creation, collection, and dissemination of written information to promote a broad understanding of, and interest in, "QWL."

*Workers' Compensation Advisory Program:* This program provides assistance to workers and employers, primarily in presenting cases before the Workers' Compensation Appeals Tribunal, as well as advice on assessment of levies and the *Workers' Compensation Act.* Other services include advice to the Workers' Compensation Board on possible industrial diseases and related eligibility rules for compensation claims.

## EXPENDITURE ESTIMATES

*Estimated Expenditures 1987–88*:

| | |
|---|---|
| Ministry Administration | $20,928,438 |
| Industrial Relations | 11,073,000 |
| Labour Relations Board | 7,115,200 |
| Occupational Health and Safety | 49,520,100 |
| Employment Standards | 8,267,900 |
| Workers Compensation Advisory Program | 7,176,500 |
| **Ministry total:** | **$104,081,138** |

## AGENCIES, BOARDS, AND COMMISSIONS

The following ABCs report to the Legislative Assembly through the Minister of Labour:

*Advisory Committee on Occupational Chest Disease:* This is a committee of the Workers' Compensation Board and its purpose is to review all WCB claimants for pneumoconioses and asbestosis.

*Advisory Council on Occupational Health and Occupational Safety:* The advisory council advises the Minister on matters relating to occupational health and occupational safety, and makes recommendations to the Minister regarding Ministry programs in occupational health and safety.

*Agricultural Industry Advisory Committee:* This committee advises the Minister of Labour on matters relating to the application of employment standards legislation to agricultural workers and the development and modification of employment standards appropriate to the agriculture industry and its different sectors.

*Boards of Conciliation:* These boards, subject to ministerial policy, function as important tools to deal with disputes involving public service, pattern-setting industries, and contentious first agreements. However, few boards of conciliation have been appointed in recent years.

*Boards of Hospital Arbitration:* The purpose of these boards is to arbitrate unresolved collective bargaining disputes between employers and trade unions representing employees in the health care field.

*Classification Ratings Committees:* These committees are designated by the chairman of the Civil Service Commission to adjudicate grievances concerning position classification from eligible employees who are excluded from the application of the *Crown Employees Collective Bargaining Act.* The committees are therefore essentially responsible for classification grievances filed by persons employed in a managerial or confidential capacity.

*Construction Industry Advisory Board:* This advisory body has been established to advise the Minister on issues of common concern to labour and management in the construction industry.

*Industrial Adjustment Committee:* Through manpower assessment and incentive agreements the Ministry of Labour, contributes financially to the support of such committees, established by the Industrial Adjustment Service of the Canada Employment and Immigration Commission. Their purpose is to assist employees affected by large-scale terminations to become re-employed.

*Industrial Disease Standards Panel:* The IDSP investigates possible industrial diseases and makes findings as to whether a probable connection exists between a disease and an industrial process, trade, or occupation. It creates, develops, and revises criteria for the evaluation of workers' compensation claims and advises on eligibility rules regarding compensation claims respecting industrial diseases.

*Industrial Standards Act Advisory Committees:* These committees administer the schedules made under the *Industrial Standards Act.* There are four advisory committees, all in the garment industry and all with province-wide schedules. They apply to the fur, ladies' cloak and suit, ladies' dress, and men's and boys' clothing industries.

*Mining Legislative Review Committee:* This committee reviews the Mining regulations and makes recommendations for revisions to the Minister of Labour.

*Minister of Labour's Labour-Management Advisory Committee:* This committee advises the Minister on matters relating to arbitration, particularly with respect to persons qualified to act as arbitrators.

*Ontario Labour-Management Study Group:* This committee, composed of senior representatives from labour, management, and government, acts as a tripartite body to develop consultative mechanisms in society.

*Ontario Labour Relations Board:* The OLRB administers the *Labour Relations Act,* which entails certifying trade unions, appointing officers to mediate complaints of contraventions of the Act, conducting hearings into unsettled complaints, granting remedial orders, issuing directions and declarations in cases of unlawful strikes and lock-outs, settling jurisdictional disputes, accrediting employees' associations and bargaining agencies, certifying employee bargaining agencies in the construction industry, conducting arbitration hearings on grievances under construction industry collective agreements, terminating bargaining rights, and providing opinions to the Minister relating to his authority to appoint conciliation officers or arbitrators.

*Pay Equity Commission:* Responsible for assisting all public sector parties in achieving pay equity in their workplaces, based on the requirements of the *Pay Equity Act, 1987.* The Commission is comprised of two bodies:

1. *The Pay Equity Office:* Provides information and guidelines for developing pay equity programs and makes staff available for conducting workshops and addressing groups on the requirements and policies of the Act. The Office also provides review officers to investigate complaints raised by employers, employees or union officials, about issues arising from pay equity plan negotiation and implementation. The review officers are responsible for reaching settlements when objections are filed with the Pay Equity Office.

2. *The Pay Equity Hearings Tribunal:* An independent tripartite adjudicative body comprised of representatives from labour, management, and neutral groups. The Tribunal ensures compliance with the Act by resolving disputes that cannot be settled by the key participants or the review officers.

*Public Service Appeal Boards:*

1. *Ontario Public Service Labour Relations Tribunal:* Administers the *Crown Employees Collective Bargaining Act*; is empowered to adjudicate matters referred to it by government employers, employee organizations or employees on such topics as representation rights, unfair labour practices, bad faith bargaining, succession rights, strikes, and lock-outs, consent to prosecute inclusions and exclusions of employees in bargaining units, exemptions from payment of union dues, and the duty of fair representation owed by employee organizations to individual employees.

2. *Crown Employees Grievance Settlement Board:* Solely responsible for the adjudication of employee organization and employer rights disputes involving matters such as dismissals, suspensions, other forms of discipline, working conditions, and classification.

*Public Service Grievance Board:* The Board operates pursuant to the *Public Service Act.* It adjudicates grievances concerning non-bargaining unit employees and may be called upon to deal with matters such as dismissal, suspension, other forms of discipline, merit increase, promotion, and transfer.

*Workers' Compensation Appeals Tribunal* (WCAT): The tribunal hears, determines and disposes of all appeals from final decisions of the WCB respecting the provision of health care, vocational rehabilitation, entitlement to compensation, employer assessments, penalties, and transfer of costs under the *Workers' Compensation Act.* The Tribunal adjudicates and determines whether a worker's right to take court action is taken away by the Act. It also considers appeals with respect to access to claim files.

*Workers' Compensation Board:* The Board, which operates 14 offices province-wide, including a Toronto head office, provides the province with three fundamental services:

1. Adjudicating claims for work-related injuries and occupational diseases, and compensating workers for the resulting time lost from work and for permanent disability;

2. Furnishing injured workers with comprehensive health care and vocational rehabilitation services to help them return to a healthy life and gainful employment;

3. Paying for these services through the collection of funds from the province's employers.

## LEGISLATION

The Ministry of Labour is responsible for the following Acts:

*Crown Employees Collective Bargaining Act:* Governs provincial government employees and their bargaining relationship with the government. Gives jurisdiction to the Grievance Settlement Board to adjudicate employee organization and employer rights disputes involving such matters as dismissals, suspensions, classification grievances, and working conditions grievances. Also gives responsibility to the Ontario Public Service Labour Relations Tribunal to adjudicate matters referred to it by government employers, employee organizations, or employees on matters such as conferring representation rights on employee organizations, fair labour practices, bad faith bargaining, and inclusions and exclusions of employees in bargaining units.

*Employment Agencies Act:* Provides for the licensing and regulating of permanent employment agencies. This includes any business that, for a fee, either assists employees or helps people find work.

*Employment Standards Act:* Establishes minimum working conditions for the protection of employees with respect to minimum wage, hours of work, home workers, public holidays, overtime pay, vacation pay, equal pay for equal work, benefit plans, pregnancy leave, and termination of employment.

*Government Contracts Hours and Wages Act:* Sets out the fair wage policy of the government of Ontario in respect of government of contracts.

*Hospital Labour Disputes Arbitration Act:* Provides for conciliation and arbitration in interest disputes between hospitals and employees.

*Industrial Standards Act:* Provides a means for employers and employees of specific industries or trades to get together and establish a schedule of wages, hours, and days of work. The schedule established then becomes law for the industry or trade in a designated zone.

*Labour Relations Act:* Furthers harmonious relations between employers and employees through collective bargaining between employers and trade unions representing the employees and chosen by them. Also provides for designation of employer bargaining agencies to represent provincial units and thus provide for bargaining on a province-wide scale.

*Ministry of Labour Act:* Establishes the Ministry of Labour and provides authority for the effective performance of its responsibilities.

*Occupational Health and Safety Act:* Provides for the safety of the total work force of the province with the exception of teachers and those engaged in farming operations. The Act requires a high degree of worker-employer cooperation to identify, control, reduce and, where possible, eliminate hazards to the health and safety of workers. It also provides for health and safety committees, refusal to work, and the regulation of toxic substances.

*One Day's Rest in Seven Act:* Provides that every employee has one day's rest in every seven.

*Pay Equity Act, 1987:* Endeavors to remove sex discrimination in the wage-setting process. The Act obliges the public sector and private sector firms with 100 or more employees to develop, post, and implement pay equity plans and to make adjustments to wage inequities. The Act covers full-time and permanent part-time employees, but does not cover casual workers, students, or private sector employers with fewer than ten employees. Under the Act, the public sector must achieve pay equity by January 1991, private sector employers of 500 or more staff by January 1992, and employers of 100–499 staff by January 1993. Pay equity is voluntary for employers with 10–99 employees.

*Rights of Labour Act:* Establishes the rights of labour and trade unions.

*Workers' Compensation Act:* Creates the Workers' Compensation Board to pay employee's claims arising from an accident in the course of employment; establishes a fund to which employers subject to the Act must contribute regularly, and out of which claims are paid; and defines employers' liability for injuries incurred by employees during the course of employment, for employees excluded from the usual workers' compensation benefits.

*Blind Workmen's Compensation Act:* Extends to blind workers the provisions of the *Workers' Compensation Act* and provides for the Ontario Government to pay the costs of it.

*Workmen's Compensation Insurance Act:* Ensures that an employee (not covered by the provisions of the Workers' Compensation Act) receives his due damages in the case where employer is privately insured.

# INNOVATIONS

The following innovations have had a positive impact on the operations of the Ministry of Labour:

1. The Industrial Relations Division's preventive mediation initiative, entitled the *Relationship Improvement Program*, has been functioning since 1975 to establish a system of formal communication between employers and unions in order to promote and maintain sound working relationships. Following a training program by Ministry of Labour mediators joint committees are established in which parties' attitudes, communications, leadership, grievance administration, and responsibilities are examined.

2. The *Quality of Working Life Centre*, established in 1978, assists labour and management in jointly designing and redesigning organizations that are both highly effective and provide a high level of human involvement and dignity.

3. The *Offices of the Worker and Employer Advisers* and an independent *Appeals Tribunal* for the province's Workers' Compensation Board system were established in 1985.

4. The *Handicapped Employment Program* assists employers to develop programs to encourage the recruitment, retention, and promotion of handicapped persons, by offering conferences, consulting services, and support to community initiatives and organized labour.

5. The *Plant Closure Review and Employment Adjustment Branch* contacts companies contemplating, or subject to, closure/layoff, to attempt to alleviate the dislocation of employees by helping to coordinate federal-provincial adjustment assistance and by providing advice concerning termination entitlement, etc.

6. The *Employee Counselling Program* provides employees affected by permanent job loss (especially due to plant closures) with professional assistance in the areas of job search techniques, career assessment, access to retraining, retirement counselling, and financial counselling.

# MINISTRY OF MUNICIPAL AFFAIRS

## ROLES AND FUNCTIONS

The Ministry of Municipal Affairs ensures municipalities have the legislative authority to respond to changing conditions and local needs. Management and administrative support is made available as required, along with financial assistance, to 839 municipalities across Ontario, which vary greatly in size, structure, and circumstances. The Ministry also encourages sound planning at the community level, and renewal activity in municipalities through operational and technical assistance. The Ministry's objectives are achieved through the regulatory and monitoring process as well as by grant and loan programs. Staff assistance and advice is also provided to municipalities and business improvement organizations.

## BACKGROUND HISTORY

In 1935, in the midst of the Great Depression, with many municipalities defaulting, Royal Assent was given to an Act to establish the Department of Municipal Affairs (DMA). The Department was assigned the general responsibility for overseeing municipalities. This included the standardizing of municipal accounting, the compiling of statistical data, the conducting of special investigations, and the providing of advice to municipalities. Policy and planning-related functions were gradually added to these roles. When ordered by the Ontario Municipal Board, DMA supervised the administration of such defaulting municipalities. As time passed, new vigour returned to municipal activities.

Local assessment, which was previously conducted by each municipality, was taken over by the province in 1970 and added to the responsibilities of the Department of Municipal Affairs. However, in 1972, DMA's major functions, except for assessment, were merged with the newly created Ministry of Treasury, Economics and Intergovernmental Affairs (TEIGA), and the assessment function was assigned to the newly formed Ministry of Revenue. Community planning functions, which were part of the local government function under TEIGA, were transferred to the Ministry of Housing when it was established in 1974.

Four years later, TEIGA was divided into two ministries: the Ministry of Treasury and Economics and the Ministry of Intergovernmental Affairs. As a result, the divisions of TEIGA concerned with municipal affairs, except for the Municipal

Finance Division, became part of the Ministry of Intergovernmental Affairs. In 1980, however, the Finance Division was also joined to Intergovernmental Affairs, but this overall structure did not remain stable for long. In 1981, the local government responsibilities were separated from the Ministry of Intergovernmental Affairs and joined with the Ministry of Housing to create the Ministry of Municipal Affairs and Housing. This new ministry brought together provincial government services and programs related to municipalities and those dealing with housing, community development, community planning, and land development.

A new provincial government in 1985 brought further changes to Municipal Affairs. With numerous local governments demanding attention in the Legislature, the province created a Ministry of Municipal Affairs to be solely responsible for municipal affairs and community planning functions. This Ministry provides a full range of services to support local government and encourages effective land use planning in Ontario. The Ministry is also responsible for the Niagara Escarpment Commission.

## GLOSSARY

(From the *Ontario Municipal Directory*.)

A *Municipality* is an area whose inhabitants are incorporated. Its powers (except in the case of an "improvement area" where powers are exercised by a board of trustees appointed by the government) are exercised by a council composed of individuals elected by the electors of the municipality.

A *County* is a municipality which is a federation of towns, villages, and townships, each with an elected council which assigns members to the county council. A county is responsible for a limited number of functions, with major roads being the most important. Cities, even though geographically located within a county, do not participate in the county political system, and are responsible for their own municipal functions.

A *Regional Municipality* (or "upper tier" municipality) is a municipality created by a special act of the Ontario Legislature, and is a federation of all the local municipalities within its boundaries. Each local municipality designates members from its council to sit on the regional council. Regions are responsible for land use planning, social services, major roads, and trunk sewers and water systems. Local councils are responsible for community services such as recreation, libraries, local roads, and garbage collection. The ten regional municipalities in Ontario are similar to counties but have more responsibilities, and the cities in a regional municipality are full participants in the regional system.

## ORGANIZATION

The Ministry of Municipal Affairs is organized into three major divisions (see organization chart):

1. *Community Planning:* Encourages effective land-use planning in Ontario so that communities develop within a sound planning framework that is consistent with provincial policies.

2. *Municipal Affairs:* Provides for liaison between municipalities; analysis of organizational, functional, and structural aspects of local government; financial analysis; a full range of advisory services to support local government; administration of transfer payments to municipalities; and the promotion and operation of local government through a network of field offices.

3. *Ontario Municipal Audit Bureau:* Provides assurance to management regarding the compliance to relevant agreements and legislation by recipients of municipality transfer payments.

In addition, the Niagara Escarpment Commission reports to the Legislative Assembly through the Minister of Municipal Affairs (see Agencies, Boards, and Commissions).

The Head Office of the Ministry of Municipal Affairs is located in Toronto. The Ministry also provides services to municipalities through ten field offices located throughout the province. The Ministry employs approximately 420 public servants.

## PROGRAMS

### Community Planning Division

The Community Planning Division is comprised of the following branches:

1. *Community Planning Advisory Branch:* Provides a wide range of technical and financial planning services to municipalities, the development industry, and the public.

2. *Community Renewal Branch:* Encourages community improvement through assistance to municipalities and the private sector; and administers ongoing projects, funded under previous renewal programs, as well as current projects under the comprehensive Program for Renewal, Improvement, Development and Economic Revitalization.

3. *Local Planning Policy Branch:* Recommends provincial policies and legislation and prepares policy statements, regulations, and guidelines to apply at the local government level.

4. *Plans Administration Branch:* Central and Southwest, and North and East. Regulates and monitors functions for a variety of planning matters.

MINISTRY OF MUNICIPAL AFFAIRS

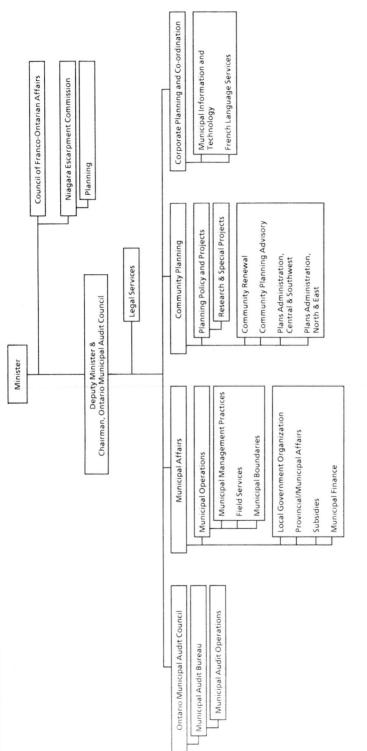

**Minister**

- Council of Franco-Ontarian Affairs
- Niagara Escarpment Commission
  - Planning

**Deputy Minister & Chairman, Ontario Municipal Audit Council**

- Legal Services

**Ontario Municipal Audit Council**
- Municipal Audit Bureau
- Municipal Audit Operations

**Municipal Affairs**
- Municipal Operations
- Municipal Management Practices
  - Field Services
  - Municipal Boundaries
- Local Government Organization
- Provincial/Municipal Affairs
- Subsidies
- Municipal Finance

**Community Planning**
- Planning Policy and Projects
- Research & Special Projects
- Community Renewal
- Community Planning Advisory
- Plans Administration, Central & Southwest
- Plans Administration, North & East

**Corporate Planning and Co-ordination**
- Municipal Information and Technology
- French Language Services

5. *Research and Special Projects Branch:* Provides technical advice on community planning, emphasizing practical approaches to community planning and development.

*Community Planning Division Programs*

*Community Planning Grant Program:* Designed to help municipalities initiate studies to resolve local planning issues. The program provides financial assistance to all municipalities, including counties and regions, and to planning boards in Northern Ontario. The program's objectives are to promote the effective operation of community planning, to support the study and resolution of local planning issues, to assist in the implementation of the *Planning Act*, and to resolve matters of provincial interest during the municipal planning process. Generally, funding is limited to 50 percent of eligible costs of one study per year with provincial funding not to exceed $35,000.

*Planning Administration Grants:* These grants are provided to planning boards in unorganized territories in Northern Ontario to cover 100 percent of the eligible costs for administration of planning functions. Grants assist such planning activities as consent approvals, and commenting on subdivision applications and zoning orders. This program is administered through field offices in Sudbury and Thunder Bay.

*Program for Renewal, Improvement, Development and Economic Revitalization* (PRIDE): This program assists municipalities in redevelopment, renovation, conservation, and development of areas in need of community improvement, and enhances their ability to attract and retain economic activity. Consultation and advisory services include:

1. Preparation of community improvement policies as part of municipal official plans;

2. Interpretation, application, and administration of community improvement legislation in the *Planning Act*;

3. The establishment and ongoing operation of *Business Improvement Areas* (BIAs) across the province;

4. The development of by-laws governing property maintenance standards which encourage property owners to maintain the physical appearance of the property in a manner which reflects local standards and needs.

Education and information exchange services include:

1. The sponsorship and participation in seminars and conferences focusing on community improvement programs and related activities;

2. The development of guidelines, manuals, and other resource materials dealing with improvement activities and legislation;

3. The publication of a newsletter and other resource materials for Business Improvement Areas.

Financial assistance provided under PRIDE has incorporated the objectives of the former Ontario Neighbourhood Improvement Program (ONIP) and the Commercial Area Improvement Program (CAIP), but, those objectives have now been broadened to include improvements in all other sections of a municipality, such as industrial and mixed land-use areas. The program provides funding for improvements to remedy a range of physical deficiencies within a defined area. Funding available to municipalities will be in the form of a provincial grant covering 50 percent of approved eligible costs.

The *Business Improvement Area* (BIA) concept is a self-help mechanism designed to assist local business and retail communities to upgrade and promote their commercial and shopping districts. A BIA can be established only on the initiative of the local business community, with the approval of the local municipal council. A board of management, appointed by council, directs the BIA with funds generated by a special tax levy which is applied to all businesses in the area.

### Municipal Affairs Division

The Municipal Affairs Division comprises the following branches:

1. *Local Government Organization Branch:* Develops policy and advises management and the Minister on issues involving the functions, organization, and accountability of local government.

2. *Provincial/Municipal Affairs Secretariat:* Acts as a liaison between the provincial government and those municipal organizations which represent local government in Ontario. It publishes an annual Municipal Directory.

3. *Subsidies Branch:* Delivers and monitors subsidy programs, totalling almost a billion dollars annually, to municipalities and farmers, including unconditional grants and payments in lieu of local taxes.

4. *Municipal Finances Branch:* Develops policy and legislation to ensure the long-term financial viability of Ontario municipalities.

5. *Municipal Management Policy Branch:* Offers a broad range of services to improve local government management effectiveness.

6. *Field Services Branch:* Operates a network of 10 field services offices to provide advice to municipalities.

7. *Municipal Boundaries Branch:* Helps municipalities resolve boundary and boundary-related issues by administering the *Municipal Boundary Negotiations Act.*

*Municipal Affairs Division Programs*

*Disaster Relief Assistance Program:* Provides grants to local disaster committees to match funds raised in order to assist the victims of natural calamities.

*Farm Tax Reduction Program:* Provides municipal tax assistance to encourage owners of properties assessed as farms to maintain their farming activities. Farm owners who meet the criteria are eligible to receive rebates of up to 60 percent of their total municipal taxes.

*Involvement in Municipal Administration:* Provides subsidies to municipalities, district school area boards, municipal associations, and some planning boards to hire students in computer science, law, administration, and planning, who are interested in municipal government.

*Managed Forest Tax Reduction Program:* Provides assistance to owners of private forests in order to reduce tax burdens and encourage proper management and preservation of forest resources. Owners must meet certain criteria in order to qualify for municipal tax rebates.

*Municipal Services in French:* Provides subsidies to municipalities for the provision of services in both French and English, including: translation of official documents; language instruction for municipal council or staff; and purchase or leasing of simultaneous translation equipment.

*Ontario Local Government Student Research Assistance Program:* Provides assistance to fourth-year university and graduate students for research costs of theses or dissertations related to local government responsibilities, structure, finance, or politics.

*Ontario Municipal Training Program:* Provides assistance in developing qualified municipal managers and in training college and university graduates in municipal government.

*Provincial Properties Program:* Under the *Municipal Tax Assistance Act,* this program provides grants in lieu of taxes to municipalities for provincially owned and non-tenanted properties, including provincial parks, historical parks, wilderness areas, and the non-tenanted portions of agricultural research stations located within their boundaries. Under the *Assessment Act,* this program provides for payment of taxes to municipalities in respect of tenanted provincial properties. These payments are recovered from tenants directly.

*Shoreline Property Assistance Program:* Provides 10-year loans at eight percent, for the repair or protection of privately-owned shoreline properties damaged by high water levels on the Great Lakes.

*Unconditional Grants Program:*

1. *Density Per Household Grant:* Provides assistance to the municipalities to alleviate the higher cost per household of servicing sparsely populated area municipalities. It is based on a schedule of per household rates (the lower the household density, the higher the rate), applied against municipal households.

2. *General Per Household Grant:* Provides assistance towards the cost of municipal services. It is based on a per household rate (currently $30 per household), applied against the municipal households.

3. *General Support Grant:* Assists municipalities, regions, and counties in the financing of municipal services. The grant is based on a fixed percentage (set at eight percent for the 1987 program year) of the net municipal levy requirements.

4. *Northern Special Support Grant:* Provides additional assistance, over and above the general support grant provided to municipalities, towards the financing of higher-cost municipal goods and services in Northern Ontario. Municipalities located north of the French River, including the Region of Sudbury, are eligible. The grant is based on a fixed percentage (set at 18 percent for the 1986 program year) of the net municipal levy requirements. Traditionally, the ratio of 3:1 is maintained between the rate for the northern special support grant and that of the general support grant.

5. *Policing Per Household Grant:* Provides assistance to municipalities that have their own local or regional police forces, or hold contracts for policing by the Ontario Provincial Police, or the police force of another municipality. There are no conditions as to the application of these grants by municipalities and the money is not necessarily spent on policing.

6. *Resource Equalization Grant:* Paid to "lower-tier municipalities" with below-average assessment bases to allow them to improve municipal services without incurring excessive property taxes. A portion of this grant is paid directly to "upper-tier municipalities" (see Glossary).

Every municipality is guaranteed to receive total unconditional grants in 1987 at least equal to their 1986 grant entitlement, increased by the enrichment in the general support and northern special support, as applicable.

## Ontario Municipal Audit Bureau

The Ontario Municipal Audit Bureau, established in 1986, contributes to the management of the provincial-municipal transfer payment programs through the provision of audit services to provincial ministries. The Bureau provides assurance to management regarding the compliance by recipients of transfer payment to relevant agreements and legislation. It also promotes good accountability and financial management practices. The Bureau works closely with such bodies as the Institute of Chartered Accountants of Ontario, providing input into management and audit standards. The Ontario Municipal Audit Bureau is involved in the auditing of transfer payment programs for the following ministries: Citizenship, Culture and Communications, Community and Social Services, Environment, Housing, Municipal Affairs, Northern Development and Mines, Tourism and Recreation, Transportation, and Treasury and Economics.

## EXPENDITURE ESTIMATES

*Estimated Expenditures 1987–88*:

| | |
|---|---:|
| Ministry Administration | $7,540,338 |
| Municipal Affairs | 879,737,700 |
| *(unconditional grants to municipalities)* | |
| Community Planning | 38,349,700 |
| Ontario Municipal Audit | 1,532,600 |
| Niagara Escarpment Commission | 1,714,700 |
| **Ministry total:** | **$928,875,038** |

## AGENCIES, BOARDS, AND COMMISSIONS

The following Commission reports to the Legislative Assembly through the Minister of Municipal Affairs:

*Niagara Escarpment Commission:* The purpose of the Commission is to assist the Minister in providing for the maintenance of the Niagara Escarpment and lands in its vicinity as a continuous natural environment, and in ensuring that any development which occurs is compatible with that natural environment. The Commission administers the development permit system, reviews, and comments on related planning applications, and intervenes at hearings on development applications. It also processes proposed amendments to the plan, and assists the Ministry in plan interpretation and in bringing local documents into conformity. The Commission comments and advises on park master plans, development plans, resource management plans, escarpment land acquisition, and heritage protection proposals; and promotes the objectives of the plan through publications, public meetings, and related information services.

## LEGISLATION

The Ministry of Municipal Affairs is responsible for the following Acts:

**Municipal Affairs**

*Barrie-Innisfil Annexation Act, 1981*

*Barrie-Vespra Annexation Act, 1984*

*Brantford-Brant Annexation Act, 1980*

*City of Cornwall Annexation Act, 1974*

*City of Gloucester Act, 1980*

*City of Hamilton Act, 1975*

*City of Hazeldean-March Act, 1978*

*City of Nepean Act, 1978*

*City of Ottawa Road Closing & Conveyance Validation Act, 1981*

*City of Port Colborne Act, 1974*

*City of Sudbury Hydro-Electric Service Act, 1980*

*City of Thorold Act, 1975*

*City of Thunder Bay Act, 1968-69*

*City of Timmins-Porcupine Act, 1972*

*County of Haliburton Act, 1982*

*County of Oxford Act*

*District Municipality of Muskoka Act*

*District of Parry Sound Local Government Act, 1979*

*International Bridges Municipal Payments Act, 1981*

*Line Fences Act*

*Local Improvement Act*

*Ministry of Municipal Affairs and Housing Act, 1981*

*Moosonee Development Area Board Act*

*Municipal Act*

*Municipal Affairs Act*

*Municipal Arbitrations Act*

*Municipal and School Tax Credit Assistance Act*

*Municipal Conflict of Interest Act, 1983*

*Municipal Corporations Quieting Orders Act*

*Municipal Elderly Residents' Assistance Act*

*Municipal Elections Act*

*Municipal Franchises Act*

*Municipal Interest and Discount Repeal Act, 1982*

*Municipal Payments in lieu of Taxes Statute Law Amendment Act, 1984*

*Municipal Private Acts Repeat Act, 1983*

*Municipal Subsidies Adjustment Repeal Act, 1976*

*Municipal Tax Assistance Act*

*Municipal Tax Sales Act, 1984*

*Municipal Unemployment Relief Act*

*Municipal Works Assistance Act*

*Municipality of Metropolitan Toronto Act*

*Municipality of Shuniah Act, 1936*

*Ontario Unconditional Grants Act*

*Ottawa-Carleton Amalgamations and Elections Act, 1973*

*Planning Statute Law Amendment Act, 1983*

*Police Village of St. George Act, 1980*

*Provincial Parks Municipal Tax Assistance Act*

*Public Parks Act*

*Public Utilities Act*

*Public Utilities Corporations Act*

*Regional Municipality of Durham Act*

*Regional Municipality of Haldimand-Norfold Act*

*Regional Municipality of Halton Act*

*Regional Municipality of Hamilton-Wentworth Act*

*Regional Municipality of Niagara Act*

*Regional Municipality of Ottawa-Carleton Act*

*Regional Municipality of Ottawa-Carleton Land Acquisition Act, 1980*

*Regional Municipality of Peel Act*

*Regional Municipality of Sudbury Act*

*Regional Municipality of Waterloo Act*

*Regional Municipality of York Act*

*Road Access Act*

*Shoreline Property Assistance Act*

*Snow Roads and Fences Act*

*Statute Labour Act*

*Tax Sales Confirmation Act, 1974*

*Territorial Division Act*

*Tom Longboat Act, 1980*

*Toronto District Heating Corporation Act, 1980*

*Toronto Islands Act, 1980*

*Town of Wasaga Beach Act, 1973*

*Township of North Plantagenet Act, 1976*

*Wharfs and Harbours Act*

**Community Planning:**

*Condominium Act*

*Land Titles Act*

*Municipal Act*

*Municipal Affairs and Housing Act, 1981*

*Niagara Escarpment Planning and Development Act*

*Ontario Planning and Development Act*

*Parkway Belt Planning and Development Act*

*Planning Act*

*Registry Act*

**Regional Municipalties Acts**
Durham
Haldimand-Norfolk
Halton
Hamilton-Wentworth
Niagara
Ottawa-Carleton
Peel
Sudbury
Metropolitan Toronto
Waterloo
York
District Municipality of Muskoka

## INNOVATIONS

The following innovations have had a positive impact on the operations of the Ministry of Municipal Affairs:

1. *Community Planning Educational Program:* A review of the educational role of the Community Planning Advisory Branch has resulted in a restructuring of the way in which community planning information is provided. As a result of the conclusion of the review and the government priority placed on excellence in education, this educational assistance is increasingly directed to elected representatives. Community planning education activity is being delivered using applied adult education theory and a variety of media. Branch resources have been reallocated, and an Education Officer position has been created to implement these changes.

2. *Computers in Planning:* Microcomputer hardware and software are being used extensively in community planning. A mainframe system of document recording intended to ensure that the process operates efficiently and effectively, has been implemented. Another initiative has been the establishment of a local area network.

3. *Legislation:* Legislation for which Municipal Affairs is responsible has to be reviewed and revised to keep it in line with the current environment in which municipalities operate. Many amendments have been made to these statutes during the last five to ten years. Examples include: simplified Tax Sales procedures and a revised *Municipal Conflict of Interest Act*. In addition, numerous amendments have been made to the *Municipal Act* and the *Regional Acts* to permit municipalities to deal with changing conditions.

4. *Local Government Week:* In 1986 and 1987, the Ministry of Municipal Affairs in cooperation with municipalities, school boards, and public utility

commissions, celebrated Local Government Week throughout Ontario. Community events across Ontario were designed to highlight the services provided to Ontario citizens by local government. In addition, many communities actively involved local school children in activities designed to increase their knowledge of the role of local government.

5. *Municipal Boundary Negotiations Process:* The *Municipal Boundary Negotiations Act, 1981* implemented a new method of resolving disputes over inter-municipal boundary and boundary-related matters. Formerly, these disputes were resolved by means of a quasi-judicial process before the Ontario Municipal Board. These disputes were often expensive, divisive, and uncompromising. They produced only winners and losers and did not enhance inter-municipal relations. The new procedure allows the municipalities to settle these matters in direct negotiations between elected representatives of the affected municipalities. The process is being used to implement municipal boundary changes that meet local priorities and needs, and agreements that are beneficial to all the party municipalities.

6. *Municipal Financial Reporting Handbook:* In January 1983, the Ministry of Municipal Affairs introduced the Municipal Financial Reporting Handbook. This handbook, the first of its kind in Canada, sets out the generally accepted accounting principles and disclosure requirements which municipalities must use when preparing their annual audited financial statements. In recognition of this accomplishment, the Government Finance Officers Association of the United States and Canada presented the Ministry of Municipal Affairs with its 1983 Award of Excellence for Accounting and Financial Reporting. This was the first time that the award was made to a government outside of the United States. Copies of the handbook have been requested by all the other provinces in Canada and has served as a model for the development of a similar handbook in the Province of Nova Scotia and one which is presently underway in the Province of Saskatchewan.

7. *Niagara Escarpment Implementation:* In 1986, the Ministry assumed responsibility for the Niagara Escarpment Commission, the Final Plan for the Niagara Escarpment, the governing legislation, and the overall program coordination. The Ministry has established a monitoring system for decisions on development permits and amendments to the Plan; formulated procedures for the delegation of development control; and published both a Consolidated Niagara Escarpment Plan and an Implementation Proposal. The Ministry's Plans Administration Branch completed a 10-year communications strategy for the escarpment. This strategy integrates the communication programs of the three ministries involved; Ministry of Culture and Communications, Ministry of Natural Resources, and Ministry of Municipal Affairs.

8. *Ontario Municipal Audit Bureau:* In an effort to streamline the auditing of the more than $3 billion in transfer payments and conditional grants

received by municipalities from several provincial ministries, the Province established the Ontario Municipal Audit Bureau in June 1986 (see under Programs). The Bureau's headquarters, located in the City of North York, will handle auditing for ten ministries: Culture and Communications, Community and Social Services, Environment, Health, Housing, Municipal Affairs, Northern Development and Mines, Tourism and Recreation, Transportation, and Treasury and Economics. While the Executive Director reports to the Deputy Minister of Municipal Affairs for day-to-day administrative purposes, the Bureau reports to a Council of Deputy Ministers (Ontario Municipal Audit Council) for overall policy direction. The Deputy Minister of Municipal Affairs is chairman of the Audit Council.

9. *Program for Renewal Improvement Development and Economic Revitalization* (PRIDE): Provincial community improvement programs have been expanded through PRIDE to provide municipalities with the flexibility and the means to address improvement needs across the community. In addition to older residential and commercial areas, PRIDE funding can now be applied to other areas such as waterfronts or mixed-use areas (see under Programs).

10. *Subsidy Programs:* Over the past eight years grants administration has been automated, mainly via Electronic Data Processing. All large programs such as Farm Tax/Managed Forest Tax Reduction, Provincial Properties, and Ontario Youth Employment Programs, have become computer dependent. This has resulted in a faster turnaround in meeting requests and making payments. Since 1984, expensive mainframe time-sharing systems have been replaced by in-house computing which has maintained the level of service, while significantly reducing costs. Furthermore, about $777.4 million in unconditional grants in the 1986/87 fiscal year were deposited directly into the municipalities' bank accounts via the Electronic Funds Transfer System. The EFT System, implemented in 1981, provides the municipal sector with guaranteed receipt of their funds on a day announced at the beginning of the year by this Ministry. Thus, the municipalities were provided with a much better environment for their financial planning, e.g. timing of cash flow with their expenditures and short-term investment decisions.

11. *"You Decide" Campaign:* In 1982 and 1985, the Ministry conducted, in cooperation with the local government associations, a campaign to increase awareness of and participation in local government elections. In 1982, the Ministry produced a film on Local Government which was widely used prior to and during the election campaign. In addition, an extensive media campaign was launched with the result of significantly improved voter turnout in 1982 over 1980. In 1985, the Ministry continued to assist the local electoral process through distribution of material highlighting both the role of local government and the importance of local government elections.

# MINISTRY OF NATURAL RESOURCES

## ROLES AND FUNCTIONS

The goal of the Ministry of Natural Resources (MNR) is to provide economic and social benefits to the people of Ontario through an effective mixture of both development and conservation of the province's natural resources. These resources include land, water, forests, and wildlife. Encouraging the development of natural resources is a particularly vital objective, since resource-based industries are essential to the health of provincial, regional, and local economies. A great many communities depend on such resource industries as fisheries, forestry, trapping, or tourism. The Ministry of Natural Resources seeks to promote the use of available supplies of fish, fur-bearing animals, aggregate and fuel minerals, and trees, by the resource products industries. The Ministry seeks to stimulate the development of Crown land, including its water resources, and to stimulate the production of fish and wildlife in order to promote tourism. The Ministry also identifies and supports new market opportunities for resource products and developments. Finally, the Ministry of Natural Resources provides Ontario with protection from forest fires, floods, and erosion.

## BACKGROUND HISTORY

In 1827, Peter Robinson was appointed the first Crown Lands Commissioner. His duties in Upper Canada (Ontario) and Lower Canada (Quebec) included granting forest tracts to prospective settlers and lumber companies, a task which had been performed for some 40 years by the Surveyor General of Canada. Between 1841 and 1860, the Crown Lands Department absorbed the old Surveyor General's office and assumed responsibilities for mining claims, Indian affairs, and fisheries. In 1852, the Woods and Forests Branch was created, to handle timber licenses and dues.

With Confederation in 1867, responsibility for fisheries and Indian Affairs passed from the province to the new federal government. In the 1880s, Ontario switched from clearing forests for roads, farms, and commerce, to managing the land and its forests, and protecting trees and wildlife from fire, insects, and disease. Part of that management involved ensuring that future generations would have adequate supplies of recreational and industrial forests through reforestation, regeneration, and maintenance of inventory records. In 1885, thirty-seven Bush and Fire Rangers were hired and posted throughout the province to educate the public about forest fire threats, and to extinguish fires.

In 1898, a large share of the jurisdiction over fisheries was returned to the provinces by the Judicial Committee of the Privy Council of Great Britain. The Fisheries Branch was established in the Ontario Public Works Department in 1899. In 1905, the Commissioner of Crown Lands became the Minister of Lands and Mines, then Minister of Lands, Forests and Mines in 1906. In 1907, the Game and Fisheries Branch was established to take over the work of the Board of Game Commissioners and the Department of Fisheries.

In 1912, E.J. Zavitz, Ontario's first professional forester, was hired. In 1917, Mr Zavitz was appointed to administer the *Forest Fires and Prevention Act*, the first important legislation which allowed for hiring a large forest fire fighting force and for control of open fires throughout the province during dry seasons.

In 1920, the Mines Bureau of the Department of Lands, Forests and Mines became the Department of Mines, and the Department of Lands, Forests and Mines became the Department of Lands and Forests.

In 1921, the Department began to use airplanes and aerial photographic equipment as a means of assessing the quality and quantity of Ontario's forest resources. In 1924, the Ontario Provincial Air Service, headquartered in Sault Ste. Marie, was formed, to provide air transportation for surveyors and forest fire spotting.

In 1946, the Game and Fisheries Department of the Provincial Secretariat merged with the Department of Lands and Forests. By the early 1950s, increased affluence and time available for recreation fishing led to greater demand for, and appreciation of, the need to protect and develop fisheries. In 1954, all existing provincial parks were brought together under a single authority, through the *Provincial Parks Act*, which provided for the establishment of more provincial parks through land purchases, grants, and setting aside Crown Land.

In 1962, the Department of Lands and Forests assumed responsibility from the Department of Planning and Development for conservation authorities, the corporate municipal bodies which preserve water resources, watersheds, and drainage basins, and create recreational areas. Also in 1962, the Department of Lands and Forests, under the new *Crown Timber Act*, assumed responsibility for reforestation on Crown Land.

In 1972, the Ministry of Natural Resources was created from components of the former Department of Lands and Forests and the Department of Mines and Northern Affairs, the Conservation Authorities Branch from the Department of the Environment, and the St. Lawrence Parks Commission and Historic Parks from the former Department of Tourism and Information, along with the Mining Commissioner, the Niagara Parks Commission, and the Ontario Energy Board.

In 1973, responsibility for the Ontario Energy Board was moved from MNR to the new Ministry of Energy. In 1975, responsibility for Historic Parks was moved from MNR to the Ministry of Culture and Recreation. In 1977, the Ministry of Northern Affairs was created from the Northern Affairs Branch of MNR, the Northern Region Priority Program of the Ministry of Treasury, Economics and Intergovernmental Affairs, and the Northern Roads Program of the Ministry of

Transportation and Communications.

In 1981, jurisdiction for the St. Lawrence Parks Commission was moved from MNR to the Tourism Division of the Ministry of Industry and Tourism. In 1982, jurisdiction for the Niagara Parks Commission was also moved from MNR to Industry and Tourism. These Commissions are now the responsibility of the Ministry of Tourism and Recreation, which was established later in 1982. In 1985, except for responsibility for aggregate resources and fuel minerals, the mining portfolio was split from MNR to form part of the new Ministry of Northern Development and Mines, which formerly had been the Ministry of Northern Affairs.

The current responsibilities of MNR include management of forest resources, conservation of land and water, and promotion of outdoor recreation.

## ORGANIZATION

The Ministry of Natural Resources is organized into five divisions (see organization chart):

1. *Forest Resources:* Responsible for development and implementation of policies and programs relating to management of Ontario forests.

2. *Lands and Waters:* Responsible for conservation, land and water management, aviation and fire management, and surveys and mapping.

3. *Outdoor Recreation:* Responsible for policies and programs concerning fish and wildlife, and recreational areas.

4. *Field Operations:* For both Northern and Southern Ontario.

5. *Administration:* Including communications, legal services, personnel, etc.

In addition, twelve agencies, boards, and commissions, including the Algonquin Forestry Authority and the Provincial Parks Council, report to the Legislative Assembly through the Minister of Natural Resources (see Agencies, Boards, and Commissions).

The head office of the Ministry is located in Toronto. The Ministry also operates 160 regional, district, and field offices, research stations, assessment units, conservation authorities, nurseries, and laboratories throughout the province, and manages Ontario's 115 provincial parks. The Ministry employs approximately 3700 public servants.

## PROGRAMS

### Forest Resources Division

The Forest Resources Division provides for an optimum contribution to Ontario's economy by the forest-based industries, and provides for other uses of the forest, through sound forest management and environmental practices. It ensures that a continuous supply of wood is available to industry through the successful

MINISTRY OF NATURAL RESOURCES

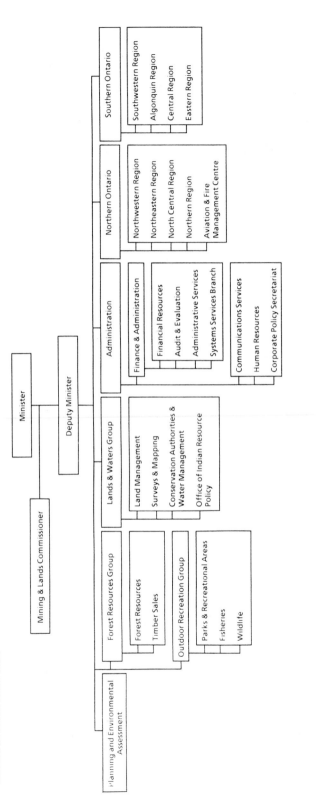

Minister

Mining & Lands Commissioner

Deputy Minister

Planning and Environmental Assessment

**Forest Resources Group**
- Forest Resources
- Timber Sales

**Outdoor Recreation Group**
- Parks & Recreational Areas
- Fisheries
- Wildlife

**Lands & Waters Group**
- Land Management
- Surveys & Mapping
- Conservation Authorities & Water Management
- Office of Indian Resource Policy

**Administration**

Finance & Administration
- Financial Resources
- Audit & Evaluation
- Administrative Services
- Systems Services Branch

Communications Services
Human Resources
Corporate Policy Secretariat

**Northern Ontario**
- Northwestern Region
- Northeastern Region
- North Central Region
- Northern Region
- Aviation & Fire Management Centre

**Southern Ontario**
- Southwestern Region
- Algonquin Region
- Central Region
- Eastern Region

marrying of harvesting and regeneration. A forest production policy, adopted in 1972, provides targets for the amount of wood that Crown forests will produce for industry.

Between 1979 and 1986, MNR established Forest Management Agreements (FMAs) for more than 50 percent of Crown lands. Under FMAs, companies harvest and reforest, in return for long-term access to the timber resource in the agreement areas.

In order to improve the management of forests by private land owners, MNR has developed a program under the *Woodlands Improvement Act*, which provides for the Minister to enter into agreements with property owners for reforestation and forest management of their lands. The Ontario Tree Improvement and Forest Biomass Institute is the centre of research activities for MNR.

The new Canada-Ontario Forest Resources Development Agreement (COFRDA) provides $150 million for forest management over five fiscal years to be shared equally by Canada and Ontario. The four major programs under COFRDA are forest management and renewal operations, forest management and renewal support, innovative programs, and administration.

**Lands and Waters Division**

*Conservation Authorities and Water Management Branch*

The Conservation Authorities and Water Management Branch provides programs, financial and administrative policy, program priorities, and technical services to Ontario's 38 autonomous conservation authorities and to the Ministry's public waters program (inland and Great Lakes). The 38 conservation authorities — 33 in Southern Ontario and five in Northern Ontario—undertake programs for watersheds to further conservation, restoration, development, and management of natural resources other than gas, oil, coal, and minerals.

Through the *Conservation Authorities Act*, a conservation authority is established by the Lieutenant Governor in Council as an autonomous corporate organization with the support of the majority of the municipalities within the watershed. Financing for conservation authorities is a cost-shared arrangement between the province, which provides transfer payments, and local municipalities, within their respective jurisdictions. The Minister of Natural Resources is responsible for the administration of the *Conservation Authorities Act*. In this respect, projects proposed by conservation authorities require both technical and financing approval by the Minister.

The role of monitoring water levels in Ontario includes developing flood contingency plans and responding to provincial emergencies. A major task of the Ministry is the operation of a stream flow forecast centre, which includes designing and maintaining a data collection system, interpreting and forecasting potential flooding, and providing for early alert and consultation among regions and conservation authorities.

The branch ensures that its water quantity policies and objectives are compatible with the programs and objectives of other ministries, municipal governments, and

Crown agencies.

*Land Management Branch*

The Land Management Branch maintains the Crown's proprietary interest in land, which includes 87 percent of the land and water base of the province; leases small waterpower generating sites and charges for the use of water for the generating of hydroelectric power to such agencies as Ontario Hydro; stimulates development and construction of access roads in Northern Ontario; issues title documents to individuals and corporations as part of the disposition of public and mining lands; ensures future availability of mineral aggregates and fuel mineral resources such as oil, gas, oil shales, peat, and lignite.

*Office of Indian Resource Policy*

The Office of Indian Resource Policy researches, negotiates, and resolves Indian land claims and other natural resources issues; coordinates all of the Ministry's involvement in matters relating to Indian people; and acts as consultant within the Ministry on all such matters.

*Surveys and Mapping Branch*

The Surveys and Mapping Branch develops and maintains a provincial geographical reference system; provides geographic names, and legal and geodetic survey services as required by the *Surveys Act*; maintains the provincial boundaries and the township framework of the province; establishes standards for the basic topographic information of the province and the Ministry of Natural Resources' cartographic services; establishes a standard for and maintains a computerized map data-base for the province; and develops the technology and applications of remotely sensed data.

**Outdoor Recreation Division**

*Fisheries Branch*

The Fisheries Branch protects, rehabilitates, and enhances Ontario's fish populations and their environment in order to provide opportunities for recreational and commercial fishing. Their objective includes protecting and rehabilitating fish habitats, monitoring fish health and populations, regulating all types of fishing, and annually raising and stocking almost nine million fish in over 1,000 public waters.

*Provincial Parks and Recreational Branch*

The Provincial Parks and Recreational Branch is responsible for managing Ontario's 115 provincial parks, including their canoe routes, water access points, snowmobile trails, campgrounds, trails, and concessions. It cooperates with federal and municipal governments in planning parks and provides financial assistance to municipalities for parks development.

*Recreational Boating Office*

The Recreational Boating Office coordinates activities of public and private boating agencies, so as to achieve maximum social and economic benefits for the people of Ontario. As well as administering the Boating Restriction Regulations, the Office assists in the public and private sectors to develop more and better marina facilities and is involved in educating the public about the safe and harmonious use of the waters of Ontario.

*Wildlife Branch*

The Wildlife Branch develops and audits policies and programs related to major game and non-game species and coordinates the management of habitat, including wetlands. The branch reviews land and resource development plans regarding wildlife.

*The Wildlife Services Section:* Coordinates the provincial fur management program, and the hunter education program. It also verifies and maintains hunter licenses and records and conducts surveys of licenses.

*The Wildlife Extension Development Section:* Provides for  programs on wildlife management for the public and special interest groups.

*The Wildlife Program Development and Audit Section:* Relates public demand and requirements of wildlife populations to wildlife management technology, and proposes resulting revisions to wildlife management programs and policy. Specialist coordinators in the Section provide information on programs and techniques and coordinate implementation of programs by training staff, periodically audit existing programs, and maintain communication with agencies providing related services.

The goal of Wildlife Research is to enhance understanding of the species and ecosystems of interest to MNR. The objectives of research projects must be to obtain results which help wildlife managers address practical problems. This means providing research information which will enable management to produce predictable results.

## EXPENDITURE ESTIMATES

*Estimated Expenditures 1987–88:*

| | |
|---|---|
| Ministry Administration | $ 64,866,738 |
| Lands and Waters | 159,830,700 |
| Outdoor Recreation | 98,995,200 |
| Resource Products (Forest Management) | 200,375,200 |
| Resource Experience | 7,084,100 |
| **Ministry total:** | **$531,171,938** |

## AGENCIES, BOARDS, AND COMMISSIONS

The following ABCs report to the Legislative Assembly through the Minister of Natural Resources:

*Algonquin Forestry Authority:* Subject to the *Crown Timber Act*, the Authority was established in 1974 as a Crown Corporation to harvest and sell Crown timber in Algonquin Park and adjacent designated parks, by contracting to local loggers and mill operators. The Authority, which currently has 11 board members, also undertakes and carries out such forest management, land management, and other programs as the Minister may authorize.

*Crown Timber Board of Examiners:* The three-member Board, established in 1970, sets written and practical examinations in wood measurement and recommends successful candidates to receive a Scaler's License.

*Game and Fish Hearing Board:* Established in 1973, the five-member Board reports to the Ministry of Natural Resources on the merits of appeals regarding the issuance or cancellation of commercial licences. The Board's assessments are made in light of the facts presented and in view of the purpose of the *Game and Fish Act.*

*Lake of the Woods Control Board:* Since its establishment in 1922, the Board has been responsible for the regulation of Lake of the Woods and Lac Seul, and for the flow in the Winnipeg River and English River between the lake outlets and their confluence. Each of the four Board members may serve as chairperson, under the present practice of rotating the position every January 1. The Board has the responsibility to

1. Secure the most dependable flow and the most advantageous and beneficial use of the waters of the Winnipeg and English Rivers;

2. Regulate the flow of Lake of the Woods to levels recommended by the International Joint Commission as agreed to by Canada and the U.S., Lac Seul, to levels recommended by the Board and approved by the Lieutenant Governors in Council of Ontario and Manitoba;

3. Regulate the flow into Lac Seul through the Lake St. Joseph diversion;

4. Regulate the flow of the Winnipeg River, between its junction with the English River and Lake of the Woods, and the English River between its junction with the Winnipeg River and Lac Seul; and

5. Regulate the flow of other waters of the watershed of the Winnipeg River as are placed under the Board's jurisdiction by the Governor General in Council and the Lieutenant Governors in Council of Ontario and Manitoba.

*Ontario Forestry Council:* The eight-member Council was established October 1, 1984 to recommend appropriate objectives, priorities, and funding for forest research and development in Ontario. September 30, 1989 is the Council's current "sunset date" (target date for dissolution).

*Ontario Geographic Names Board:* The seven-member Board was established in 1970 to provide consultative services to the Ontario Government on the official names of places and geographical features; specifically, to consult with and advise agencies and persons on nomenclature selections; to recommend changes to existing names; and to collaborate with the Canada Permanent Committee on Geographic Names. In addition, the Board supplies information about the foregoing to ministries, agencies, and individuals. The group also recommends, for the Minister's approval, the names of geographical features. The current sunset date for the Board is March 31, 1991.

*Ontario Renewable Resource Research Review Board:* Established in 1983, the eleven-member Board ensures that research proposals received from universities are treated in an equitable manner, that program outlines are adhered to, and that appropriate and relevant research is recommended to the Ministry for funding, and carried out with commensurately high standards. The current sunset date for the Board is December 1, 1988.

*Ottawa River Regulation Planning Board:* The objectives of the seven-member Board are to prepare guidelines and criteria to coordinate the operation of reservoirs; to achieve an improved level of flood protection; to audit reservoir operation and channel flows; and to manage the operation of a flow forecast model. The Board also advises governments on action during extreme flow periods (high or low) and studies possible schemes to reduce flood damage in the basin. Established March 2, 1983, the Board's current sunset date is March 31, 1990.

*Provincial Parks Council:* The seven-member Council was formed December 11, 1974 to advise, make recommendations, and report to the Minister of Natural Resources on matters the Minister refers to it regarding policy in the areas of planning, management, and development of the provincial parks system. The current sunset date for the Council is March 31, 1989.

*Rabies Advisory Committee:* Established August 1, 1979. The seven-member Council is responsible for advising the Minister on steps necessary to develop an effective vaccine and delivery system for immunizing wild animal populations against rabies. The Committee's current sunset date is November 30, 1988.

*Shoreline Management Review Committee:* Established on April 17, 1986, the seven-member Committee holds public meetings throughout Ontario along the shoreline of the Great Lakes. The committee provides the Minister of Natural Resources and the Minister of Municipal Affairs with recommendations on a long-term approach to the management of the Great Lakes' shorelines.

*Sturgeon River/Lake Nipissing/French River Watershed Management Advisory Board:* Established April 8, 1982, the nine- member Board participates and makes recommendations to the Minister of Natural Resources on the development of a watershed management plan, and reviews the plan regularly. In addition, it recommends to the Minister such changes as the Board deems appropriate and plays a role in public education and information. The current sunset date for the Board is March 31, 1990.

## LEGISLATION

The Ministry of Natural Resources is responsible for the following Acts:

*Ministry of Natural Resources Act:* Effective as of April 1, 1972, this Act created the new Ministry of Natural Resources by amalgamating the former Department of Lands and Forests and the Department of Mines and Northern Affairs, and repealed the provisions of a number of Acts on which the departments depended for administrative authority. Effective October 30, 1973, the Act provides for the appointment of a Mining and Lands Commissioner and advisory committee.

### Lands and Waters Group

*Beach Protection Act:* Prohibits the removal of sand from the bed, bank, beach, shore, or waters of any lake, river, or stream in Ontario except under the authority of a licence issued under the Act or written consent of the local municipality.

*Beds of Navigable Waters Act:* (Sometimes referred to as the "Cochrane Act"). Declaratory legislation relating to title in the beds of navigable waters.

*Conservation Authorities Act:* Provides for the establishment of conservation authorities for the purpose of establishing and undertaking in the area over which they are given jurisdiction, programs designed to further conservation, restoration, development, and management of natural resources other than gas, oil, coal, and minerals.

*Gas and Oil Leases Act:* Sets out the procedure whereby a lessor under a gas or oil lease may, upon default by the lessee under the terms of the lease, obtain an order declaring the lease void.

*Indian Lands Act, 1924:* Relates to administration and disposition of surrendered Indian Reserve land.

*Lakes and Rivers Improvement Act:* Deals with the construction, repair, and use of dams, timber driving, and timber slide companies. The Act prohibits construction of dams without Ministry approval.

*Lake of the Woods Control Board Act:* Complementary to a Federal Act of 1921. It deals with the regulation of the water levels of the Winnipeg River, the English River, Lac Seul, and Lake St. Joseph.

*Mining Act:* Certain portions, not under the jurisdiction of the Ministry of Northern Development and Mines, remain under the jurisdiction of the Land Management Branch. The areas under MNR control include signing and executing all patents, licenses, and contracts; signing the instrument terminating a licence of occupation or a mining lease; prescribing and discharging the registration of forms of notice for the erection of fences; registering voluntary surrender of mining lands and lands forfeited to the Crown; exempting lands from tax and referring any related disputes to the Mining and Lands Commissioner; exempting mining rights from tax; deciding if surface rights are being used for purposes other than mining; and authorizing title searches in registry offices free of charge.

*Ontario Geographic Names Board Act:* Provides for the establishment of a Geographic Names Board for Ontario, which has the duty to gather information respecting the names of places and geographic features, make recommendations thereon, collaborate with the Canada Permanent Committee on Geographic Names, and provide information to the government departments.

*Ontario Harbours Agreement Act, 1962–63:* Confirms on behalf of Ontario, the agreement between Ontario and Canada establishing the harbours which were public harbours at Confederation, providing that mines and minerals therein are administered by Ontario, and confirming grants and quit claims listed therein. Federal harbours are Amherstburg, Belleville, Brockville, Chatham, Collingwood, Fort William, Gananoque, Goderich, Kincardine, Kingston, Kingsville, Leamington, Oshawa, Owen Sound, Penetanguishene, Port Arthur, Port Burwell, Port Hope, Port Stanley, Prescott, Rondeau Bay, Sarnia, Sault Ste. Marie, Southampton, Toronto, Whitby, and Windsor.

*Petroleum Resources Act:* Sets out licensing requirements for various aspects of oil and natural gas exploration, drilling, and production; and provides for the making of regulations respecting oil and gas conservation and the safe operation of drilling and production facilities.

*Pits and Quarries Control Act:* Provides for the regulation of pit and quarry operations in designated parts of Ontario. Operations in designated areas must be licensed under the Act and are subject to periodic review to ensure compliance with the provisions of the Act, the regulations, and site plan.

*Public Lands Act:* Provides for (1) the disposition of Crown land for a variety of purposes by sale, lease, or licence, and by auction or tender; (2) the management of Crown land by the Ministry through zoning for land use, setting apart for public use, research, etc., and through agreements with municipalities on beaches and water lots; (3) the administration of roads on Crown lands, including the designation of public forest roads and agreements with occupiers of private forest roads respecting the use by the public of private forest roads; (4) the granting of water powers and privileges; (5) the establishment of a Public Agricultural Lands Committee to recommend on agricultural lands and their settlement, replacing the regulations on this subject.

*Surveys Act:* Defines the system of surveys and the rules for surveys. The Minister may order surveys made on his own volition or upon application in order to settle disputes or lost lines, etc.; and, after hearing evidence, he confirms the surveys, with or without amendment. His decision is subject to appeal to a judge of the Divisional Court.

*Surveyors Act:* Deals with the Association of Ontario Land Surveyors and the rules governing membership and conduct. The Minister or his appointee and the Surveyor-General are members of the Council of the Association.

### Forest Resources Group

*Algonquin Forestry Authority Act:* Establishes a Crown corporation called the Algonquin Forestry Authority to harvest Crown timber in Algonquin Park and public lands adjacent to the park, to sell the logs, and to carry out such forestry, land management, and other programs and projects as the Minister of Natural Resources authorizes.

*Arboreal Emblem Act, 1984:* Adopts the Eastern White Pine as the arboreal emblem of the Province of Ontario.

*Crown Timber Act:* Enables the granting of the following four types of licenses to cut Crown timber: a licence based on a call for tenders; a licence to salvage timber; a licence for areas that do not exceed 64.75 hectares (160 acres); and a licence approved by Order-in-Council for large areas. The Act also enables the Minister to enter into comprehensive Forest Management Agreements with forest companies, which ensure that forests under the agreements are harvested and regenerated by the company to produce successive crops of timber on a sustained yield basis, in return for long-term access to those resource areas. Other subjects dealt with under the Act are: forest management, operating and annual plans; examination and licensing of scalers; licensing of mills; penalties for wasteful practices, unauthorized cutting, removal of timber for scaling, and other violations; and a protection of the Crown's interests through seizure of timber and a statutory lien for Crown charges.

*Forest Tree Pest Control Act:* Provides for the control of outbreaks of forest tree insects and diseases on private lands.

*Forestry Act:* Under this Act (1) the Minister enters into agreements with landowners such as municipalities, conservation authorities, and the National Capital Commission (Ottawa) to manage the forest lands; (2) Ministry tree nurseries are established and nursery stock is distributed; (3) Private forest reserves are set up on private lands with the consent of the owners; (4) the Minister, with the approval of the Lieutenant Governor in Council, may establish programs for the encouragement of forestry. At present, a managed forest tax- reduction program has been established by the Minister.

*Industrial and Mining Lands Compensation Act:* Provides for agreements between the owner or operator of a mine, and the owner or lessee of any land, for payment of compensation for any damage or injury resulting or likely to result to the land or to its use and enjoyment from the operation of the mine.

*Settlers' Pulpwood Protection Act:* Provides for the regulation of the sale and of the price of pulpwood cut from settlers' land.

*Spruce Pulpwood Exportation Act:* Provides for exportation under the authority of an Order-in-Council of unmanufactured spruce pulpwood from lands granted under special Acts which prohibit such export.

*Trees Act:* Provides that, with the Minister's approval, municipalities may pass by-laws restricting and regulating destruction of trees and appoint enforcement officers. Generally, through by-law, municipalities may acquire land for forestry purposes and enter into agreements with the Minister for the management of such lands and related matters.

*Woodlands Improvement Act:* Provides for the Minister to enter into agreements with owners of private forest lands for the planting of nursery stock or stand improvement.

*Woodmen's Employment Act:* Authorizes appointment of inspectors and making of regulations respecting conditions in lumber camps. It also provides that Crown timber license holders are responsible for the acts and omissions of their jobbers and sub-contractors who carry out operations.

*Woodmen's Lien for Wages Act:* Provides a lien and a procedure to enforce such lien for persons performing labour on timber.

### Outdoor Recreation Group

*Endangered Species Act:* Provides for the conservation, protection, restoration, and propagation of species of flora and fauna of the Province of Ontario that are threatened with extinction.

*Fish Inspection Act:* Complementary to the Federal Act.

*Fisheries Act (Canada):* Ontario Fishery Regulations are made under this Act. They relate to open seasons for angling and commercial fishing and the licenses required. The form of the licenses and the fees are prescribed under the Game and Fish Act. Protection of fish habitat is also based primarily on this act.

*Fisheries Loan Act:* Provides for loans to persons carrying on commercial fishing or any other business which depends in whole or in part on the taking of fish from waters where such taking has been prohibited by reason of the contamination of fish resulting from pollution of the water. Provision is made for federal-provincial agreements respecting the sharing of such loans.

*Freshwater Fish Marketing Act* (Ontario): Complements the *Freshwater Fish Marketing Act* (Canada). Through these Acts and the federal-provincial agreement, the Freshwater Fish Marketing Corporation, established under the Federal Act, is the sole purchaser of commercial fish, as defined in the Federal Act, taken in that part of Ontario designated in the regulations.

*Game and Fish Act:* Deals with the management of wildlife resources; game animals; upland game birds; fur-bearing animals; frogs; sale and rearing of game fish; and offences and enforcement. Regulations made under the Act establish open seasons for hunting and trapping; bag limits; Crown game preserves; the licensing of hunters, trappers, guides, persons operating game bird hunting preserves, and persons selling game fish for stocking and human consumption. Regulates dogs used in hunting, aircraft transporting hunters, the conduct of hunters (hunter safety); and farmer-hunter relations. The Game and Fish Hearing Board was established under the Act on November 15, 1973.

*Migratory Birds Convention Act:* Open seasons for migratory birds are set under this Act.

*North Georgian Bay Recreational Reserve Act, 1962-63:* Establishes the North Georgian Bay Recreational Reserve and provides for the planning and development thereof and the appointment of a committee to advise the Minister thereon.

*Parks Assistance Act:* Provides for the establishment of parks in municipalities or in territory without a municipal organization. The Minister may, with the approval of the Lieutenant Governor in Council, make grants not exceeding 50 percent of the cost of acquiring land and developing such parks. The parks established under the Act are to be maintained and operated in a manner complementary to provincial parks.

*Provincial Parks Act:* Provides for the establishment of provincial parks and their management and for certain employees to have the authority of the Ontario Provincial Police in a provincial park. Advisory committees for one or more provincial parks may be appointed by the Minister with the approval of the Lieutenant Governor in Council. Parks may be classified as a natural environment park, a nature reserve park, a wilderness park, a recreational park, a waterways park, or an historical park. Mining is prohibited in provincial parks except as provided in the regulations. Hunting is prohibited in provincial parks except as provided in regulations under the *Game and Fish Act* or where prohibition is removed. This Act does not apply to any park under the management of the Niagara Parks Commission, the St. Lawrence Parks Commission, or the St. Clair Parkway Commission.

*Wilderness Areas Act:* Passed on March 26, 1959, to preserve areas having some unique feature. Development, or use of the natural resources in an area more than 260 hectares (640 acres) in size, is not affected by this Act.

*Wild Rice Harvesting Act:* Permits the harvesting of rice on Crown land under the authority of a licence.

### Aviation and Fire Management Centre

*Forest Fires Prevention Act:* Applies to the seven fire regions set up by regulation. The fire season from April 1 to October 31, may be extended by regulation. Fire permits are required during the fire season to (a) start fires in a fire region except for fires lit for cooking or warmth or to (b) ignite fireworks in or within 300 metres of a forest or woodland. Work permits are required at any time of the year for carrying on any logging, mining, industrial operation or clearing in or within 30 metres of a forest or woodland. Areas may be established as restricted fire zones in which fires for cooking or warmth will be restricted to portable stoves and barbecues, or as restricted travel zones in which a travel permit will be required except on public roads, cities, towns, villages, police villages, supervised camping grounds, and water adjacent thereto. The Minster may declare emergency areas and may take orders for suppression and the safety and evacuation of persons. The Minister may enter into agreements with Canada, any province, and any federal or provincial agency or municipality respecting forest fire prevention and control. The regulations establish fire precautions.

### General

*Algonquin Provincial Park Extension Act, 1960–61:* Adds the public lands in the Geographic Townships of Bruton and Clyde in the Provincial Country of Haliburton, to the park, subject to hunting.

*Lands Act, 1961:* Vests certain lands in the town of Gananoque in the Crown and authorizes the sale of encroachments to adjoining owners for a fee of $50 and the granting of the balance of the land.

*Lac Seul Conservation Act, 1928:* Provides for the execution of an agreement between the Government of the Province of Ontario, represented by the Minister of Lands and Forest (now Natural Resources), the Government of Canada, and the Government of the Province of Manitoba, regarding the construction of a dam at the outlet of Lac Seul.

*Manitoba-Ontario Lake St. Joseph Diversion Agreement Authorization Act, 1958:* Provides for entry by Ontario and the Hydro-Electric Power Commission of Ontario into an agreement with Manitoba and the Manitoba Hydro-Electric Board in respect to the diversion of waters into the Winnipeg River and electrical power generated from such waters in Ontario and Manitoba.

*Mineral Emblem Act, 1975:* Adopts the amethyst as the mineral emblem of the Province of Ontario.

*National Radio Observatory Act, 1962-63:* Provides for the transfer of the administration and control of certain public lands in the Township of White, District of Nipissing, to Canada for the maintenance and operation of a national radio observatory.

*Ottawa River Water Powers Act, 1943:* Ratifies and confirms an agreement between the Province of Ontario, the Province of Quebec, the Hydro-Electric Power Commission of Ontario, and the Quebec Streams Commission respecting the development of water power on the Ottawa River.

*Seine River Division Act, 1952:* Confirms the partial diversion of the Seine River and authorizes the completion and operation of the diversion by Steep Rock Iron Mines Limited.

# MINISTRY OF NORTHERN DEVELOPMENT AND MINES

## ROLES AND FUNCTIONS

The Ministry of Northern Development and Mines is partially or wholly responsible for the delivery of Ontario Government programs in the North relating to: road, rail, air, and water transportation, medical, fire protection, dental services, water, sewage, and drainage systems. The Ministry's Northern Development Division maintains administrative and program implementation staff in the North, as well as a network of 30 Northern Officers providing "one window" government service to residents of communities across the North. The Ministry's Mines and Minerals Division is responsible for encouraging and regulating the orderly development and utilization of the Province's mineral resources.

## BACKGROUND HISTORY

The Ministry of Northern Development and Mines was established in November, 1985 to respond to the needs of the relatively dispersed population living in the northern part of the province, an area comprising almost 90 percent of the land mass of Ontario. The Northern Development section replaces the former Ministry of Northern Affairs, which was created in 1977; the Ministry's Division of Mines and Minerals was transferred from the Ministry of Natural Resources. Although there are now two Cabinet ministers responsible for the activities of the Ministry (the Minister of Northern Development and the Minister of Mines), the Ministry of Northern Development and Mines will continue to operate as one organization under a single deputy minister.

## ORGANIZATION

The Ministry of Northern Development and Mines is organized into three major divisions (see organization chart):

1. *Planning and Administration:* Includes Financial and Administrative Services, Human Resources, Audit, Information Technology, and Corporate Planning Branches, and a Ministry Relocation Unit.

MINISTRY OF NORTHERN DEVELOPMENT

MINISTRY OF MINES

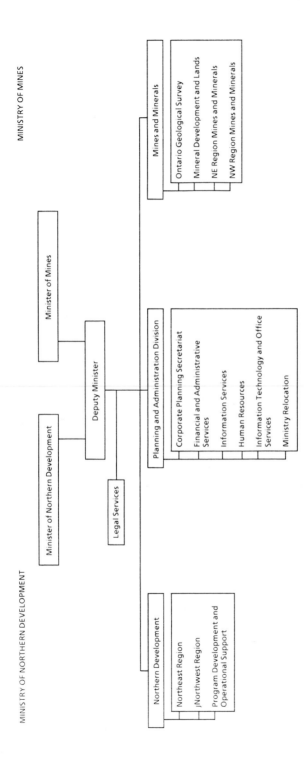

Minister of Northern Development

Minister of Mines

Deputy Minister

Legal Services

Northern Development
- Northeast Region
- JNorthwest Region
- Program Development and Operational Support

Planning and Administration Division
- Corporate Planning Secretariat
- Financial and Administrative Services
- Information Services
- Human Resources
- Information Technology and Office Services
- Ministry Relocation

Mines and Minerals
- Ontario Geological Survey
- Mineral Development and Lands
- NE Region Mines and Minerals
- NW Region Mines and Minerals

2. *Northern Development:* Delivers programs designed to meet the needs of residents of Northern Ontario, and operates 30 Community Relations Offices throughout the north.

3. *Mines and Minerals:* Responsible for encouraging the development of Ontario's mineral resources.

In addition, the Ontario Northland Transportation Commission reports to the Legislative Assembly through the Minister of Northern Development (see Agencies, Boards, and Commissions).

The Ministry of Northern Development and Mines employs approximately 440 public servants. In July 1986, it was announced that the Ministry will be relocated to Sudbury. This move, expected in 1988, will involve two hundred and seventy-five positions, including the Deputy Minister's office, the Planning and Administrative branches, and the Mines and Minerals Division. A new building is being constructed in Sudbury to house the Ministry as well as the staff of the Ministry of Labour's Mining Health and Safety Branch.

## PROGRAMS

*Capital Assistance Program for Designated Small and Remote Secondary Schools in Northern Ontario* (EDUCAP): Provides assistance toward the purchase of equipment for regular curriculum programs in Technical Studies, Computer Literacy, Business, the Arts, and Home Economics. Eligible recipients for this program are 32 small, isolated secondary schools in Northern Ontario with fewer than 400 students, located at least 70 kilometres from another secondary school.

*Extended Care Capital Assistance Program for Small and Remote Communities in Northern Ontario* (ELDCAP): Provides assistance towards capital and equipment costs for the construction of an addition to a local hospital of up to twenty beds for extended care, or for the renovation of existing hospital space to the same purpose and extent. Operating costs are provided by the Ministry of Health according to established formulae.

*Industrial Infrastructure Program:* Provides assistance toward removing the physical constraints to the development of identified small-scale private sector projects. Assistance may include mapping, power and water supply, waste disposal, access, and other public services.

*Mines and Minerals Programs:* Include development of mineral resource policies, maintenance of statistics, provision of incentives to encourage mineral exploration (grants equal to 25% of expenses), licensing, development of standards for management and protection of public lands for mining purposes, and provision of information on the geology and mineral resources of Ontario.

*Northern Community Economic Development Assistance Program:* Assists communities in Northern Ontario, particularly single industry communities, to identify and pursue opportunities to develop and diversify their local economies with the private sector, and to work effectively with other government agencies providing specific industrial development support programs. In addition, the program will provide the basis for any special or capital development assistance not normally available from either the private or public sector. The Ministry of Northern Development and Mines works in conjunction with other provincial ministries to fund highway construction programs and remote airport programs throughout Northern Ontario. The Ministry also contributes funds for a range of social, medical, and dental clinics, bursaries for medical and dental students, audiologists and speech pathologists, and capital support for air ambulance service. The Ministry of Northern Development and Mines has also taken an interest in improving the quality of life, and in this regard, promotes and makes contributions to the arts and undertakes other cultural initiatives as opportunities arise.

*Ontario Geological Survey:* Provides information on the geology and mineral resources of Ontario to encourage mineral exploration, and provides a basis for land-use planning and aid in the development of resource policy. Activities of the Survey include geological, geophysical, and geochemical surveys, mineral deposit studies, development of new exploration techniques, chemical analysis, and identification of mineral, rock, and ore samples, and presentation of classes and lectures on minerals and rocks.

*Operating Grants to Local Services Boards for Basic Services:* Provides assistance to territories without municipal organization in Northern Ontario towards the operations and maintenance costs for providing basic services in an unorganized area in which a Local Services Board (see under Agencies, Boards, and Commissions) has been elected and duly authorized with one or more of the following powers: water supply, garbage collection, street or area lighting, fire protection, sewage disposal, and recreation. The Ministry of Northern Development and Mines provides a matching dollar-for-dollar grant, based on monies raised locally through eligible sources (e.g. local taxation, via a surcharge on the Provincial Land Tax bill, user fees or fund-raising events) which are expended on operating and maintenance.

*Provision of Receiving and Transmitting Facilities for TVOntario:* Provides assistance to communities in Northern Ontario towards the purchase of a three metre receiving dish, transmitting equipment, installation, and maintenance. Eligible recipients are communities of not less than 100 who have three or less TV signals and no service from TVOntario. This program is restricted to the area of jurisdiction of the Ministry of Northern Development and Mines.

*Unincorporated Communities Assistance Program* (UCAP): Provides assistance towards the capital costs of providing basic services in unincorporated communities, mainly for fire protection and minor capital projects (e.g. fire halls, community wells, street lighting):

1. *Fire Protection:* The Ministry of Northern Development and Mines provides fire equipment through the Solicitor General, Office of the Fire Marshal. Equipment provided includes fire vehicles and smaller packages of fire equipment depending on the needs of the community.

2. *Direct Grants:* Up to 75 percent for capital projects such as septic systems, community wells, street lighting.

## EXPENDITURE ESTIMATES

*Estimated Expenditures 1987–88*:

| | |
|---|---|
| Ministry Administration | $ 7,671,806 |
| Northern Development | 73,726,000 |
| Northern Transportation | 129,291,300 |
| Mines and Minerals | 32,717,300 |
| **Ministry total:** | **$243,406,406** |

## AGENCIES, BOARDS, AND COMMISSIONS

The following ABCs report to the Legislative Assembly through the Minister for Northern Development and Mines:

*Local Services Boards:* A Local Services Board is a legally constituted body of members elected to act on the behalf of an unincorporated Northern Ontario community to ensure that basic services such as water supply, fire protection, and garbage collection, are provided for them on a continuing basis. Establishment of a Local Services Board is optional, as are the services it may choose to offer. Currently there are 42 LSBs in operation.

*Northern Development Councils* (NDCs): Five NDCs are being established across the North to act as a sounding board and advisory group to the Government on new programs and initiatives. The NDC membership includes representatives from municipalities, local business, labour, education facilities, and other groups.

*Ontario Northland Transportation Commission* (ONTC): The Ministry of Northern Development and Mines provides rail, bus, air, ferry, and telecommunications services to Northern Ontario through the Ontario Northland Transportation Commission:

1. Rail passenger services include the Polar Bear Express between Cochrane and Moosonee, the Northlander between Toronto and Timmins, the North Bay and Cochrane component of the Toronto to Kapuskasing Northland train service, and a mixed passenger-freight train between Cochrane and Moosonee.

2. Bus services are regularly scheduled between North Bay, Hearst, Sudbury, Timmins, and other locations throughout Northeastern Ontario.

3. Rail freight services are provided between North Bay and other points in Northeastern Ontario.

4. Highway freight services are the responsibility of Star Transfer Ltd., a subsidiary of the ONTC that operates throughout Northeastern Ontario and south to Toronto and Hamilton. Another subsidiary, Ontario Northland Express Services, makes deliveries from six terminals located in the Northeast.

5. The Commission operates a provincially-owned airline, NorOntair, which services 21 communities, and serves as a feeder for Air Canada, and Nordair in Northeast and Northwest Ontario.

6. A passenger, car, and truck ferry, the M.S. Chi-Cheemaun, is operated by the Owen Sound Transportation Company, a subsidiary of the ONTC, between Tobermory on the Bruce Peninsula and South Baymouth on Manitoulin Island, from May to October. The Marine Services Department of the ONTC operates the Chief Commanda, a cruise boat on Lake Nipissing, from spring to fall, and manages a freight and passenger service between Moosonee and Moose Factory Island during the same period.

7. The ONTC also provides telecommunications services in the Northeast: long distance telephone, private wire voice, and teletype, radio, and television transmission.

## LEGISLATION

The Ministry of Northern Development and Mines is responsible for the following Acts:

*Local Services Boards Act:* This act was passed in 1979 in response to the need to find some means whereby residents of unincorporated communities in Northern Ontario could provide basic services for themselves. It allows inhabitants of territory without municipal organization to establish legally constituted bodies to speak for them and to raise funds for certain basic community services to improve quality of life.

*Ministry of Northern Affairs Act:* In recognition of the different conditions and special needs existing in Northern Ontario and the desire of northern residents to have a stronger voice in government, the Ministry of Northern Affairs was established in 1977 by this Act. It defines Ministry's functions to coordinate government activity and to initiate policies and programs for the government in Northern Ontario.

*Ontario Northland Transportation Commission Act:* The Ministry of Northern Development and Mines provides subsidies for rail, bus, ferry, air, and telecommunications services to Northern Ontario through the Ontario Northland Transportation Commission, which was established by this act.

*Mining Act:* This act provides for the administration of mining exploration and development in Ontario.

*Ontario Mineral Exploration Act:* Originally enacted in 1980, this act provides for tax credits and grants to encourage mineral exploration in Ontario.

# MINISTRY OF TOURISM AND RECREATION

## ROLES AND FUNCTIONS

The mandate of the Ministry of Tourism and Recreation is to strengthen, maintain, and assist the recreation and tourism industries in the province of Ontario. The Ministry of Tourism and Recreation has two main purposes; first, to enhance and encourage the tourism industry; second, to ensure adequate opportunities for recreation, sport, and fitness are available to all residents of the province.

## BACKGROUND HISTORY

The current Ministry of Tourism and Recreation was created in 1982 in response to a perceived need for a ministry responsible for development of tourism in Ontario, and a recognition of the complementary and collateral relationships of sports and recreation to that objective. It brought together the tourism function formerly with the Ministry of Industry and Tourism (now the Ministry of Industry, Trade and Technology) and the sports and recreation function formerly with the Ministry of Culture and Recreation (later the Ministry of Citizenship and Culture, now the Ministry of Culture and Communications).

## ORGANIZATION

The Ministry of Tourism and Recreation is organized into four divisions (see organization chart):

1. *Community Programs/Sports and Recreation Division:* Concerned with providing advice and leadership in the development of community recreation activities and facilities, and the promotion of sport and fitness, principally through its support of amateur athletic associations.

2. *Tourism Division:* Deals with tourism development and marketing, and the operation of Huronia Historical Parks and Old Fort William.

3. *Tourism and Recreation Operations:* Delivers Ministry programs and administers financial assistance programs through a network of 23 field offices throughout the province. Each office is staffed with consultants who provide information and assistance on either tourism or recreation development.

MINISTRY OF TOURISM & RECREATION

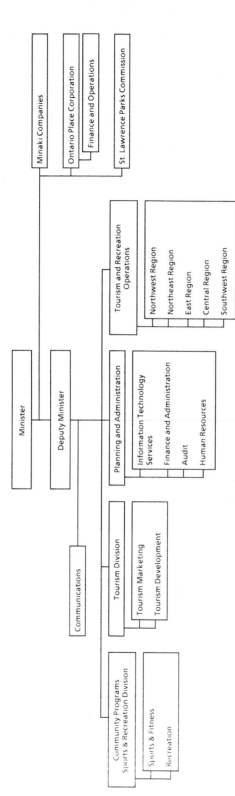

Minister

Deputy Minister

Minaki Companies

Ontario Place Corporation
- Finance and Operations

St. Lawrence Parks Commission

Communications

Community Programs
Sports & Recreation Division
- Sports & Fitness
- Recreation

Tourism Division
- Tourism Marketing
- Tourism Development

Planning and Administration
- Information Technology Services
- Finance and Administration
- Audit
- Human Resources

Tourism and Recreation Operations
- Northwest Region
- Northeast Region
- East Region
- Central Region
- Southwest Region

4. *Planning and Administration Division:* Provides staff support to the Minister and Deputy Minister, and for a number of Ministry agencies.

In addition, twelve agencies, boards, and commissions, including the Metro Toronto Convention Centre, Ontario Lottery Corporation, Ontario Place Corporation, and Niagara Parks Commission report to the Legislative Assembly through the Minister of Tourism, and Recreation (see Agencies, Boards, and Commissions).

The head office of the Ministry is located in Toronto. The Ministry also operates 23 regional and field offices, and 20 Travel Information Centres. The Ministry employs approximately 650 public servants.

## PROGRAMS

### Community Programs/Sports and Recreation Division

The purpose of the Recreation Division is to provide leadership to municipalities and private and public recreation organizations by operating training programs, publishing recreation manuals, and arranging direct financial assistance; to promote professional training for recreation workers and volunteers by establishing certification programs and sponsoring workshops on topics ranging from the provision of recreation opportunities for the elderly to maintenance and management of municipal recreation facilities; assist community organizations and province-wide groups with leadership training, seminars on improving their effectiveness, skills training, and methods of recruiting and using volunteers; and publish a newsletter, a series of recreation bulletins, training manuals, information kits, and brochures to provide a medium for the exchange of ideas, and to assist local groups in improving recreational opportunities in their communities. The division gives grants and other forms of assistance to municipalities and community groups to help maintain recreation facilities, and provides about $5 million a year to fund 72 sports governing bodies. Recreation division programs include:

*Recreation Programs*

*Community Recreation Program:* Includes a recognition program for recreation volunteers, and the Municipal Recreation Committee Training (through Operations Division), which provides a consistent recreation training format.

*Grants to Non-Profit Camps:* Provides grant to non-profit camps in accordance with the guidelines set forth in the legislation. Although the number of these grants is high, the dollar value per grant is quite low.

*Grants to Provincial Recreation Programs:* Provides support for projects of recreation organizations (funding is not provided for ongoing or administrative costs); these grants are awarded on a cost-sharing basis.

*Grants for Recreation Development:* Provides support for projects of local and regional recreation organizations. Projects may be submitted to the Branch through the Operations Division staff or may be developed by the client in consultation with the Operations consultant and the Branch consultant to address a need related to specific portfolio in the Branch (e.g. pilot projects, innovative projects, resource development).

*Grants for Research:* Provides grants for research projects which are initiated by the Ministry through the Recreation Research Committee or grants for research projects which clients submit to the Ministry for support.

*Leadership Development Program:* Includes a program to develop trainers who can return to their organizations to develop leaders in their home setting, workshops to improve the group facilitation skills of local recreationists, and workshops to improve skills in managing and maintaining recreation facilities.

*Older Adults Program:* Workshops to assist organizations to provide recreation services for older adults, offered at the local level.

*Wintario Development Program:* Reviews and makes recommendations on Wintario Development Program grants received from provincial recreation organizations according to established guidelines.

### Sports and Fitness Programs

*Assessment:* Coordinates and facilitates fitness testing in Ontario; allows the Ministry to consult with community agencies in the design and development of testing programs and consult with practitioners, medical associations, and educators regarding issues in stress testing; and standardizes a safe, basic physical fitness testing procedure across Ontario.

*Athletic Achievement Awards:* Recognizes the nominees for Ontario Amateur Athlete of the Year through financial grants toward development of programs or projects in their sports, and motivates provincial sports associations to nominate qualified athletes for the award. This program contributes to ongoing talent identification and training of future athletes.

*"Best Ever Ontario" Program:* Objectives are to encourage the best ever performance of Ontario athletes at the 1988 Winter Olympics in Calgary, and Summer Olympics in Seoul, South Korea; to increase the level of participation in sport throughout Ontario; and to ensure that economic spin-offs created by success in athletics are fully capitalized upon.

*Corporate Challenge:* Promotes a more active lifestyle for the residents of Ontario, leading to an increased sense of well-being and health by improving the fitness level of the employees of participating private sector corporations.

*Development:* Increases participation in sports activities at the recreational and elite athlete level by providing consultation and funding to some 76 provincial sport governing bodies.

*Elite Athlete Assistance Program:* Encourages and increases Ontario representation at the Commonwealth, Pan American, and Olympic Games and increases the number of Ontario athletes on the National Team and Federal Athlete

Assistance Program by identifying top athletes in the province, assisting them in meeting personal training and competition needs, and providing them with opportunities to attain National Team standing or "Card" status within the Federal Athlete Assistance Program.

*Employee Fitness:* Encourages business and industry in the promotion of a positive orientation toward fitness/recreation and lifestyle development among their employees.

*Fitfive Program:* Promotes a more active lifestyle for the residents of Ontario, leading to an increased sense of well-being and health by improving fitness levels; administers a fitness awards system which encourages and rewards individual and family participation in physical activity.

*Fitness Grants:* Provides assistance to provincially based fitness organizations which support the development of fitness programs at the community level and coordinates the delivery of fitness leadership training programs provided by provincially based fitness associations.

*Fitness Leadership:* Upgrades the present level of expertise of fitness professionals in Ontario; standardizes the basic level of expertise of fitness leaders in Ontario; increases the number of such fitness leaders; provides professional development opportunities for fitness personnel; develops a nucleus of trainers capable of providing training in the fitness field; and allows the Ministry to consult with communities, agencies, and special client groups requiring assistance related to fitness training for leaders.

*Fitness Resource Services:* Assists local agencies in the design and delivery of effective and appropriate fitness and physical activity programs.

*Francophone Initiative:* Assists provincial sports governing bodies in the operation of pilot projects which entail the provision of francophone services. This program develops resources (written material such as brochures, bulletins, rule books, as well as audio-visual resources) appropriate for Franco-Ontarians participating in these sport activities.

*Grants to Sports Governing Bodies:* Assures that the physical recreation and sport needs of participants throughout the province are met through provincial sports organizations and other related agencies. This program also assists sport organizations to develop programs, fosters a wide base of participation throughout the province, develops excellence through higher levels of competition and training for promising athletes; assists sport organizations in the creation and maintenance of an organization which allows for maximum membership participation in democratic decision-making and for development of strong regionally-based affiliates; and assists sport organizations in the development and improvement of volunteer association management to serve the needs of their membership and the amateur sporting public.

*Junior Olympics:* Provides local groups with a ready-made program to promote a grass roots participation program involving Olympic and Pan

American games sports.

*National Coaching Certification Program Community Coaching Development:* Promotes and develops coaching education in Ontario; provides coaches at all levels with a standardized system for improving their knowledge and skills in the theory, techniques, and practice of coaching through delivery and administration of the National Coaching Certification Program; increases the number of coaches taking certification courses in the province.

*Ontario Sports Centre:* Facilitates the operation of the Ontario Sports Centre by providing assistance for the cost of office space; support staff salaries, reproduction services, mail service, personnel services for support staff, telephone services, computerized accounting, and sports marketing.

*Ontario Sports Heritage Display:* Located in the Legislature Building, this display provides a graphic, sustained exhibit of aspects of amateur sport in Ontario—history, personalities, events, and sport art. This program illustrates the partnership in sport development between public and private agencies and is a showcase for Ontario's Amateur Athletes of the Year. The exhibit is a series of display cases focus on various aspects of amateur sport in Ontario—past, present, and future—through audio-visual presentations of graphics, artifacts, etc., including examples of sport depicted in various media by Ontario artists.

*Ontario Sport Medicine and Safety Advisory Board:* Develops recommendations for the Minister of Tourism and Recreation concerning a coordinated approach to the delivery of sport medicine information and/or programs in Ontario.

*Participation Development:* This program increases the level of participation in sports and fitness activities at all levels throughout the province. Central to this direction is a desire to introduce new sport activities, and to expand existing programs.

*Promotion:* Increases awareness of the benefits of physical activity through fitness and participation in amateur sports; motivates people to achieve fitness through their own initiative. This program encourages participation in amateur sports as a means to achieving improved fitness as well as strengthening Ontario's performance in amateur sports.

*Regional Development:* Increases participation and strengthens provincial sport governing bodies through the development of strong regional affiliates. Financial assistance is given to projects focused on the sport infra-structure at the regional level.

*Regional Fitness Grants:* Promotes regional campaigns leading toward increased motivation, education, and opportunities for fitness; provides support to community agencies in the development and delivery of fitness programs at the local/regional level.

*Regional Sports Councils/Advisory Committee:* Improves the coordination of delivery of sports programs to the regional and community levels, provides a forum for assessing the status of sport development in the regions, and assists the Recreation Operations Division in identifying sport development needs in the regions.

*Sports Awards Program:* Recognizes achievement, participation, and contribution to fitness and amateur sport; certificates are presented to athletes who win championships at all levels, and to individuals or groups other than athletes who have contributed to the development of fitness and amateur sport in the province.

*Sport Sciences and Testing:* Ensures the provision of scientific testing protocol services to athletes to enhance high performance development and training.

*Sports Travelcade:* Provides a mobile resources centre including comprehensive audio-visual information about sports and fitness to residents of Ontario who might not otherwise have access to such information.

*Training Institutes:* Assists the Recreation Operations Division in the provision of training for volunteers in the sport administration field. This training can take place at the regional, area or local levels.

*Youth and Special Populations:* Promotes and encourages physical fitness programs for children and other special population groups. Allows the Ministry to consult with education institutions and youth, sports and recreation centres in the design and development of youth fitness programs. Provides information to parents regarding the importance of physical activity in the growth and development of their children. Identifies special populations (e.g. seniors) which may require attention to encourage them to become physically active.

**Tourism Division**

The role of the Tourism Division is to develop new tourism attractions, improve existing tourism facilities, market Ontario as a tourism destination, provide information about Ontario to tourists, assist tourist operators, trade associations, and regional tourism associations in their marketing programs, both by providing marketing expertise and assistance, and through direct grants to offset some of the costs. The division assists tourist operators and associations by arranging displays of literature in high traffic locations, promotes Ontario as a destination for conventions and groups through Government of Ontario offices in Frankfurt, Paris, London, Tokyo, Boston, New York, Los Angeles, and Chicago. Trade missions are regularly sent to international travel trade shows. Tourism Division programs include:

*Marketing Programs*

*Advertising and Promotions Program:* Includes tourism advertising in Ontario, U.S., Quebec, and Overseas; travel publications (including Accommodation Guide, Camping Guide, and Travellers Encyclopedia); public relations such as the Visit Ontario Program, sports and travel shows, special events, travel news releases, and familiarization tours for out-of-province and foreign journalists; an audio-visual library, photo library, and film distribution.

*Customer Sales and Service:* Includes telephone lines in English and French, a network of 20 year-round and seasonal travel information centres, and distribution of MTR tourism publications.

*Market Research Program:* Studies traveller demand and economic impact; monitors the tourism trade, using both past and current statistics; and evaluates marketing branch programs for return on investment.

*Travel Trade and Convention Program:* Promotes travel to Ontario through tour operators, wholesalers, carriers, and group influencers in North American and overseas markets. Works with Ontario Convention Bureaux to promote meetings.

*Tourism Development Programs*

*Canada-Ontario Subsidiary Agreement for Tourism Development* (COTDA): An agreement was signed in November 1984, for development of major destination resorts and attractions on a 50:50 cost sharing basis. Each level of government is to provide $22 million, for a total of $44 million over five years. The agreement is administered by a joint management committee comprised of representatives from the federal Department of Industry, Science and Technology, the Ontario Ministry of Treasury and Economics, and MTR.

*Help for Entrepreneurs Loan Program* (HELP): Administered through the Ontario Development Corporations; provides first-year interest-free and principal-payment-free loans, up to $50,000 for staged developments of tourism enterprises.

| | |
|---|---|
| Stage 1 assistance | $ 5,000 |
| Stage 2 assistance | $15,000 |
| Stage 3 assistance | $30,000 |

*Small Business Development Corporations Program* (SBDC): Administered through the Ministry of Revenue; cash or tax grants provided for equity investments in businesses involved in the activities of accommodation, recreation, or attractions, primarily for use by tourists. This program was announced in June 1979. In the October 24, 1985 budget, a funding increase of $5 million was announced (total program funding now $30 million).

*Tourism Grading Term Loan Program:* Administered through the Ontario Development Corporations; provides term loans up to $50,000 at an interest rate two percent below the ODC's base lending rate with repayment terms up to eight years.

*Tourism Redevelopment Incentive Program* (TRIP): Administered through the Ontario Development Corporations; provides loan guarantee and interest subsidy up to $1 million for new projects, or up to $750,000 for existing operations.

*Tourism Term Loan Program:* Administered through the Ontario Development Corporations; provides term loans up to $500,000 at two percent below the ODC's base lending rate for up to 15 years, for new development, expansion, or improvement of tourist accommodation establishments, attractions, tourist marinas (must provide slips for transients), campgrounds (30 percent transient sites), and tourist restaurants.

## Tourism and Recreation Operations Division

Programs offered by the Ministry of Tourism and Recreation are accessed through the 23 field offices organized into five regions. Each office is staffed by consultants who work with municipal recreation and planning departments, with tourism associations, and operators, and with agencies and volunteer associations to improve local services.

Ministry consultants manage financial assistance programs targeted for both tourism and recreation clients at the local level and offer a wide range of consulting services to local tourism and recreation clients, In addition:

1. *Recreation consultants:* Provide services in human resources development, organizational development, fiscal development, program development, and facility development; provide leadership to municipalities and private and public recreation organizations by operating training programs; promote professional training for recreation workers; assist community organizations with leadership training, seminars on improving their effectiveness, skills training, and methods of recruiting and using volunteers; assist corporations in establishing employee fitness programs.

2. *Tourism consultants:* Provide services in marketing, product development, fiscal development, management assistance, and municipal consulting; assist tourist operators, trade associations, and regional tourism associations in their marketing programs, both by providing marketing expertise and assistance, and through direct grants to offset some of the costs; and, act as advocate to assist Ontario's tourist operators in dealing with the provincial and federal governments.

### Tourism and Recreation Operations Programs

*Capital Conservation Program:* Intended to encourage the updating of existing community recreation facilities to meet new user needs. The program provides assistance with fees and construction costs according to a regional formula.

*Capital Program for New Recreation Facilities:* Designed to provide support for the development of new and innovative sports, fitness, and recreational facilities. Assistance is provided for the purchase of land, design costs, professional fees, and construction costs according to a regional formula.

*Community Recreation Planning Program:* Increases the effectiveness of community recreation services. Assists municipalities and organizations by funding planning studies. The program shares up to a maximum of 50 percent of costs in communities with populations over 5,000 and up to a maximum of 75 percent of costs in communities of 5,000 or less.

*Destinations East Initiative:* Administered by the Eastern Ontario Development Corporation (EODC) and the Ministry of Tourism and Recreation offices in Eastern Ontario. Announced September 23, 1986, this program includes:

1. *Capital Construction Assistance Program:* Encourages more investment in the Eastern Ontario tourism industry, stimulates job creation and attracts increased visitation. Eligible operations include accommodation establishments, tourist campgrounds, ski resorts, and attractions.

2. *Commercial Tourist Marina Program:* Provides incentive loans up to 50 percent of approved capital costs or $100,000 for renovations, transient dock construction, on-shore facilities, infrastructure, and projects necessary to conform with environmental and government regulations.

3. *Feasibility and Planning Studies Program:* Allows non-repayable contributions for up to 50 percent of feasibility study costs. Maximum assistance $25,000. Private sector developers and municipalities are eligible. Also, gives non-repayable contributions for up to 75 percent of tourism planning study costs. Maximum assistance $40,000. Municipalities which have established a Tourism Development Committee of Council are eligible.

4. *Festivals and Special Events Program:* Allows non-repayable contributions for up to 50 percent of eligible costs. Maximum assistance $50,000. Municipalities and non-profit organizations are eligible.

5. *Investment Sourcing Program:* Allows non-repayable contributions for up to 50 percent of investment-sourcing costs for private sector developers, and up to 75 percent of costs, for municipalities. Maximum assistance $50,000.

6. *Major Capital Projects Program:* Provides funds for major developments such as canals, parks, waterfront enhancement, and large scale attractions.

7. *Marketing Assistance Program:* Allows non-repayable contributions for up to 50 percent of incremental marketing expenditures over $1,500. Maximum assistance $50,000. Eligible operations include licensed accommodation establishments, tourist campgrounds, tourist marinas, ski resorts, and attractions.

*Destinations North Initiative:* Administered by the Northern Ontario Development Corporation (NODC) and the Ministry of Tourism and Recreation offices in Northern Ontario. Announced July 8, 1986. Program includes:

1. *Large Scale Tourism Development:* Identifies development opportunities for major travel generators and funds tourism related projects which can attract increased numbers of visitors from longer distances.

2. *Tourism Capital Construction Assistance Program:* Encourages more investment in the Northern Ontario tourism industry, stimulates job creation and attracts increased visitation.

3. *Working Capital Assistance Program:* Assists tourist operators in meeting fluctuating working capital requirements and unexpected expenses. This

program emphasizes small establishments (roofed accommodations and attractions).

*Development Program:* Designed to increase participation in recreation activities, improve the quality of leadership in recreation activities, and increase the organizational stability and effectiveness of recreation organizations. Assistance is provided to projects which address one or more of these objectives, through grants of up to 50 percent of eligible costs.

*Facility Management Program:* Enhances the technical and human-oriented expertise of facility personnel, and provides assistance for the development and delivery of facility management training opportunities and for the development of facility management systems to a maximum of 75 percent of eligible costs.

*Grants for Municipal Recreation Programs:* Financial support provided to municipalities, Indian Bands, and local service boards to assist with the provision of recreation programs and services.

*Nor-Dev* (Northern Ontario Regional Economic Development Program): Administered through the Ministry of Northern Development and Mines. Established in July 1983; provides $1.5 million funding for cost-sharing of incremental marketing expenses and planning/feasibility studies.

*Northern Marketing Program:* Builds tourism in northern Ontario as a means of strengthening the economy in a time of severe industrial dislocation. This program is a marketing campaign including advertising that features northern attractions, communities, hospitality, and outdoor adventure. It will target southern Ontario and border U.S. states.

*Ontario Travel Association Program* (OTAP): Partially funded by the Ministry of Tourism and Recreation according to a three-part system. There is an administrative grant; a promotion grant; and an experience grant, which pays for the summer staff program.

*Quebec Marketing Program:* Increases tourism expenditure from Quebec visitors through a fully integrated advertising campaign including outdoor billboards, English and French radio stations, and newspapers. Other components include extensive research, French publications, and increased French travel counselling service.

## EXPENDITURE ESTIMATES

*Estimated Expendutures 1987–88*:

| | |
|---|---|
| Ministry Administration | $24,943,538 |
| Tourism Development | 36,921,600 |
| Parks and Attractions | 27,725,400 |
| Recreation, Sports and Fitness | 25,338,900 |
| Tourism and Recreation Operations | 70,171,500 |
| **Ministry total:** | **$185,100,938** |

## AGENCIES, BOARDS, AND COMMISSIONS

The following ABCs report to the Legislative Assembly through the Minister of Tourism and Recreation:

*Huronia Historical Advisory Council:* Responsible for advising the Minister on matters respecting the historical sites of Sainte-Marie among the Hurons, and the Historic Naval and Military Establishments.

*Metropolitan Toronto Convention Centre:* A world-class convention facility which attracts Canadian, U.S., and international conventions, tradeshows, and meetings to Metro Toronto.

*Niagara Parks Commission:* Operates a 56 kilometre parkway along the Niagara River from Lake Erie to Lake Ontario. Included are: recreation areas, scenic attractions, a campground, a marina, restaurant, gift shops, historic sites, golf courses, and horticultural school.

*Old Fort William Advisory Committee:* Responsible for advising the Minister on matters concerning the operation, expansion, and development of Old Fort William. It is not responsible for direct operation. Old Fort William, in Thunder Bay, is a reconstruction of a major Northwest fur trading trans-shipment depot. A living museum, it serves as a major tourist attraction and educational resource for Northwestern Ontario.

*Ontario Lottery Corporation:* Manages Wintario, Lottario, Instant, Provincial, Super Loto, and Lotto 6/49 lotteries. The net profits of the corporation, after provision for prizes and the payment of operating expenses, are paid into the Consolidated Revenue Fund to be available for the promotion and development of physical fitness, sports, recreational, and cultural activities and facilities.

*Ontario Place Corporation:* Operates a 96-acre cultural, entertainment, and recreation complex on three man-made islands in Lake Ontario at Toronto, which includes exhibition pavilions, the Forum, theatres, the giant screen Cinesphere, live entertainment, the waterfall showplace, restaurants, snack bars, boutiques, a marina, pedal boats, bumper boats, boat tours, the Wilderness Adventure Ride, the Canadian destroyer HMCS Haida, land rides, mini-golf, picnic areas, a theme pavilion "Ontario North Now," and a children's village with a water-play area and play apparatus, including a 370 foot, four-flume waterslide. Throughout the year, Ontario Place arranges banquets and receptions, and shows films for conventions and other groups of residents or tourists.

*Ontario Sport Medicine and Safety Advisory Board:* Advises the Government of Ontario through the Minister of Tourism and Recreation on matters pertaining to safety in amateur sport, personal fitness, and physical recreation.

*Ontario Trillium Foundation:* In September, 1982, the Ontario Government created the Trillium Foundation as an innovative approach to providing voluntary social service organizations with access to lottery revenues. The Foundation, which is run by an independent voluntary Board of Directors, receives $15 million a year from the province from proceeds generated by the Ontario Lottery Corporation. The Foundation makes available time-limited grants for specific projects or the unfunded portions of ongoing programs to organizations providing direct social services across the province.

*Ottawa Congress Centre:* An world class convention centre facility which promotes and develops the convention tourist industry in the the National Capital Region.

*St. Clair Parkway Commission:* Responsible for the establishment of a parkway along the St. Clair River from Point Edward on Lake Huron to Mitchell's Bay on Lake St. Clair. The St. Clair Parkway Commission is a joint program of parks and recreation development by the Province of Ontario, Country of Lambton, County of Kent, City of Chatham, and the City of Sarnia.

*St. Lawrence Parks Commission:* Operates and maintains parks, campgrounds, and historic sites from the Ontario-Quebec border to 48 kilometers west of Kingston on Highway 33. Historic sites are Old Fort Henry at Kingston; Fairfield House at Amherstview; and Upper Canada Village, 11 kilometers east of Morrisburg. Other facilities include a Wildfowl Sanctuary, an 18-hole golf course, a paved air strip, a railroad museum, nature trails, a marina, Pioneer and Loyalist memorials, and winter recreation facilities (including cross-country skiing, snowmobiling, tobogganing, snowshoeing). Skating and horse-drawn sleigh rides are available at Upper Canada Village. A riding stable, summer theatre, and paddleboat rentals are available on Commission lands.

*Thunder Bay Ski Jumps Ltd.:* Operates Big Thunder National Ski Training Centre. The training centre is sanctioned by the International Ski Federation to hold World Cup Ski Jumping events. Both its 70 metre and 90 metre hills are built to exact tolerances and have the world's longest landing area for maximum safety. The two jumps and the surrounding area are used as a provincial ski-training site.

## LEGISLATION

The Ministry of Tourism and Recreation is responsible for the following Acts:

*Community Recreation Centres Act:* The council of a municipality may provide for the establishment, maintenance, and operation of one or more recreation centres. Provincial grants may be provided in respect of such recreation facilities as community halls, playing fields, swimming pools, skating areas, skiing facilities, tennis courts, fitness trails, gymnasiums, and cultural centres.

*Historical Parks Act:* The province may set apart for the use of its citizens as an historical public park any lands in which there is an object, site or land of historical significance. Land may be acquired for this purpose under the *Ministry of Government Services Act.* Such recreational facilities as golf courses, bowling greens, camping facilities, and other facilities for sports or amusement may be constructed or operated. As well, boats, vehicles and other means of transportation can be acquired or operated in connection with the parks. Three such areas have been designated in the province: Old

Fort William Historical Park, Thunder Bay, Ontario; Historic Naval and Military Establishment Historical Park, Penetangueshene, Ontario; and Sainte-Marie among the Hurons Historical Park, Midland, Ontario.

*Ministry of Tourism and Recreation Act:* The Ministry was created in 1982 to promote tourism and recreation in Ontario, stimulate employment and income opportunities in the tourism and recreation sector, encourage the use of parks and tourist attractions, ensure adequate opportunities to pursue recreational activities, provide sports and recreational resources to municipalities, and promote standards of accommodation, facilities, and services offered to the travelling and vacationing public.

*Niagara Parks Act:* Established the Niagara Parks Commission (see Agencies, Boards, and Commissions) to manage the Niagara Parks.

*Ontario Lottery Corporation Act:* Created the Ontario Lottery Corporation to manage lotteries in the province (see Agencies, Boards, and Commissions).

*Ontario Place Corporation Act:* Created the Ontario Place Corporation to manage Ontario Place in Toronto (see Agencies, Boards, and Commissions).

*St. Clair Parkway Commission Act:* Created the St. Clair Parkway Commission to manage the St. Clair Parkway (see Agencies, Boards, and Commissions).

*St. Lawrence Parks Commission Act:* Created the St. Lawrence Parks Commission to manage the St. Lawrence Parks (see Agencies, Boards, and Commissions).

*Tourism Act:* Requires permits and licenses to be obtained for the construction, addition to, alteration or operation of information centres and tourism establishments in the province.

# MINISTRY OF TRANSPORTATION

## ROLES AND FUNCTIONS

The Ministry of Transportation is responsible for the operation and maintenance of the province's highway system, and for most forms of transportation which receive financial support from the province. It manages the municipal transfer payment programs, which provide subsidies for the construction, rehabilitation, and maintenance of municipal roads, as well as the capital and operating costs of municipal transit systems. Through its regional and district staff, the Ministry also provides guidance and expertise to the municipalities in identifying their road and transit needs. Among its other areas of responsibility are fuel conservation and alternative fuels research, inter-city transportation, and goods distribution systems. In addition, it operates three "modal" offices, which promote Ontario's interest in the federally-regulated jurisdictions of air, marine, and rail transportation.

## BACKGROUND HISTORY

Ontario's Ministry of Transportation was created in 1896, when the Ontario Cabinet passed an Order-in-Council creating the new position of Provincial Instructor for Roadmaking. Archibald William Campbell, later known as "Good Roads" Campbell, was appointed to the position. Canada's first motor cars arrived in Ontario in 1898. At the time, Campbell predicted that as soon as motor cars were sold competitively, they would become a major challenge to the then-dominant railroad. In 1900, Campbell was appointed Ontario Commissioner of Highways in the Department of Public Works; in 1906, Administrator of Colonization Roads, which were being constructed by settlers in northern Ontario; in 1910, Deputy Minister of Railways and Canals for the federal government.

In the early 1900s, railways were predominant; the system of roads was used largely for the transport of farm produce to market. Between 1901 and 1903, Ontario introduced the "Good Roads Train," an instruction project in road-building. Its message—"Commerce can flourish without railways, but never without good roads"—was well-received by the populace. By 1907, there were only 2,600 motor vehicles in Ontario, but work continued, with model roads being built in the Windsor and Aylmer areas. A Toronto firm laid down a thoroughfare in Islington and paid for its upkeep as a goodwill gesture.

Following World War I, the demands of industry over agriculture underscored an increase in the importance of good roads. By the end of World War II, there was

MINISTRY OF TRANSPORTATION

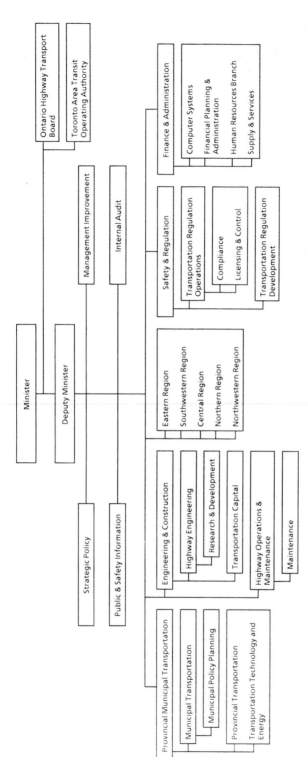

Minister

Ontario Highway Transport Board

Toronto Area Transit Operating Authority

Management Improvement

Deputy Minister

Internal Audit

Strategic Policy

Public & Safety Information

**Provincial Municipal Transportation**
- Municipal Transportation
- Municipal Policy Planning
- Provincial Transportation
- Transportation Technology and Energy

**Engineering & Construction**
- Highway Engineering
- Research & Development
- Transportation Capital
- Highway Operations & Maintenance
- Maintenance

**Eastern Region**
- Southwestern Region
- Central Region
- Northern Region
- Northwestern Region

**Safety & Regulation**
- Transportation Regulation Operations
- Compliance
- Licensing & Control
- Transportation Regulation Development

**Finance & Administration**
- Computer Systems
- Financial Planning & Administration
- Human Resources Branch
- Supply & Services

evidence that a massive highway-building program would be needed to meet the needs of the post-war economic boom. Road-building in Ontario took on a formalized approach with the organization of the Department of Public Works and Highways in 1916. The name was changed to the Department of Public Highways a few years later. In 1930, it was finally shortened to the Department of Highways, Ontario.

In 1917, the first section of Ontario's modern highway system, a 72 kilometre stretch of Highway 2 from Rouge River to Port Hope, was brought under the Department's administration. In 1923, the first Ontario road map was produced: 2,976 kilometers of provincial roads (1,664 km paved, 1,312 km gravel). A speed limit was established: 25 m.p.h. In 1952, the Toronto-Barrie Freeway (now Highway 400) opened. It was widened to six lanes in 1972. In 1958, the Burlington Bay Skyway (James N. Allan Skyway) was opened—Ontario's longest at 2,562 metres. In 1960, the Trans-Canada Highway opened. In 1968 the final section of the Macdonald-Cartier Freeway (Highway 401) opened between Ivy Lea and Brockville. Highway 401 carries more than 180,000 vehicles per day in up to 12 lanes along its 816-km length from the U.S. border to the Quebec boundary. In 1975, construction started on Highway 404, the northern extension of the Don Valley Parkway. In 1977, Highway 401 was widened east and west of Toronto.

## ORGANIZATION

The Ministry of Transportation is organized into a number of divisions (see organization chart):

1. *Finance and Administration:* Includes the Computer Systems, Financial Planning and Administration, Human Resources, and Supply and Services Branches.

2. *Engineering and Construction:* Includes the Highway Engineering and Transportation Capital Branches.

3. *Highway Operations and Maintenance:*

4. *Provincial/Municipal Transportation:* Includes the Municipal Transportation, Municipal Policy Planning, Provincial Transportation, and Transportation Technology and Energy Branches.

5. *Safety and Regulation:* Includes the Transportation Regulation Operations and Transportation Regulation Development Branches.

Regional Directors for Central, Southwestern, Eastern, Northern, and Northwestern Ontario regions report to the Deputy Minister, as do the Strategic Policy, Internal Audit, and Public and Safety Information Branches.

In addition, three agencies, boards, and commissions, including GO Transit and the Ontario Highway Transport Board, report to the Minister of Transportation.

The head office of the Ministry of Transportation is located in Downsview, Ontario. The Ministry also delivers its programs through five regional and 18 district offices, 259 highway maintenance patrol stations, and over 300 motor vehicle and drivers license issuing agents throughout the province. Employing approximately 8,500 public servants, the Ministry of Transportation is one of the largest ministries in the province.

## PROGRAMS

### Engineering and Construction

One of the Ministry's most important functions is to build and expand the provincial highway network. The Engineering and Construction Division is responsible for the design and construction of these facilities, from property acquisition to installation of traffic systems.

The Division's mandate encompasses research in such areas as pavement, structures, engineering materials, and systems. It maintains a number of test laboratories to provide controlled conditions for these purposes. It also develops specifications for chemicals, concrete, soils, aggregates, and asphalt—as well as evaluating any post-construction problems with these materials. This Division's activities include the following programs:

*Engineering Materials:* The Ministry ensures that Ontario's provincial highways are built to provide the maximum in operational efficiency, safety, and durability. To this end, the engineering materials office investigates new products and applications, along with maintaining strict standards for materials used on Ministry projects. It also prepares foundation reports and final design drawings; offers advice to Ministry and municipal staff; and makes recommendations for remedial action.

*Environmental Assessment:* Environmental concerns are of importance to the Ministry in all its activities—from road construction to rehabilitation and maintenance. In cooperation with the Ministry of the Environment, the Ministry prepares environmental assessment reports before undertaking most new road projects. Special attention is paid to preserving the natural habitats of wildlife and ensuring that rare species of plants are relocated. The environmental staff also make recommendations on ways to overcome the potentially harmful effects of highway construction and maintenance operations.

*Property:* The Ministry attempts to negotiate amicable settlements with owners of property required for highway construction. Efforts are made to ensure that future projects create a minimum of disruption in residential, industrial, and farming areas.

*Research and Development:* The Ministry maintains close ties with Ontario universities and independent consultants working in research and development. It has contacts at the national and international levels and has been invited to participate in numerous conferences and projects with other members of the public and private sectors. The Research and Development Branch focuses its activities in such areas as pavements, structures, traffic systems, and technology applications. As a result of its studies, it publishes technical reports and manuals which are made available to other jurisdictions and the public.

*Structures:* The structural office is involved in the construction, inspection, maintenance, and rehabilitation of all bridges within the provincial highway system. In addition, the office is responsible for approval of municipal bridge projects, including the restoration of a number of "heritage" structures being preserved for their historical significance.

*Surveys and Plans:* The surveys and plans office uses a variety of methods to collect data for highway construction and mapping purposes. Through aerial photography and remote sensing techniques, detailed three-dimensional images of the Ontario landscape are obtained for assembly into "mosaics," or composite maps.

## Equipment Engineering

The Equipment Engineering Office is responsible for developing policies and providing training in the selection, operation, and maintenance of Ministry vehicles and road maintenance equipment. One of its functions is to keep a computerized inventory of the ministry's fleet, including usage and operating costs. This information is useful in establishing maintenance schedules and determining whether new acquisitions are warranted. In addition, the Equipment Engineering Office oversees the operation of the head office equipment garage and the government garage at Queen's Park, where the vehicles owned by other ministries and government agencies are fueled and serviced.

## Modal Offices

The Ministry's Air, Marine and Pipeline, and Rail Offices fulfill an advocacy role in what are essentially federally-regulated transportation modes:

The *Air Office* has a similar mandate to influence federal government policy, but its responsibilities also encompass two other areas: remote airport development and municipal airport assistance. Ontario's 12 remote airports provide access to isolated settlements, some of which are served by no other means of transportation. The Ministry of Northern Development and Mines covers the capital cost of these projects, with the Ministry contributing planning and design expertise, and maintenance funding.

The *Marine and Pipeline Office* plays a major role in the promotion of shipping in the Great Lakes/St. Lawrence Seaway System. It also assists in the development and marketing of Ontario ports and the province's three shipbuilding facilities at Collingwood, Port Arthur (Thunder Bay), and Port Weller (St. Catharines). In addition, it cooperates with the federal government and its agencies to conduct studies related to marine and pipeline issues within the province.

The *Rail Office* assists in the development of an efficient provincial rail transportation system for both passengers and freight. Among its primary concerns are route abandonments or branch line rationalizations which affect Ontario residents. It also reviews the level and quality of passenger services, as well as maintaining an active involvement in federal regulatory activities and safety issues. Position papers are submitted regularly to the federal government on a wide variety of issues, including commuter rail legislation, domestic deregulation, freight rates, and inter-switching limits.

## Municipal Roads

The Ministry provides subsidies at varying rates to all municipalities within the province. Provincial funds are used for the construction of new roads and bridges, the rehabilitation of existing facilities, and ongoing maintenance operations. These subsidies are granted on the entire year's road budget and decisions as to what projects will receive priority are left up to the individual municipality. However, work of special benefit to the area is often eligible for separate funding through the development road program or the new municipal improvement fund. The Ministry also sets aside funds for its highway connecting link program, which provides local residents with more direct access to the provincial highway system. In addition, the municipal roads program supports seven ferry services.

## Policy Planning

The Ministry operates four separate offices which support its policy development process.

The *Goods Distribution Systems Office* promotes the efficient and cost-effective movement of Ontario-produced goods, both within the province and beyond its borders. It provides advice to shippers with transportation or distribution problems and maintains satellite offices in Timmins and Thunder Bay to handle the unique difficulties experienced by northern Ontario businesses. Besides representing Ontario's interests in relation to federal legislative changes, it also has encouraged the establishment of a computerized information bank of goods-transportation services.

The *Inter-City Transportation Policy Office* represents the interests of public transportation users and private vehicle passengers through research and analysis. It is responsible for provincial policy proposals concerning the line-haul bus system, regional air services, and passenger rail services.

The *Transportation Demand Forecasting Office* monitors travel and land use trends to establish future demand for roads, transit, and other transportation services. It supplies municipalities with such data as place-of-work and place-of-residence relationships for use in their own planning processes.

The *Urban Transportation Policy Office* identifies opportunities for improving the planning of urban transportation initiatives. It is responsible for the preparation of position papers on a variety of issues, including rapid transit and land development proposals.

## Safety and Regulation Division

One of the most important areas under the Ministry's jurisdiction is road safety. Through an ongoing program of education, the Safety and Regulation Division promotes good driving practices among all Ontario motorists. Its efforts have been rewarded in recent years with a steady decrease in the number of highway fatalities, along with an improvement in seat-belt usage, and a reduction in impaired driving convictions. It is also responsible for the regulation and licensing of drivers and vehicles, as well as the province's involvement with inter-city busing, trucking, and for-hire transport. Programs include:

*Compliance:* The staff of this branch are responsible for regulating compliance with the various acts which the Ministry administers. Its areas of involvement include the licensing of commercial vehicles, the supervision of weight and dimension guidelines and the adoption of vehicle standards. Through this branch, the ministry also licenses Motor Vehicle Inspection Stations and monitors the issuing of Safety Standards Certificates. In addition, it oversees the inspection of dump trucks, buses, and propane-powered vehicles.

*Transportation Regulation Development:* Staff of the Safety Coordination and Development Office are responsible for the development and implementation of a broad range of highway safety policies. Their areas of concentration includes seat-belt and child-restraint usage, driver education, driver improvement, voluntary 24-hour headlight use, and bicycle and motorcycle safety programs. The emphasis is on raising public awareness of the need for responsible behaviour among all drivers and cyclists. This message is spread through the distribution of safety materials—including a high school driver education textbook—and participation in seminars, workshops, and conferences dealing with traffic safety concerns. Existing programs are constantly being evaluated for ongoing effectiveness and data gathered through frequent surveys is used to establish new safety initiatives. The research and recommendations of this office play an important role in the legislative review process. Similarly, the Bus and Truck Transportation Offices contribute their input to regulatory changes in their areas. All three offices are in consultation with industry, the public, and other levels of government to ensure that diverse interests are represented.

## Signs and Building Permits

Owners of all property bordering on provincial highways must seek permits from the Ministry before using that land for any purpose. Permits are issued for building and land use, as well as for the posting of advertising signs visible from the highway. In addition, land owners need access permits to create new entrances onto a highway or to do any other work in the right-of-way.

## Traffic Management and Engineering

The primary goal of Traffic Management and Engineering is to ensure the safe and effective flow of traffic on Ontario highways. This is accomplished through a combination of traffic analysis, signing, signals, electrical design, and accident data management.

A recent addition to this list is the Freeway Traffic Management System (FTMS). Using changeable overhead message signs, the FTMS relays up-to-the-minute traffic information to motorists, enabling them to avoid trouble spots ahead. It also detects and responds to accidents and breakdowns through direct communications links with emergency services. The FTMS has the added capability of directing traffic from one freeway to another, as well as balancing the flow between express and collector lanes. All these functions result in a vast improvement in safety and service for Ontario motorists.

## Transit

Ontario has a far-reaching reputation for excellence in transit. A total of 73 municipalities have helped the province gain high marks in three important categories: number of residents served, ridership, and percentage of costs recovered in revenue. As well, there are other areas where the average passenger recognizes even greater achievements—namely, comfort, reliability, and cleanliness. The Ministry's contribution to the performances of Ontario's transit systems has earned it the prestigious Government Agency Achievement Award from the American Public Transit Association. The award is presented for the outstanding execution of public transportation responsibilities and contributions to the industry as a whole.

In addition to providing provincial funding, the Ministry assists municipalities in meeting high standards for transit service through research and development, and the provision of operational and management expertise. The staff of the Ministry's Transit Office is also available to help in the planning of municipal and provincial transit system improvements.

Recent projects supported by the Ministry include the City of Scarborough's new rapid transit line, the exclusive busway currently under construction for Ottawa-Carleton Transport, and the purchase of new subway cars, streetcars, and buses for the Toronto Transit Commission.

Because the Ministry believes in providing access to transit services for all residents of the province, it encourages the establishment of services for the physically disabled within the municipalities. A total of 50 such services are now receiving provincial assistance, resulting in much-improved mobility for the handicapped.

The Ministry is continuing its work on the Transit Information, Communications and Control System (TICCS) project. The aim of this project is to develop a range of computer-based support packages to assist in managing and controlling many of the important functions of transit.

## Transportation Technology and Energy

The Ministry is involved in the research, development, and application of advanced technology which improves the efficiency of Ontario transportation systems, while at the same time fostering strong economic growth. These activities are performed in relation to transit, commercial vehicles, control and information systems, and automotive energy. They include the testing of vehicle systems and equipment, the exploration of new applications for existing technology, and the promotion of new products and innovations.

In an effort to support Ontario industry, the Ministry also assists local businesses in product development and marketing. Contracts have been made with other provinces and several foreign governments seeking Ontario-produced goods and services.

Another important technological initiative undertaken by the Ministry is the Transportation Energy Management Program (TEMP). A joint effort with the Ministry of Energy, TEMP aims at reducing Ontario's dependence on petroleum-based fuels through the development of alternative energy sources and marketing of energy management techniques.

TEMP works with private industry, municipal government, and the public to encourage fuel-saving and the use of alternative fuels such as propane, methane, and natural gas. Its efforts at promoting car-pooling and van-pooling through the Share-A-Ride project have been successful in conserving energy and curbing rush-hour traffic density in urban centres. The program has also been active in reducing fuel consumption among transit systems and truck fleets, as well as conducting applied research into alternative fuels.

## EXPENDITURE ESTIMATES

*Estimated Expenditures 1987–88*:

| | |
|---|---|
| Ministry Administration | $ 50,653,938 |
| Municipal Roads | 618,836,600 |
| Municipal Transit | 333,635,200 |
| Policy Planning and Research | 12,975,800 |
| Provincial Highways | 563,332,900 |
| Provincial Transit | 148,500,000 |
| Provincial Transportation | 12,073,400 |
| Safety and Regulation | 92,695,200 |
| **Ministry total:** | **$1,832,730,038** |

## AGENCIES, BOARDS, AND COMMISSIONS

The following ABCs report to the Legislative Assembly through the Minister of Transportation:

*GO Transit: The Toronto Area Transit Operating Authority:* An inter-regional transit system serving Metro Toronto and the surrounding Regions of Durham, York, Peel, Halton, and Hamilton-Wentworth. The objects of the authority include the establishment and operation of inter-regional transit systems with associated parcel express service, facilitation of the operational integration of such systems, and provision of transit services within a regional area at the request of its council. GO Transit (for "Government of Ontario") administers the system; contracted operators handle most of the day-to-day service: CN Rail, and CP Rail for GO Train Service, and Gray Coach Lines, Travelways, and Charterways for GO Bus Service.

*License Suspension Appeal Board:* Hears appeals from persons whose driver or vehicle license has been suspended under the *Highway Traffic Act*, and other appeals concerning the refusal, revocation or conditions of motor vehicle inspection station licenses under the *Highway Traffic Act*.

*Ontario Highway Transport Board:* A regulatory tribunal which approves issuance of, and charges for, licenses for bus and truck for-hire services. It recommends to the Minister of Transportation approval or rejection of transfers of operating licenses and public vehicle tariffs. Acts such as the *Public Commercial Vehicles Act* and the *Motor Vehicle Transportation Act (Canada)* require that for-hire bus and truck operators hold an operating license.

## LEGISLATION

The Ministry of Transportation is responsible for the following Acts:

*Dangerous Goods Transportation Act, 1981:* Complementary to the *Transportation of Dangerous Good Act* (Canada); regulates the transportation of dangerous goods in vehicles on highways with respect to safety requirements, safety standards and safety marks. Penalties for contravention range up to $100,000 or imprisonment for less than two years. The regulations under the federal Act have been adopted by reference and deal with such matters as the designation of commodities which are dangerous goods, driver training, documentation, etc.

*Highway Traffic Act:* An omnibus Act, which establishes the rules with regard to such matters as vehicle permits, driver licenses, vehicle equipment standards, load, dimension and weight limitations, speed limits, rules of the road, civil actions, municipal by-laws, suspension for failure to pay civil judgments, records, and reporting of accidents and convictions, offences involving arrest powers, penalties, etc.

*Ontario Highway Transport Board Act:* Establishes the Board, administrative rules, provisions with respect to the holding of hearings, receipt of evidence, making of orders, award of costs, rights of appeal or petition. Authorizes the Lieutenant Governor in Council to make regulations governing the practice and procedure in proceedings before the

Board.

*Public Commercial Vehicles Act:* Provides for the economic regulation of those transporting the goods of others for compensation in commercial vehicles beyond urban zones, with certain exemptions. Operating licenses are required, such licenses being issued by the Minister on the basis of certificates of public necessity and convenience issued by the Ontario Highway Transport Board after a hearing. Certificates of intercorporate exemption may be issued to corporations having a minimum of 90 percent common ownership. Tariffs must be filed with the Board 30 days prior to their taking effect. There are operating requirements with respect to such matters as bills of lading and insurance. The Act contains powers of investigation and suspension or cancellation of operating licenses subject to a hearing by the Board and decision by the Minister. The Act currently also requires freight forwarders to be licensed as such.

*Public Vehicles Act:* Provides for the economic regulation of the transportation of passengers for compensation beyond municipal boundaries except in taxi cabs and car pool vehicles as defined. Operating licenses are issued by the Minister pursuant to a certificate of public necessity and convenience issued by the Ontario Highway Transport Board after a hearing. Tariffs must be approved by the Minister. There are operating rules with respect to safety matters, insurance, number of standees, etc. There are investigation powers and authority to suspend or cancel operating licenses with a right to a hearing before the Board.

*Toronto Area Transit Operating Authority Act:* Establishes the Toronto Area Transit Operating Authority and its area of jurisdiction. The composition of the authority membership is prescribed and administrative matters provided for. There is provision for the authority to establish and operate transit systems in other areas with the approval of the Lieutenant Governor in Council. The authority has power to make regulations with approval of the Lieutenant Governor in Council regarding operational matters, including payment of fares, parking on authority property, etc.

**Statutes Administered by the Ministry of Transportation by Responsible Program**

*Ministry*

*Ministry of Transportation and Communications Act*

**Policy Planning and Research**

*Ontario Transportation Development Corporation Act* (part)

*Public Transportation and Highway Improvement Act* (part)

*Urban Transportation Development Corp. Act* (part)

**Transportation Regulation**

*Dangerous Goods Transportation Act*

*Highway Traffic Act*

*Motorized Snow Vehicles Act*

*Off-Road Vehicles Act*

*Ontario Highway Transport Board Act*

*Public Commercial Vehicles Act*

*Public Vehicles Act*

*Motor Vehicle Transport Act (Canada):* Delegated responsibility.

**Provincial Highways**

*Highway Traffic Act*

*Ministry of Transportation and Communications Creditors Payment Act*

*Public Service Works on Highways Act* (part)

*Public Transportation and Highway Improvement Act* (part)

*Toll Bridges Act*

**Provincial Transit**

*Commuter Services Act* (part)

*Ontario Transportation Development Corporation Act* (part)

*Public Transportation and Highway Improvement Act* (part)

*Toronto Area Transit Operating Authority Act* (part)

*Urban Transportation Development Corp. Act* (part)

**Provincial Transportation**

*Airports Act*

*Bluewater Bridges Act*

*Bridges Act*

*Commuter Services Act* (part)

*Ferries Act*

*Ontario Transportation Development Corporation Act* (part)

*Public Commercial Vehicles Act* (part)

*Public Transportation and Highway Improvement Act* (part)

*Public Vehicles Act* (part)

*Railways Act, R.S.O. 1950, c.331* (part)

*Toronto Area Transit Operating Authority Act* (part)

*Township of Pelee Act*

*Urban Transportation Development Corp. Act* (part)

**Municipal Roads**

*Local Roads Boards Act*

*Public Service Works on Highways Act* (part)

*Public Transportation and Highway Improvement Act* (part)

*Statute Labour Act*

*Municipal Transit*

*Municipal Electric Railways Act, R.S.O. 1950, c.248*

*Public Transportation and Highway Improvement Act* (part)

*Railways Act, R.S.O. 1950, c.331* (part)

*Toronto Area Transit Operating Authority Act* (part)

# Section 5
# JUSTICE MINISTRIES

The Justice Ministries administer justice and regulate business and commercial activity in the province. The Justice Ministries are the Ministries of the Attorney General; Consumer and Commercial Relations; Correctional Services; Financial Institutions; and the Solicitor General.

The Ministry of Citizenship might also be described as a Justice Ministry because it is responsible for the administration of the Ontario Human Rights Commission and its minister presently sits on the Cabinet Committee on Justice. However, the programs delivered by this ministry are focussed primarily on encouraging multicultural expression and assisting newcomers to settle into Ontario society. Accordingly, the Ministry of Citizenship is described in the section on the Social Policy Ministries.

MINISTRY OF THE ATTORNEY GENERAL

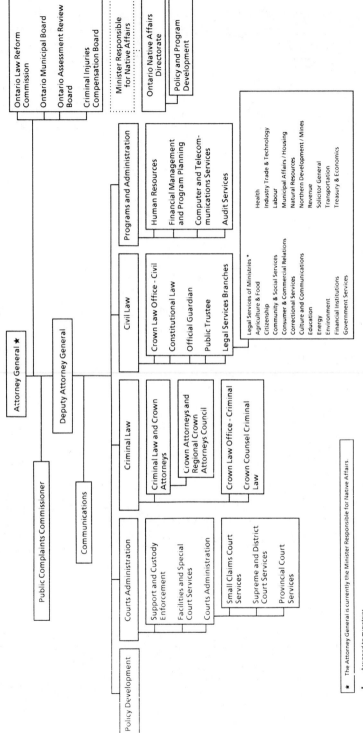

Attorney General ★

Public Complaints Commissioner

Deputy Attorney General

Communications

Ontario Law Reform Commission
Ontario Municipal Board
Ontario Assessment Review Board
Criminal Injuries Compensation Board

Minister Responsible for Native Affairs

Ontario Native Affairs Directorate

Policy and Program Development

Policy Development

Courts Administration

Support and Custody Enforcement
Facilities and Special Court Services
Courts Administration

Small Claims Court Services
Supreme and District Court Services
Provincial Court Services

Criminal Law

Criminal Law and Crown Attorneys
Crown Attorneys and Regional Crown Attorneys Council

Crown Law Office - Criminal
Crown Counsel Criminal Law

Civil Law

Crown Law Office - Civil
Constitutional Law
Official Guardian
Public Trustee
Legal Services Branches

Legal Services of Ministries *
Agriculture & Food
Citizenship
Community & Social Services
Consumer & Commercial Relations
Correctional Services
Culture and Communications
Education
Energy
Environment
Financial Institutions
Government Services

Health
Industry Trade & Technology
Labour
Municipal Affairs / Housing
Natural Resources
Northern Development / Mines
Revenue
Solicitor General
Transportation
Treasury & Economics

Programs and Administration

Human Resources
Financial Management and Program Planning
Computer and Telecommunications Services
Audit Services

★ The Attorney General is currently the Minister Responsible for Native Affairs.

* Assigned to ministries.

# MINISTRY OF THE ATTORNEY GENERAL

## ROLES AND FUNCTIONS

The Ministry of the Attorney General is responsible for the administration of justice in Ontario and ensures the effective operation of the courts across the province. The Ministry conducts and regulates all civil litigation and criminal prosecutions for and against the Crown. Ministry lawyers advise heads of departments and agencies of government on their legal concerns. The Attorney General is the law officer of the Executive Council and attends to all matters of a legislative nature.

For a discussion of the roles and functions of the Supreme Court, District Court, and Provincial Courts in Ontario, refer to the Judiciary Section in Part I.

## BACKGROUND HISTORY

The Office of Attorney General in Ontario predates Confederation. Before 1972, the Office of Attorney General was recognized in the *British North America Act*, although there was no place that the power, functions, or duties of the office were set out by statute.

In 1966, the Ministry of Financial and Commercial Affairs was created and thirteen Acts not related to the Office of the Attorney General were transferred to that Ministry. The Ministry of Financial and Commercial Affairs is now known as the Ministry of Consumer and Commercial Relations.

The *Ministry of the Attorney General Act*, which was introduced in 1972, set out specified duties of the office. The original Department of Justice was renamed Ministry of the Attorney General. Also, in 1972, the Ministry of the Solicitor General was created, and the responsibility for the supervision of law enforcement was transferred from the Attorney General to that Ministry.

## ORGANIZATION

The Ministry of the Attorney General is organized into five divisions (see organization chart):

1. *Civil Law:* Provides the Ontario Government with legal services in the matter of civil litigation in all courts, boards, and tribunals, and provides legal

advice to all government ministries and agencies. This division also includes the Official Guardian, Public Trustee, and the Constitutional Law Office. The Ministry of the Attorney General provides Legal Services to 22 Ontario Government ministries through the Legal Services Branch.

2. *Courts Administration:* Responsible for civil and criminal courts and court offices, including the Supreme Court, District Court, and Provincial Courts systems.

3. *Criminal Law:* Responsible for the activities of Crown Attorneys and Crown Law offices, which conduct prosecutions under the Criminal Code or other provincial or federal statutes in all 49 counties and judicial districts in the province.

4. *Policy Development:* Conducts research and analysis of all aspects of the administration of justice in Ontario, and reviews the statutes administered by the Attorney General.

5. *Programs and Administration:* Delivers support services to the Ministry, including Human Resources, Financial Management, Computer Services, and Audit.

As well, six agencies, boards, and commissions report to the Legislative Assembly through the Attorney General, including the Ontario Law Reform Commission, the Ontario Municipal Board, and the Criminal Injuries Compensation Board (see Agencies, Boards, and Commissions).

The head office of the Ministry of the Attorney General is located in Toronto. The Ministry operates a network of over 375 courts, court offices, and crown attorneys' offices in every county and judicial district in the province. The Ministry employs over 3300 public servants.

## PROGRAMS

*Compensation for Victims of Crime:* With the introduction and passage in 1986 of amendments to the *Compensation for Victims of Crime Act*, payments that are made to victims of crime were substantially increased. Decisions with regard to claims made by the victims of crime and the amount of payment are made by the Criminal Injuries Compensation Board following a hearing held by the Board.

*Drinking and Driving Countermeasures Office:* This office was established in September 1983, to coordinate provincial efforts to combat drinking and driving, including the encouragement of community-based programs and the review of policy issues. The Drinking and Driving Countermeasures Office encourages new and expanded forms of community action on drinking and driving and, through direct awareness campaigns, further increases the public's perception so that changes in attitudes and behaviour become permanent. Also through this Office, Ontario's representation at federal-provincial meetings discussing related federal Criminal Code amendments and federal plans for related anti-drinking and driving campaigns are coordinated.

*French Language Services:* The right of Ontario's francophone population to have equal opportunity to pursue legal rights in the language of their choice, regardless of geographical or jurisdictional barriers is reflected in the *French Language Services Act.* This act requires that provincial Ministries and agencies provide services to the public in French and English in those areas where a significant number of French speaking Ontarians reside. These rights have been extended to all courts in Ontario.

*Legal Aid:* Generally, the government gives the legal profession control over the provision of legal services to the public because it believes that a self-regulating profession is the best way to secure an independent profession and a high standard of public service. However, Legal Aid is a partnership between the government and the legal profession. The government has worked to gain increases in the tariff rate, to establish new community legal aid clinics, to obtain federal cost-sharing for civil legal aid and has negotiated an improved agreement wherein the federal government shares some of the costs of criminal legal aid. The Ministry of the Attorney General has an active involvement in policy and financial matters affecting the Ontario Legal Aid Plan through: its membership on a joint committee of senior ministry and plan officials; its representation on the Clinic Funding Committee, which is responsible to the Law Society of Upper Canada for administering and developing legal aid clinics in Ontario; its efforts which have led to federal cost-sharing for civil legal aid and to an improved agreement by which the federal government shares some of the costs of criminal legal aid; its participation in the Legal Aid Mediation Project, whose purpose is to monitor the cost and social benefits of mediation in the legal aid context; and, its contribution, with the Law Society of Upper Canada and the Legal Aid Plan officials, to the devlopment of amendments to the Legal Aid Regulation and tariff.

*Office of the Public Complaints Commissioner:* With the establishment in 1981 of this office, through the *Metropolitan Toronto Police Force Complaints Act,* a new degree of openness and accountability to police discipline matters has been demonstrated. Members of the public in Metropolitan Toronto have the benefit of an outside, impartial review of the way in which their complaints about police misconduct are handled. At the same time, police officers against whom an improper allegation is made can be cleared in a process which is open, visible, and credible to the public. Legislation has been recently introduced proposing to make this important justice initiative available to municipalities which elect to have the Office of the Public complaints Commissioner exercise jurisdiction in respect to local complaints.

*Official Guardian:* Represents the civil rights of persons under a legal disability, usually children under 18 years of age, the mentally incompetent, as well as unborn and absentee persons. The Official Guardian also makes recommendations to the Court regarding the care, custody, and maintenance of children in divorce cases, and provides them with legal protection.

*Ontario Native Justice of the Peace Program:* Promotes the appointment of justices of the peace of native ancestry in areas of the province where high numbers of aboriginal people are residing or appearing before the courts.

*Provincial Offences Act:* This legislation substantially improved established procedures for dealing with the very large number of offences committed annually under provincial statutes, the largest number being violations under the *Highway Traffic Act.* Through the Provincial Offences Act, the process is made more efficient and effective. The act also provides persons charged with offences with important new procedures to exercise their rights to dispute the charges in a more convenient and accessible forum.

*Public Trustee:* Manages the estates of mentally incompetent persons (mainly those in psychiatric hospitals and facilities for the developmentally handicapped), and the estates of Ontarians who die intestate, without adult next-of-kin in Ontario.

*Support and Custody Enforcement:* Following the proclamation of the *Support and Custody Orders Enforcement Act,* the Office of the Director of Support and Custody Enforcement was established. This Branch is responsible for locating support defaulters; investigating the ability to pay; enforcing payments, through discussions with defaulters, garnishments, seizure of assets, and liens on property; attending at court; enforcing custody; and, is responsible for handling more than a hundred million dollars of payments. There are six regional offices throughout the province. Besides benefitting more than 100,000 persons who are owed support payments and are expected to register with local enforcement offices in the province, the program also reduces costs to municipal and provincial welfare systems.

*Impact Statement Pilot Project:* The Ministry of the Attorney General, in January of 1987, announced, in coordination with the Metropolitan Toronto Police Force, the development of this project. The Project's purpose is to provide the victim with the opportunity to express his or her views regarding the physical, emotional, and economic impact of the offence directly to the prosecutor and/or the presiding judge. This Project is designed to last for eighteen months during which a formal evaluation will be conducted to ascertain whether the Ministry of the Attorney General, in conjunction with the Solicitor General of Ontario, will work toward a province-wide implementation of the introduction of these statements.

*Victim/Witness Assistance Program:* This program provides a more comprehensive service to victims and witnesses in order to enhance their understanding of and participation in the criminal justice process. Ten victim/witness coordinators are located across the province and work in cooperation with the local Crown Attorney. These coordinators work in conjunction with available community services to provide valuable assistance to victims and witnesses through addressing specific requests for information and assistance and coordination of existing community resources.

## EXPENDITURE ESTIMATES

*Estimated Expenditures 1987–88*:

| | |
|---|---:|
| Law Officer of the Crown | $ 7,537,238 |
| Administrative Services | 95,389,000 |
| Guardian and Trustee Services | 13,107,300 |
| Crown Legal Services | 42,336,100 |
| Legislative Counsel Services | 2,663,900 |
| Courts Administration | 169,617,700 |
| Administrative Tribunals | 16,031,400 |
| **Ministry total:** | **$346,682,638** |

## AGENCIES, BOARDS, AND COMMISSIONS

The following ABCs report to the Legislative Assembly through the Attorney General:

*Assessment Review Board:* Responsible for the processing and scheduling of complaints and appeals against assessments, appeals against school support and for the certification of the last revised assessment roll of each municipality in Ontario. The board accepts appeals from its decisions for transmittal to the Ontario Municipal Board.

*Board of Negotiation:* Responsible for providing an informal tribunal, to either a property owner or an expropriating authority, which may act as a mediator to negotiate a settlement when real property is expropriated and no agreement can be reached on compensation for the expropriation.

*Criminal Injuries Compensation Board:* Responsible for providing compensation to eligible applicants when a person is injured or killed in Ontario as a result of an unprovoked act of criminal violence. The board administers the *Compensation for Victims of Crime Act, 1971.* Hearings are held in Toronto and at other centres across the province at various times throughout the year.

*Office of the Public Complaints Commissioner:* Responsible for receiving, recording, and investigating complaints from the public against police officers on the Metropolitan Toronto Police Force; monitors and reviews the completed investigations and the discipline decisions taken by the force; may recommend changes in police practices and procedures and law; and, if in the public interest, can order that an independent civilian board of inquiry hold a public hearing into a case.

*Ontario Law Reform Commission:* Responsible for maintaining a continuous review of the law of Ontario. The commission inquires into any matter relating to law reform, the administration of justice, or judicial and quasi-judicial procedures, and conducts legal research. Reports containing recommendations for changes in the law are submitted to the Attorney General.

*Ontario Municipal Board:* Responsible for hearing applications and appeals concerning municipal and planning matters such as: zoning by-laws, subdivision plans, official plans and consents, and minor variances under the *Planning Act*; assessment appeals under the *Assessment Act*; land compensation matters under the *Expropriations Act*; and municipal capital expenditures and debentures under the *Municipal Act*. The Ontario Municipal Board is an independent administrative tribunal.

## LEGISLATION

The Ministry of the Attorney General is responsible for the following Acts:

*Absconding Debtors Act:* Sets out the procedures in law for dealing with the property of those who leave Ontario with the intent to defraud their creditors, or to avoid being arrested or served with process.

*Absentees Act:* Provides a mechanism for the management of property of a person who has disappeared.

*Accidental Fires Act:* Prohibits the bringing of an action against a person on whose property there has been an accidental fire.

*Accumulations Act:* Limits the power of a trust to accumulate the proceeds of its investments.

*Administration of Justice Act:* Authorizes the making of regulations establishing fees for services related to the administration of justice.

*Age of Majority and Accountability Act:* Sets out the age of majority as 18 years of age.

*Aliens' Real Property Act:* Provides that aliens have the same rights to own and transfer real property as Canadian citizens.

*Arbitrations Act:* Provides basic rules governing the private settlement of disputes by arbitration.

*Architects Act, 1984:* Establishes the Architects Association as the self-governing licensing organization for architects and provides for their governance and discipline.

*Assessment Review Board Act:* Sets up the Assessment Review Board which reviews the assessments of real property.

*Bail Act:* Provides for the registration of security on land for the payment of bail.

*rristers Act:* Provides for the order in which counsel will be heard in the courts and for the appointment of Queen's Counsel.

*Blind Persons' Rights Act:* Requires the admission of a blind person together with his or her guide dog to any place to which the public is customarily admitted and prohibits discrimination in accommodation and services.

*Bulk Sales Act:* Sets out the requirements necessary in a sale of the stock of a business.

*Business Records Protection Act:* Restricts the ability of businesses to remove business records from Ontario.

*Charitable Gifts Act:* Requires a charity to dispose of gifts to it that involve a substantial interest in an operating business.

*Charities Accounting Act:* Provides for the supervision of charities by the Public Trustee of Ontario and allows the court to control the process.

*Children's Law Reform Act:* Declares that all children have equal status regardless of whether they are born inside or outside marriage; ensures that applications with respect to custody are determined on the basis of the best interests of the child; discourages child abduction; and, provides for enforcement of custody and access orders.

*Commissioners for Taking Affidavits Act:* Provides for the appointment of Commissioners for Taking Affidavits and regulates their activities.

*Compensation for Victims of Crime Act:* Establishes the Criminal Injuries Compensation Board and provides it with the authority to compensate victims of crime.

*Construction Lien Act, 1983:* Protects the interests of those who supply services and materials for the improvement of immovable property.

*Conveyancing and Law of Property Act:* Amends, qualifies, and supplements the common law rules that deal with the ownership and transfer of property.

*Costs of Distress Act:* Regulates the amount of fees and the costs payable to a person that seizes goods.

*Courts of Justice Act, 1984:* Sets up the courts in Ontario and states what their jurisdiction is.

*Creditors' Relief Act:* Regulates the distribution of money that the Sheriff receives as a result of garnishment or seizure.

*Crown Administration of Estates Act:* Provides that the Crown may administer estates of people dying without wills and with no known next-of-kin and sets out the rules for doing so.

*Crown Agency Act:* Provides that companies, boards, and certain other entities owned or controlled by the Crown are agents of the Crown.

*Crown Attorneys Act:* Provides for the appointment of Crown Attorneys and their responsibilities.

*Crown Witnesses Act:* Provides for the payment of fees and expenses of witnesses who appear at the request of the Crown.

*Disorderly Houses Act:* Permits the court to order the closing of gaming or bawdy houses.

*Dog Owner's Liability Act:* Governs the liability of dog owners for the actions of their dogs.

*Dower and Miscellaneous Abolition Act:* Formerly known as the Family Law Reform Act. Important only in terms of family law transition, (see Family Law Act, 1986).

*Escheats Act:* Regulates the disposal of property which has escheated to the Crown. (i.e. reverted to Crown because there are no legal heirs).

*Estates Administration Act:* Contains a number of provisions governing executors and trustees administering the estate of a deceased person.

*Evidence Act:* Provides rules for the admissibility of evidence in court proceedings.

*Execution Act:* Sets out the property which a Sheriff may or may not seize under a writ of seizure and sale issued by a court.

*Expropriations Act:* Provides safeguards for compensation where legislation authorizes the taking of property.

*Family Law Act, 1986:* Provides rules for the division of family property upon the breakdown of a marriage or death of one spouse, rules governing the matrimonial home, support obligations between the spouses, provisions with respect to domestic contracts, and dependant's claims for damages.

*Fines and Forfeitures Act:* Provides for the collection of fines where there is no other mechanism available to the Crown.

*Foreign Arbitral Awards Act, 1986:* Implements in Ontario the New York Convention on the recognition and enforcement of foreign arbitral awards.

*Fraudulent Conveyances Act:* Allows the courts to set aside transactions that were completed with the intention of defrauding or hindering the creditors of a person.

*Fraudulent Debtors Arrest Act:* Provides for the arrest of persons who are about to leave the province with the intention of defrauding their creditors.

*Frustrated Contracts Act:* Provides rules relating to the rights of the parties to a contract, if, after entering into the contract, it becomes impossible to keep.

*Gaming Act:* Provides that gambling debts cannot be enforced.

*Habeas Corpus Act:* Allows a person to apply to the Supreme Court of Ontario to determine whether they are being lawfully detained.

*Hospitals and Charitable Institutions Inquiries Act:* Permits the Lieutenant Governor in Council to establish an inquiry into any matter connected with hospitals or charitable institutions.

*Hotel Registration of Guests Act:* Requires hotels to keep registers of guests and to post notices of room rates.

*Innkeepers Act:* Gives innkeepers power to seize and sell goods of guests who do not pay their bills and deals with the liability of an innkeeper for loss or injury to goods of a guest.

*Interpretation Act:* Used as a tool to interpret other acts of the legislature. It contains a guide to interpretation and a number of definitions of terms used in other acts.

*Interprovincial Subpoenas Act:* Allows the courts in Ontario to summon witnesses in other provinces to appear and also allows for the courts in other provinces to have their witnesses summoned. This statute operates on a reciprocal basis.

*Judicial Review Procedure Act:* Sets out the procedure to have the Supreme Court of Ontario review the decision of an administrative tribunal. Comparable to an appeal, the review can only be for fundamental errors of law made by the tribunal.

*Juries Act:* States who is eligible and who is not, to be on a jury, and provides the procedure for summoning people to serve on a jury.

*Justices of the Peace Act:* Provides for the appointment and powers of Justices of the Peace.

*Landlord and Tenant Act:* Provides some statutory regulation of both commercial and residential tenancies.

*Law Society Act:* Establishes the Law Society of Upper Canada as the self-governing licensing organization for lawyers and provides for their governance and discipline.

*Legal Aid Act:* Sets up the Ontario Legal Aid Plan and provides some of the basic rules of eligibility for legal aid.

*Libel and Slander Act:* Governs the bringing of an action for defamation.

*Limitations Act:* Establishes time periods governing the time within which various claims must be made to the court.

*Master and Servant Act:* Sets out some procedures for the recovery of wages which have not been paid by an employer.

*Mechanics' Lien Act:* The law recognizes the right of persons who improve personal property to retain that property until paid for the improvement. Section 52 provides for a sale to recover the value of the improvement.

*Mental Incompetency Act:* Authorizes the courts to appoint a committee of the estate (manager) and a committee of the person (guardian) for a person who is found mentally incompetent.

*Mercantile Law Amendment Act:* Provides certain rules to interpret commercial agreements.

*Metropolitan Toronto Police Force Complaints Act, 1984:* Establishes the Office of the Public Complaints Commissioner and the procedure for the independent investigation of complaints against the Metropolitan Toronto Police Force.

*Ministry of the Attorney General Act:* Sets out by statute a number of the powers, functions, and duties of the Attorney General.

*Minors' Protection Act:* Prohibits the sale of tobacco to minors.

*Mobility Rights Statute Law Amendment Act, 1985:* This act amends eight Ontario statutes containing a provincial residency requirement as a condition of employment, in order to bring Ontario legislation into line with section 6 of the Canadian Charter of Rights and Freedoms.

*Mortgages Act:* Provides the procedures for enforcing a mortgage when the mortgagor does not pay on time.

*Negligence Act:* Provides rules for the sharing of liability among parties to negligence claims.

*Notaries Act:* Provides for the appointment of Notaries Public.

*Occupiers' Liability Act:* Replaces the common law duties of an occupier of property with a duty of occupiers to take reasonable care for the safety of entrants on their property.

*Ontario Law Reform Commission Act:* Establishes the Ontario Law Reform Commission.

*Ontario Municipal Board Act:* Creates the Ontario Municipal Board and gives it the power to review municipal official plans, zoning by-laws, and other land use policies.

*Partition Act:* Provides for the physical division or the division of the sale proceeds of any property that is jointly owned by two or more people.

*Pawnbrokers Act:* Regulates pawnbrokers.

*Perpetuities Act:* Important in estates and trusts. Invalidates gifts if the identity of the recipient of the gift is not definitely known within a prescribed period of time.

*Powers of Attorney Act:* Regulates the giving of powers of attorney.

*Proceedings Against the Crown Act:* Provides procedures for suing the Government of Ontario.

*Professional Engineers Act, 1984:* Establishes the Professional Engineers Association as the self-governing licensing organization for engineers and provides for their governance and discipline.

*Property and Civil Rights Act:* Contains some provisions from the Magna Carta that is part of the law of England, and now Ontario, since 1215.

*Provincial Offences Act:* Establishes the procedures applicable to the prosecution of offences against provincial statutes and municipal by-laws.

*Public Accountancy Act:* Provides for the licensing and regulation of public accounting which is the provision of a statement by an accountant to add credibility to the accounting records of an individual or corporation.

*Public Authorities Protection Act:* Establishes a six-month limitation period for suing a person acting in pursuance of a public duty and deals with circumstances in which a Justice of the Peace will be liable.

*Public Halls Act:* Requires a licence for the use of a public hall as a place of public assembly.

*Public Inquiries Act:* Provides for the powers and procedures applicable to commissions appointed to conduct public inquiries.

*Public Institutions Inspection Act:* Provides for the inspection of public institutions.

*Public Officers Act:* Requires persons holding public office to swear allegiance to Her Majesty the Queen.

*Public Trustee Act:* Establishes the Public Trustee as a manager of the property of mentally incompetent persons, absentees, and persons dying in Ontario who have no other person willing to undertake the function of manager. The Public Trustee also supervises charities.

*Reciprocal Enforcement of Judgments Act:* Allows the registration and enforcement in Ontario of the judgment of other courts in the provinces and territories in Canada.

*Reciprocal Enforcement of Judgments (U.K.) Act, 1984:* Allows the registration and enforcement in Ontario of the judgment of other courts in the United Kingdom.

*Reciprocal Enforcement of Maintenance Orders Act:* Provides a framework for the enforcement of maintenance orders between jurisdictions which have entered into agreements with Ontario to do so.

*Regulations Act:* Provides for the procedures involved in the making and indexing of regulations.

*Religious Freedom Act:* Declares that every person is free to practice his or her religion.

*Religious Organizations' Lands Act:* Provides a convenient way for religious congregations to own land for the purpose of a place of worship.

*Sale of Goods Act:* Provides rules to govern contracts for the sale of goods.

*Settled Estates Act:* Provides that a court may order that lands tied up in certain ways by wills and trusts may be used by certain persons under a court-approved lease.

*Sheriffs Act:* Provides for the appointment of Sheriffs and regulates their activities.

*Short Forms of Conveyances Act:* Provides short forms of language that may be used in land deals.

*Short Forms of Leases Act:* Provides short forms of language that may be used in leases.

*Short Forms of Mortgages Act:* Provides short forms of language that may be used in mortgages.

*Solicitors Act:* Prohibits the unauthorized practice of law and provides a procedure by which clients of lawyers can have lawyers fees assessed by an independent officer.

*Statute of Frauds:* Requires certain legal documents to be in writing.

*Statutes Act:* Principle purpose is to require statutes to be printed by the Queen's Printer.

*Statutory Powers Procedure Act:* Provides minimum procedural standards that must be complied with by administrative tribunals.

*Succession Law Reform Act:* Establishes rules for the division of property on the death of a person with or without a will, and a dependent's claims for support from an estate as well as technical provisions for the drafting of wills.

*Support and Custody Orders Enforcement Act:* Provides for the creation of an office that has the power to enforce support and custody orders on behalf of a spouse or parent at no cost.

*Surrogate Courts Act:* Sets up and states the jurisdiction of our Surrogate Courts which are responsible for probating wills and appointing persons to administer estates.

*Ticket Speculation Act:* Prohibits speculation in selling tickets to attractions.

*Time Act:* Prescribes the hour observed in Ontario's two time-zones and provides for the observance of standard and daylight-saving time.

*Transboundary Pollution Reciprocal Access Act, 1985:* Permits persons injured outside Ontario by pollution originating from Ontario to sue in Ontario provided their jurisdiction affords similar rights to Ontario residents.

*Trespass to Property Act:* Permits the occupier of property to control access and use of that property.

*Trustee Act:* Governs the standard of conduct of trustees and limits the investments in which they may put trust funds.

*Unconscionable Transactions Relief Act:* Allows a court to alter the terms of loan contracts if the court finds that the cost of the loan is excessive and the transaction is harsh and unconscionable.

*University Expropriation Powers Act:* Gives Universities the power to expropriate land.

*Variation of Trusts Act:* Permits a court to vary the terms of a trust in certain circumstances.

*Vendors and Purchasers Act:* Provides for an application to court to determine any question arising out of a contract for the sale of land.

*Wages Act:* Provides certain protections for wage earners in that it exempts a portion of wages from garnishment and gives wage earners priority over other creditors of an employer.

*Warehouse Receipts Act:* Regulates transactions involving warehouse receipts.

*Warehousemen's Lien Act:* Gives a warehouseman a lien on goods it stores and provides for its enforcement.

## INNOVATIONS

A major aim of the Ministry of the Attorney General is to make the court system more comprehensible to and convenient for the general public. The administration of justice must not merely be efficient, it must be understandable and accessible, to citizens across Ontario.

One way in which the Ministry has tried to help the public understand our court system and any new legislation is through the Communications Branch, which is responsible for all public education and media relations activities within the ministry. It coordinates the researching, writing, designing, printing, and distribution of all public information materials emanating from the Ministry. This material includes films, brochures, pamphlets, and promotional items.

*Courthouses Facilities Planning and Maintenance:* Throughout the years the Ministry of the Attorney General has been concerned with the ever-increasing demands placed on the courts as a result of constitutional and legislative changes. These increasing demands have caused, in some instances, overcrowded court facilities and increased demands on legal officers, the judiciary, and administrative personnel.

With the need for the Ministry to be represented province-wide in order to provide the citizens of Ontario with convenient access to the courts, there has been a strain placed on the administration of justice due to greater burdens continually being placed on the existing system. To this end, the Ministry has undertaken to establish a strategic plan, based on consistent principles, to provide and maintain courtroom facilities over the next generation that are consistent with the needs shown in each judicial district.

In 1986, the Ministry appointed the Honourable Mr Justice Thomas Zuber to conduct an Inquiry into the organization, jurisdiction, and structure of the courts of Ontario. The report from this Inquiry, released in the August 1987, has provided the Ministry of the Attorney General with the groundwork upon which Ontario's court system can be rebuilt. Mr Justice Zuber was asked to examine all matters dealing with access to the courts by the public, the provision of service by the courts to the public, and to make recommendations for the provision of a simpler, more convenient, more expeditious, and less costly legal system. It is anticipated by the Ministry that the impact of Mr Justice Zuber's report on the Ontario court system will be significant.

# MINISTRY OF CONSUMER AND COMMERCIAL RELATIONS

## ROLES AND FUNCTIONS

The Ministry of Consumer and Commercial Relations regulates interactions between consumers and businesses in Ontario. The Ministry is responsible for over fifty Acts and related regulations which affect many businesses and virtually every citizen in the Province. The Ministry's objectives include licensing, registration, and inspection of business establishments to promote a high level of ethical business conduct; licensing and inspection of technical and operational situations to ensure public safety; registration of documents related to all aspects of real and personal property ownership; collecting data, and providing an efficient system of public information in the registration of vital statistics, property, and companies; applying standards for public entertainment in the areas of film, lotteries, athletics, and horse-racing; and developing and operating an efficient and socially responsible system of liquor distribution and licensing by controlling the use and availability of beverage alcohol.

## BACKGROUND HISTORY

The Ministry of Consumer and Commercial Relations (MCCR) was established in November, 1966, as the Department of Financial and Commercial Affairs. It consisted of three divisions: Consumer Protection, Superintendent of Insurance, and the Ontario Securities Commission. It was assigned the responsibility for thirteen Acts previously assigned to the Attorney General and the Ministry of Justice. The Department pioneered the first Consumer Protection Bureau in 1967 to administer the *Consumer Protection Act.*

The importance of consumer protection issues grew as the Ontario economy expanded through the 1970s, and the scope of the activities of the Ministry of Consumer and Commercial Relations (as the Department was renamed after an extensive reorganization in 1972) kept pace. The Ontario Pension Commission was established in 1976, and the Ministry grew in size with the creation of the Business Practices Division, the Technical Standards Division, and the Registration Division.

By the mid-1980s, MCCR was responsible for administering over seventy pieces of legislation dealing with registration, public safety, and consumer protection. The Financial Institutions Division was separated from the Ministry in March 1986, to create the Ministry of Financial Institutions (MFI). MCCR continues to provide administrative support to the new Ministry, and, until the September 1987 election in Ontario, the Minister of Consumer and Commercial Relations was "double-hatted" as Minister of Financial Institutions. MCCR and MFI now have separate ministers and deputy ministers.

## ORGANIZATION

The Ministry of Consumer and Commercial Relations is organized into four divisions (see organization chart):

1. *Business Practices:* Ensures ethical business practices in a variety of industries, such as real estate, automobile dealers, debt collection, mortgage brokers, and paperback and periodical publishers, and operates the Consumer Advisory Bureaux.

2. *Registration:* Provides for the registration of interests in property through a network of registry offices, and is responsible for the collection of vital statistics in the province.

3. *Technical Standards:* Responsible for setting design standards for equipment and machinery which may affect public safety, and for carrying out inspections to ensure that safety standards are met.

4. *Support Services:* Coordinates communications, finance and administration, audit, and personnel support for the Ministry of Consumer and Commercial Relations and the Ministry of Financial Institutions.

In addition, five agencies, boards, and commissions, including the Liquor License Board, the Commercial Registration Appeals Tribunal, and the Ontario Film Board report to the Legislative Assembly through the Minister of Consumer and Commercial Relations (see Agencies, Boards, and Commissions).

The head office of the Ministry of Consumer and Commercial Relations is located in Toronto, with branches spread out among six locations in the city. The Ministry also delivers its programs through five regional offices, eight Consumer Advisory Bureaux, and 65 land registry offices located throughout Ontario. The Ministry employs approximately 1,700 public servants.

## PROGRAMS

**Business Practices Division**

Consumer protection is the primary role of the Business Practices Division. Questionable business practices are investigated and consumer concerns are monitored as they develop. The Division administers 15 Acts, including the *Business Practices Act*, which prohibits companies from making representations that are false, unconscionable, deceptive, or misleading; the *Bailiffs Act, Cemeteries Act,*

MINISTRY OF CONSUMER AND COMMERCIAL RELATIONS

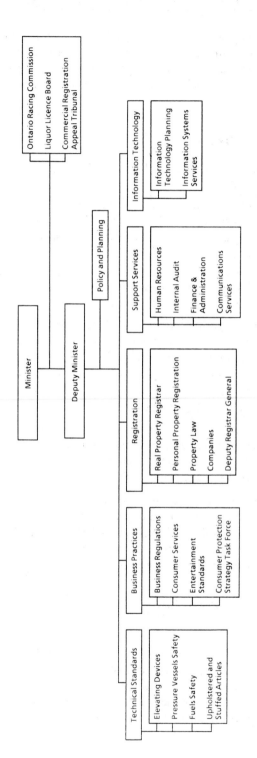

*Collection Agencies Act, Condominium Act, Consumer Protection Act, Consumer Reporting Act, Discriminatory Business Practices Act, Motor Vehicle Dealers Act, Paperback and Periodical Distributors Act, Prearranged Funeral Services Act, Real Estate and Business Brokers Act, Residential Complex Sales Representation Act,* and *Travel Industry Act.* The Division is comprised of five Branches and a Commissioner:

*Bailiffs, Collection Agencies, Condominiums, Consumer Reporting, Debt Collectors, Discriminatory Business Practices, Mortgage Brokers, Paperback and Periodical Distributors:* Administers the corresponding Acts. The Branch ensures the protection of Ontario consumers through controls and supervision of bailiffs, collection agencies, consumer reporting agencies (credit and personal information investigation), mortgage brokers, and distributors of paperback books and periodicals. This office also arranges appointments of bailiffs.

*Consumer Advisory Services Branch:* Provides advice and mediation of consumer complaints under eleven Acts dealing with consumer protection. The Central Registration Section maintains a central file of registered businesses and answers public inquiries as to whether a business is registered under the appropriate Acts. The Branch operates a network of Consumer Advisory Bureaux in eight locations (Toronto, Ottawa, Hamilton, London, Windsor, Thunder Bay, Sudbury, and Peterborough) to answer consumer inquiries and attempt to mediate disputes arising from the purchase of goods or services, borrowing money, and deceptive or unfair business practices.

*Investigation and Enforcement Branch:* Assists in the administration of various registration Acts by conducting investigations and inspections of businesses and persons covered under the Acts administered by the Ministry.

*Athletics Commissioner:* Administers the *Athletics Control Act,* and is responsible for the proper conduct of all professional combative sports (boxing, kickboxing, wrestling) in Ontario.

*Lotteries Branch:* Supervises, controls, and issues licenses to all lottery, bingo, raffle, and games of chance operators in Ontario covered by the *Criminal Code of Canada.* The Ontario Lottery Corporation reports to the Ministry of Tourism and Recreation.

*Theatres Branch:* Administers the *Theatres Act,* and is responsible for ensuring the safety of theatre-goers in Ontario by licensing and inspecting theatres, testing projectionists, and licensing film distributors and retailers; is responsible for the approval for public exhibition and distribution of all films and videos through the Ontario Film Board, and the approval of all printed advertising related to the public exhibition of film.

## Registration Division

*Companies Branch:* Provides for the incorporation, dissolution, and revival of companies and non-profit organizations, and for the registration of partnerships and proprietorships.

*Personal Property Registration Branch:* Manages the Personal Property Registration System, whereby the seller of personal property or a lender of money can secure the purchase price or the loan by registering a financial statement at any of 49 of the 65 Registry Offices in the province. As well, purchasers can determine, when buying personal property or accepting it as collateral for a loan, whether there is a security interest (lien) on the property by filing an inquiry.

*Real Property Registration Branch:* Is responsible for the management and operation of 65 land registry offices in Ontario, which register, store, and preserve documents, deeds, mortgages, and surveys relating to the ownership of real property. All records are available to the public, for a fee.

*Registrar General Branch:* Registers and records Ontario births, deaths, marriages, name changes, adoptions, and divorces. Statistics are compiled annually. Wallet-size, paper, and certified photocopies of birth, marriage, and death certificates are provided to entitled applicants for a fee.

## Technical Standards Divison

*Elevating Devices Branch:* Licenses, inspects on a regular basis and develops a safety code for elevating devices, including elevators, escalators, dumbwaiters, moving walkways, platform lifts, ski lifts, lifts for the disabled, and construction hoists under the *Elevating Devices Act.* Contractors installing, maintaining, and repairing such devices must be registered with the Branch. Accidents and consumer complaints are also investigated.

*Fuels Safety Branch:* Administers the *Ontario Energy Act* and the *Gasoline Handling Act.* This Branch strives to prevent loss of life, bodily injury, and property damage by controlling potential safety hazards in the transportation, handling, storage, and utilization of hydrocarbon fuels (natural gas, propane, fuel oil, and gasoline). The Branch issues licenses to service stations; propane facilities; and natural gas and propane handlers, fitters and mechanics.

*Pressure Vessels Safety Branch:* Administers the *Boilers and Pressure Vessels Act* and the *Operating Engineers Act.* This Branch strives to prevent loss of life, bodily injury, and property damage arising from the operation of boilers and pressure vessels by ensuring safety in design, welding procedure, fabrication, installation, and repair. The Branch issues licenses to welders and to operating engineers in steam, refrigeration, and compression plants, and investigates accidents.

*Upholstered and Stuffed Articles Branch:* Administers the *Upholstered and Stuffed Articles Act* and ensures safety by registering renovators and manufacturers, and inspecting premises of registrants and retailers of upholstered and stuffed articles. The Branch also investigates consumer complaints about upholstered and stuffed furniture, mattresses, pillows, clothing materials, and toys.

## EXPENDITURE ESTIMATES

*Estimated Expenditures 1987–88*:

| | |
|---|---|
| Ministry Administration | $13,325,738 |
| Commercial Standards | 10,986,000 |
| Technical Standards | 10,597,500 |
| Public Entertainment Standards | 36,498,900 |
| Registration | 46,965,200 |
| Liquor Licence | 8,238,600 |
| **Ministry total:** | **$126,611,938** |

## AGENCIES, BOARDS, AND COMMISSIONS

The following ABCs report to the Legislative Assembly through the Minister of Consumer and Commercial Relations:

*Commercial Registration Appeals Tribunal:* Holds public hearings on appeals to review administrative decisions denying, refusing to renew, suspending, or revoking registration of individuals and corporations. It also hears appeals to review government-originated cease and desist orders respecting advertising, selling, and unfair business practices, by real estate brokers and agents, mortgage brokers, motor vehicle dealers and salespersons, bailiffs, consumer credit reporting agencies, collection agencies, itinerant sellers, manufacturers and renovators of upholstered and stuffed articles, distributors of paperback books and periodicals, travel agents, and wholesalers. The Tribunal also holds public hearings on appeals from persons aggrieved by Liquor Licence Board decisions on licensing.

*Liquor Control Board of Ontario* (LCBO): Through over 600 retail stores across Ontario, the LCBO distributes and retails spirits, wine, and beer to consumers and licensed establishments. The LCBO also places private orders for brands not normally carried in its stores, offers free product advice to consumers by experienced wine consultants, and provides a wide selection of fine wines and spirits in its Vintage stores and the "Vintage Sections" of regular liquor stores. For travellers leaving the country, the LCBO operates two duty-free stores at Pearson International Airport. The LCBO also authorizes the sale of Ontario beer through the Brewers' Retail stores and Ontario wine through Ontario winery stores. Unlike the majority of ABCs in the Government of Ontario, the operations of the LCBO are financed by its own revenue.

*Liquor Licence Board of Ontario* (LLBO): Issues licenses, renews, transfers, suspends, and revokes liquor licenses for on-premise sale and consumption of alcoholic beverages. The LLBO also regulates alcoholic beverage advertising and inspects all licensed establishments in Ontario.

*Ontario Film Review Board:* The Board approves and classifies films and videos shown to the public in Ontario, on the basis of guidelines established by the *Theatres Act.* The Board is administered by the Theatres Branch of the Business Practices Division.

*Ontario Racing Commission* (ORC): Supervises and controls the racing of horses in Ontario. The ORC licenses all racetrack operators and racing participants. The Commission holds public hearings on appeals to review rulings issued by Commission Judges and Stewards officiating at races. The ORC also administers the *Race Tracks Tax Sharing Arrangement,* a program which returns approximately $20 million a year to the racing industry in the form of purse supplements, breeding incentive programs, and research grants.

## LEGISLATION

The Ministry of Consumer and Commercial Relations is responsible for the following Acts:

*Apportionment Act:* Defines and provides for the accrual, apportionment, and payment of dividends, rents, annuities, and other payments in the nature of income.

*Assignments and Preferences Act:* Provides that assignments take preference over attachments, garnishee orders, and judgements, and sets out a scheme for the distribution of money and determination of claims arising out of an assignment.

*Athletics Control Act:* MCCR is responsible for administering those parts of the Act which relate to boxing and wrestling, specifically the supervision of professional contests and exhibitions including the licensing of boxing and wrestling contests and of the participants.

*Bailiffs Act:* Provides for the appointment of bailiffs by the Lieutenant Governor in Council on the recommendation of the Minister. It also requires that bailiffs be bonded and that they keep certain accounting records.

*Bills of Sale Act:* Provides that every sale of goods not accompanied by an immediate delivery and followed by a change of possession shall be evidenced in writing and registered.

*Boundaries Act:* Provides for the establishment and confirmation of undefined, dubious, and disputed boundaries on the application of an owner, municipal council, or other official.

*Bread Sales Act:* Requires the council of every city, town, village, or township to license bakers and to appoint an inspector to enforce the provisions of the Act with respect to bread weights and contents.

*Business Corporations Act:* Provides the basic statutory framework governing private and public commercial share capital corporations in Ontario. Corporate information regarding incorporation, fundamental changes, and dissolutions are made available to the public.

*Business Practices Act:* Prohibits unfair business practices, including false, misleading, deceptive, unreasonable, and unconscionable consumer representations, and permits the rescission of contracts induced by unfair practices.

*Cemeteries Act:* Requires approval by the Ministry for the establishment or enlargement of cemeteries, provides for the licensing of salesmen of cemetery plots, and sets rules for the administration of cemeteries and perpetual care funds.

*Certification of Titles Act:* Provides that an owner of land which is subject to the *Registry Act* may apply for a certificate guaranteeing the title of that land, and establishes the Certification of Titles Assurance Fund to compensate persons having interest in land who suffer a loss by reason of a title having been certified under the Act by error or oversight.

*Collection Agencies Act:* Provides for the registration of collection agencies and collectors, for the handling of complaints, and for inspection of a registrant's financial affairs.

*Condominium Act:* Provides for the creation, operation, management, and termination of condominium corporations and establishes rules for the registration and sale of condominium units.

*Consumer Protection Act:* Provides for the registration of itinerant sellers, for the investigation of complaints, and for the inspection of a registrant's financial affairs. The Act also provides for the disclosure of information in a credit transaction, and restricts the right of repossession by a seller after two-thirds of the purchase price has been paid.

*Consumer Protection Bureau Act:* Establishes the Bureau as a branch of MCCR to disseminate consumer information, promote credit counselling services, investigate consumer complaints, and enforce legislation for the protection of consumers.

*Consumer Reporting Act:* Provides for the registration of consumer reporting agencies, and prescribes rules concerning information that may be provided, persons to whom information may be given, and mechanisms for correcting information.

*Corporation Securities Registration Act:* Provides a register of mortgages and charges of chattels in Ontario created by corporations, and assignments of book debts made by corporations engaged in business in Ontario

*Corporations Act:* Provides for the basic statutory framework governing not-for-profit non-share charities and social clubs.

*Corporations Information Act:* Provides for the filing of information notices by corporations regarding officers and directors, and for the registration of corporate business style names. Information is maintained for public inquiry.

*Debt Collectors Act:* Prohibits the printing, publishing, or use of forms which imitate any form appended to the *Small Claims Court Act* or which imitate forms used in any other legal process.

*Discriminatory Business Practices Act:* Designed to prevent discrimination in the business community on the basis of race, creed, colour, nationality, ancestry, place of origin, sex, or geographical location of a person. The Act provides for orders for compliance, and for rights to compensation for loss or damage incurred.

*Elevating Devices Act:* Provides for the inspection and licensing of all elevating devices and for the approval of specifications and plans for their construction.

*Energy Act:* Provides for the licensing of persons who handle hydrocarbons and contractors who install or repair appliances that use hydrocarbons.

*Extra-Provincial Corporations Act:* Provides for the licensing of corporations incorporated under the laws of a jurisdiction outside Canada and carrying on business in Ontario.

*Factors Act:* Validates the sale of goods by a mercantile agent who is in possession of the goods with the consent of the owner, whether or not the owner has consented to the sale of the goods.

*Gasoline Handling Act:* Provides for the approval of equipment and containers used in the handling of gasoline and associated products, and for the licensing of persons: who operate service stations, marinas, and bulk plants; who install equipment in such locations; and who transport gasoline.

*Land Registration Reform Act:* Provides simplified procedures and forms for the registration of interests in land.

*Land Titles Act:* Establishes a system for the registration of interests in land, and provides a procedure for unregistered Crown land or land subject to the *Registry Act* to be certified and dealt with under the Act.

*Limited Partnerships Act:* Provides for the basic statutory framework governing limited partnerships created in Ontario or carrying on business in Ontario, and provides for a central registry of information available to the public.

*Liquor Control Act:* Authorizes the Liquor Control Board of Ontario to buy and sell liquor in Ontario and to authorize manufacturers of beer or Ontario wine to operate stores to sell their products.

*Liquor Licence Act:* Establishes the Liquor License Board of Ontario to issue licenses and permits for the sale of Liquor. The Act also provides that a municipal vote may be taken to determine whether government liquor stores be established or licenses to sell liquor issued within a municipality.

*Marriage Act:* Requires the issuance of a license prior to the solemnization of a marriage, empowers certain persons to issue marriage licenses, and provides for the registration of persons authorized to solemnize marriage.

*Ministry of Consumer and Commercial Relations Act:* Establishes and continues the Ministry, sets out the legislation for which the Ministry is responsible, constitutes the Commercial Registration Appeals Tribunal, and provides for the appointment of officers, clerks, and servants as are necessary for the proper conduct of the business of the Ministry.

*Motor Vehicle Dealers Act:* Provides for the registration of motor vehicle dealers and salesmen.

*Ontario New Home Warranties Plan Act:* Empowers a non-profit corporation to administer the Ontario New Home Warranties Plan. All vendors and builders of new homes are required to be registered; all new homes and the warranties concerning their construction must also be registered. Where an owner suffers financial loss resulting from the bankruptcy of the vendor or damage resulting from a breach of warranty, the owner is entitled to compensation from the Plan.

*Operating Engineers Act:* Provides for the registration, classification, and inspection of boilers, compressors, and plants, and prescribes requirements that must be fulfilled to obtain certificates of qualification as an operating engineer.

*Paperback and Periodical Distributors Act:* Provides for the registration of distributors of paperback and periodical publications.

*Partnerships Act:* Provides the basic statutory framework governing partnerships in Ontario, including formation and dissolution, as well as the relationships among partners and between partnerships and the public.

*Partnerships Registration Act:* Provides for a central registry of partnerships and sole proprietorships using business style names and engaged in business in Ontario in trading, manufacturing, or mining.

*Personal Property Security Act:* Establishes a system for the registration of security interests and assignments of book debts. It also prescribes rules governing the validity of security interests and outlines the rights of parties.

*Petroleum Products Price Freeze Act, 1975* (unrepealed): provided a mechanism for prescribing the sale price of petroleum products for the period June 23, 1975 to November 30, 1975.

*Prearranged Funeral Services Act:* Prohibits and provides penalties for anyone who pre-arranges funeral services while not licensed under the *Insurance Act.*

*Racing Commission Act:* Continues the Ontario Racing Commission and provides that the Commission govern, direct, control, and regulate horse racing in Ontario.

*Real Estate and Business Brokers Act:* Provides for the registration of all real estate brokers and sales agents. Trading in land located outside Ontario is prohibited unless a prospectus has been filed and a certificate of acceptance issued.

*Registry Act:* Establishes a system for registering notice of interests in land throughout Ontario, and provides for survey standards, plans, and descriptions of land.

*Residential Complex Sales Representation Act:* Prohibits vendors of apartment buildings containing more than six dwelling units from leading people to believe that they are buying a residential unit and/or the right to occupy a residential unit, if in fact they are only acquiring an interest in the building, unless the vendor makes a clear statement in respect of the right to occupancy.

*Theatres Act:* Provides for the appointment of the Ontario Film Board to approve films shown in Ontario, inspect and license theatres, license projectionists, and approve theatre building plans.

*Travel Industry Act:* Provides for the registration of travel agents and travel wholesalers, and establishes a compensation fund for clients who have not received the travel services for which they contracted.

*Unclaimed Articles Act:* Outlines the procedures to be followed for the disposal and sale of articles that have been deposited for storage, cleaning, repairing, or other treatment, and which have been unclaimed or for which the services remain unpaid after a period of time.

*Upholstered and Stuffed Articles Act:* Provides for the registration of manufacturers and renovators of upholstered and stuffed articles, and requires that prescribed labels be attached to upholstered and stuffed articles. The Act also prohibits certain kinds of stuffing.

*Vital Statistics Act:* Provides for the registration of births, still-births, marriages, deaths, adoption orders, changes of name, and divorce decrees which occur or have been granted in Ontario and aboard ships whose port of registry is Ontario. The Act also provides for the deposit of church records with the Registrar General, the correction of errors in registration, and for the issue of birth, death, and marriage certificates.

*Wine Content Act:* Permits the fixing of quotas and proportions of grapes grown outside of Ontario which may be used in the manufacture of wine in Ontario.

# MINISTRY OF CORRECTIONAL SERVICES

## ROLES AND FUNCTIONS

The role of the Ministry of Correctional Services is two-fold: to provide opportunities for offenders under sentence to adjust their behaviour in keeping with society's expectations, and to provide society with protection from unlawful behaviour.

The Ministry is responsible for male and female persons 18 years of age and over who are sentenced by the courts to prison terms of less than two years or probation terms of up to three years. It is also responsible for persons on remand awaiting trial or sentencing, persons being held for immigration hearings or deportation, and those awaiting transfer to federal institutions to serve sentences of two years or more. Under the federal *Young Offenders Act*, the Ministry also holds the responsibility for sixteen- and seventeen-year-old offenders, up to their eighteenth birthday. Those offenders under sixteen years of age are the responsibility of the Ministry of Community and Social Services.

## BACKGROUND HISTORY

The Ministry of Correctional Services was established in 1946. Known then as the Department of Reform Institutions, it operated facilities for male and female adults, and juvenile offenders.

In 1968, the name was changed to the Department of Correctional Services with the passing of the *Department of Correctional Services Act*, which consolidated all of the Acts relevant to the Ministry's operations. That year, the Province took over responsibility for all county and city jails in Ontario. In 1972, the name was changed to the Ministry of Correctional Services, and the Ministry gained responsibility for probation services from the Ministry of the Attorney General. In 1977, responsibility for juvenile offenders (those under 16 years of age) was transferred to the Ministry of Community and Social Services. Since that time, the Ministry has grown in size very rapidly. Today, the Ministry's Operations Division administers to close to 70 correctional institutions and detention facilities, and a network of 112 probation offices throughout the province.

MINISTRY OF CORRECTIONAL SERVICES

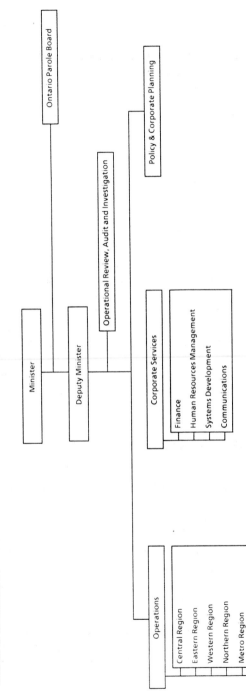

Ontario Parole Board

Minister

Deputy Minister

Operational Review, Audit and Investigation

Policy & Corporate Planning

Corporate Services
- Finance
- Human Resources Management
- Systems Development
- Communications

Operations
- Central Region
- Eastern Region
- Western Region
- Northern Region
- Metro Region
- Offender Programming & Operational Support

## ORGANIZATION

The Ministry of Correctional Services is organized into two major divisions (see organization chart):

*Corporate Services:* Provides services, such as finance and administration and human services, which support the Ministry in its activities.

*Operations:* Includes regional directors and the administration of jails, detention centres, correctional centres, and forestry camps:

1. *Detention Centres and Jails:* Adult offenders enter the correctional system through one of the province's jails or detention centres. These facilities provide secure settings for those remanded for court appearances or other judicial proceedings; inmates awaiting transfer to other institutions; and offenders serving sentences of less than 124 days. Detention centres and jails hold a complete spectrum of types of offenders and are therefore designed for maximum security (cell accommodation).

2. *Correctional Centres:* Persons sentenced to terms of incarceration greater than 124 days are generally transferred to a correctional centre. Those sentenced to two years or more are transferred to a federal penitentiary.

3. *Forestry Camps:* Two forestry camps provide outdoor work environments in minimum security settings. The camps provide accommodation for 40 to 60 male inmates each. Work projects include pruning, thinning and clearing of county forests and conservation areas. Camp inmates also perform community work such as cutting firewood for provincial parks and other institutions.

In addition, the Ontario Parole Board reports to the Legislative Assembly through the Minister of Correctional Services (see Agencies, Boards, and Commissions). The head office of the Ministry of Correctional Services is located in Scarborough, Ontario. The Ministry delivers its programs through five regional offices, which administer 49 correctional institutions, 18 young offender detention facilities, and a network of 112 probation offices. The Ministry employs approximately 5,900 public servants.

## PROGRAMS

### Community Programs

Institutional custody or "imprisonment" only makes up a fraction of the ministry's scope of activity. On any given day, more than 85 percent of offenders under the Ministry's care are serving their sentences under community supervision by Ministry probation and parole personnel.

*Probation:* Some offenders are judged by the courts not to require imprisonment and are sentenced to terms of probation. A probation order specifies the conditions under which the offender may remain in the community. Conditions may include: regular reporting to a probation/parole officer, a requirement to perform community service, orders that the offender make direct restitution to the victim, or restrictions on personal freedoms such as alcohol consumption and right of association.

*Temporary Absence:* Offenders completing sentences in the community include those released from institutions on temporary absence permits for employment, education, health or personal reasons. Temporary absence is considered to be an effective means of keeping inmates in touch with the realities of the community, in anticipation of their re-integration into society.

*Parole:* As inmates are eligible for parole after having served at least one-third of their sentence, community correctional services are also directed to those released from institutions on parole.

*Community Resource Centres:* These resource centres house offenders serving sentences in Ontario correctional institutions. The centres are operated by community organizations under contract to the ministry. An inmate wishing to pursue an education or employment program outside the institution can apply for a transfer to a community resource centre.

*Bail Verification and Supervision:* Aimed at reducing the numbers of those who are in institutions on remand (awaiting court proceedings). The program provides information to the courts on the accused's ability to post bail or obtain a surety and confirms community ties. In certain cases bail supervision is offered as an alternative to incarceration, pending disposition of charges.

*Community Service Orders* (CSOs): Given to some non-violent offenders as a condition of a probation order. The work performed would not otherwise be carried out except by volunteers. Organizations with projects of benefit to the community can obtain volunteer help from the CSO Project.

*Volunteer Coordination Program:* This program is a central resource to volunteer coordinators who recruit, screen, train, and supervise volunteers involved in correctional programs operated by the Ministry. Opportunities for volunteer participation exist in all geographic areas of the province.

*Fine Options Program:* This program is a pilot project intended to offer an alternative to incarceration for the non-payment of fines under the *Provincial Offences Act.* Individuals volunteer to do community service work at the minimum wage rate to accumulate credits towards fine payment. The program is available to individuals in the pilot areas when a fine is in default. The pilot projects are being carefully studied for possible expansion.

*Restitution Program:* Selected probationers with the possibility of making restitution are often encouraged to meet with the victims of the crimes and with a third party mediator to determine how the victims will receive restitution—in cash or kind. Similar programs are encouraged for selected inmates in Ontario correctional institutions, whereby they are placed in a Community Resource

Centre, obtain suitable employment, and make restitution to their victims.

*Victim Assistance Program:* A project alerting victims of crime to available social services such as crisis counselling and information on the criminal justice process.

### Institutional Programs

*Treatment Facilities:* The Ontario Correctional Institute is a 220-bed treatment facility providing clinical services including general medicine, psychotherapy, group counselling, dentistry, self-awareness training and other therapeutic programs. Treatment services are also available at the 50-bed Guelph Assessment and Treatment Unit, which is part of the Guelph Correctional Centre. Both facilities accept inmates on a referral basis from other correctional institutions.

*Health and Professional Services:* This program provides consultation and coordination in the following areas: dentistry, food and nutrition, medicine, nursing, pharmaceuticals, psychiatry, psychology, recreation, and social work. It is managed by the senior medical advisor, and has recently been expanded to include a coordinator of nursing services and a coordinator of professional services.

*Medical Services:* The senior medical advisor ensures that medical, psychiatric, and dental care are available to those under the supervision of this ministry.

*Psychologists and Psychometrists:* Psychologists and psychometrists work alone and in conjunction with others in providing a variety of assessment, treatment, and research services.

*Alcohol and Drug Abuse Programs:* Established in institutions, probation/parole offices, and community resource centres across the province.

*Native Program Coordination:* Assists in the development of policies and training related to the problems of Native peoples who are inmates in Ontario correctional institutions. It is also responsible for the development of institutional and community-based programs directed to the needs of Native inmates, and it provides liaison with Native organizations of Ontario.

*Education and Training:* Educational programs for offenders in correctional institutions include academic, technical, vocational, and life-skills courses. Apprenticeship and secondary school credits can be earned. Boards of Education provide programming for offenders aged 16 and 17 years who are the responsibility of the Ministry under the *Young Offenders Act.* They also operate continuing education programs for adult offenders in a number of jails and detention centre sites.

*Industrial Programs:* Institutional industries provide work and on-the-job training for inmates in correctional centres. Manufactured products are sold to other ministries or governments and are also used in correctional institutions.

*Self Sufficiency Program:* This program is responsible for projects in which of-fenders help produce food and other items to supply the needs throughout the province's institutions. The program supplies a substantial part of the meat, vegetable, and poultry requirements of institutions.

## EXPENDITURE ESTIMATES

*Estimated Expenditures 1987–88:*

| | |
|---|---|
| Ministry Administration | $ 19,346,300 |
| Operations | 344,495,700 |
| *(including institutional services, community services, and offender programming)* | |
| **Ministry total:** | **$363,842,000** |

## AGENCIES, BOARDS, AND COMMISSIONS

The following Board reports to the Legislative Assembly through the Minister of Correctional Services:

*Ontario Parole Board:* Considers for parole those inmates serving sentences of up to two years less a day in provincial institutions. Offenders who have served one third of their sentences are eligible for parole consideration. Those sentenced to six months or more are automatically scheduled to be seen by the Board. Those sentenced to less than six months must apply in writing to the board for parole consideration.

## LEGISLATION

The Ministry of Correctional Services is responsible for the following acts:

*Ministry of Correctional Services Act:* The statute which defines the operations of the Ministry, and prescribes some provincial-specific stipulations for federal acts (e.g. *Young Offenders Act*).

**Federal Statutes**

There are a number of *federal* statutes that affect the Ministry's operation:

*Criminal Code of Canada:* Describes criminal offences and procedures for dealing with adult offenders. Its has a procedural impact on the Ministry, e.g. content of war-rants, terms of probation orders, etc.

*Parole Act:* Prescribes parole eligibility and procedural rules for granting of parole, supervision, suspension, and revocation.

*Penitentiary Act:* Governs management and operation of federal penitentiaries. The provincial impact is evident in certain areas (e.g. offenders do not enter federal peniten-tiaries until appeal period complete, and remain in provincial custody).

*Prisons and Reformatories Act:* Provides for certain matters to which all provincial prisons prescribe, e.g. granting of remission.

*Young Offenders Act:* A procedural statute for dealing with offenders under 18 years of age.

MINISTRY OF FINANCIAL INSTITUTIONS

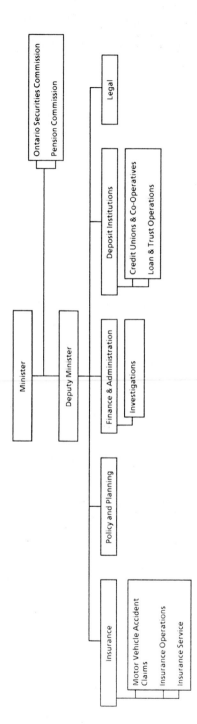

- Minister
  - Ontario Securities Commission
  - Pension Commission
- Deputy Minister
  - Policy and Planning
  - Insurance
    - Motor Vehicle Accident Claims
    - Insurance Operations
    - Insurance Service
  - Finance & Administration
    - Investigations
  - Deposit Institutions
    - Credit Unions & Co-Operatives
    - Loan & Trust Operations
  - Legal

# MINISTRY OF FINANCIAL INSTITUTIONS

## ROLES AND FUNCTIONS

The purpose of the Ministry of Financial Institutions is to consolidate and strengthen the functions pertaining to the regulation, supervision, and policy direction of financial institutions operating in Ontario. The Ministry is responsible for regulation and policy concerning loan and trust companies, insurance companies, credit unions and cooperatives, and mortgage brokers; and works closely with the Ontario Securities Commission and the Ontario Pension Commission.

## BACKGROUND HISTORY

Until March 1986, the current functions of the Ministry of Financial Institutions (MFI) were the responsibility of the Financial Institutions Division of the Ministry of Consumer and Commercial Relations (MCCR). The Ministry was established from programs formerly administered by MCCR in order to increase the domestic and international competitiveness of Ontario in the financial services sector and to improve the regulatory protection provided to consumers. Responsibility for the administration of 22 Acts, the Ontario Securities Commission, and the Ontario Pension Commission were transferred to the new Ministry by an Order-in-Council dated March 26, 1986.

The new Ministry continues to receive some policy development, legal, and administrative support from the Ministry of Consumer and Commercial Relations. Until September 1987, the Minister of Financial Institutions was also the Minister of Consumer and Commercial Relations. MFI and MCCR now have separate ministers and deputy ministers.

## ORGANIZATION

The Ministry of Financial Institutions is organized into two operating divisions (see organization chart):

1. *Deposit Institutions Division:* Includes the Credit Unions and Cooperatives Branch and the Loan and Trust Operations Branch.

2. *Insurance Division:* Includes the Insurance Operations Branch and the Motor Vehicle Accident Claims Fund.

In addition, a Finance and Administration Division provides support services for the Ministry; and the Ontario Pension Commission and the Ontario Securities Commission report to the Legislative Assembly through the Minister of Financial Institutions. The head office of the Ministry of Financial Institutions is located in Toronto. The Ministry employs approximately 300 public servants.

## PROGRAMS

### Deposit Institutions

Headed by the Superintendent of Deposit Institutions, the Deposit Institutions Division strives to ensure a high level of ethical business conduct on the part of individuals and organizations operating within Ontario's deposit-taking industry. This Division consists of two main areas of responsibility:

*Credit Unions and Cooperatives Services Branch:* Administers the provisions of the *Credit Unions and Caisses Populaires Act* and the *Cooperative Corporations Act.* Activities include improving the financial management standards of credit unions and credit leagues by establishing and enforcing standards on an individual and systems basis; enforcing sound business and financial practices; monitoring established standards for reserves, retained earnings, and levels of liquidity in order to protect members' deposits; performing field examinations of all leagues and undertaking on-site reviews of problem areas in credit union operations; and, reviewing requests for incorporation. Deposits in credit unions and "caisse populaires" are insured with the Ontario Share and Deposit Insurance Corporation.

*Loan and Trust Corporations Branch:* Administers the provisions of the *Loan and Trust Corporations Act.* Activities include supervising the incorporation, registration, and operations of all Ontario loan and trust corporations and reviewing compliance with regulations and legislation; monitoring loan and trust companies' financial status and economic soundness to protect and maintain the Ontario public's confidence in deposit institutions; and, conducting loan and trust industry investigations. Deposits in all loan and trust institutions are insured with the Canada Deposit Insurance Corporation.

### Insurance Division

Headed by the Superintendent of Insurance, the Insurance Division strives to ensure a high level of ethical business conduct by individuals and organizations operating within Ontario's insurance industry. This Division consists of two areas of activity:

*Insurance Operations Branch:* Administers the provisions of the *Guarantee Companies Securities Act,* the *Insurance Act,* the *Investments Contracts Act,*

*Marine Insurance Act,* and *Prepaid Hospital and Medical Services Act.* Activities include supervising the incorporation, licensing or registration, and operations of insurance companies, fraternal societies, mutual benefit societies, farm mutual and insurance agents carrying on business in Ontario; conducting insurance industry examinations and checking and monitoring all financial filings; reviewing the actuarial liabilities of all provincial insurance companies and extra-provincial life insurance companies on a regular basis; and investigating consumer complaints.

*Motor Vehicle Accident Claims Fund:* Administers the *Motor Vehicle Accident Claims Act* and the *Compulsory Auto Insurance Act.* This branch provides automobile accident compensation: to victims injured by motor vehicles who are without insurance coverage, in hit-and-run situations, for stolen vehicles, and to innocent parties where two uninsured vehicles are involved.

## EXPENDITURE ESTIMATES

*Estimated Expenditures 1987–88:*

| | |
|---|---|
| Ministry Administration | $ 3,421,400 |
| Financial Standards | 34,143,300 |
| **Ministry total:** | **$37,564,700** |

## AGENCIES, BOARDS, AND COMMISSIONS

The following ABCs report to the Legislative Assembly through the Minister of Financial Institutions:

*Ontario Pension Commission:* Administers the *Pension Benefits Act,* which requires the registration and regulation of all private (i.e. company) pension plans covering employees in Ontario. The Commission also provides information and advice to the general public, pension plan administrators, and the pension industry regarding Ontario's legislated requirements for pension plans.

*Ontario Securities Commission:* Maintains a list of reporting securities issuers; records filings of insider trading, proxy solicitation material, financial statements, and take-over bids for the benefit of investors. It processes prospectus offerings of securities and applications for exemption, transfer, or release of securities from escrow. The Commission registers and investigates consumer complaints about stockbrokers, investment advisors, and commodity futures dealers. It also investigates complaints about actions by companies which affect the value of securities. It answers consumers' inquiries concerning commodity futures trading.

## LEGISLATION

The Ministry of Financial Institutions is responsible for the following Acts:

*Central Trust Company Act:* Provides for the transfer of the trusteeship and agency business of the Crown Trust Company to the Central Trust Company.

*Commodity Futures Act:* Provides for the regulation of trading and advertising in commodity futures and options by the Ontario Securities Commission.

*Compulsory Automobile Insurance Act:* Requires every owner of a motor vehicle which is to be driven on a highway to have the vehicle insured. The Act also requires all automobile insurance agents and companies to make automobile insurance available for every resident of Ontario seeking to obtain the mandatory coverage.

*Cooperative Corporations Act:* Provides for the creation, management, operation, and dissolution of cooperative corporations.

*Credit Unions and Caisses Populaires Act:* Provides for the incorporation, management, operation, and dissolution of credit unions and credit union leagues, and establishes the Ontario Share and Deposit Insurance Corporation.

*Crown Trust Company Act:* Facilitates the preservation of certain assets and obligations of the Crown Trust Company, including deposit accounts and trust property, through arrangements for their sale or management.

*Deposit Regulation Act:* The Act, which does not apply to banks, trust companies, and other specified enterprises, prohibits the solicitation of deposits in any manner that is false and misleading.

*Guarantee Companies Securities Act:* Defines a "guarantee company" as one approved by the Lieutenant Governor in Council and empowered to grant guarantees, bonds, policies, or contracts for the integrity and fidelity of employed persons.

*Insurance Act:* Provides for the appointment of a Superintendent of Insurance and the licensing of insurance companies and agents. The Act regulates capital requirements, investments, and reserves, and provides for the inspection of the operation of insurance companies.

*Investment Contracts Act:* Provides for the registration of persons who issue or sell investment contracts, and for the filing of forms of investment contracts with the Superintendent of Insurance.

*Loan and Trust Corporations Act:* Provides for the incorporation, operation, management, and registration of loan and trust companies.

*Marine Insurance Act:* Provides a method for determining insurable value and states the regulations concerning marine insurance.

*Mortgage Brokers Act:* Provides for the appointment of a Registrar, for the registration of mortgage brokers, for the handling of complaints, for the inspection and investigation to ensure compliance with the Act, and for the filing of prospectuses concerning mortgages on land located outside of Ontario.

*Motor Vehicle Accident Claims Act:* Establishes an Accident Claims Fund financed by fees collected for drivers' licenses. Payouts from this fund have declined since the 1979 enactment of the *Compulsory Automobile Insurance Act.* However, payments are still made out of the Fund for pedestrians who have no automobile insurance, and uninsured parties injured in an accident.

*Ontario Credit Union League Act:* Permitted the League to purchase the business and undertaking of the Ontario Cooperative Credit Society in 1972.

*Ontario Deposit Insurance Corporation Act:* Provides for the management and operation of the Ontario Deposit Insurance Corporation, whose objective is to provide insurance for deposits in loan and trust corporations. The Act requires all trust companies to have deposit insurance under the provincial Act or the *Canada Deposit Insurance Act.* All corporations are insured under the federal Act, but the provincial Act is still enforced because it sets out the requirement for carrying deposit insurance.

*Pension Benefits Act:* Establishes and continues the Pension Commission of Ontario, which requires registration of all pension plans covering employees in Ontario and regulates the management of pensions.

*Prepaid Hospital and Medical Services Act:* Provides for the registration of corporations established to provide medical services to members.

*Registered Insurance Brokers Act:* Establishes the Registered Insurance Brokers of Ontario as a self-governing body of insurance brokers. All insurance brokers in Ontario must be registered under this Act or the *Insurance Act.* The legislation sets out requirements for the composition of the governing body, a committee dealing with qualifications and registration of members, a complaints committee, and a discipline committee.

*Securities Act:* Establishes the Ontario Securities Commission and requires the registration of securities salespersons, dealers, underwriters, and advisors. The Act prescribes rules concerning content of a prospectus, issuing receipts, trading in securities, methods of making takeover bids, soliciting proxies, insider trading, and financial disclosure. It also prohibits a stock exchange from carrying on business unless recognized by the Commission.

*Toronto Futures Exchange Act:* Creates a corporation without share capital known as the Toronto Futures Exchange, to operate an exchange in Ontario for trading in commodity futures contracts by members of the corporation. The corporation is subject to the regulatory supervision of the Ontario Securities Commission and to the provisions of the *Commodity Futures Act.*

*Toronto Stock Exchange Act:* Establishes and continues the Toronto Stock Exchange Corporation, the object of which is the operation of a stock exchange in Ontario for trading by members of the corporation.

# MINISTRY OF THE SOLICITOR GENERAL

## ROLES AND FUNCTIONS

In fulfilling its responsibilities for law enforcement and public safety in Ontario, the Ministry of the Solicitor General provides the following services: supervision of police services and training throughout the province; a provincial police force with expertise in criminal and traffic law enforcement; specialized scientific criminal analysis; the maintenance of an adequate standard of fire safety services in the province; the determination of causes of death in unusual circumstances; forensic pathology services; and the provision of anatomical materials to schools of anatomy in Ontario.

The Ministry is also responsible for ensuring that municipal police forces and the Ontario Provincial Police (OPP) are effective in preventing and detecting crime and that they enforce the law in a fair and impartial manner. The Ministry is assisted in this supervisory role by the Ontario Police Commission and local police governing bodies (boards of commissioners of police and committees).

The Ministry's role as civilian authority for police services in Ontario, (as the Ministry responsible for the *Police Act*) is direct with respect to the OPP and indirect with respect to the 127 municipal and regional police forces. Responsibilities are shared with the Ministry of the Attorney General, which provides legal and other prosecutorial advice to all forces in Ontario. In the area of relations with municipal and regional police forces, much of the Ministry's work is carried out by its civilian agency, the Ontario Police Commission.

## BACKGROUND HISTORY

The Ministry of the Solicitor General was created in 1972 by the *Ministry of the Solicitor General Act*. Prior to this date, the responsibility for law enforcement and public safety in Ontario was held by the Department of the Attorney General. The Ministry's present programs include supervision of the Ontario Provincial Police, the Ontario Police Commission, the Ontario Police Arbitration Commission, the Chief Coroner's Office, the Centre of Forensic Sciences, the Office of the Fire Marshal, Forensic Pathology and Emergency Planning.

# ORGANIZATION

The Ministry of the Solicitor General is organized into four major divisions (see organization chart):

1. *Program Resources:* Provides support services to the Ministry.

2. *Public Safety:* Promotes adequate standards for fire safety services, attempts to determine causes of fires, and reviews fire safety standards of building plans through its Fire Safety Services Branch; attempts to determine causes of death in unnatural circumstances, and helps prevent or minimize future loss of life through the Coroner's Branch; provides services and expertise in forensic pathology through the Forensic Pathology Branch.

3. *Policy Development:* Includes the Ministry's Legal Services, Policy Development, and Coordination, and Communications Services Branches.

4. *Ontario Provincial Police:* Includes administration, investigations, and field operations divisions, and over 180 detachments and 17 district headquarters.

As well, the Ontario Police Commission, the Ontario Police Arbitration Commission, and several other boards report to the Legislative Assembly through the Solicitor General (see Agencies, Boards, and Commissions).

The head office of the Ministry of the Solicitor General is located in Toronto. The Ministry employs approximately 6,200 public servants, including 4,500 uniformed Ontario Provincial Police officers.

# PROGRAMS

In addition to its public safety and law enforcement roles, the Ministry has developed a number of specialized initiatives, including:

*Crime Prevention:* A full-time crime prevention bureau was established within the Ontario Police Commission to assist the province's municipal police forces to initiate and develop effective crime prevention programs and to serve as a monitoring agency to assess their effectiveness. The Ministry has seconded experienced police officers to coordinate the program, which has proven extremely successful.

*Victim Assistance:* Based on the success and insight of the Crime Prevention Program, in 1984 a police officer was seconded to the OPC to serve as Victim Assistance Coordinator for the Ministry. This officer advises and assists the OPC and the Solicitor General in formulating, developing, and promoting an acceptable and uniform level of victim assistance by police forces throughout Ontario.

The Ministry of the Solicitor General, along with four other Ministries, contributes towards a grant to the Ontario Coalition of Rape Crisis Centres. Studies are also under way with respect to missing children, fire prevention, and computer crime.

MINISTRY OF THE SOLICITOR GENERAL

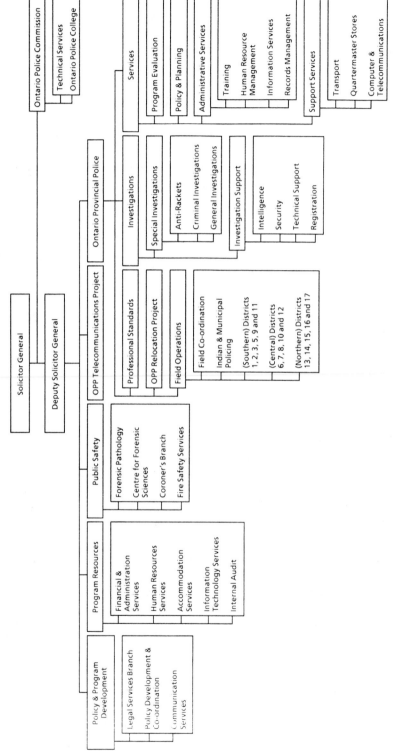

## EXPENDITURE ESTIMATES

Estimated Expenditures 1987–88:

| | |
|---|---|
| Ministry Administration | $ 16,072,538 |
| Public Safety | 34,458,500 |
| Policing Services | 11,827,200 |
| Ontario Provincial Police | 331,211,400 |
| **Ministry total:** | **$393,569,638** |

## AGENCIES, BOARDS, AND COMMISSIONS

The following ABCs report to the Legislative Assembly through the Solicitor General:

*Advisory Committee on Crime Prevention:* Consists of 23 members and was established in 1984 by Order-in-Council. The purpose of the Committee is to assist and advise the Solicitor General in formulating strategies for the development, implementation, and evaluation of the province's Crime Prevention Program. Representation on the committee is from government, police, private industry, and the general public.

*Animal Care Review Board:* Established in 1968 under authority of the *Ontario Society for the Prevention of Cruelty to Animals Act.* The Board, consisting of three members, is a regulatory agency providing the public with an independent review of the orders and actions of inspectors or agents of the Ontario Society for the Prevention of Cruelty to Animals.

*Coroners Council:* Reviews and investigates complaints against coroners; makes recommendations to improve the system.

*Fire Code Commission:* Established under the *Fire Marshals Act;* hears and determines appeals with respect to the Fire Marshals Orders issued under that Act.

*Ontario Police Arbitration Commission:* Administers the arbitration process between municipalities and municipal police forces throughout Ontario. Has the general responsibility for monitoring the police arbitration system and making recommendations for its improvement in order to promote more harmonious police contract bargaining and arbitration. The Commission consists of five members appointed by the Lieutenant Governor in Council. Other than the chairman, two members of the Commission represent municipal police governing bodies and two represent police forces.

*Ontario Police Commission:* Established in 1962 under authority of the *Police Act.* The Commission is charged with ensuring the adequacy of policing across the province. The functions of the Commission include supervising, monitoring, training, and offering technical and operational advice and assistance to the province's 127 municipal and regional police forces in order to maintain adequate police services.

## LEGISLATION

The Ministry of the Solicitor General is responsible for the following Acts:

*Anatomy Act:* Provides for the appointment of general and local inspectors of anatomy and imposes a public duty to deliver up control of unclaimed bodies not intended for use under the *Human Tissue Gift Act* to local inspectors, who may then authorize their use for the purposes of anatomical dissection by designated schools.

*Coroners Act:* Establishes the Office of the Chief Coroner and governs the appointment, tenure, and functions of both the chief and regional coroners. A general public duty to report to the coroner certain types of death is stipulated in the Act. The powers and duties of a coroner are also set out, as are the procedures and purposes of an inquest.

*Egress from Public Buildings Act:* Stipulates that the doors of public buildings are to open outward.

*Emergency Plans Act, 1983:* Provides for municipal emergency plans; enables a municipality to declare that an emergency exists and to make orders for the protection of property and persons within the area. The Act requires the Lieutenant Governor in Council to formulate an emergency plan for nuclear facilities and requires provincial government bodies to do so for their respective ministries, such plans to be monitored by an Emergency Planning Coordinator. Plans are to be made available to the public.

*Fire Accidents Act:* Deems that where there is a duty imposed on the owner or occupant of a building to provide fire safety equipment and such requirements have not been met, any death resulting from fire in such a building will be presumed to be the result of the non-compliance.

*Fire Departments Act:* Empowers the Fire Marshal to establish a central fire college and regional fire schools for the training of fire fighters and officers. Governs their hours of work, bargaining powers, and arbitration procedures.

*Fire Fighters Exemption Act:* Exempts members of municipally-approved fire-fighting companies from serving as jurors or constables during the term of their membership.

*Fire Marshals Act:* Creates the Office of the Fire Marshal to further fire prevention and public safety in Ontario. The Office is empowered to investigate fires and explosions and to inspect buildings to ensure compliance with Fire Code. Procedures are set out governing appeals from orders of the Fire Marshal to the Fire Code Commissioner and to Divisional Court.

*Hotel Fire Safety Act:* Requires that all hotel plans be approved by the Fire Marshal and meet specifications as to alarm and extinguishing systems, exist, etc. Provides for inspections of premises with a right of appeal from orders of inspectors or the Fire Marshal and ultimately the courts.

*Human Tissue Gift Act:* Governs inter-vivos and post-mortem transplants of human tissue and the giving of consent. Prohibits the sale of human tissue for profit.

*Lightning Rods Act:* Prohibits the sale of lightning rods except under licence of the Fire Marshal. Sets out procedures governing the issuance of licenses and appeals of suspended licenses.

*Ministry of the Solicitor General Act:* Continues the existence of the Ministry; sets out the statutes for which the Solicitor General is responsible; and requires that an annual report of Ministry affairs be submitted to the Lieutenant Governor in Council.

*Ontario Society for the Prevention of Cruelty to Animals Act:* Continues the existence of the Society whose object is to protect and prevent cruelty to animals and provide relief to them. Enumerates the powers of the Society, including the right to pass by-laws; confers on inspectors the powers of police officers, enabling them to search premises where animals are believed to be in distress, issue orders, take possession of, destroy, or sell such animals. The Animal Care Review Board is also created as an appeal body from orders of the Society, and its procedures outlined.

*Police Act:* Ensures adequate policing across the province at both the municipal and provincial levels. The Act mandates a provincial force, the Ontario Provincial Police, and provides administrative direction to that force as well as municipal forces. The Act provides for the Ontario Police Commission, which assists in coordination of policing in the Province and adjudicates disputes among members of the Ontario forces. Allows for the appointment of auxiliary members to a police force.

*Private Investigators and Security Guards Act:* Prohibits anyone from operating as a private investigator or security guard without a licence from the Registrar of Private Investigators and Security Guards, while at the same time exempting certain types of activity from operation of the Act. The legislation also sets out procedures relating to licence application, suspension, cancellation, and appeal.

*Public Works Protection Act:* Defines "public work," provides for the appointment of guards for the protection thereof, and enumerates the powers and duties of such guards in relation to their appointment.

*Retail Business Holidays Act:* Lists the statutory holidays and prohibits retail businesses from carrying on business on those days. Certain businesses, depending on size and nature of goods or services offered, are exempt from the prohibition.

## INNOVATIONS

A number of major innovations in policies or administrative procedures introduced during the last 5–10 years affected Ministry objectives positively. They include: The Ontario Fire Code; the Royal Commission on High-rise Fire Safety; the Crime Prevention Program (see Programs); the Emergency Plans Act (see Legislation); developing a new OPP radio communications system; increased resources for systems development staff; improvement of Ministry information technology; and a Management Services Branch to deal with non-technical issues of management.

# Section 6
# SOCIAL POLICY
# MINISTRIES

The Social Policy Ministries promote and support the development of the education, health, cultural expression, and social welfare of the people of Ontario. Social policy accounts for the majority of spending on government programs and services in Ontario. The seven Social Policy Ministries are the Ministries of Citizenship; Colleges and Universities; Community and Social Services; Culture and Communications; Education; Health; and Skills Development; plus the Office for Disabled Persons and the Office for Senior Citizen's Affairs.

# MINISTRY OF CITIZENSHIP

## ROLES AND FUNCTIONS

The Ministry of Citizenship is responsible for encouraging individuals to participate in the Province's economic, political, social, and cultural life by ensuring that ethnocultural groups, immigrants, newcomers, Francophones and native people are able to participate fully in Ontario society through programs that promote equality of opportunity and access to services, the retention and sharing of cultural traditions, and community development. The Ministry of Citizenship is also responsible for the Ontario Human Rights Code.

## BACKGROUND HISTORY

The Ministry of Citizenship and Culture was established on February 13, 1982 by an Act of the Ontario Legislature, which received Royal Assent on June 7, 1982. The Ministry succeeded the former Ministry of Culture and Recreation which was first formed in 1975 out of the Cultural Affairs Division of the Ministry of Colleges and Universities, and other programs from a variety of different ministries. An Order-in-Council dated October 8, 1987 created the Ministry of Citizenship, which is now comprised of the Citizenship Division of the former Ministry of Citizenship and Culture, and the Ontario Human Rights Commission, transferred from the Ministry of Labour.

## ORGANIZATION

The Ministry of Citizenship is organized into one division:

*Citizenship:* Includes the Citizen Development, Native Community, and Newcomer Services Branches.

Administrative support services, such as finance, internal audit, and human resources, are provided by the Ministry of Culture and Communications. The Ontario Human Rights Commission and the Advisory Council on Multiculturalism and Citizenship report to the Legislative Assembly through the Minister of Citizenship (see Agencies, Boards, and Commissions).

The head office of the Ministry of Citizenship is located in Toronto. The Ministry employs approximately 260 public servants.

## PROGRAMS

### Citizenship Development Branch

The Citizenship Development Branch supports programs aimed at developing and improving ethnic and intercultural relations. These include: developing an appreciation for different ethnocultural groups in Ontario; encouraging information through intercultural workshops; assisting in the development within institutions of a sensitivity to cultural differences. The branch provides consulting services (to community groups and institutions) and an ethnocultural data base; develops and distributes print and audio/visual materials; supports workshops and seminars; and administers grants. It also encourages and assists with the implementation of the province's multi-cultural policy within the Ontario Government. The branch further administers the Volunteer Awards program on behalf of the Ministry of Citizenship. This program recognizes years of service and outstanding achievements in the area of volunteerism related to the mandate of the Ministry. The branch supports the promotion and recognition of volunteerism and the development of leadership within volunteer organizations. Included are leadership training/volunteer development workshops, stimulation of volunteer activity and encouragement of volunteer recognition. Francophone initiatives also include the stimulation of leadership development and volunteerism.

The grants administered by the branch are:

*Citizenship Development Branch Grants Program:* Promotes community participation, responsible citizenship, cultural sharing and understanding, leadership, organizational development, and volunteerism.

*Multiculturalism and Citizenship Community Projects Grants:* Assists projects that promote one of the following: citizenship in a multicultural society; cultural, social, and linguistic integration into Ontario's society; cultural heritage preservation and sharing; leadership skills and organizational effectiveness development for organizations delivering multicultural and citizenship services, voluntary action, and participation in multicultural and citizenship activities.

### Newcomer Services Branch

The Newcomer Services Branch provides assistance related to settlement, orientation, and language training for immigrants and refugees, and helps other government ministries to provide better access to their services. The branch offers direct multilingual settlement services to newcomers through the Ontario Welcome House network, develops orientation information and language training aids, and provides support to voluntary organizations and educational institutions in the delivery of settlement and language training programs. The branch also acts as a policy and information resource to the government and the public in the development and adaptation of programs for newcomers.

Community support is provided through transfer payments, consultation, training, and program development to community based organizations, boards of education, and community colleges, for the development and delivery of settlement orientation language training for newcomers.

Informational, language training, and multilingual materials and programs are developed for newcomers and to assist teachers and counsellors working with newcomers (e.g. TESL Talk—a professional journal for teachers of English as a Second Language (ESL); Newcomer News—a graded English newspaper distributed to teachers and students in ESL programs; Newcomers Guide to Services in Ontario, available in 20 languages; Living in Ontario—multilingual slide/tape cassette kits, used in settlement and orientation programs).

The Branch has an up-to-date ESL multicultural and adult education collection in the Ministry Resource Centre. The collection is available on loan to ESL teachers throughout Ontario. Branch staff locate, assess, organize, and update information about programs and services relating to immigrants and refugees. In cooperation with community-based information providers, the Branch provides information support and resource materials for settlement officers at Ontario Welcome House, government staff and others working with newcomers. A call collect line is available to provide information to newcomers, their sponsors and helping agencies. The same number can be used to order Branch publications, lists of publications and other resources available through the Ministry.

Government and community organizations are striving to adapt their policies and programs to meet the needs of multicultural society. Through "New Beginnings", a newsletter for Ontario Government personnel, the Branch highlights issues, information, and innovations in service delivery to newcomers.

The Newcomer Services Branch responds to requests for grants, consultation, training, and resources related to all aspects of newcomer settlement and language training brought to their attention by the regional staff. Information and support is also provided directly to provincial organizations involved in newcomer services.

In order to facilitate requests, consultants provide generalist support through a regional liaison system. The liaison consultant for each region receives all requests for funding, consultation and/or training, and identifies resources in the Branch or elsewhere to assist in meeting the needs identified.

Programs administered by the Newcomer Services Branch include:

*Newcomer Integration Grants Program:* Grants assist voluntary organizations in developing projects such as volunteer development, community outreach, and a variety of settlement services and special projects which facilitate newcomer integration. Specialist consultation in areas related to newcomer settlement and integration is available to organizations providing services to newcomers in the community.

*Newcomer Language Orientation Classes Grants Program:* Through the newcomer language/orientation classes (NLOC) grants programs, voluntary organizations (e.g. community agencies, immigrant aid agencies, YMCAs, church groups) receive assistance in operating language programs in the community locations, in cooperation with boards of education and community colleges. A variety of approaches is used in these programs such as: parent and preschool programs, English as a Second Language (ESL), and English as a Standard Dialect (ESD) programs, citizenship preparation/ESL programs, programs with special orientation content (i.e. job preparation), programs for one language group taught by a teacher who speaks the language of the students (i.e. Chinese/English), one-to-one tutoring programs (i.e. "HAFLE"--Help a Friend Learn English), French as a Second language (FSL) programs, and programs operated in the workplace.

Resources and professional development through workshops, seminars, and certified courses are provided for staff and volunteers in NLOC-supported programs across the province. Consultative assistance and workshops for community organizations, boards of education, and colleges are offered on special programs such as ESL/Literacy, HAFLE programs and multicultural/ESL preschool programs. Assistance is also provided to organizations implementing ESL teacher-training programs.

Programs to improve communications in multicultural workplaces are delivered by community colleges, boards of education, and community groups to business and labour. Programs and services delivered included language training, intercultural community training, communications needs assessments. The Branch, in cooperation with the Citizenship Development Branch provides coordination, resources, training, and consultation for deliverers of the programs. Special community project grants have been provided for the development of pilots and models.

*Ontario Welcome House:* A multi-service centre for new immigrants and refugees in the Golden Horseshoe (Oshawa to St. Catharines) area. Ontario Welcome House operates four locations in and around Metropolitan Toronto, and one in Hamilton. Services include orientation and settlement counselling at all locations and a language school, nursery, and translation bureau at the Downtown Toronto location. All services are free and confidential. As a "first stop for service," multilingual Settlement Officers provide initial information and guidance about education, employment, health care, housing, recreational facilities, government, and community services, along with general orientation to life in Ontario. Clients receive help from the settlement officers in completing applications such as those for Family Allowance. Counsellors work with, and refer clients to, community-based agencies and government departments as required.

Settlement services are available at all Ontario Welcome House locations. Ontario Welcome House—Downtown Toronto also offers a language school with six levels of classes, lasting for six weeks. The Multilingual Section, which is part of the Ministry of Government Services, but is located at Ontario Welcome House, is responsible for the translation into English of personal documents needed for employment or further education. Documents translated include educational certificates and diplomas, trade credentials, work testimonials, marriage certificates, birth, and baptism certificates. Canadian citizens and landed immigrants living in Ontario are eligible for this free service. Translations bear the official stamp of the Government of Ontario and are officially recognized throughout the province.

*Training Program:* Training programs for front-line settlement workers are being developed in cooperation with other levels of government, educational, and community organizations.

## Joint programs

Two programs are the joint responsibility of the Citizenship Development and Newcomer Services Branches:

*Community Facilities Improvement Program:* Provides support for the planning, purchase, construction, improvement, and renovation of cultural, multicultural or citizenship facilities and for the conservation of heritage buildings in Ontario.

*Multicultural Service Program Grants:* Supports, by assisting with operating costs, community organizations that deliver, on an ongoing basis, services and programs within the multicultural mandate of the Ministry.

## Native Community Branch

The Native Community Branch consults and works with Native communities and organizations to support aspirations for self-reliance and economic independence. Its programs include consultative assistance, research, information, publications, policy advisory services, and grants. Consultation is provided to more than 500 Native groups by the Branch's native Development Consultants throughout Ontario. Consultation services include: assisting native communities in identifying local problems and in developing appropriate projects; advising Native communities and organizations of services and programs which could help their development, and assisting them in securing resources necessary to conduct community development projects; linking Native communities and organizations with the appropriate provincial ministries and agencies; and providing assistance to native leaders on the preparation, submission, and evaluation of project proposals to government.

Programs administered by the Native Community Branch include:

*Communications Grants:* Support Native-initiated projects in a variety of media, including radio, video-tape, television, and print—providing they support community and leadership development through the native community.

*Constitutional Funding Program:* The process of defining "Aboriginal and Treaty Rights" in the *Constitution Act, 1982* requires aboriginal organizations to consult widely with their membership and with the provincial and federal governments through the First Ministers Conferences. The Constitutional Funding Program provides financial assistance to defray the costs associated with the constitutional discussions.

*Leadership Training Program:* Funds are available to Native communities concerned with the development of leadership potential among its people. Support is also provided for projects that provide skill training to Native people.

*Meeting Grants:* Funding is available for Native groups to gather and discuss issues of common concern. Priority is given to meetings of Native groups at the local and regional level.

*Native Community Branch Feasibility Studies Grants:* Funding is available for feasibility studies assisting groups in exploring the potential for undertaking a specific project or business. These projects may be in any of the grant category areas.

*Native Community Branch Social Development Grants:* Funds are available to Native communities and organizations for projects that address particular social problems in the community.

*Native Heritage Grants:* Projects of an innovative nature that support Native community and leadership development through cultural activities can be funded by a Native heritage grant. Eligible projects range from heritage preservation, crafts, and cross-cultural relations, to visual and performing arts.

*Ontario Native Economic Support Program*: a specialized version of the Community Facilities Improvement Program. It provides financial support for Native projects which will assist in community facility development, enhance economic opportunities, and strengthen management capacities. ONESP can provide support for the planning, purchase, construction, improvement, and renovation of Native community facilities. It can assist in the purchase of equipment needed to advance economic objectives.

*Provincial Organizations Support Program:* The Ontario Native Women's Association, Chiefs of Ontario, and the Ontario Federation of Indian Friendship Centres receive funding to cover basic administrative costs. To receive funding, each organization must represent members throughout the province and their mandate must support the objectives and the priorities of the Ministry.

*Research Grants Program:* Native-initiated projects that deal with areas of original research related to Native people are considered for funding. Priority is given to demographic research and community needs documentation. Consideration is also given to Native organizations to undertake detailed research design.

## EXPENDITURE ESTIMATES

*Estimated Expenditures 1987–88*:

| | |
|---|---|
| Ministry Administration | 2,414,858 |
| Citizenship and Multicultural Support | 20,493,100 |
| Capital Support and Regional Services | 9,158,475 |
| Ontario Human Rights Commission | 8,152,400 |
| **Ministry total:** | **$40,218,833** |

## AGENCIES, BOARDS, AND COMMISSIONS

The following ABCs report to the Legislative Assembly through the Minister of Citizenship:

*Advisory Council on Multiculturalism and Citizenship:* The Council consists of sixty members from across Ontario, appointed by Order-in-Council. The members represent a wide range of ethnocultural backgrounds and occupations, selected on the basis of their sensitivity to the multicultural nature of Ontario society and knowledge of the ethnocultural communities. The Council's role is to advise the Government of Ontario on those matters within the authority of the government which pertain to multiculturalism and citizenship for all residents of the province.

*Ontario Human Rights Commission:* The commission administers the Human Rights Code and formulates policies on all issues affecting human rights in the province. It implements programs of compliance, conciliation, and mediation with employers, unions, landlords, suppliers of services, goods, and facilities, trade or occupational associations, and self-governing professions. It conducts public education in the provisions and principles of the Code.

## LEGISLATION

The Ministry of Citizenship is responsible for the *Ontario Human Rights Code.* The Code protects individuals from discrimination in employment, housing, and public accommodation, contracts, services, goods, and facilities, and vocational associations on the grounds of race, creed, colour, ethnic origin, citizenship, ancestry, places of origin, age, sex, marital status, sexual orientation, handicap, record of offences (in employment where an individual has been pardoned under the *Criminal Records Act* or convicted of a provincial offence), and receipt of public assistance (accommodation only). This includes membership in unions and professional associations.

# MINISTRY OF COLLEGES AND UNIVERSITIES

## ROLES AND FUNCTIONS

The role of the Ministry of Colleges and Universities (MCU) is to help universities and colleges achieve their goals through programs of operating and capital support. The Ministry administers support funds to 15 provincially assisted universities, Ryerson Polytechnical Institute, the Ontario College of Art, the Ontario Institute for Studies in Education, and 22 colleges of applied arts and technology (CAATs). It also administers student financial assistance programs.

To promote accessibility to post-secondary education, funding is provided to all qualified students to remove financial barriers and assist them in obtaining a post-secondary education. The Ministry provides both need-based and merit-based funds to meet the educational needs of those who have completed their secondary school programs.

The 22 Colleges of Applied Arts and Technology operate from 96 campuses throughout the province. Their goals for education are:

1. To provide types and levels of courses beyond, or not suited to, the secondary school setting through vocationally oriented courses;

2. To meet the educational needs of graduates from any secondary school program, apart from those wishing to attend university;

3. To meet the educational needs of adults and out-of-school youths, whether or not they are secondary school graduates; and

4. To act as delivery agents of programs for people with special needs.

The Ministry's role with respect to the CAATs is to ensure the effective operation of the college system through the development and implementation of administrative policies and funding mechanisms.

In the case of universities, the Ministry's role is more limited, since the autonomy of the university system in Ontario is guaranteed by law. Each institution is responsible for determining programs, courses, entrance requirements, academic standards, and internal budget allocations. According to the Ontario Council on Universities Affairs the goals for Ontario universities are:

1. To develop a more educated populace;

2. To educate and train people for their professions;

3. To provide for study at the highest intellectual level;
4. To conduct basic and applied research; and
5. To provide service to the community.


## BACKGROUND HISTORY

In 1958 a group of senior civil servants formed the "University Committee" to give advice to Minister of Education on problems of support for higher education. In 1961 the name of the committee was changed to the Advisory Committee on University Affairs, and members from the academic and education community outside the government were added. In May 1964, an Act was passed to establish the Department of University Affairs. The Advisory Committee on University Affairs was enlarged, and the word "Advisory" was dropped from title. In May 1965, legislation was introduced to authorize the Minister of Education to establish Colleges of Applied Arts and Technology (CAATs).

In October 1966, when the federal government announced a decision to cease direct financial support for universities, the responsibilities of the Department increased. By April 1967, the Department of University Affairs assumed full responsibility for funding provincially assisted universities. In the period from 1966–67, the Department also assumed responsibility for the planning and administration of the newly instituted Ontario Student Awards Program.

In 1969, the Commission on Post-Secondary Education was established. Its report was released in December 1972. In response to this report, responsibility for CAATs was transferred to Department of University Affairs from the Department of Labour.

In April 1972, following the recommendations of the Committee on Government Productivity, the Department's name was changed to the Ministry of Colleges and Universities, and the Industrial Training Branch was transferred to MCU from the Ministry of Labour.

In September 1974, the Ontario Council on University Affairs was appointed, replacing its predecessor, the Council on University Affairs. In January 1975, responsibilities of the recently created Cultural Affairs Division were transferred to the Ministry of Culture and Recreation. In 1979, MCU and the Ministry of Education, while remaining separate portfolios, came under jurisdiction of the same Minister. This arrangement continued until June 1985, when the incoming government appointed separate Cabinet ministers to each of these two ministries.

At that point, the Minister of Colleges and Universities was also appointed as Minister of Skills Development and assumed responsibility for that new ministry. With the appointment of a new Cabinet in September 1987, the Honourable Lyn McLeod is now the Minister for Colleges and Universities.

MINISTRY OF COLLEGES AND UNIVERSITIES

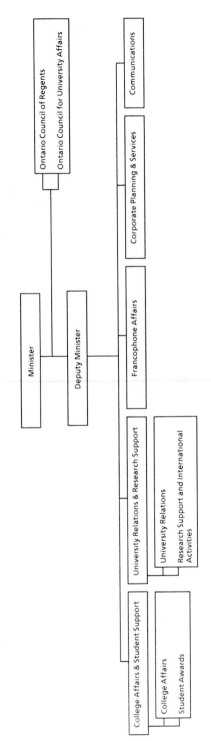

Minister

Deputy Minister

Ontario Council of Regents

Ontario Council for University Affairs

College Affairs & Student Support
- College Affairs
- Student Awards

University Relations & Research Support
- University Relations
- Research Support and International Activities

Francophone Affairs

Corporate Planning & Services

Communications

# ORGANIZATION

The Ministry of Colleges and Universities is organized into two major divisions (see organization chart):

1. *College Affairs and Student Support Division:* Composed of the College Affairs Branch, the Student Awards Branch, and the Office of the Superintendent of Private Vocational Schools.

2. *University Relations and Research Support Division:* Consisting of the University Relations Branch and a unit responsible for research support.

There are also the following support units: Corporate Planning and Services; Communications; Legal Services; International Activities; Franco-Ontarian Affairs; and the Executive Secretariat. In addition, the Ontario Council on University Affairs and three other councils and commissions report to the Legislative Assembly through the Minister of Colleges and Universities (see Agencies, Boards, and Commissions).

The head office of the Ministry of Colleges and Universities is located in Toronto. The Ministry employs approximately 240 public servants.

# PROGRAMS

## Colleges Affairs and Student Support Division

*College Affairs Branch*

The College Affairs Branch develops and administers the operational and administrative policies relating to the 22 colleges of applied arts and technology, and monitors the operation of existing policies. Programs include:

*Operating Grants:* Including

1. *General purpose operating grants.*

2. *Special purpose grants,* including grants for the rental of premises, grants for the incremental costs of programs delivered in French in designated colleges, grants in support of Ontario-Quebec exchange, grants in support of defined Francophone activities, grants in support of accumulated credits, and other ad hoc grants.

*Capital Grants:* Capital assistance to colleges.

*Coordination and development of Francophone services.*

*Support of the collective bargaining process* with the Faculty and Support Staff bargaining units in colleges.

*Supplying consulting services to colleges* in all matters relating to terms and conditions of employment of staff.

*Program approval* and related processes.

*College operational reviews.*

*Approval of property related transactions of colleges.*

*Development and promotion of programs for students with special needs:* E.g. women, the disabled, and native people.

### Student Awards Branch

The Student Awards Branch administers a number of programs for student support under which students receive grants, loans, bursaries, work-study funds, and scholarships/fellowships. This Branch maintains liaison with the financial aid offices in Ontario's universities and colleges, which receive students' applications for assistance, screen them, and forward them to the Ministry for processing. A small financial aid office at this Branch handles applications from students enrolled in post-secondary institutions other than Ontario universities and colleges. Student support programs include:

*Need-based Programs:* Ontario Student Assistance Program (OSAP, which includes Ontario Study Grant Plan, Ontario Student Loans Plan, Ontario Special Bursary Plan, and Ontario Work Study Plan); and the Canada Student Loan Program.

*Merit-based Programs:* Ontario Graduate Scholarship Program; Ontario-Quebec Exchange Fellowship; Queen Elizabeth II Ontario Scholarship; Sir John A. Macdonald Graduate Fellowship in Canadian History; Teachers' Winter Bursary Program; the Ontario-Jiangsu Scholarship; and three federal programs—the Summer Language Bursary Program, Fellowships for studying in French, Teachers' Summer Bursary Program—which are administered by the Province of Ontario.

*The Superintendent of Private Vocational Schools:* Responsible for registering and regulating private vocational schools throughout the province.

## University Relations and Research Support Division

### University Relations Branch

The University Relations Branch administers support to the 15 provincially-assisted universities, the Ontario College of Art, the Ontario Institute for Studies in Education, Ryerson Polytechnical Institute, Dominican College, and the Bar Admission Course of the Law Society of Upper Canada. In addition, the Branch is concerned with the development, planning, and coordinating of policies which affect these institutions. Programs include:

*Operating Grants:* Including

1. *Formula Operating Grants.*

2. *Extra-Formula Operating Grants:* Bilingualism Grants; Northern Ontario Grants; Differentiation Grants; and Grants to the Law Society of Upper Canada (for Bar Admission Course).

3. *Non-formula Operating Grants:* Grants for the Development and Start-up of New French Courses in the Bilingual Universities; grants for Projects in French as a Second Language; grants in support of the Ontario-Quebec Exchange Program; grants for Off-Campus Programs; grants to Faculties of Education; Sustaining grants (University of Toronto Schools, and Ontario Educational Communications Authority); and other Grants (on the basis of line-budget review).

4. *Other Envelopes:* Enrollment/Accessibility Fund; Research Overheads/Infrastructure Funds; Instructional Equipment and Library Enhancement; Faculty Renewal; Program Adjustment Fund; and Special Northern Institutions Fund.

*Capital Grants:* Capital Assistance to Universities.

*Other Grants:* University Research Incentive Fund.

## EXPENDITURE ESTIMATES

*Estimated Expenditures 1987–88:*

| | |
|---|---|
| Ministry Administration | $ 6,122,300 |
| University Support | 1,525,995,900 |
| College Support | 673,558,900 |
| Student Affairs | 188,725,700 |
| **Ministry total:** | **$2,394,402,800** |

## AGENCIES, BOARDS, AND COMMISSIONS

The following ABCs report to the Legislative Assembly through the Minister of Colleges and Universities:

*College Relations Commission:* Established in 1975 to oversee the collective bargaining process between the Ontario Council of Regents for Colleges of Applied Arts and Technology and the Ontario Public Service Employees Union representing both academic and support staff. The Commission monitors and assists in negotiations, supervises staff voting, and advises the Lieutenant Governor in Council when a strike or lock-out is jeopardizing student education.

*Council for Franco-Ontarian Education* (Le Conseil de l'Education Franco-Ontarienne): Established by Order-in-Council in 1972. The role of the Council is to advise the Minister of Colleges and Universities and the Minister of Education on all matters relating to Franco-Ontarian education. It recommends the allocation of funds to bilingual universities for the development and start-up of new French courses or programs.

*Ontario Council of Regents for Colleges of Applied Arts and Technology:* Advises the Minister on a wide range of policies related to the colleges; it appoints

Boards of Governors of colleges, and approves procedures for the election of elected members; it is responsible for collective bargaining under the *Colleges Collective Bargaining Act* and establishes terms and conditions of employment for college staff. The Director of the College Affairs Branch of the Ministry is the Executive Secretary of the Council, and secretariat services are provided by that Branch.

*Ontario Council on University Affairs* (OCUA): Established in 1974 as an advisory body to the Minister of Colleges and Universities and the Lieutenant Governor in Council. The OCUA is composed of a full-time chairman and 19 others who serve on a part-time basis. A small research staff supports the work of the Council. The OCUA may advise on any matters pertaining to the university system but regularly advises on the funding required, the allocation of funds, graduate and professional program approval, and the Ontario Graduate Scholarship funding.

## LEGISLATION

The Ministry of Colleges and Universities administers the following Acts:

*Colleges Collective Bargaining Act*

*Degree Granting Act, 1983*

*Lakehead University Act, 1965*

*Ministry of Colleges and Universities Act*

*Ontario College of Art Act, 1968-69*

*Ontario Institute for Studies in Education Act, 1965*

*Private Vocational Schools Act*

*Ryerson Polytechnical Institute Act, 1977*

*University of Guelph Act, 1964*

*University of Ottawa Act, 1965*

*University of Toronto Act, 1971*

*Wilfrid Laurier University Act, 1973*

*York University Act, 1965*


A number of institutions receiving provincial operating support, either directly or through another provincially assisted university, have private acts which are monitored by the Ministry of Colleges and Universities. These include:

*Assumption University Act, 1964* (federated college of University of Windsor)

*Brock University Act, 1964*

*Carleton University Act, 1952*

*Dominican of Friar Preachers of Ottawa College Act, 1976*

*Huntington University Act, 1960* (federated college of Laurentian University)

*Huron College Act, 1958* (affiliate of the University of Western Ontario)

*Knox College Act, 1948* (federated college of the University of Toronto)

*Laurentian University of Sudbury Act, 1960*

*McMaster University Act, 1976*

*McMaster Divinity College Act, 1951* (affiliate of McMaster University)

*Osgoode Hall Law School Scholarship Act, 1968-69*

*Queen's University, Royal Charter, 1841*

*Regis Act, 1978* (federated college of the University of Toronto)

*Royal Military College of Canada Degrees Act, 1959*

*St. Augustine's Seminary Act, 1983* (federated college of the University of Toronto)

*University of St. Jerome's College Act, 1986* (federated with the University of Waterloo)

*University of St. Michael's College Act, 1958* (federated college of the University of Toronto)

*Saint Peter's Seminary Corporation of London, in Ontario Act, 1972* (affiliate of King's College, University of Western Ontario)

*University of Sudbury Act, 1960* (federated with Laurentian University)

*Thorneloe University Act, 1960* (federated with Laurentian University)

*Trent University Act, 1962-63*

*University of Waterloo Act, 1972*

*University of Western Ontario Act, 1982*

*University of Windsor Act, 1962-63*

*Victoria University Act, 1951* (federated with the University of Toronto)

*An Act Respecting Wycliffe College, 1916* (federated with the University of Toronto)


Some privately run bible colleges and theological seminaries were also incorporated by statute and the following acts are monitored by the Ministry of Colleges and Universities:

*Baptist Bible College Canada and Theological Seminary Act, 1984*

*Canadian Reformed Theological College Act, 1981*

*Central Baptist Seminary and Bible College Act, 1984*

*Eastern Pentecostal Bible College Act, 1983*

*Emmanuel Bible College Act, 1981*

*Institute for Christian Studies Act, 1983*

*London Baptist Bible College and London Baptist Seminary Act, 1981*

*Maimonides Schools for Jewish Studies Act, 1968-69*

*Ontario Bible College and Ontario Theological Seminary Act, 1982*

*Redeemer College Act, 1980*

*Toronto Baptist Seminary Act, 1982*

**Regulations**

In addition to the Acts detailed above, a number of regulations formulated under the *Ministry of Colleges and Universities Act* are also of relevance to the Ministry. These are:

*Ontario Study Grant Regulation*

*Ontario Student Loan Regulation*

*Ontario Special Bursary Plan Regulation*

*Ontario Graduate Scholarship Regulation*

# MINISTRY OF COMMUNITY AND SOCIAL SERVICES

## ROLES AND FUNCTIONS

The Ministry of Community and Social Services is one of the largest ministries in the Ontario Government. It serves over half a million adults, children, and families across the province who have special needs. The Ministry offers a broad range of services—from ensuring that the basic needs for food, clothing, and shelter are met, to providing counselling, rehabilitation services, and residential care.

The Ministry's primary goal is to maintain the stability and quality of life of Ontario society, by strengthening the capacity of communities to cope with change and to respond to the needs of families and individuals in ways that reinforce their dignity and independence. Six operating principles define the Ministry's general approach to developing polices and programs:

*Accessibility:* Support services are designed to be accessible in order to be useful to families and individuals. The appropriate support needs to be reasonably close at hand and organized so that people can readily find help.

*Affordability:* The Ministry plans ways of supporting communities while also trying to restrain cost increases.

*Community:* The local community is the focus when planning services for families and is the centre of responsibility for delivering services. Improving services for people with varying special needs involves integrating both services and people into local communities. The Ministry's job is to ensure that the local community is equipped to support its own residents.

*Diversity:* Wherever possible, supports to families and individuals recognize and respect differences of culture, religion, and heritage.

*Equal Treatment:* While service planning is designed to be flexible, an attempt is also made to protect clients from negative discrimination. The rights of people under the law--as well as standards of service--should not be affected adversely by local prejudices or special interest groups. This basic principle requires that policies and programs be developed with care and caution.

*Flexibility:* Meeting needs appropriately and efficiently requires planning a range of measures to help people cope with their own particular problems. Services are designed to be sensitive to the needs of individuals and groups.

This statement of goals and operating principles is basic to the strategic agenda adopted for the Ministry. Central to the Ministry's six operating principles are the major roles of providing family services and income maintenance, and community services.

### Family Services and Income Maintenance

*Child Care:* Through municipalities, Indian bands, and approved corporations, the Ministry provides child care services in home settings and with informal child care providers.

*Family Support Services:* The Ministry funds a number of support programs for families with special needs. These include residential and support services for battered women and their children, for people who are temporarily homeless, and for families under social or economic stress, among others.

*Income Maintenance:* Approximately $1.5 billion, half of the Ministry's total budget, goes to income maintenance programs. The objective of these programs is to provide a basic income to people in financial need. The *General Welfare Assistance* program provides shorter-term financial help to individuals and families suffering a temporary loss of income because of illness, unemployment or other misfortune. Fifty percent of the cost of General Welfare Assistance is funded by the federal government, thirty percent by the provincial government, and twenty percent by local governments. The *Family Benefits* program provides assistance on a longer-term basis to individuals and their families in financial need--primarily single parents and disabled people. This program is funded by the provincial and federal governments on a 50/50 per cent basis. Family Benefits recipients throughout Ontario who return to full-time jobs can continue to get financial assistance and benefits for up to two years, through the Ministry's Work Incentive (WIN) program. In addition, with the aim of helping single parent families to become self-sufficient, the Ministry has introduced Employment Support Initiatives in test municipalities across the province. Under this program, Family Benefits clients receive help in preparing their own employment and training plans; information about and referrals to training and employment programs; pre-training and pre-employment assistance; job search assistance and counselling; and assistance with their child care requirements.

### Community Services

*Children's Services:* One of the Ministry's prime responsibilities is to ensure the well-being and safety of all children in Ontario. To accomplish this, it funds and supervises a range of services including services for emotionally disturbed children, and correctional services for young offenders under the age of sixteen. In addition, the Ministry regulates and funds 51 Children's Aid Societies across the province whose responsibilities include assisting children in need of protection, arranging foster care and adoption placements, and providing parent education and counselling for children and families.

*Elderly Services:* The Ministry provides funding to a variety of home support services for seniors designed to help seniors continue to live in their own homes in the community as long as possible. For seniors who can no longer live on their own, the Ministry also funds almost 200 homes for the aged across the province.

*Services for the Physically Disabled:* Services aimed at ensuring that disabled people have the help they need to live as independently as possible are provided by the Ministry. Vocational rehabilitation services for those capable of entering the competitive labour market, and sheltered employment for others, are offered. In addition, the Ministry provides support services to enable physically disabled people to live in non-institutional settings.

*Services for the Developmentally Handicapped:* To help them to develop to their full potential, the Ministry provides programs for developmentally handicapped adults and children in a range of settings including institutions, developmental day care centres, group homes, sheltered workshops, and their own homes.

## BACKGROUND HISTORY

The forerunner of the Ministry of Community and Social Services was originally established in 1930 as the Department of Public Welfare. This department was formed as a result of the Ross Commission on Public Welfare and comprised an amalgamation of the Old Age Pensions, the Mother's Allowance, and the Children's Aid Branches which previously were administered by the Provincial Secretary, along with the Unemployment Relief Branch from the Department of Labour.

The Depression of the 1930s put enormous financial pressure on municipalities to provide relief, and as a result, the provincial government became involved. Over the following 30 years, "welfare" and child welfare programs were the core of the government's programs. During these years income maintenance designs were based on the assumption that the industrial workforce was stable. Welfare was provided to categories of people, such as those who were "not employable" or were "deserted mothers."

Beginning in the 1960s, social policy began to respond to other kinds of demands. Community services were inaugurated, including family support and day care programs, which began to grow. In 1967, the name of the Department was changed to the Department of Social Family Services, a name which was maintained until 1972. In that year, the current Ministry was established under the *Community and Social Service Act.*

In 1974, the Ministry added the care of the mentally retarded to its responsibilities. In 1979, it became responsible for all children's services, including mental health programs and corrections.

In November 1985, the new *Child and Family Services Act* was proclaimed. It eliminated inconsistencies, simplified the law, addressed the new legal issues, and ensured that the legislation conformed with the equality provisions of the Charter of Rights and Freedoms.

MINISTRY OF COMMUNITY AND SOCIAL SERVICES

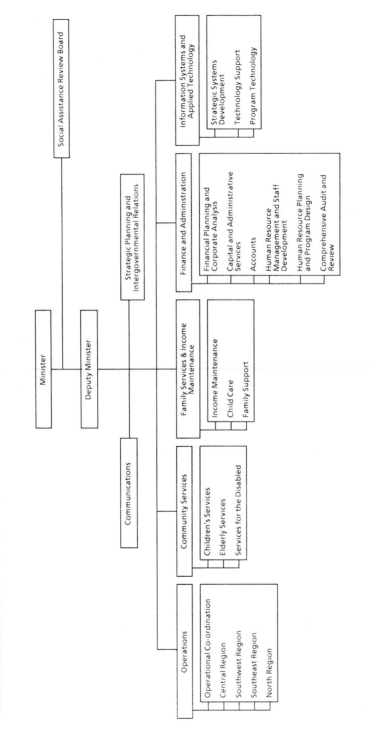

The current trend within the Ministry is to encourage and support community living programs which enable physically and mentally handicapped persons and elderly citizens to live independently. Ministry-operated and Ministry-funded programs are moving towards smaller residential setting with support networks.

Administration of Ministry-funded and direct-delivery programs across the province are decentralized to four administrative regional offices and 13 area offices within these regions.

## ORGANIZATION

In 1986, the Ministry of Community and Social Services underwent a major reorganization, which resulted in the establishment of five functional divisions: Operations, Community Services, Family Services and Income Maintenance, Finance and Administration, and Information Systems and Applied Technology. In addition, a new office of Strategic Planning and Intergovernmental Relations was created. The top executives in those six areas report directly to the deputy minister.

The reorganization was based on a number of principles. First, the intent was to create a structure with a clear system of accountability. With that in mind, the organization was built around two central functions: design and delivery. The design is handled by the program development part of the Ministry (the Community Services and the Family Services and Income Maintenance Divisions), which is responsible for strategic thinking and design of new programs up to the point of implementation. At that point, responsibility is transferred to the Operations Division, which is completely responsible for the delivery of Ministry programs, as well as annual budgeting and financing.

Another important principle in the reorganization was the need for a strong program focus. The Ministry is responsible for approximately $3 billion worth of programs delivered to half a million clients, many of whom are served through the 1,800 agencies which receive Ministry support. That is why distinct program areas were created (Children's Services, Elderly Services, Services for the Disabled, Income Maintenance, Child Care, Family Support). This will allow each of the areas to focus their attention exclusively on the matters for which they are responsible.

In order to keep bureaucracy to a minimum, it was recognized that any reorganization must reduce the layering of management within the Ministry. As a result, the number of senior management levels have been reduced from four to three, which puts the Deputy Minister closer to the front line activity of the Ministry.

As the Ministry receives a large portion of its funding from the federal government, the reorganization examined the importance of relations with other governments. This resulted in the establishment of the Office of Strategic Planning and Intergovernmental Relations, which will provide the strategic thinking and planning so important in this vital area.

During the reorganization, the importance of information systems and technology was recognized. Technology has a huge potential not only to increase Ministry efficiency, but also to help the Ministry's clients. In order to harness that potential, the new division of Information Systems and Applied Technology was created. This will be a permanent part of the Ministry, working to make use of the latest technological developments.

The reorganization of the Ministry of Community and Social Services has not led to any change in day-to-day contact with clients but it has resulted in a better organization. It frees senior management to spend more time on long-term planning and makes it clearer to everyone who is responsible for what in the Ministry.

Finally, the reorganization also enables Ministry staff to develop strategic management principles which should assist in demonstrating that money spent on social services is money well spent. The reorganization should also give the Ministry a greater chance to listen to the needs and ideas of everyone involved in social services.

The accompanying organization chart illustrates the organization of the Ministry. The Ministry of Community and Social Services employs approximately 8,900 public servants.

## PROGRAMS

The services of the Ministry of Community and Social Services, which are provided both directly and through funded agencies, can be grouped into two main categories: Children and their Families, and Adults.

Services to children and/or their families include: group or foster homes; adoption or foster parents; help with physical, emotional, or developmental disabilities; temporary or long-term help for children in need of protection; and probation and aftercare programs.

Services to adults include: senior citizens' centres, homes, and community programs; job preparation for people with physical, emotional, or developmental disabilities; benefits for those in financial need--either temporary or long-term; group homes for ex-offenders, alcoholics, or people who are emotional or developmentally disabled; and residential and community programs for people with developmental disabilities.

Ministry programs include:

### Adult Services

*Services for the Developmentally Handicapped*

There are many support services available to assist developmentally handicapped adults to live independently in the community. For others whose handicaps necessitate a more structured environment, there are a number of specialized facilities operated by the Ministry or community agencies. Services to the developmentally handicapped include: accommodation in special residences and group homes, employment and training, adult protective services, communications (specialized communication skills), life-skills training, behaviour management, adult education programs, recreational and social activities, and financial assistance to meet special needs.

### Rehabilitation for Physically and Socially Disabled

*Employment Programs:* Aid for disabled persons is provided with the goal of preparing them for and obtaining them employment. Employment may be sheltered, in the open labour market, or at home. Under the *Vocational Rehabilitation Services Act*, the following services are provided by the Ministry to individuals with a physical, emotional, or intellectual disability which inhibits their ability to get a job:

1. Counselling services to support an individual through the rehabilitation process until suitable employment is found;

2. Assessment services to determine aptitudes and the kind of work that the disabled person is best suited for;

3. Restoration services and devices such as artificial limbs, braces, or wheelchairs; and

4. Vocational training which may involve training at a community college, university, private, or business school, workshop, or an on-the-job training program.

The Ministry shares with municipal governments the cost of work-activity projects which give participants an opportunity to develop social and educational skills within a working environment. Work-activity projects are aimed at removing personal, family, and environmental barriers to employment.

*Residential Programs:* Halfway houses, for persons needing interim help to adjust to normal living, are funded by the Ministry and include halfway houses for alcoholics, ex-offenders, ex-psychiatric patients, and adults with other social adjustment problems. The Ministry also funds attendant care services for physically disabled people who live in specially operated apartments and group homes.

### Seniors Programs

*Aids for Independence:* Most senior citizens in Ontario live in their own homes or with relatives. The Ministry helps local municipalities and non-profit organizations operate services for seniors such as meals-on-wheels, homemakers' and nurses' services, and senior volunteer-in-service which help seniors remain at home. The Ministry also assists older people in applying for the Ontario Senior Citizens' Privilege Card and the Drug Benefit program.

*Elderly Persons' Centres:* Offer social, recreational, and other activities to encourage seniors to remain active in the community. The Ministry gives grants to municipalities and other non-profit organizations which operate these centres.

*Homes for the Aged:* Subsidies are paid to charitable and municipal homes which offer residential or extended health care for seniors unable to remain in their own homes. Charge for accommodation, meals, and services are levied, and a subsidy is provided if needed. Facilities in home for the aged usually include games and crafts rooms, gift and tuck shops, hair salons, and chapels. Many newer homes offer private accommodation for married couples.

### Family and Children's Services

*Adoption Aids:* The Ministry, using various adoption aids, assists in bringing together adoptable children and prospective parents. "Today's Child", a syndicated column, is distributed to newspapers across Ontario. Many of the children featured in the column are older or wish to be adopted with their brothers or sisters as a family. The television show, "Family Finder," features adoptable children who come from children's aid societies all over Ontario.

*Adoption Disclosure Registry:* A registry was created in 1978, for those adoptees and natural parents of adoptees who may wish to contact each other or share information. If the natural parents, the adoptee, and the adopting parent agree to the disclosure, information may be exchanged following counselling.

*Child Abuse and Neglect:* Public education is an important part of child abuse prevention. The Ministry has produced a number of pamphlets and booklets for public use, as well as guidelines and research reports for professional use. The Ministry funds a variety of demonstration projects and programs aimed at preventing child abuse. In addition, a central child abuse register has been set up to record the names of all children who have suffered abuse and the people who have inflicted or permitted abuse. This information is then available to children's aid societies throughout the province as a means of "tracking" the child, and thereby assisting the Children's Aid Society in its attempt to prevent any repetition of child abuse within the family.

*Children Requiring Emotional Care:* Children with behavioural or psychological problems may receive care and treatment at children's mental health centres located throughout the province. These centres provide services for emotionally disturbed children, youths, and their families, with a view to returning them as contributing members of society. The Ministry is attempting to ensure that each child with emotional problems has reasonable access to a range of mental health services. The Ministry supervises these centres and provides operating funds.

*Children Requiring Residential Care:* The Ministry funds and supervises homes for children and youths unable to live with their families or on their own. Temporary accommodation is sometimes necessary during a family crisis such as illness, separation, or loss of housing. Long-term needs are filled by a variety of group and foster homes and institutional care.

*Children's Aid Societies:* Children's Aid Societies (CAS) are non-profit corporations. The Ministry supervises and provides major funding for them in partnership with local government. The services of the CAS include: programs to prevent family breakups, including parent education and family counselling; protection of children from abuse and from situations of distress; guidance for mothers-to-be who are on their own; foster homes for children needing temporary or long-term placement; and adoption services, including all aspects involved in helping a family arrange for and adjust to the adoption.

*Day Nurseries:* The Ministry ensures that all daycare centres and nurseries meet accepted standards of child care, educational stimulation, fire safety, health, nutrition, and child guidance. It licenses and supervises all group programs for normal children up to 10 years of age and for developmentally handicapped children, ages two to 18 years.

*Developmentally Handicapped Children:* Services to developmentally handicapped (also called mentally retarded) children are administered by the Ministry, community agencies, and facilities for the mentally retarded. Some facilities are owned and operated by the Ministry; others are funded by the Ministry and operated by local boards. Services include: assessment and diagnostic facilities; family counselling; day nurseries; parent relief; nursing and medical care; behaviour modification programs; educational, recreational, and social activities; life-skills training; community outreach programs; and special programs for retarded children with additional disabilities such as hearing or sight loss.

*Disabled Children At Home:* Families who care for severely disabled children in their own homes may qualify for a special monthly allowance. The Handicapped Children's Benefits program is designed to help defray the extraordinary costs related to the special assistance and treatment needed for the severely disabled child.

*Young People in Trouble with the Law:* The Ministry supervises a number of programs and facilities for young people in trouble with the law. For instance, a young offender placed on probation is supervised by a probation and aftercare officer. The young offender may continue to live at home, or be placed in a foster or group home funded by the Ministry. The Ministry operates a small number of training schools for young offenders who need a structured setting. There are also a number of centres for assessing offenders.

## Financial Assistance—Temporary or Long-Term

*Family Benefits Assistance* (FBA): This program, similar to municipal general welfare assistance, is provided to individuals and their families who need help on a long-term basis. To qualify, the recipient must usually be in need and be: a sole-support parent; a person who is blind, disabled, or permanently unemployable; a foster parent (on behalf of the foster child in limited circumstances); a single woman between 60 and 64 years old; or an elderly person who is not in receipt of old-age security payments. In some instances, parents of handicapped children are eligible. Family benefits are paid monthly, by cheque. The amount depends on incomes, expenses, family size, and the ages of the children. The program also covers health aids. Families with dependent children are limited to dental care for the children and emergency care for the parents, as well as back-to-school benefits.

*General Welfare Assistance:* Available at municipal social service offices to people in temporary financial need who are: unemployed and looking for work; supporting children alone; caring for foster children (under limited circumstances); sick; physically, mentally, or emotionally disabled; elderly; or attending elementary or secondary school with no other means of support. The amount of assistance depends on the recipient's income, expenses, family size, and ages of the children. General Welfare Assistance provides money for basic living costs and other expenses such as special diet food if needed, and fuel. In addition, recipients and their dependents receive health insurance coverage and prescription drugs.

*Part-time Employment:* Because more recipients are only able to work part time, the Family Benefits program allows recipients to retain a portion of the earnings.

*Temporary Financial Problem:* The Ministry also sponsors programs, usually through municipalities and/or private agencies, to help people get through periods of temporary financial distress. They include: financial eligibility assessment for those unable to pay fees for necessary legal services, which are provided through the province's legal aid program; credit/debt counselling, provided through private agencies; and subsidies for homemakers to enable those who are elderly, disabled, ill, or convalescent to remain in their own homes and prevent serious family disruption, provided through municipalities, except in unorganized territories. Homemaker services are available on a daily or periodic basis, under the direction of a physician or visiting nurse.

*Training Allowance:* Special provisions may be made for those with dependent children who are taking approved Canada Manpower job-training courses. They may be able to continue to receive a minimal allowance plus coverage for medical, dental, and drug expenses. When entering full-time employment, such recipients may also be eligible for the phase-out allowance and Work Incentive Program.

*Work Incentive Program:* Designed to encourage and to assist those recipients on Family Benefits to return to full-time employment. It is a voluntary program that provides allowances and health-related benefits, for up to two years, to FBA recipients who start full-time employment.

## EXPENDITURE ESTIMATES

*Estimated Expenditures 1987–88:*

| | |
|---|---|
| Ministry Administration | $ 38,692,438 |
| Adults' and Children's Services | 3,457,768,700 |
| **Ministry total:** | **$3,496,461,138** |

## AGENCIES, BOARDS, AND COMMISSIONS

The following ABCs report to the Legislative Assembly through the Minister of Community and Social Services:

*Boards of Management of Homes for Aged:* There are 10 Boards of Management, one for each District throughout Northern Ontario. The council of a municipality, in the process of establishing and maintaining a home, appoints a committee of management from among members of the council. In addition, the province appoints, by Order-in-Council, two or three members-at-large to each Board.

*Child Welfare Review Committees:* Where the council of a municipality or a District Child Welfare Budget Board does not agree with the amount of the estimate submitted to it by a society, or where the Ministry through notice of filing, variance, or refusal alters a Children's Aid Society's estimate, either the municipality, Budget Board, or society may request the Minister to refer the matter to a Child Welfare Review Committee. The Committee may review the evidence, and the findings and recommendations shall be made available to the parties concerned. After reviewing the findings and recommendations the Minister may approve, vary, or determine the amount of the estimates.

*Children's Services Review Board:* Provides an appeal mechanism for specific decisions regarding licenses made by the Director under the Child and Family Services Act, 1984, and the Day Nurseries Act, and recommendations about residential placements made by Residential Placement Advisory Committees. Additionally, in certain specified situations, the Board is mandated to review a service provider's refusal to provide access to records, refusal to correct a record, and allegations of unauthorized disclosure of a record. The Board is established as an independent body and its decisions are not subject to review by the Minister or an official of the Ministry.

*Custody Review Board:* Operates jointly with the Ministry of Correctional Services. Young persons, while in a custody facility, may apply to the Custody Review Board for reviews of Provincial Directors' decisions regarding their placement. As part of their review, the Board may hold a hearing. Recommendations are made in writing to the Provincial Director who makes the final decision. The duties of the Training Schools Advisory Board are assumed by the Custody Review Board so that the progress of the remaining training school wards may continue to be reviewed.

*District Welfare Administration Boards:* A board is established and maintained by all towns, villages, etc. in a district when by-laws, authorizing the establishment of the Board, have been passed by a majority of municipalities in the district. All powers, duties, and responsibilities associated with administration of welfare services are vested in the board. The Board appoints a welfare administrator and staff. In addition, the province appoints by Order-in-Council several members-at-large.

*Medical Advisory Board:* Provides adjudication on medical issues arising from applications for disability benefits. The Board reports to the Director as to whether an applicant or recipient of Family Benefits is a blind person, a disabled person, or a permanently unemployable person. The Board also reports on whether or not an applicant may benefit from vocational rehabilitation services and whether or not vocational training would be detrimental to the health of the applicant.

*Social Assistance Review Board:* Holds hearings of appeals throughout the province which have been requested by individuals regarding decisions on General Welfare Assistance, Vocational Rehabilitation Services, Family Benefits (financial allowances for single mothers, the blind and disabled, permanently unemployable fathers, foster children, severely handicapped children), Guaranteed Annual Income System GAINS-D (income supplement for the blind and disabled), and co-payment (exemption from payment for chronic care services provided under the *Health Insurance Act*).

*Soldiers Aid Commission:* Provides emergency aid to veterans of World War I, II, and the Korean War who have exceptional circumstances and who have exhausted all other sources of funds. The Commission is self-funded by three trusts. The Ministry is responsible for providing administrative support including the preparation of cheques and maintenance of financial records. Members are appointed by Order-in-Council.

## LEGISLATION

The Ministry of Community and Social Services is responsible for the following Acts:

*Child and Family Services Act:* This Act consolidated many separate pieces of legislation which provided services to children (see Innovations). The consolidated Act includes the *Child Welfare Act, Children's Residential Services Act, Children's Mental Health Services Act, Children's Institutions Act, Developmental Services Act,* and *Homes for Retarded Persons Act.*

*Child Welfare Municipal Payments Continuance Act, 1976*

*Child Welfare Validation of Adoption Orders Act*

*Day Nurseries Act*

*Charitable Institutions Act*

*Developmental Services Act*

*District Welfare Administration Boards Act*

*Elderly Persons Centres Act*

*Family Benefits Act*

*General Welfare Assistance Act*

*Homemakers and Nurses Services Act*

*Homes for Retarded Persons Act*

*Homes for the Aged and Rest Homes Act*
*Indian Welfare Service Act*
*Jewish Family and Child Services of Metropolitan Toronto Act*
*Ministry of Community and Social Services Act*
*Soldiers' Aid Commission Act*
*Soldiers' Aid Commission Amendment Act*
*Vocational Rehabilitation Services Act*
*Young Offenders Act*

## INNOVATIONS

The new *Child and Family Services Act* is one of the most significant pieces of social policy legislation passed in recent years. It is the result of several years of public consultation. Under the new Act, the services provided to children by the Ministry of Community and Social Services that were previously governed by many separate acts, are now consolidated under a single piece of legislation. It eliminates the inconsistencies, simplifies the law, addresses new legal issues, and ensures that the legislation conforms with the equality provisions of the Charter of Rights and Freedoms.

The Act attempts to present one cohesive philosophy for services to children and families and for the protection of children. It reinforces the philosophy that community living is preferable to institutional living and open facilities to locked ones through guidelines that direct the courts and service providers to seek out the least restrictive or drastic alternative when intervention is necessary.

Other issues addressed in the legislation include access to and confidentiality of records; the use of extraordinary measures such as secure treatment and secure isolation or intrusive procedures; the rights, special heritage, and culture of Canada's Indian and native peoples; and review of residential placements, particularly in institutions. Based on the assessment of change in the economy and society, and on the historical development of social services in Ontario, the Ministry is embarking on strategies in three major areas: a new approach to income support for families; a comprehensive approach to the needs of the elderly; and a community-based, preventive approach to supporting families with special needs.

The following are a number of innovative measures being taken by the Ministry to address the identified social needs within Ontario:

*De-institutionalization:* The Ministry recognizes the need to gradually transfer developmentally handicapped people from institutions to the community, and to provide a range of service supports. A need still exists to ensure a decent quality of life for those who now live in institutions. The Ministry is reconciling these conflicting needs and pressures by developing a comprehensive plan to place developmentally handicapped people in the community, while maintaining decent standards of living for people remaining in institutions.

*Employment Support Initiatives Program:* This program offers a "one window" approach to employment services. It has been introduced in over 19 municipalities throughout the province.

*Federal/Provincial Agreement on Enhancing the Employability of Social Assistance Recipients:* The Federal Government's Canadian Jobs Strategy, a consolidation of a number of former programs, is important to social assistance recipients. It provides training programs for women and youth, and work experience programs for the long-term unemployed. Canada Employment and Immigration has made a commitment to give priority to social assistance recipients in two of these programs: job entry and job development. The Federal Government has established a national fund of $100 million for each of the next three years to expand employment and training opportunities for social assistance recipients, or to develop new ones. The Provincial Governments will match the Federal contributions. The signing of this agreement will enhance existing employment programs and provide more training and jobs for those who, up to now, have been unable to take part.

*Integrated Homemaker Program:* The aim of the Integration program is to coordinate provincial and municipal homemaker services to the elderly in order to enable the individual to live at home. The program will relieve municipalities of a significant financial responsibility, as about two-thirds of the cases previously cared for by municipal homemaker programs are frail elderly and physically disabled adults. However, the new Integrated Homemaker Program has a maximum monthly service limit of 60 hours. It is hoped that local governments will continue to provide additional services over and above the 60 hours in those situations where this is deemed appropriate to maintain the individual at home. The program is a positive step towards filling a real need for frail elderly and physically disabled adults who wish to remain at home, but who are ineligible for other services. It is hoped that municipalities which enjoy savings as the result of this new program will redirect these savings to other community support services for elderly and disabled people. The outcome is expected to be a coherent and coordinated system of programs, such as appropriate home supports, that help the elderly remain independent as long as possible. This includes an assessment, placement, and monitoring system to control access to residential care, to reduce the demand for new residential beds, and to ensure ready availability of services matched to individual needs.

*Integration of Income Maintenance Delivery:* Since 1982, several municipalities have undertaken test projects integrating General Welfare Assistance and Family Benefits Assistance at the municipal level. Final agreements have been signed with a number of these communities. The Ministry continues to fund all Family Benefits Assistance at 100 per cent. The aim of integration is to rationalize and streamline the delivery of income maintenance services.

## SUMMARY

In summary, the Ministry is embarking upon three major strategic directions:

1. A new design for income support that ensures help and incentives to those who can return to work, while assisting the permanently unemployed in a dignified way;

2. A reliable, organized, and expanded system of community support services for seniors, complemented by a system of quality, long-term care; and

3. A system of appropriate supports and policies that enhance families' capacity to care for their children, the elderly, and the handicapped. Emphasis is on prevention in all program areas and a child care system that is accessible, affordable, and flexible. This includes a planned approach to placing developmentally handicapped people in communities. Included is the intention to apply technology to helping the physically handicapped, and to program design and management.

These strategies will also require special attention to cost-sharing with municipalities, Native services, the use of technology, and organizational structures. The comprehensive and systematic strategies described above are an effective long-term response to the strategic concerns facing society.

MINISTRY OF CULTURE AND COMMUNICATIONS

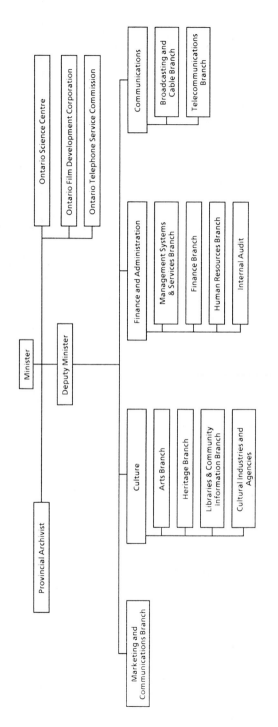

Minister

Provincial Archivist

Deputy Minister

Ontario Science Centre

Ontario Film Development Corporation

Ontario Telephone Service Commission

Marketing and Communications Branch

Culture
- Arts Branch
- Heritage Branch
- Libraries & Community Information Branch
- Cultural Industries and Agencies

Finance and Administration
- Management Systems & Services Branch
- Finance Branch
- Human Resources Branch
- Internal Audit

Communications
- Broadcasting and Cable Branch
- Telecommunications Branch

Support services shared with the Ministry of Citizenship

# MINISTRY OF CULTURE AND COMMUNICATIONS

## ROLES AND FUNCTIONS

The Ministry of Culture and Communications promotes shared values, cultural expression, and a pluralistic cultural heritage by supporting cultural and multicultural development in Ontario. The Ministry attempts to support and strengthen all sectors of the cultural community through programs that promote cultural expression and diversity, heritage preservation, library and information services, and formal and informal learning opportunities. The Ministry also represents Ontario's interests in the communications field through its involvement in the federal policy-making process.

## BACKGROUND HISTORY

The Ministry of Citizenship and Culture was established on February 13, 1982, by an Act of the Ontario Legislature, which received Royal Assent on June 7, 1982. The Ministry replaced the former Ministry of Culture and Recreation which had been formed in 1975, out of the Ministry of Colleges and Universities and other programs from a variety of different ministries.

An Order-in-Council dated October 8, 1987, created the Ministry of Culture and Communications, which now comprises of the Culture Division of the former Ministry of Citizenship and Culture, and the Communications Division of the former Ministry of Transportation and Communications. Broadcasting policy is considered to be more closely related to cultural issues than transportation, and the two areas are combined at the federal level. It is felt that the pairing of the culture and communications functions will smooth future federal-provincial negotiations. The new Ministry of Citizenship will continue to receive administrative support from the Ministry of Culture and Communications.

## ORGANIZATION

The Ministry of Culture and Communications is organized into three divisions (see organization chart):

1. *Finance and Administration:* Provides support services such as Finance, Internal Audit, and Human Resources to the Ministry.

2. *Culture:* Includes the Arts, Heritage, Library and Community Information, and Cultural Industries and Agencies Branches.

3. *Communications:* Includes the Broadcasting and Cable, and the Telecommunications Branches.

In addition, thirteen agencies, boards, and commissions, including The Art Gallery of Ontario, the Royal Ontario Museum, and the Ontario Science Centre, report to the Legislative Assembly through the Minister of Culture and Communications (see Agencies, Boards and Commissions).

The head office of the Ministry of Culture and Communications is located in Toronto. The Ministry also delivers its programs through a network of 18 regional and field offices. The Ministry employs approximately 400 public servants.

## PROGRAMS

### Archives of Ontario

The basic objectives and responsibilities of the Archives are to provide archival service to the Government of Ontario, its ministries, and agencies. It acquires significant unpublished documents to preserve Ontario's historical heritage. By law, the Archives obtain important non-current records from Ontario agencies. From other sources important historical manuscripts, maps, pictures, early newspapers, audio-visual archives etc. are obtained by donation or purchase. The Archives of Ontario maintain a conservation laboratory for document restoration of Archive's holdings, and operate a library and public reading room for those doing historical, administrative, legal, or other research. Information on the location of historical material is sought and welcomed.

### Regional Services

The Ministry is responsible for encouraging and developing increased opportunities for public involvement in cultural activities in all communities across the province in order to strengthen cultural expression. The Regional Services staff provides consultation services at the community level to municipalities, to community organizations, associations, and interest groups. Consultants also administer the Ministry's grants programs.

### Communications Division

The Communications Division keeps in touch with the opinions and aspirations of private industry and the general public while developing a provincial position on a variety of communications issues. Federal decisions are influenced through consultation, participation in hearings, and written submissions. Proposals by the Ministry have been included in changes to Canadian content legislation and FM radio regulations; in the guidelines for licensing Canadian "superstations" and cellular mobile radios; and in the debates over telephone competition and rates. The Ministry has three major objectives in this area: to ensure that Ontario residents have access to a reasonable choice of communications services at fair prices; to promote efficiency and effectiveness in the communications network; and to contribute to the province's economic growth in the communications sector.

## Culture Division

### Arts Branch

The Arts Branch develops policies and programs to encourage excellence and wider participation in the arts. The Arts Branch maintains close liaison with the Ontario Arts Council to support the development of the arts in Ontario and Canada. Programs administered by the branch are:

*Arts Abroad Program:* Provides assistance to both professional and community-based non-profit organizations touring outside the province.

*Arts Education Institutions Program:* Two national professional arts training institutions, the National Ballet School in Toronto and the National Theatre School in Montreal, are assisted.

*Arts Services Organizations Operating Grant Program:* To facilitate the ongoing operation and growth of the arts service organizations, the Ministry provides operating grants to provincial and national groups.

*Festival Ontario/Outreach Ontario:* Festival Ontario coordinates exhibitions from major cultural and arts institutions and makes these available free of charge to communities to augment festivals or special events. Festival Ontario helps the organizers of community events and festivals to tap resources of various provincial cultural agencies. Festival Ontario does not organize festivals but assists at the request of the communities. Outreach Ontario is designed to decentralize the Province's resources by encouraging Toronto area cultural institutions to diversify their programs, expand extension services, and undertake cooperative projects.

*Films Festival/Theatre Awards:* The annual Festival of Festivals and the International Animation Festival, both of which showcase the products of Canadian film professionals in an international context, receive support.

*Investment in the Arts Program:* A new three-year $10 million program, Investment in the Arts, will match one dollar for every fundraising dollar raised above the fundraising base. And if the dollar comes from a new corporate donor, the Ministry will match it two to one. In general, Ontario-based arts organizations are eligible if they have been serving the community for three years, have operating budgets in excess of $75,000 and are currently receiving assistance through the Ontario Arts Council; arts organizations in northern Ontario are eligible with an operating budget of $50,000 and over.

*Ontario/Quebec Permanent Commission:* Cooperative Ontario-Quebec joint ventures include a number of promotional activities, exhibitions, festivals, resource sharing, and tours.

*Operating Grant Program For Art Galleries:* Eligible nonprofit community art galleries are assisted through grants for basic operating and administrative expenditures.

*Provincial Fine Arts Insurance Program:* This program is designed to aid art galleries and museums with insurance costs associated with travelling exhibits.

### Cultural Agencies and Enterprises Branch

*Book Publishing Program:* Canadian-owned, Ontario-based book publishers may be eligible for assistance from the Province of Ontario, whether through a guarantee of a loan made by a commercial lending institution or a rebate of interest paid on such loans.

### Heritage Branch

The Branch assists in the conservation, protection, and preservation of Ontario's historical resources and heritage. The Branch also provides staffing and administrative support to the Ontario Heritage Foundation, an agency of the Ministry of Culture and Communications.

*Heritage Programs Section:* Administers Ontario Heritage Foundation and Ministry grants programs and advises individuals and organizations in matters related to local/regional historical research and promotion, architectural conservation, archaeological excavation, and natural preservation. There are three units within the section:

1. *The Historical Resources and Museum Unit:* Provides heritage grants and professional advice to community museums and historical societies; undertakes projects designed to highlight the province's Franco-Ontarian and Multicultural heritage and to promote heritage/tourism; and operates a conservation program for museum and archival collections.

2. *The Architecture and Heritage Planning Unit:* Provides grants, technical assistance, and advice regarding building conservation techniques. Also, on behalf of the Ontario Heritage Foundation, grants are awarded for the conservation of heritage properties designated under the *Ontario Heritage Act.* These properties are usually publicly-owned by non-profit corporations. Grants are occasionally given for properties in private ownership. The directors of the Ontario Heritage Foundation judge the property on the basis of its architectural or historical significance.

3. *The Archaeology and Heritage Planning Unit:* Provides grants and advice for archaeological research and excavation and natural heritage preservation. The unit maintains an archaeological research data base. The six regional offices monitor archaeological sites and carry out excavations.

*Heritage Administration Section:* Responsible for the restoration, development, and management of historic and natural heritage properties owned by the Ontario Heritage Foundation (OHF). It also administers the OHF collection of movable properties (artworks and artifacts) and the Foundation's heritage easements program. In addition, this section through its Grants Services Unit, is responsible for the coordination of Ministry granting programs in the heritage field.

## Heritage Branch Programs

*Community Facilities Improvement Program:* The program provides support for the planning, purchase, construction, improvement, and renovation of cultural, multicultural, and citizenship facilities and for the conservation of heritage buildings in Ontario.

*Community Museum Operating Grant Program:* To encourage and improve the standard of operation of community museums in the province, the Community Museum Operating Program provides financial assistance to museums owned and maintained by municipalities, Indian band councils, conservation authorities, libraries, and non-profit corporations.

*Exhibit Support Program:* The Ontario Heritage Foundation awards grants to assist with technical expenses to non-profit groups producing exhibits which promote significant aspects of the province's heritage and are based upon solid, scholarly research.

*Heritage Festival/Regional Conference Grants:* In an effort to stimulate wide participation in the study of local history and in the preservation and utilization of heritage resources, the Ontario Heritage Foundation awards grants to assist in the staging of heritage festivals or regional conferences. Applicants must be non-profit groups; annual conferences are not eligible; the festivals must be open to the general public.

*Heritage Organization Development Grant Program:* The Ministry program is designed to encourage and assist incorporated heritage activity within their communities. Eligible expenses include administration costs and the operation of heritage resource centres, but emphasis is placed on expenses incurred in outreach or extension activities.

*Heritage Support Grant Program:* Financial support is provided under this Ministry program to help offset the operating and extension activity expenses of provincial heritage organizations.

*Local Marking Assistance Program:* Non-profit organizations and municipalities are eligible to receive funding under this Ministry program towards the manufacturing and installation costs in the erection of local plaques.

*Multicultural History Society of Ontario:* The Ministry provides financial support to the MHSO to assist it with operating, extension, publishing, organizational development, and archival collections' management expenses in promoting wider appreciation of the provinces' multicultural past.

*Natural Heritage Program:* The Natural Heritage program fulfills the Ontario Heritage Foundation's heritage protection mandate by carrying out three basic objectives: the protection of natural areas representing a wide range of earth and life science resources; the support of natural heritage protection methods through the coordinating mechanisms of the Natural Heritage League; and the provision of financial assistance through loans to individuals, groups, private and to public agencies for research, public education, publications, and conferences related to natural heritage projects.

*Ontario Historical Studies Series:* The Ministry provides financial support to assist the Ontario Historical Studies Series with the operating and publishing expenses in producing biographies of Ontario premiers and works related to various aspects of the province's heritage.

*Provincial Historical Plaque Program:* Upon request from individuals, organizations, and municipalities, the Ontario Heritage Foundation erects provincial historical plaques to commemorate persons, places, buildings, and events judged by Foundation directors to be of provincial significance.

*Publications Awards Program:* This Ontario Heritage Foundation program is designed to assist individuals and organizations in publishing works, that might not otherwise be produced, on aspects of Ontario's heritage. Only manuscripts judged by the directors of the Foundation to meet acceptable standards of scholarship and organization receive support.

*Research Grant Program:* The Ontario Heritage Foundation research grant program provides financial assistance to individuals and organizations to help offset technical expenses incurred in researching aspects of Ontario's past. Grants are awarded only to those applicants judged by the directors of the Foundation to be capable of completing high quality projects.

*Libraries and Community Information Branch*

The Libraries and Community Information Branch administers the Ontario Library Service, established under the *Public Library Act, 1984,* to deliver programs and services on behalf of the Ministry.

*The Libraries Section* is responsible for administering the Library Act. The section provides consultative assistance to Indian Band Councils, library boards, and municipalities regarding the establishment, organization, management, accommodation, and rules of county libraries, public libraries, and Ontario Library Service areas. It administers the operating grants formula and provides special financial assistance for the purpose of developing a province-wide network of library services, and assists in the provision of library service in areas without municipal organization. The section publishes statistical reports and other publications on public library service for distribution to the general public.

*The Technical Development Section* provides a range of advisory services aimed at increasing the use of computers and telecommunications to bring about communication and cooperation between libraries. It is currently implementing the Ontario Public Libraries Information Network (OPLIN). The Technical Development Unit administers the library automation grants programs, provides province-wide support for automation activities, including manuals, directories, and workshops, and will assist with library planning activities upon request.

### Libraries and Community Information Branch Programs

*Automation For Small Libraries Program:* Assists small libraries in the creation of databases and in the implementation of automated systems suitable to their needs. Automated projects will assist the library with accessing and managing library collections and will result in the creation of a machine-readable database which will be available for Automation for Small Libraries grants.

*Communities Facilities Improvement Program:* Provides support for the planning, purchase, construction, and improvement of citizenship facilities and for the conservation of heritage buildings in Ontario.

*Community Information Services Program:* Provides grants to fund eligible community information centres (CICs). It advises them on such matters as information management, policy, staffing, and volunteer training. The unit also produces resource materials and provides developmental assistance to CICs.

*Grants to Public Libraries:* The program awards grants to assist public library boards in providing, in cooperation with other boards, a comprehensive and efficient public library service that reflects the community's unique needs. Grants are calculated on a per household basis for municipal libraries and a per capita basis for Indian band libraries; the program guarantees a minimum increase over the previous year's grant.

*Larger Units of Public Library Services:* The program awards grants to assist county or municipal councils in evaluating the benefits of larger units of library service.

*Library Cooperative Automation Program:* Assists in the development of local public library networks. Projects considered include improvements to existing cooperative library automation projects and the extension of an existing library automation project to include additional participating jurisdictions.

*Northern Libraries Automation Program:* The program is designed to assist the development of automation in libraries located in Northern Ontario where cooperation is not economically feasible.

*Northern Native Library Development Program:* The Northern Native Library Development Program provides special assistance to Native Band Libraries in Northern Ontario. The program assists with the salary of the Band Librarian, acquisitions of collections, and equipment purchases.

*Operating Grants For Ontario Library Services Areas:* Provide operating grants to facilitates coordination of public libraries, interlibrary van and direct library service.

*Project Grants Program:* Public libraries may apply or assistance under the following categories:

1. Acquisition of Collections
2. Equipment
3. Events/Festivals
4. Internship Training
5. Organizational Development
6. Skills Training
7. Writers-In-Residence

Community Information Centres may apply for assistance under the following categories:

1. Acquisition of Collections
2. Equipment
3. Internship Training
4. Organization Development
5. Skill Training

## EXPENDITURE ESTIMATES

*Estimated Expenditures 1987–88*:

| | |
|---|---:|
| Ministry Administration | 7,244,574 |
| Heritage Conservation | 16,764,000 |
| Communications | 3,395,600 |
| Cultural Development and Institutions | 126,712,700 |
| Libraries and Community Information | 39,702,200 |
| Capital Support and Regional Services | 27,475,425 |
| **Ministry total:** | **$221,294,499** |

## AGENCIES, BOARDS, AND COMMISSIONS

The following ABCs report to the Legislative Assembly through the Minister of Culture and Communications:

*Art Gallery of Ontario:* The Gallery cultivates and advances the cause of visual arts in Ontario with programs, lectures, and films on the origin, development, appreciation, and techniques of visual arts. The Gallery exhibits works of art from its permanent collection and invitational and loan exhibitions in the art gallery and the Grange, a restored historic Toronto house. Exhibitions are also circulated to Ontario communities. The Gallery offers an art rental service, art book shop, audio-visual library, art reference library, art classes, tours and speakers bureau.

*CJRT-FM Incorporated:* CJRT-FM provides educational opportunities for the citizens of Ontario by offering adult education through credit courses at the university level as well as programming designed to provide a better understanding and appreciation of such fields of interest as the arts, music, and literature. All program content is presented without commercial sponsorship.

*Conservation Review Board:* The Board holds hearings at the request of a municipality if owners object to municipal designation of property for historic or architectural conservation. The Board reports its opinion to the municipal council. Hearings are also held if there are appeals against the Minister's designation of archaeological or historical sites or against the Minister's refusal of archaeological licenses.

*McMichael Canadian Collection:* The Collection exhibits one of Canada's most important collections of paintings by the Group of Seven painters and other Canadian masters, plus sculptures, paintings, and prints by native Indian artists and their contemporaries.

*Ontario Arts Council:* Promotes the study, enjoyment, and production of works in the arts. It provides grants in response to applications from performing and creative arts groups such as theatre and dance companies, orchestras and concert societies, art galleries and schools, publishing houses and periodicals, local and regional art councils and festivals, arts service groups, and community arts projects. Individual artists (e.g. choreographers, poets, film -makers, video artists, and photographers) may also apply. The Council has officers on staff who represent various arts disciplines and pursuits.

*Ontario Educational Communications Authority* (TVOntario): TVOntario is responsible for educational broadcasting in Ontario. TVOntario designs and produces TV-based learning systems in English and French for in-school, pre-school, and adult education. The TVOntario educational television broadcast reaches 95 percent of the Ontario population. It is delivered via an ANIK C3 satellite to 15 major transmitters, and through this same satellite is also delivered to 30 low-power transmitters to communities across northern Ontario and cable companies throughout the province. TVOntario also distributes video and audio tapes, maintains a library, and publishes print materials supporting educational programming.

*Ontario Film Development Corporation:* A new corporation to foster the development of Canadian-owned, Ontario-based film producers, the Ontario Film Development Corporation (OFDC) has established an investment fund to assist producers, writers, and directors. Film companies may be eligible for financial assistance to maintain ongoing financial stability.

*Ontario Heritage Foundation:* The Ontario Heritage Foundation advises the Minister of Culture and Communications on the issuance of archaeological licenses and on the designation of significant archaeological and historic sites. The Foundation provides grants to encourage innovative work in archaeology and to help complete artifact analysis; for architectural conservation to encourage renovation of buildings of historic and architectural significance; and to assist historians with the preparation and printing of manuscripts of local, regional, and specialized interest related to Ontario's heritage. It erects historic plaques which recognize people, places, buildings, and events of significance to the history of the province, and acquires, usually by donation, heritage properties, parkland, works of art, and historical artifacts.

*Ontario Science Centre:* Through innovative methods, the Ontario Science Centre makes science and technology appealing to children of all ages. The Centre invites visitor participation in its unique exhibits, demonstrations, workshops, and theatre presentations. It provides special exhibitions, films, and free education programs for Canadian school classes (booked in advance of their visit). Four major travelling exhibits visit shopping malls, schools, libraries, and recreation centres throughout Ontario. The Centre also houses a reference and information centre, the Ontario Film theatre, which screens films, and the Ontario Film Archives.

*Ontario Telephone Service Commission:* A regulatory body which is responsible for regulating the providers of the 30 telephone systems under provincial jurisdiction (e.g. Manitoulin Island Telephone Company, Dryden Municipal Telephone System). Bell Canada is *not* under this jurisdiction, as it reports to the Canada Radio-Television and Telecommunications Commission (CRTC).

*Royal Botanical Gardens:* The Royal Botanical Gardens in the Hamilton-Wentworth and Halton regions is 2,000 acres of developed gardens featuring world-renowned plant collections complemented by extensive natural areas served by 27 miles of interpretive nature trails. Educational programs include courses on horticulture, botany and design with plant materials, and instruction for school classes, as well as university credit courses. The Royal Botanical Gardens also offer the public extensive horticultural information on ornamental, native, and poisonous plants, edible and poisonous mushrooms, and information on birds.

*Royal Ontario Museum* (ROM): Located in Toronto, the ROM is the largest of Canada's public museums and a major research institution with collections in twenty departments. These include the arts, archaeological studies (e.g. Chinese, Egyptian), and science (e.g. mammalogy, mineralogy). The departments identify objects related to their fields such as birds, insects, works of art. The ROM maintains specialized libraries and offers group tours, a Discovery Room, traveling exhibitions, museum mobiles, a speakers bureau, lectures and art instruction, showings of films, and clubs for senior citizens and children.

*Science North:* Located in Sudbury, Science North provides science and technology programs through a combination of exhibitions, films, and demonstrations. Science North also operates the Big Nickel Mine for the only public tour of an actual working mine in Ontario.

## LEGISLATION

The Ministry of Culture and Communications is responsible for the following Acts:

**Culture**

*Archives Act:* The Archivist is responsible for the safekeeping of all original documents, manuscripts, papers, records, and other matters of the government; and the collection and the preservation of papers of historical value to the people of Ontario.

*Art Gallery of Ontario Act:* The Art Gallery of Ontario is established as a corporation with the following objectives: to cultivate and enhance the visual arts in Ontario; to conduct educational programs in the history and the techniques of visual arts; and to exhibit works of art.

*Arts Council Act:* The Ontario Arts Council is established to promote the study and production of works in the arts by: assisting, cooperating, and enlisting the help of organizations with similar goals to the council; providing grants, scholarships, and loans for study or research of the arts in Ontario; and making awards to persons in Ontario for outstanding accomplishments in the arts.

*Centennial Centre of Science and Technology Act:* The Ontario Science Centre is established as a corporation whose objectives including conducting an educational program in the history and progress of science and technology, collecting and exhibiting displays and objects, and maintaining and operating a museum.

*Foreign Cultural Objects Immunity from Seizure Act:* Works of art or other objects of cultural significance brought into Ontario for temporary exhibits or displays are given immunity from seizure while in Ontario.

*George R. Gardiner Museum of Ceramic Art Act, 1981:* The George R. Gardiner Museum is established as a corporation for the purpose of collecting, conserving, and exhibiting works of ceramic art. The museum is also responsible for promoting research and education in the history and the techniques of ceramic art.

*McMichael Canadian Collection Act:* The McMichael Canadian Collection is established as a corporation for the purpose of maintaining and operating an art gallery. The focus of the art collection is the works and objects created by Tom Thomson, Emily Carr, David Milne, A. Y. Jackson, Lawren Harris, A. J. Casson, Frederick Varley, Arthur Lismer, J. H. MacDonald, Franklin Carmichael, and the indigenous people of Canada.

*Ministry of Citizenship and Culture Act:* The Act creates a ministry of the public service known as the Ministry of Citizenship and Culture. The function of the Ministry is to encourage full, equal, and responsible citizenship among the residents of Ontario and to ensure the creative and participatory nature of cultural life in Ontario.

*Ontario Educational Communications Authority Act:* TVOntario is established under this act as an authority to initiate, acquire, produce, distribute, and exhibit programs and materials in the education and communications field.

*Ontario Heritage Act: Part I* designates the Minister of Citizenship and Culture to be responsible for the programs and policies directed at the conservation, protection, and preservation of the heritage of Ontario. *Part II* establishes the Ontario Heritage Foundation to: advise and make recommendations to the Minister regarding heritage matters; receive, acquire, and hold property in trust for the people of Ontario; support and facilitate the conservation, protection, and preservation of the heritage of Ontario; and ensure proper care for properties of historical architectural, archaeological, and scenic interest. *Part III* establishes the Conservation Review Board as the hearing body to which matters concerning designations of archaeological or historical properties are referred to under this legislation. *Part IV* authorizes municipalities to designate properties of architectural value in the province and grant permission to property owners to make alterations or to demolish these properties. *Part V* authorizes municipalities to designate districts or a group of buildings of architectural value and to grant permission to owners to make alterations or to demolish these buildings. Under *Part VI*, the Minister has the power to designate sites of archaeological significance and is authorized to grant licenses and permits to conduct archaeological field work in the province.

*Public Libraries Act, 1984:* Clarifies and strengthens the accountability between municipal council and a public library board. It allows the council to appoint board members, and to approve a board's estimates in the format decided by council. The Act clarifies free public library service. All library materials including print material and talking books for the blind must be free. The Act deletes reference to non-operative certification program and definition of librarian. The Ministry is supportive of professional development and is investigating a self-administered certification program. The Act places emphasis on the Boards' responsibility to respond to unique community needs and provides for confidentiality of patron records, French language for Board members, and open meetings.

*Royal Botanical Gardens Act:* Under this Act, a corporation is established to maintain and develop the Royal Botanical Gardens.

*Royal Ontario Museum Act:* The Act established the Royal Ontario Museum and the McLaughlin Planetarium as a corporation to collect and exhibit objects, documents, and books to illustrate to the public the natural history of Ontario, Canada, and the world. The corporation also operates the planetarium and promotes the research and education of all fields related to the objects of the museum.

*Science North Act:* Science North, formerly known as Sudbury Science Centre, is established under this act. The centre collects, develops, and exhibits objects and displays. It is also responsible for the maintenance and operation of a museum/science centre.

### Communications

*Muskoka and Parry Sound Telephone Co. Ltd. Acquisition Act.*

*Ontario Telephone Development Corporation Act.*

*Telephone Act.*

# MINISTRY OF EDUCATION

## ROLES AND FUNCTIONS

The Ministry of Education oversees the provision of elementary and secondary school education through over 750 school boards throughout Ontario. It also operates correspondence courses and schools for the deaf, blind, and handicapped. The Ministry is responsible for determining general education policy in the elementary and secondary schools of the province.

Other Ministry responsibilities include providing broad guidelines for the curriculum of Ontario schools; approving the list of textbooks from which school boards make selections for schools; establishing requirements for student diplomas and certificates; setting requirements for and issuing teaching certificates; distributing the funds allocated by the Legislature for assisting school boards with the costs of operating schools; and making regulations to govern the school year and holidays of students, the organization of schools, and the duties of teachers and school board officials.

## BACKGROUND HISTORY

One of the oldest ministries in the Ontario Government, the Ministry of Education was established in 1867. At that time, the Education Department consisted of a chief superintendent, Egerton Ryerson, his deputy, a senior clerk and accountant, a clerk in charge of statistics, a clerk in charge of correspondence, and a messenger. In addition, there were 269 local superintendents of commons schools who submitted regular reports to the department.

A Minister of Education was appointed in 1876, upon the retirement of Ryerson. The first Minister of Education was the Honourable Adam Crooks, who held the office for eight years. The Honourable George Ross, Minister of Education from 1884–1899, who went on to become Premier of Ontario, had been a public school teacher, and took a lead role in directing the development of education policy.

The Ross Government was defeated at the polls in 1905, and one of the first actions of the new Whitney Government was to reorganize the Department of Education. The Office of the Superintendent was revived, and an Advisory Council on Education was created. The latter was abolished in 1915. Over the next 30 years, a series of reorganizations made for confusion within the Department, as its size and mandate grew to include Public Libraries, Separate Schools, Industrial Training, and Agricultural Education.

MINISTRY OF EDUCATION

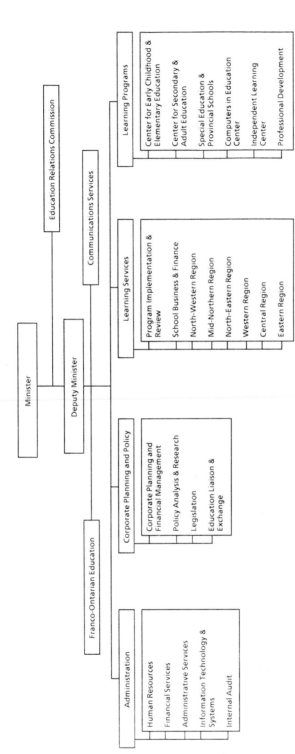

Minister

Deputy Minister

Education Relations Commission

Communications Services

Franco-Ontarian Education

**Administration**
- Human Resources
- Financial Services
- Administrative Services
- Information Technology & Systems
- Internal Audit

**Corporate Planning and Policy**
- Corporate Planning and Financial Management
- Policy Analysis & Research
- Legislation
- Education Liaison & Exchange

**Learning Services**
- Program Implementation & Review
- School Business & Finance
- North-Western Region
- Mid-Northern Region
- North-Eastern Region
- Western Region
- Central Region
- Eastern Region

**Learning Programs**
- Center for Early Childhood & Elementary Education
- Center for Secondary & Adult Education
- Special Education & Provincial Schools
- Computers in Education Center
- Independent Learning Center
- Professional Development

The Drew Government, upon assuming office in 1943, decided it was time to return to the organization of 1906, which had a clearly distinguished division between responsibility for administration and for educational policy. The complexity of the Department increased through the 1950s and '60s with the enormous increase in school enrollments which followed the rising birth rate, the heavy immigration of the post World War II period, and the development of post-secondary education in the province.

In 1972, the Department was renamed Ministry of Education. Since that time, the Ministry has evolved into two parts: administration and educational policy. Also, in the past 15 years, the Ministry has established a more clearly defined mandate. The Ministry now works in conjunction with local school boards and related Ministries such as Colleges and Universities, and Skills Development in an effort to rationalize and standardize education for the population of the province.

## ORGANIZATION

The Ministry of Education is organized into four divisions (see organization chart):

1. *Corporate Planning and Policy:* Includes the Policy Analysis and Research, Education Liaison and Exchange, and Corporate Planning and Financial Management Branches.

2. *Learning Programs:* Includes the Centres for Early Childhood Education, Computer Education, Independent Learning, and for Secondary and Adult Education; and the Special Education Branch for schools for the learning disabled, blind, and deaf, young offenders in custody, and for training nursing assistants.

3. *Learning Services:* Includes Program Implementation and Review, School Business and Finance, and School Board Services Branches, and six regional offices throughout Ontario.

4. *Administration:* Provides corporate services, such as communications, human resources, internal audit, and information technology, to the Ministry.

In addition, five agencies, boards, and commissions, including the Provincial Schools Authority and the Languages of Instruction Commission, report to the Legislative Assembly through the Minister of Education (see Agencies, Boards, and Commissions).

The head office of the Ministry of Education is located in Toronto. The Ministry also delivers its programs through six regional offices in Toronto, London, North Bay, Sudbury, Thunder Bay, and Ottawa, and operates five schools for the blind and deaf, five schools for training nursing assistants, four schools for young offenders in custody, and three schools for children with severe learning disabilities and language learning disorders. The Ministry employs approximately 1500 public servants.

## PROGRAMS

### Corporate Planning and Policy Division

*Education Liaison and Exchange Branch*

The Education Liaison and Exchange Branch encourages educational and cultural exchanges of students and teachers, and provides grants for the International Student Exchange, Ontario-Quebec Student Exchange, Ontario-Quebec School Twinning Project, Ontario Young Travellers, and International and Inter-provincial Teacher Exchange Programs. In cooperation with the federal Department of External Affairs, the Branch administers the Canadian Studies Seminars for European Teachers and coordinates seminars in Europe for Ontario educators. It administers the Second Language Monitor Program in which bi-lingual university students act as monitors to teachers of French or English as a Second Language, the Ontario Student Leadership Centre, the Ontario Secondary School Students Association, and the Summer Employment for Students program. The Branch assists school boards in coordinating Education Week and maintains liaison with other provincial education ministries, the federal government, and the Council of Ministers of Education (Canada). The Branch also maintains liaison with all Native bands, concerning education for and about Native people.

*Corporate Planning and Financial Management Branch*

The Corporate Planning and Financial Management Branch consists of four sections:

1. *Financial Management and Control:* Assists senior Ministry management with budgetary problems and administers funds allocated to the Ministry;

2. *Operational Planning and Development:* Assists in designing and implementing improvements in managements procedures;

3. *Strategic Planning:* Identifies current trends and determines long-range issues relevant to public education in Ontario; and

4. *Teachers' Superannuation:* Provides liaison with the Teachers' Superannuation Commission.

*Policy Planning and Research Branch*

The Policy Planning Research Branch provides analysis and advice on Ministry policies and identifies current issues to be addressed; regulates the contracting of education research and informs school boards of the results; gathers, validates, and analyses data on school boards, schools, colleges, and universities; develops and maintains statistics; and operates an Information Centre and an Information Service.

## Learning Programs Division

*Centre for Early Childhood and Elementary Education*

The Centre for Early Childhood and Elementary Education establishes, reviews, and extends policies and practices affecting English and French Primary and Junior Education and the first two years of Intermediate Education (i.e. kindergarten to grade eight) by disseminating circulars, guidelines, memoranda, and curriculum resource materials to school boards and elementary schools throughout the province.

*Centre for Adult Education*

The Centre for Adult Education develops, produces, and disseminates circulars, curriculum guidelines, memoranda, and resource materials in both English and French for Intermediate and Senior Education (grades nine to twelve) to assist school boards in developing programs and courses. The Centre also recommends policies for adult continuing education programs in the province, and administer the Student Guidance Information Service, which provides students with computerized career and post-secondary institution information.

*Computers in Education Centre*

The Computers in Education Centre provides leadership in the development and use of information technologies to support the curriculum in Ontario's elementary and secondary schools. It assists companies in producing educational software licensed for use in schools and offers assistance to teachers and school administrators on the effective use of electronic technology.

*Independent Learning Centre*

The Independent Learning Centre provides free home-study courses for Ontario residents who wish to obtain credits toward a high school diploma, upgrade basic skills, or study for enjoyment. More than 160 secondary school courses are offered in French or English, and may be started, completed, and diplomas awarded at any time of the year. The Centre also offers a non-credit basic adult education program in English as a Second Language (ESL), and provides an elementary program for children unable to attend school due to illness, distance from school, or lack of transportation facilities.

*Special Education and Provincial Schools Branch*

The Special Education and Provincial Schools Branch advises the Minister on program policy regarding the education of exceptional pupils in elementary and secondary schools for the trainable mentally retarded. Special education resource materials are produced to assist school board personnel, and guidelines are developed for special education courses in faculties of education. The branch operates the following special schools:

*Demonstration Schools for the Learning Disabled:* Designed for children with severe learning disabilities and language learning disorders and who cannot otherwise receive an appropriate education in their local schools. The three demonstration schools are residential, and are located in Ottawa, Belleville and Milton.

*Schools for the Deaf and Blind:* Five schools, in London, Brantford, Milton, Belleville, and Ottawa, provide day and residential programs for the blind and deaf. The Centre also operates a teacher education centre in Belleville for teachers for the deaf.

*Training Schools:* Provide Young Offender Services and Programs to youths (under age sixteen) who are confined to secure custody or temporary detention under the *Child and Family Services Act* at four centres, in Oakville, Cobourg, Simcoe, and Sudbury.

*Regional Schools for Nursing Assistants:* Offer programs for training nursing assistants in Toronto, Hamilton, London, Sudbury, and Thunder Bay.

## Learning Services Division

### Program Implementation and Review

Program Implementation and Review advises on policies and procedures for evaluation of student achievement program effectiveness, personnel performance, school safety, health, and inspection of private schools.

### Regional Offices

The Regional Offices inform school systems about Ministry programs and policies on education, and ensure, in collaboration with local school boards, that these policies are carried out. Regional offices are located in Toronto, London, Ottawa, Sudbury, North Bay, and Thunder Bay.

### School Business and Finance Branch

The School Business and Finance Branch develops and administers the grant formulas which support school boards throughout the province, sets financial accounting and enrollment reporting standards, and oversees the audit of financial statements of school boards. Architectural and construction advice is offered to school boards. The branch issues final approval for costs of school board capital projects approved for provincial funding.

### School Board Services Unit

The School Board Services Unit serves members of the Educational Computing Network of Ontario, which is a cooperative of school boards that share administrative software related to student administration, payroll/personnel, finance, bus transportation planning and management, enrollment projection, grants calculation, audio/visual booking, and student guidance information.

## EXPENDITURE ESTIMATES

*Estimated Expenditures 1987–88*:

| | |
|---|---|
| Ministry Administration | $ 39,730,438 |
| Education | 3,836,195,200 |
| *(Provincial Support for Elementary and Secondary Education)* | |
| Services to Education | 490,968,600 |
| **Ministry total:** | **$4,366,894,238** |

## AGENCIES, BOARDS, AND COMMISSIONS

The following ABCs report to the Legislative Assembly through the Minister of Education:

*Council for Franco-Ontarian Education:* The twelve-member Council advises the Minister of Education and the Minister of Colleges and Universities on all matters concerning the education of Franco-Ontarians at the elementary, secondary, and post-secondary level.

*Education Relations Commission* (ERC): Established in 1975 to administer the collective bargaining process between teachers and school boards, and to further harmonious relations between the parties. The seventeen-member ERC monitors and assists in negotiations, supervises voting by teachers, provides a common database for collective bargaining, and advises the Lieutenant Governor in Council (i.e. Cabinet) when a strike or lockout is jeopardizing students' education.

*Languages of Instruction Commission of Ontario:* Established to help resolve disputes over the provision of education programs in the language of a French or English minority group. The Commission intercedes in conflicts between school boards and their language advisory committees, or between language councils and groups of rate-payers in communities throughout the province.

*Provincial Schools Authority:* Established in 1975 under the *Provincial Schools Negotiations Act*. The Authority is the legal employer of teachers in educational programs operated by the Ministry of Education and the Ministry of Correctional Services. It negotiates, on behalf of those Ministries, with the organization representing the teachers, who have the same bargaining rights as teachers employed by school boards. The Authority is also responsible for the administration of the collective agreement.

*Teachers' Superannuation Commission:* Provides pensions under the *Teachers' Superannuation Act* for teachers in elementary and secondary fields, who hold a valid Ontario Teachers Certificate. These pensions are provided upon retirement or early retirement because of physical or mental disability. The Commission is composed of five people appointed by the Ministry of Education and one member elected from each of the Ontario Public School Teachers' Federation, the Ontario

English Catholic Teachers' Association, the Association des Enseignants Franco-Ontariens, the Ontario Secondary School Teachers' Federation, and the Federation of Women Teachers' Associations of Ontario.

## LEGISLATION

The Ministry of Education is responsible for the following Acts:

*Education Act:* Sets out the legislative framework for the provision of elementary and secondary education in Ontario.

*Essex County French-language Secondary School Act, 1977*

*Lake Superior Board of Education Act*

*Ontario Institute for Studies in Education Act, 1976*

*Ontario School Trustees' Council Act:* Provides for the establishment of the Ontario School Trustees, which is comprised of representatives from local school boards throughout the province.

*Provincial Schools Negotiations Act:* Provides the legislative framework for contract negotiations between the Provincial Schools Authority and the organizations representing teachers.

*School Boards and Teachers Collective Negotiation Act:* Provides the legislative framework for contract negotiations between local school boards and teachers, under Education Relations Commission.

*School Trust Conveyances Act*

*Teachers' Superannuation Act:* Provides for the establishment of the Teachers' Superannuation Commission to administer pensions for the teaching profession.

*Teaching Profession Act:* Provides for the licensing of teachers in the province.

*Leeds and Grenville County Board of Education and Teachers Dispute Act, 1981*

*Wellington County Board of Education and Teachers Dispute Settlement Act, 1985*

# MINISTRY OF HEALTH

## ROLES AND FUNCTIONS

The Ontario Ministry of Health is responsible for legislation, policy, funding, programs, services, and facilities deemed essential and appropriate for the prevention of disease, the promotion of health, the protection of community health, and the care, treatment, and rehabilitation of the sick and disabled in the province.

More specifically, the Ministry ensures that communities are covered by, or have access to, basic health services and programs, and that there are the boards, commissions, and agencies needed to oversee their successful operation, provincially and locally; it determines the appropriate allocation of government funds needed for the provision of essential health programs, services, and facilities in accordance with established needs and priorities for prevention and treatment; and it establishes and maintains the provision of insured hospital, medical care, and related services for all residents of Ontario.

The Ministry of Health provides research, analysis, and planning for determining the most effective utilization of manpower and fiscal and material resources necessary for the operation of the province's health care system; establishes standards, guidelines, and minimum requirements for community health services and programs, and the provisions for monitoring and maintaining such standards; monitors and assesses health and disease trends and population factors in the province with reporting and statistical systems so as to anticipate and respond in an effective way to changes, trends, or health emergencies as they arise; and ensures that the public is provided with information on Ministry policies, programs, and services as well as information on health hazards and health practices for protecting and promoting health.

The Ministry funds and administers such programs as health insurance, care for the mentally ill, extended health care, home care services, drug programs, and the regulation of hospitals and nursing homes. It operates psychiatric hospitals and medical laboratories and provides funding and professional support for local public health services.

## BACKGROUND HISTORY

The Ontario Ministry of Health had its beginning in 1882 when a provincial Board of Health was formed. The Board was specifically charged with distributing information about sanitation; making sanitary inspections; advising local health officials about public health, water supplies, and sewage improvement; maintaining supplies of vaccines; and studying vital statistics.

In 1884, the *Public Health Act* was passed which set out the requirements for local boards of health and the imposition of health and sanitary regulations. During this period, additional legislation was enacted to combat the diseases of the time, including a *Smallpox Regulation*, a *Vaccination Act*, and an act to control disease in animals. One of the Board's most pressing concerns was the control and treatment of tuberculosis, which led to legislation for licensing and inspecting meat and milk supplies as well as the establishments for tubercular patients.

Legislative changes were frequent throughout the Board's early history reflecting the growing complexity and range of public health needs and concerns in the province. In 1919, the Provincial Board of Health was transferred from the Department of the Provincial Secretary to the Department of Labour. The increased range of responsibility and function of the Board was apparent, when, in 1920, it adopted a divisional form of administration which included the following: sanitary engineering, laboratories, venereal diseases and epidemiology, maternal and child welfare, public health nursing, public health education, and industrial hygiene.

A change in the status of the Board of Health was imminent in 1923 when, for the first time, a physician, Dr Forbes Godfrey, was appointed Minister of Health and Labour. The following year, by an act of the legislature, the Board of Health became the Department of Health, the title it retained until 1971, when the present Ministry of Health designation was adopted.

The history of the Department and Ministry of Health involves major and significant undertakings which have led to the growth and complexity of the Ministry. For example, in 1930, the Department assumed responsibility for the province's public hospitals, hospitals for incurables, and sanitoria, and in 1931, the Hospital's Branch of the Department took charge of mental hospitals. In 1952, the Department became responsible for the construction and operation of clinics and premises for cancer research and the diagnosis and treatment of cancer.

The growth and expansion of the Department was offset at different periods by shifting of responsibility in some areas to other agencies of government For example, in 1957, the functions of the Division of Sanitary Engineering were taken over by a Water Resources Commission. Other, equally significant shifts in responsibility, in later years were made to the Ministry of Environment (water quality and air purity), the Ministry of Labour (occupational health), and the Ministry of Community and Social Services (mental retardation and children's services).

Perhaps the most significant phase in the Ministry's history was its gradual assumption of responsibility for the provision of hospital and medical care, which led to our present health care plan. A major restructuring of the Ministry occurred in 1972, to accommodate the development of the single comprehensive health insurance plan, in keeping with the *Medical Care Act* of Canada. The Ministry also continued, throughout the 1970s, to initiate and expand projects such as its Drug Benefit Plan, the air ambulance service, detoxification centres, the formation of district health councils, and the amalgamation of local health units and departments.

## ORGANIZATION

The Ministry of Health has recently undergone a major reorganization aimed at strengthening its corporate structure so that it may work more closely with health care providers in meeting the health care needs of Ontarians. The reorganization has been designed to improve long-term corporate planning and policy development; to create better groupings and relationships among program areas; to establish a more equitable balance in the workload among Ministry management; and to strengthen the operation of the Ministry.

The new organization divides the corporate structure into six major functional groupings each headed by an assistant deputy minister (see organization chart):

1. *Administration, Finance and Health Insurance:* Includes administration of the Ontario Health Insurance Plan, and corporate services for the Ministry including Audit, Human Resources, and Finance.

2. *Community Health:* Includes the Community and Public Health, Laboratory Services, and Health Promotion Branches.

3. *Emergency and Special Health Services:* Includes Ambulance Services and the Drugs and Devices Branches.

4. *Institutional Health:* Includes the Institutional Services and the Nursing Homes Branches.

5. *Mental Health:* Includes the Mental Health Operations, Community Health, and Mental Health Planning Branches.

6. *Policy Planning and Systems:* Includes the Policy Development and Research Branch, the Information and Systems Branch, and six District Health Councils.

In addition, 32 agencies, boards, and commissions report to the Legislative Assembly through the Minister of Health. The head office of the Ministry of Health is located in Toronto; the Ministry also delivers its programs through OHIP regional offices, psychiatric hospitals, six district health councils, public health agencies, public health laboratories and ambulance services throughout the province. The Ministry of Health is the largest ministry in the Government of Ontario, employing approximately 10,400 public servants.

## PROGRAMS

The following listing and description of programs or services includes those which are delivered and directly benefit the community and population for which they are intended. It excludes the support programs and functions of branches involved with the planning, organization, funding, and implementation of health programs.

*Alternative Payment Program:* Negotiates contracts for medical services in circumstances where contract arrangements are believed by the individual parties

MINISTRY OF HEALTH

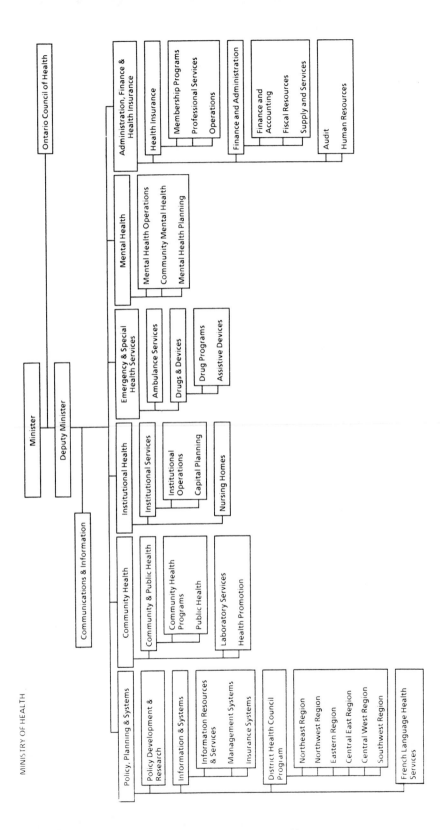

to be more suitable than application of the current OHIP Schedule of Benefits.

*Ambulance Services:* The Ontario Ministry of Health Ambulance Services provides ambulance services in Ontario on a co-payment basis; licenses private, municipal, and hospital-based ambulance services; and directly operates nine services staffed by Ministry of Health personnel. It also provides coordination of air ambulance transfers through central communications.

*Arthritis Society Treatment Program:* The Ontario Ministry of Health provides 100 percent funding for a home occupational and physiotherapy treatment program, with 41 professional staff, for arthritis patients in Ontario.

*Assistive Devices Program:* Provides Ontario residents, who have long-term physical disabilities, with assistance in paying for certain necessary equipment and supplies (wheelchairs, artificial limbs, respiratory equipment, braillers).

*Canadian Hearing Society Program:* The Ontario Ministry of Health funds the Canadian Hearing Society Program which provides audiological services support through the provision of staff to consult in rural areas, to operate its mobile facility, and to service its main headquarters clinic.

*Chest Disease Service:* Provides diagnostic services for tuberculosis and respiratory disease and ambulatory treatment for tuberculosis through district chest clinics; conducts chest examination of miners and prospective immigrants with chest disease.

*Cleft Lip and Palate Program:* The Ministry of Health pays 75 percent of the costs of specialized dental treatment for children and young people with cleft lip and palate. Patients must be under 21, register at a designated clinic of their choice, and attend a multi-disciplinary assessment program.

*Communications and Information Program:* Provides the public with health education materials and interpretation of health policies and issues.

*Community Mental Health Program:* Funds a range of both hospital- and community-based mental health services, including out-patient and day care treatment programs, supportive housing, vocational training, and detoxification services.

*Disease Control and Epidemiology Service:* Collects statistics on disease trends and environmental hazards. It provides vaccines, anti-rabies treatment, and drugs for the treatment of leprosy and sexually-transmitted diseases and snake anti-venom.

*District Health Council Program:* Develops and promotes district health councils which serve as local health planning bodies, coordinating and consolidating health services and planning new programs for their areas.

*Drug Benefit Program:* Provides selected prescribed drugs at no charge to senior citizens 65 years and older and others covered by special social benefits.

*Drug Product Selection and Quality Assurance:* The new legislation relating to drug production selection is aimed at developing economies throughout the pharmaceutical industry and health professions by encouraging fair competition and more efficient methods of distribution and utilization of quality pharmaceutical preparations available to the people of Ontario through community pharmacies or while in hospitals.

*French Language Health Services:* Coordinates the provision of French language services in the Ministry of Health, including the provision of these services to the Franco-Ontarian community.

*Health Insurance Plan:* The Ontario Health Insurance Plan funds a number of separate but related programs including:

1. *Extended Health Care Program:* Provides payments for residents of nursing homes who require up to two hours of nursing care per day and are unable to be maintained in their own home.

2. *Hospital Insurance Program:* Provides payments to hospitals and related facilities for patient services.

3. *Professional Services Program:* Provides for payment by OHIP of services by physicians, dentists, optometrists, chiropractors, osteopaths, chiropodists, and physiotherapists in accordance with predetermined schedules and conditions of payment.

*Health Service Organization and Community Health Centre Program:* Provides physician groups, hospitals, and other organizations with capitation payments for medical services in lieu of OHIP fee-for-services. The *Community Health Centre Program* provides funding for primary health care treatment services to a specified population who have a higher disease burden or are in need of improved access to care. Community Health Centres that provide the services are community-sponsored and operate under a community board.

*Home Care Program:* The Ontario Home Care Program provides coordinated delivery of multi-disciplinary services to eligible residents in their own homes. There are two components to this program which are available province-wide: *Acute Home Care,* oriented to short-term active-treatment, and *Chronic Home Care* (long term). In September 1984, the Home Care Program's mandate was expanded to allow services to be provided in the school setting. The *School Health Support Services Program* is available to students with special health care needs in the school setting. Among the services provided under the Home Care Program on medical referral are: visiting nursing care, physiotherapy, occupational therapy, speech therapy, medical/social work services, and nutritional counselling. Support services include: visiting homemaker services, diagnostic laboratory services, transportation, meals-on-wheels, drugs, dressings, and medical supplies, as well as hospital and sick room equipment.

*Homes for Special Care Program:* Provides nursing home and residential home care to former patients of Ontario psychiatric hospitals.

*Licensing and Inspection of Nursing Homes:* The licensing and inspection of nursing homes in Ontario is a function of the Ministry to ensure that they operated in compliance with the *Nursing Home Act* and that care is provided in accordance with residents' needs. Construction plans for new nursing homes are also approved by the Ministry.

*Mobile Dental Coach Program:* Provides children's dental services in very small and under-serviced communities.

*Northern Health Travel Grant Program:* Helps pay for transportation costs for northern Ontario residents who must travel a one-way distance of 300 kilometers or more for medically necessary specialist services.

*Northern Medical Specialist Incentive Program:* Provides financial incentives for approved medical specialists to locate in Thunder Bay, Sault Ste. Marie, Sudbury, Timmins, and North Bay.

*Placement Co-ordination Services:* Provides a single channel to help people requiring placement in long-term medical care facilities obtain suitable accommodation and the most appropriate services.

*Psychiatric Hospitals Program:* Administers the province's 10 psychiatric hospitals with a total bed capacity of approximately 4,600. The hospitals provide a range of adult psychiatric services including acute care, rehabilitation, long-term care, alcohol detoxification, and psychogeriatrics.

*Public Health Laboratories Program:* Laboratories operating throughout the province perform tests to assist in diagnosis, prevention, and treatment of disease. They serve doctors, hospitals, health units, and other ministries, and analyze drinking water for the general public.

*Public Health Resource Service:* Provides technically competent consultative support in the practice of public health to Boards of Health and field organizations in nursing, nutrition, public health inspection, dentistry, and veterinary medicine and offers engineering advice on the design and operation of recreational camps. It also administers regulations regarding public swimming pools.

*Telehealth (Telemedicine Program):* Provides a communications network among hospitals and other health care facilities in smaller communities and regional centres. The program enhances access to high quality health care for Ontario residents and continuing education for health professionals.

*Underserviced Area Program:* Designed to provide dentists' and physicians' services in northern and remote communities of Ontario. Physicians, dentists, physiotherapists, occupational therapists, audiologists, and speech pathologists are encouraged to practice in these areas by a program of bursaries in their undergraduate years and incentive grants after completing their studies.

## EXPENDITURE ESTIMATES

*Estimated Expenditures 1987–88*:

| | |
|---|---|
| Ministry Administration | $ 103,848,538 |
| Institutional Health | 6,063,251,200 |
| Emergency and Special Health Services | 650,160,600 |
| Mental Health | 502,865,600 |
| Community Health | 420,175,000 |
| Health Insurance | 3,491,371,700 |
| **Ministry total:** | **$11,231,672,638** |

## AGENCIES, BOARDS, AND COMMISSIONS

The following ABCs report to the Legislative Assembly through the Minister of Health:

*Addiction Research Foundation* (ARF): Conducts research and demonstration treatment, provides educational and consultative services, and publishes material in the field of alcohol and drug addiction.

*Advisory Committee on Inborn Errors of Metabolism in Children:* Provides advice on programs relating to inborn errors of metabolism in infants with the objective of preventing the development of mental retardation in these infants.

*Advisory Committee on Reproductive Care:* Develops an integrated program to decrease perinatal morbidity and mortality, through coordination of public health, including nutrition, clinical, and social services.

*Advisory Medical Board of the Ontario Mental Health Foundation:* Considers whether or not recommended applications referred to it by either the Research Committee or the Fellowship and Sundry Awards Committee are to be submitted to the Foundation for approval for support.

*Assistive Devices Advisory Committee:* Advises the Minister on the most effective and efficient methods of providing service including prescribing and assessment procedures.

*Chiropody Review Committee:* Makes recommendations on all or part of insured services rendered by a chiropodist which were not in fact rendered, were not therapeutically necessary, were not provided in accordance with accepted professional standards and practice, or where the nature of the service was misrepresented.

*Clarke Institute of Psychiatry:* The Institute maintains, manages, and operates, a hospital with facilities for psychiatric research, education, diagnosis, and treatment.

*Dental Personnel Selection Committee:* Selects and approves undergraduate dental students for bursaries; and graduate dentists for the establishment-of-practice grants or contract service.

*Dentistry Review Committee:* Makes recommendations on all or part of insured services rendered by a dentist or dental surgeon which were not in fact rendered, were not therapeutically necessary, were not provided in accordance with accepted professional standards and practice, or where the nature of the service was misrepresented.

*Denture Therapists Appeal Board:* Reviews decisions of the Complaints Committee of the Governing Board of Denture Therapists when either the complainant or the licensee complained against is not satisfied with the decision.

*Drug Quality and Therapeutics Committee:* Based on established criteria and requirements, evaluates the quality and therapeutic value of pharmaceutical manufacturers' drug products.

*Funeral Services Review Board:* Reviews decisions of the Complaints Committee, when either the complainant or the licensee complained against is not satisfied with the decision.

*Healing Arts Radiation Protection Commission:* Advises the Minister on matters relating to the health and safety of persons regarding irradiation by X-rays, and to the continuing development of an X-ray Safety Code; and reviews the contents of courses in the operation of X-ray machines and X-ray equipment.

*Health Care Systems Research Review Committee:* Makes recommendations to the Ministry regarding applications to the Health Care Systems Research and the Public Health Research and Development programs.

*Health Disciplines Board:* Reviews decisions of the complaints committee of any of the colleges, (dentistry, medicine, nursing, pharmacy, optometry)

*Health Facilities Appeal Board:* Holds hearings under the *Ambulance Act*, under the *Private Hospitals Act*, under the *Health Facilities Special Orders Act*, and under the *Healing Arts Radiation Act.*

*Health Protection Appeal Board:* Under the *Health Protection and Promotion Act*, hears appeals of orders made by Medical Officers of health and public health inspectors. Under the *Immunization of School Pupils Act*, hears appeals of suspension orders.

*Health Research and Development Council of Ontario:* Advises the Minister on research priorities, policy, and principles of program design.

*Health Research Personnel Committee:* Reviews applications received from Ontario universities, for health research personnel development awards.

*Health Services Appeals Board:* Hears appeals of decisions involving refusals of applications to become or to continue to be an insured person.

*Hospital Appeal Board:* Conducts hearings regarding appointment or reappointment to the medical staff of a hospital, if requested, by an applicant who is not satisfied with the decision of the Board not to appoint or reappoint him, or, if requested, by any member of the medical staff of a hospital who is not satisfied with any decision to revoke or suspend his appointment, or to cancel, suspend or alter his hospital privileges.

*Laboratory Review Board:* Under the *Laboratory and Specimen Collection Central Licensing Act,* holds hearings, if requested, on the refusal to issue a license; or on the imposition of conditions on the existing license. Also holds hearings under the *Health Facilities Special Orders Act,* where the Minister proposes to revoke a license or to require a licensee to cease carrying on an activity; or suspends the license or requires a licensee to suspend activity.

*Medical Eligibility Committee:* Examines and reports with its recommendations on the decision that an uninsured person is not entitled to an insured service in a hospital or health facility because such service is not medically necessary.

*Medical Review Committee:* Makes recommendations on any matter involving all or part of insured services rendered by a physician which were not in fact rendered, were not medically necessary, were not provided in accordance with accepted professional standards and practice, or the nature of the service is misrepresented.

*Medical Personnel Selection Committee:* Responsible for the selection and approval of graduate physicians for establishment-of-practice grants or contract service.

*Nursing Homes Review Board:* Holds hearings where the Director proposes to refuse to issue a license.

*Ontario Cancer Treatment and Research Foundation:* Supports programs of diagnosis, treatment, and research in cancer. It is affiliated with the Ontario Cancer Institute (Princess Margaret Hospital).

*Ontario Council of Health:* Advises the Minister on health matters and the needs of the people of Ontario and performs such other duties as referred to it by the Minister.

*Ontario Mental Health Foundation:* The Ontario Mental Health Foundation provides grants for mental health research.

*Optometry Review Committee:* Makes recommendations on all or part of insured services rendered by an optometrist which were not in fact rendered, were not therapeutically necessary, were not provided in accordance with the accepted professional standards and practice, or the nature of the service is misrepresented.

*Professional Services Management Committee:* Employs qualified medical practitioners or dental practitioners and enters into contracts with them or their services.

*Psychiatric Review Board:* Holds hearings on receipt of an application from: an involuntary patient to establish whether the patient should remain in the custody of a psychiatric facility; the attending physician to obtain an order authorizing treatment to the patient, in the case where the involuntary patient refuses to consent to treatment; a patient or outpatient to inquire whether or not a patient or outpatient is competent to manage his estate.

## LEGISLATION

The Ministry of Health is responsible for the following Acts:

*Ambulance Act:* Governs and regulates the operation of private ambulance services in Ontario.

*Alcoholism and Drug Addiction Research Foundation Act:* Governs the organization and operation of the Foundation.

*Cancer Act:* Sets out the purposes and powers of the Ontario Cancer Treatment and Research Foundation and the Ontario Cancer Institute in respect of cancer research, diagnosis, and treatment.

*Cancer Remedies Act:* Provides for the establishment of a Commission for the investigation of cancer remedies; objectives are to investigate, approve, or disapprove of any substances or treatment that are held out as cancer remedies.

*Chiropody Act:* Provides for a Board of Regents that is responsible for the registration, standards of practice, and discipline of chiropodists.

*Community Psychiatric Hospitals Act:* Provides for the establishment and approval of community psychiatric hospitals and their powers.

*Dental Technicians Act:* Provides for a Governing Board of Dental Technicians that is responsible for the registration, standards of practice, and discipline of dental technicians.

*Denture Therapists Act:* Provides for a Governing Board of Denture Therapists that is responsible for the licensing, standards of practice, and discipline of denture therapists.

*Drugless Practitioners Act:* Provides for five Boards of Directors that register, establish standards of practice, and discipline for five classes of drugless practitioners, namely, chiropractors, masseurs, physiotherapists, drugless therapists, and osteopaths.

*Fluoridation Act:* Enables local municipalities and Metropolitan Toronto Corporation to fluoridate public water supplies or to discontinue the fluoridation of same in accordance with the legal authorities conferred in the Act.

*Funeral Services Act:* Provides for a Board of Funeral Services that licenses funeral directors and funeral services establishments.

*Health Disciplines Act:* Provides for the government of five health professions by their respective Colleges in respect of registration, standards of practice, investigation of complaints, and discipline of dentists, physicians, nurses, optometrists, and pharmacists. A lay Health Disciplines Board, composed of lay persons, is authorized, on request, to review dismissal of complaints by College Complaints Committee and to hear proposed registration refusals.

*Health Facilities Special Orders Act:* Permits the Ministry to act expeditiously in order to suspend or revoke the license of a health facility.

*Health Insurance Act:* Provides for the operation of the Ontario Health Insurance Plan.

*Health Protection and Promotion Act, 1983:* Requires boards of health or their agents to protect community health by providing and controlling the spread of communicable disease and health hazards and by providing or ensuring the delivery of preventive health programs and services prescribed in the Act to residents in the boards' territorial health unit jurisdiction.

*Healing Arts Radiation Protection Act:* Governs and regulates X-ray operators and the installation and operation of X-ray machines that are used for diagnostic or therapeutic purposes on human beings.

*Homes for Special Care Act:* Provides for the licensing or approving of special homes to care for persons discharged from mental hospitals.

*Hypnosis Act:* Governs and regulates the practice of hypnosis in Ontario.

*Immunization of School Pupils Act, 1982:* Provides for the mandatory immunization of school pupils against certain designated diseases.

*Laboratory and Specimen Collection Centre Licensing Act:* Governs and regulates the operation of laboratories and specimen collection centres in Ontario.

*Mental Health Act:* Provides for the admission, treatment, and discharge of patients in psychiatric facilities.

*Mental Hospitals Act:* Provides for institutions for the mentally ill that are owned and operated by the Crown.

*Ministry of Health Act:* Governs and regulates the duties and functions of the Minister of Health.

*Nursing Homes Act:* Governs and regulates the operation of private nursing homes in Ontario.

*Ontario Drug Benefit Act, 1986:* Provides for the operation of the Ontario Drug Benefit Plan.

*Ophthalmic Dispensers Act:* Provides for a Board of Ophthalmic Dispensers that is responsible for the registration, standards of practice, and discipline of ophthalmic dispensers.

*Prescription Drug Cost Regulation Act:* Governs and regulates the dispensing of interchangeable drugs on prescription.

*Private Hospitals Act:* Governs and regulates the operation of private hospitals in Ontario.

*Psychologists Registration Act:* Provides for an Ontario Board of Examiners in Psychology that is responsible for the registration, standards of practice, and discipline of registered psychologists.

*Radiological Technicians Act:* Provides for a Board of Radiological Technicians that is responsible for the registration, standards of practice, and discipline of radiological technicians.

*Sanitoria for Consumptives Act:* Sets out the authority of medical officers of health, provincial judges, and others to confine to medical facilities those individuals with actual or suspected cases of tuberculosis .

*War Veterans Burial Act:* Requires that specified persons make reimbursement to a War Veterans Burial Fund for expenses incurred in the burial of indigent war veterans.

## INNOVATIONS

The following innovations have had a positive impact on the operations of the Ministry of Health:

*District Health Council Program:* District Health councils play an important role in decentralizing the health care planning process, allowing the planning and coordination of local health care services to respond to local needs. A total of 26 councils serve more than 90 percent of Ontario's population. All proposals for new health care programs are reviewed by councils.

The *Immunization of School Pupils Act, 1982:* Requires that all students attending school in Ontario have proof of immunization against diphtheria, tetanus, polio, measles, mumps, and rubella.

The *Health Protection and Promotion Act:* Passed in 1983, this Act replaced the former *Public Health Act* and is intended to create uniform minimum standards for all public health units. The new Act ensures that core programs emphasize preventive medicine, immunization, home care, and other community-based initiatives.

*Business Oriented New Development Program* (BOND): Introduced in 1982, allows hospitals to keep any surplus funds instead of having to return such funds to the Ministry at the end of the fiscal year.

*Strategic Planning for Health Promotion:* A Health Promotion Unit was established in 1978 to develop priorities and strategies for health promotion as an alternative to high cost health care. This led to the development of health promotion projects. In December 1984, the Office of Health Promotion was established to develop programs on behalf of an Ontario Implementation Group on Health Promotion and Disease Prevention. The unit has since become a branch.

*Establishment of Community Advisory Boards for Psychiatric Institutions:* Community Advisory Boards for Psychiatric Hospitals reporting directly to the Ministry of Health were established in 1982 to increase regional involvement in management.

*Health Professions Legislation Review:* A review of legislation governing all health professionals, which began in 1982 to update and restructure legislation for the 16 health professions regulated by six statutes, continues. The Minister has decided to regulate 25 professions; draft legislation has been circulated.

*Introduction of Global Budgeting for Health Units and Hospitals:* Global operating budgeting for health units and hospitals was introduced in the mid-

1970s to provide for better planning, utilization, and control of transfer payments received by these institutions from the Ministry.

*High-Tech Advisory Committee:* In 1983, an Advisory Committee on High Technology was established to keep the Ministry abreast of the latest advances and to make recommendations for the proper use of new devices and techniques in Ontario. The committee is assisted in its work by a series of expert advisory panels in specific fields.

*Current Innovations:* A series of new policies and programs has been introduce to provide health care for the people in Ontario. The legislation on extra-billing, passed on June 20, 1986, underscores the principles and priorities of all Ministry of Health actions: that all Ontarians are entitled to the best possible health care without regard to their financial means.

The recently announced $850 million capital funding program will allow modernization and expansion of the hospital system. It will ensure that Princess Margaret Hospital is rebuilt, that three regional cancer clinics are developed, and that 3,082 new chronic care beds and 1,375 new acute care beds are added to Ontario hospitals.

The Ministry has taken other actions recently that will significantly expand health care services:

1. A travel grant program has been introduced for the people of Northern Ontario who must travel significant distances to receive necessary health care services. Program costs will be from $10–13 million each year;

2. The new pharmacy legislation will help eliminate artificially high drug prices and increase consumer protection in the marketplace;

3. At a cost of $1.2 million, the air ambulance program has been expanded to 24-hour service and a program to upgrade the skills of air ambulance crews has been started;

4. The assistive devices program has been expanded to include young people up to 22 years of age. The program also covers 75 percent of the costs of prostheses and respiratory equipment for all age groups. Total expenditures for the program, this year, are expected to reach some $18 million;

5. The Red Cross blood screening/blood testing program for AIDS antibodies was funded at a cost of $1 million. An additional $200,000 was used to establish a public education program about this disease;

6. Community-based residential addiction programs were funded for the first time, and total funding for all addiction programs was increased from $9.9 million to $14.2 million;

7. With funding of approximately $2 million, a Cleft Lip and Palate program for children and young adults was introduced;

8. Thirty-four new community mental health programs were begun. Total spending for community mental health now stands at $48 million annually

and 276 programs are operating;

9. Paramedic services in Toronto and Hamilton were expanded and the program will be extended to five other centres throughout the province. Initial funding for this paramedic expansion will be approximately $2.8 million;

10. A task force aimed at making midwifery a regulated health profession and a recognized part of health care in Ontario has been appointed;

11. $5 million has been provided for the establishment of five regional geriatric units, and $500,000 to community health centres (CHCs) to develop services specifically oriented to the elderly; and

12. A major re-development of the Hospital for Sick Children is underway with Ministry funding of $72.5 million.

MINISTRY OF SKILLS DEVELOPMENT

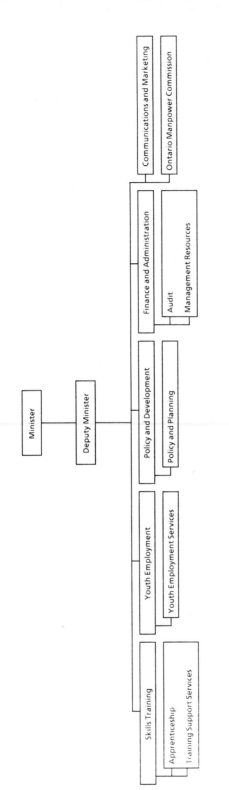

# MINISTRY OF SKILLS DEVELOPMENT

## ROLES AND FUNCTIONS

The objectives of the Ministry of Skills Development (MSD) are: to develop and upgrade skills which will enhance the employability of individuals; to contribute to Ontario's economic growth by helping employers develop the skills of their staff; to improve access to training and employment opportunities for persons with special needs and for targeted groups that encounter particular employment barriers; and to coordinate institutional and on-the-job training programs in order to increase training effectiveness and employment mobility.

## BACKGROUND HISTORY

Although the matter of skills development has been the subject of governmental concern and programs for more than a decade, the establishment of a separate ministry did not occur until 1985. The creation of the Ministry of Skills Development, announced on March 22, 1985, reflected the urgent need to consolidate and improve the many different programs of the government in skills development, training, and job creation. It also simplified its dealings with the public and the federal government. The Ministry was formed from component parts of the Ministries of Treasury and Economics, Labour, Colleges and Universities, Municipal Affairs, and the now defunct Provincial Secretariat for Social Development.

## ORGANIZATION

The Ministry of Skills Development is organized into four major divisions (see organization chart):

1. *Finance and Administration:* Provides corporate financial, personnel, audit, and administrative support services to the Ministry.
2. *Policy and Planning:* Develops skills programs administered by the Ministry. This Division is comprised of the Policy and Planning Branch, the Federal/Provincial Relations Group, and the Planning and Development Group.

3. *Skills Development:* Administers the skills development programs offered by the Ministry through the Training Support Services Branch and the Apprenticeship Branch. The division offers its programs through 28 field offices located throughout the province.

4. *Youth Employment:* Administers the youth employment programs through the Youth Employment Services Branch.

In addition, the Institute for Skills Development (the Ontario Manpower Commission) reports to the Minister of Skills Development (see Agencies, Boards, and Commissions). The head office of the Ministry of Skills Development is located in Toronto. The Ministry employs approximately 480 public servants.

## PROGRAMS

### Apprenticeship Branch

The Apprenticeship Branch administers apprenticeship training in Ontario, through the Ontario Modular Training System, and the Trades Updating program.

*Apprenticeship:* Apprenticeship training in Ontario is established by the *Apprenticeship and Tradesmen's Qualification Act* and its regulations. Of 66 regulated occupations, 20 require compulsory certification. In other regulated trades, it is not necessary to hold a Certificate of Qualification in order to practise the trade. In addition to the regulated trades, there are approximately 568 employer-established trades designed to meet the needs of individual employers. The occupations are not subject to specific regulation; they fall, however, within the jurisdiction of the Act and apprenticeship is available. All apprentices, whether in an employer-established or regulated trade, receive a Certificate of Apprenticeship after completing training. Following successful completion of an assessment examination, apprentices are eligible for Certificates of qualifications in regulated trades only. Currently there are approximately 274,000 certificate holders and 38,200 apprentices being served by the Ministry.

*Modular Training:* Provides an effective means of registering, training, and accrediting workers at all levels, with the emphasis on common skills and self-paced learning for skilled tradespeople. A training module is a unit of two or more homogeneous skill/competencies expressed in performance terms. Modules are developed to meet the acceptance level of training identified by industry. Trainees may progress at their own rate of learning. Competency of trainees may be assessed with modular written examinations or by performance-demonstrated guidelines attested to by Ministry-designated personnel.

*Trades Updating Program:* In order to provide competitive skills to those journeymen who have been unable to keep pace with technological change, the Trades Updating Program provides specific courses to upgrade and/or update their skills.

## Training Support Services Branch

The Training Support Services Branch conducts the Ministry's activities in support of employer-based and pre-employment training. Under the umbrella of Ontario's Training Strategy, this Branch administers the following programs:

*Community Industrial Training Committees (CITC) Support and Surveys:* Community Industrial Training Committees are autonomous advisory groups, representing business and labour, organized at the community or sector level. They assess local supply and demand for skills and recommend to the Ministry the best use of existing programs, services, and facilities to meet current and anticipated skills training requirements. Financial support is provided to CITCs to conduct labour-market needs surveys. The information collected through these surveys is used to identify training needs by occupation. The data is also used in the development of annual federal-provincial training purchase plans. There are 46 CITCs across Ontario, including 13 in Northern Ontario.

*Employer Sponsor Training:* Funds are provided to finance pilot projects in areas where skills training is required but cannot be funded under existing federal or provincial programs.

*Information Outreach and Employer Training Hotline:* This province-wide, bilingual hotline has been set up to provide employers and the general public with information on training and retraining. It is modelled after the "Youth Hotline".

*International Marketing Intern Program:* This program provides financial assistance to firms that have an exporting base in Ontario and that have the facilities, experience, and personnel to train an intern in international marketing. The Ministry pays 50 percent of an intern's salary, up to $15,000 per year for two years. The program is jointly administered by the Ministry of Industry, Trade and Technology, and the Ministry of Skills Development.

*Ontario Basic Skills (OBS):* Delivered through Ontario's college system, OBS is designed for adults who require upgrading to enter the work force directly or after additional training. The goals of OBS are to improve literacy and numeric skills, increase the participation of those who are traditionally under-represented, and encourage women to enter non-traditional occupations.

*Ontario Help Centres Program:* Provides funding to community-based organizations which provide employment counselling, job readiness assistance, and follow-up support to unemployed adults.

*Ontario Skills:* An incentive fund to assist with direct costs of job-related training undertaken by Ontario businesses. Ontario Skills will cover 80 percent of direct instruction costs for firms with fewer than 200 employees and 60 percent for larger firms.

*Ontario Skills Development Offices* (OSDOs): Through the OSDOs training consulting service, Ontario firms are provided with assistance in the identification of their training needs and the development of training plans. The program, delivered through Ontario's 22 colleges of applied arts and technology, is targeted to small and medium-sized firms.

*Special Project Fund:* This fund will support innovative approaches and/or projects that will enhance the effectiveness of skill development programs, especially those for groups with special needs.

*Special Support Allowances:* Assist individuals to overcome financial barriers to training. Allowances are based on need and may apply to childcare, transportation, and accommodation. Initially, Ontario Skills, Trades Updating, and OBS participants are being served with the intention of later extending these allowances to other MSD programs.

*Training Trust Fund Program:* Training trust funds are joint employer/employee mechanisms used to fund industrial activities. They are aimed at assisting experienced workers adapt to changes in the workplace through the establishment of training trust funds which encourage employers and employees to work together to provide ongoing training activities. The Ministry matches the employers' contribution to a maximum of $100,000 per eligible trust.

*Transitions:* Provides up to $2,000.00 over two years to support the training of any person, 45 years or older, who is permanently laid off due to work shortage, plant closure, or failure of a business.

### Youth Employment Services Branch

The Youth Employment Services Branch administers youth employment programs and operates a telephone hotline to provide related information to youth and employers. The Branch administers the following youth employment programs:

*Futures Program:* Provides disadvantaged young people with on-the-job training and work experience to enhance their skills and employability. Under certain circumstances placements are guaranteed for up to one year in exchange for a young person's commitment to educational upgrading on their own time. Futures is administered through local youth employment counselling centers and Futures offices at colleges of applied arts and technology.

*Summer Programs:* The Ontario Youth Employment Program (OYEP), provides subsidies to employers to create summer jobs for young people.

*Start Up:* Encourages entrepreneurial activity among young people and helps them develop entrepreneurial skills. Two loan programs, Student Venture Capital (SVC) and Youth Venture Capital (YVC), are operated under Start Up. The SVC program provides interest-free loans up to $2,000 per venture to students who wish to plan and operate their own summer business. The YVC program provides young people with interest-free business start-up loans up to $5,000.

*Youth Employment Counselling Centres* (YECCs): The Ministry funds community-based Youth Employment Counselling Centres (YECCs) which help unemployed young people develop the skills necessary to secure employment.

*Youth Hotline:* The province-wide, bilingual Hotline provides a single point of contact for the Ministry's youth programs and services. Young people, parents, employers, counselling services, educators, and others can call the toll-free Hotline.

## EXPENDITURE ESTIMATES

*Estimated Expenditures 1987–88:*

| | |
|---|---|
| Ministry Administration | $ 5,192,938 |
| Skills Training | 242,598,100 |
| Youth Employment | 198,456,900 |
| **Ministry total:** | **$446,247,938** |

## AGENCIES, BOARDS, AND COMMISSIONS

The following Commission reports to the Legislative Assembly through the Minister of Skills Development:

*Institute for Skills Training* (Ontario Manpower Commission): As part of Ontario's Training Strategy, the Government established an Institute for Skills Training in the summer of 1987. The research and labour-market analysis capacity of the Ontario Manpower Commission has been redirected in support of the Institute's objectives.

The Institute for Skills Training has undertaken four functions necessary to encourage the development of sophisticated training products and services:

1. Through the *Skills Bank*, industry, government, and labour cooperate, on a sectoral basis, to identify needs for training materials and coordinate their production. Businesses will obtain access to the Skills Bank data via the OSDOs. Sectoral advisory groups, comprised of representatives from companies which are training leaders, are responsible for identifying specific training needs. In addition, learning packages are developed in certain generic skills areas which are important across all industries. Learning materials are created by experts contracted through an open bidding process.

2. Through the *Skill-Technology Fund*, the Institute promotes the use of technology as a tool for training. It demonstrates the efficiency of technology-based training to businesses, particularly smaller ones. Partial funding is provided to select private and public producers to counter "front-end" barriers to the development of training materials, and to support research and development, adaptation, testing, packaging, and implementation of skills training programs. Up to 80 percent of the costs will be eligible for support.

3. Through *Train the Trainers*, the Institute coordinates existing and new programs to provide professional schooling to instructional trainers and training consultants. It also develops a standard, accessible curriculum of courses for training specialists.

4. *Research and Labour Market Analysis:* The Ontario Manpower Commission coordinates research efforts with the sectoral activities of the Skills Bank. The Institute also maintains broader labour-market analysis responsibilities to provide advice to the Ministry.

## LEGISLATION

The Ministry of Skills Development is responsible for the following Acts:

*Apprenticeship and Tradesmen's Qualification Act:* Provides a system of on-the-job training in skilled occupations in the construction, industrial, motive power, and service industries. This system establishes entrance requirements, training definitions, and descriptions of the training to be offered, criteria for qualification as tradesman, and accreditation procedures. Provision also exists for the establishment of advisory networks which play an instrumental role in the development of policy.

*Ontario Youth Employment Act:* This Act provides for the establishment of a youth employment program that encourages farming and business communities in Ontario to create new summer jobs for young people that will give them work experience skills and better equip them for full-time jobs. The Ontario Youth Employment Program (OYEP) is established by an annual regulation made pursuant to the Act.

## INNOVATIONS

*The Futures Program* went into effect on November 4, 1985. The program is designed to provide on-the-job training, work experience, and educational upgrading for young people who face severe disadvantages in seeking and keeping a job.

*The Ontario Training Strategy* (OTS) was announced on September 4, 1985. OTS is designed to provide employer-sponsored, on-the-job or job-related training. By increasing the participation of business and workers in ongoing, work-related training, OTS will strengthen the competitive position of Ontario firms and develop individual economic opportunities.

# OFFICE FOR DISABLED PERSONS

## ROLES AND FUNCTIONS

On October 2, 1985, the Premier announced that a Cabinet minister without portfolio was to be given special responsibility for issues relating to disabled persons. This assignment includes increasing awareness of the abilities and needs of disabled persons in society as a whole and enhancing government responsiveness to issues of concern to these individuals. This latter responsibility is facilitated by the Minister's membership on the Cabinet Committee on Social Policy and the Cabinet Committee on Regulation, in addition to Cabinet itself.

The Minister Responsible for Disabled Persons performs a key role with respect to community liaison with the various service provider agencies, consumer groups, and the Ontario Advisory Council for Disabled Persons. The Minister also advocates on behalf of the interests of disabled persons. Other assignments as assigned by the Premier from time to time are undertaken by the Minister.

On October 29, 1985, a Senior Advisor to the minister was appointed. The Senior Advisor and the Office are responsible for supporting the Minister in his responsibilities relating to disabled persons. The Office acts as a focal point to promote an awareness of the government's programs and to encourage the responsiveness of the policy development process to the needs of disabled persons.

*Policy:* The Office, under the direction of the Minister, sees to the development and implementation of coordinated policies and programs which favour the integration of disabled persons in the mainstream of society. It monitors Ministry activities and initiates action and identifies options for dealing with issues or concerns which cross traditional ministerial lines of responsibility. The Office maintains close liaison with the Ontario Advisory Council for Disabled Persons.

*Information:* The Office acts as a central information source for government's policies and programs. Inquiries are received on a wide range of issues such as income maintenance, disability pensions, transportation, attendant care, and community living. As part of its information role, the Office produces a number of publications including the "Guide to Ontario Government Programs and Services for Disabled Persons," "Guide for Disabled Drivers in Ontario," "Inventory of Ontario Government Programs and Services for Disabled Persons," and "Courier," a quarterly newsletter.

*Awareness:* The Office identifies opportunities of a corporate nature to increase awareness throughout government and the public of the abilities and needs of disabled persons. Within this context, the Office coordinates special projects that include awards programs, such as the Premier's Awards for Accessibility and Community Action Awards, and undertakes special events such as the Proclamation of the Decade of Disabled Persons. The Office maintains contact with the news media and government information personnel on issues related to the Office and disabled persons.

*Community liaison:* The Office maintains working relationships with the Ontario Advisory Council for Disabled Persons, various service providers, and consumer groups representing disabled persons.

In June 1987, the Office secured funding of $5 million per year over three years conjointly with the Office for Senior Citizens Affairs. This allocation is for an Access Fund that will provide financial assistance for capital renovation in the non-profit sector, within organizations serving disabled persons and senior citizens.

## BACKGROUND HISTORY

In December, 1975, an Inter-ministerial Council on Rehabilitation Services was established by Cabinet. The Council served to focus a single provincial source for rehabilitation services.

In May, 1978, Cabinet established the appointment of a Provincial Coordinator for the Secretariat for Disabled Persons to coordinate activities of an Inter-ministerial Team of Coordinators of Rehabilitation. The Secretariat started its activities in January 1979. The Provincial Coordinator, Secretariat for Disabled Persons reported to the former Provincial Secretariat for Social Development.

Three main functions for the Secretariat were identified, including policy review, information and awareness, and development of consultative working relationships with the disabled community.

In addition, the Ontario Advisory Council for the Physically Handicapped was established in 1976. This Advisory Council was established as a body representing various components of the disabled community in the province. The role of the Advisory Council was to advise government on policy issues relating to disabled persons. The Advisory Council reported to the Secretariat for Social Development via the Secretariat for Disabled Persons.

In October 1985, Premier David Peterson appointed the first Minister Responsible for Disabled Persons, and established a new position of Senior Adviser to the Minister Responsible for Disabled Persons, through whom the Secretariat for Disabled Persons and the Provincial Coordinator report to the Minister. Under the new reporting relationship, the Ontario Advisory Council for the Physically Handicapped also reports to the Minister Responsible for Disabled Persons.

The title of the Secretariat for Disabled Persons and the Ontario Advisory Council on the Physically Handicapped were changed in 1987 to Office for Disabled Persons and Ontario Advisory Council for Disabled Persons, respectively.

The Office employs approximately 30 public servants.

# PROJECTS

*Community Action Fund:* Established in June, 1986, with an annual allocation of $500,000. It funds community-based organizations serving disabled persons on a project basis.

*Access Fund:* Announced in June, 1987, with a $5 million allocation every year for three years. It will fund non-profit groups serving disabled persons and senior citizens for capital renovation projects to improve physical access.

# EXPENDITURE ESTIMATES

*Estimated Expenditures 1987–88:*

Office for Disabled Persons       $4,432,825

# OFFICE FOR SENIOR CITIZENS' AFFAIRS

## ROLES AND FUNCTIONS

The Office for Senior Citizens' Affairs (formerly known as the Ontario Seniors Secretariat from July, 1985 until April, 1986) is responsible for developing a broad policy framework for services for senior citizens, and for insuring appropriate coordination of existing policy and programs for seniors (e.g. health and social services). The office also provides information to senior citizens and promotes the recognition of the contributions seniors make to their communities. It publishes the "Guide for Senior Citizens", the Directory of Accommodation, and two song books for seniors.

## BACKGROUND HISTORY

Ontario's first Minister without Portfolio Responsible for Senior Citizens' Affairs was appointed in July 1985. His role at that time was to review programs and services for seniors in Ontario. A special focus of this review was an examination of the programs and services offered to seniors by both the Ministry of Health and the Ministry of Community and Social Services. The objective was to determine the ways and means of rationalizing responsibility for funding, delivery, and management of services for seniors.

Having recently completed this review, the Minister without Portfolio is currently undertaking policy development in the following areas: a single location for community services for the elderly; a new extended care act; a complementary study of care requirements in homes for the aged and nursing homes; and regulation of the quality of care in rest homes.

## ORGANIZATION

The Minister is supported in his role by the Office for Senior Citizens' Affairs, which includes the following staff sections:

1. Policy Development and Strategic Planning;
2. Corporate Services;
3. Communications; and
4. Office of the Special Advisor.

The Office employs approximately 20 public servants.

## PROGRAMS

While the Minister's office does not directly administer programs, the Minister consults with the Minister of Health and the Minister of Community and Social Services in the development of programs for the elderly. The following are programs on which the Minister has consulted. Please note that all of these programs are funded and run by other ministries.

1. The *New Integrated Homemaker Program* makes homemaking assistance available to seniors free of charge. Eligibility is based solely on need. Neither medical nor financial tests are required. This program is funded by Ministry of Community and Social Services and delivered by local home care units of the Ministry of Health.

2. Extension of existing community support services such as Meals-on-Wheels, escorted transportation services, friendly visiting, and home help.

3. Fifty additional centres for elderly people.

4. Funding for volunteers who deliver home support services for seniors and for the establishment of new Senior Talent Banks throughout the province.

5. Funding to establish special home support services for elderly people in isolated communities.

6. Funding of projects related to Alzheimer's disease including the provision of day care for those with the disease, relief services at home for families caring for someone with the disease, and counselling and training for caregivers. These projects are being developed with the cooperation of local Alzheimer's societies.

7. Funding for public education to encourage a more positive public attitude towards aging and the aged and for the recruitment of additional volunteers for agencies serving the elderly.

8. Funding to increase the provincial share of funding for agencies for a maximum of 50 percent up to a maximum of 60 percent of their operating expenses.

## EXPENDITURE ESTIMATES

*Estimated Expenditures 1987–88*:

Office Responsible for Senior
Citizens' Affairs                    $4,591,825

## AGENCIES, BOARDS, AND COMMISSIONS

The Minister works with the *Ontario Advisory Council on Senior Citizens*, which was established in April 1974. The Council consists of a Chairman, two Vice-Chairmen and eleven members selected from across the province. Members are from diverse backgrounds and occupations; most of them are seniors. The mandate of the Council is to advise the Government of Ontario, through the Minister of Senior Citizens' Affairs, on matters pertaining to the well-being of the aged and aging persons, and:

1. To further promote self-help for the aged, to their satisfaction and advantage as members of society as a whole;

2. To review current policies that have a bearing on aging and the economy, and that involve employment, preparation for retirement, income maintenance, health measures, services, and facilities of government, and other related services; and,

3. To respond to requests from the Minister for Senior Citizens' Affairs for advice and consideration on matters relating to senior citizens.

The Council meets five or six times a year. It is not a funding body, does not undertake case management, and is not involved in the delivery of programs. Since July 1985, the Council's newspaper, "Especially for Seniors," has been sent directly to all Ontario residents 65 years of age and older.

In April 1987, the Minister appointed two additional advisory committees to provide advice to the government on developing an extended-care act and regulations to govern the standard of care in rest homes. Both the Advisory Committee on Rest Homes and the Advisory Committee on Extended Care consist of a Chairman and members representing related service providers and seniors groups. The members offer their expertise on a voluntary basis.

## LEGISLATION

The Minister and the Office are responsible for the development of new extended care legislation which will apply to all providers and establish uniform criteria in such areas as inspection services, programming, staffing, quality of care, and physical plant standards. The Office is also preparing a complementary study to establish care requirements in homes for the aged and nursing homes and to develop policy in respect to regulating the quality of care in rest homes.

The Policy Development and Strategic Planning Unit recently completed a consultation tour and is developing a "one-stop shopping" approach to the provision of community health and social services to seniors which will: serve as a single point of entry; provide comprehensive functional assessments; provide or arrange necessary services; monitor and adjust services as needs change; and allow devolution to an appropriate local authority with a mandate to ensure the provision of services.

Future plans include the development of a provincial policy framework for services to the elderly, including initiatives in areas such as transportation and housing. Coordinating and monitoring provincial policy initiatives for seniors will continue.

## INNOVATIONS

One year after appointment, the Minister released a White Paper entitled "A New Agenda: Health and Social Service Strategies for Ontario's Seniors." This was the first time in Ontario that the government had set down a broad strategic plan to meet the needs of seniors now and in the future. The central theme of the White Paper was to help seniors live active and independent lives in their own communities and to prevent unnecessary institutionalization.

The *first* strategy is to improve and maintain the functional state of all Ontario's senior citizens. This strategy proposes:

1. Improvements in health promotion and illness prevention programs for the elderly;

2. Enhancement of geriatric training and education;

3. Ensuring an adequate supply of geriatric specialists in all disciplines; and

4. Encouraging basic and clinical research on the aging process and related diseases.

The *second* strategy is to assist the elderly to live independently in the community by:

1. Significantly expanding and improving community services with priority given to northern, underserviced, rural, and remote areas; and by

2. Improving accessibility and delivery of community services through a single access or a "one-stop shopping" approach.

The *third* strategy is to enhance geriatric care in acute and chronic hospitals. This strategy involves:

1. Introduction of regional geriatric units across the province;

2. Development of specialized out-patient and in-patient services including day hospitals and outreach clinics; and

3. Expansion of rehabilitation and convalescent services for the elderly in chronic care facilities.

The *fourth* strategy is to ensure high-quality, long-term care for those who are no longer able to live independently in their communities. The main thrust of this strategy is the revision and rationalization of the extended care program, beginning with the development of new, comprehensive extended care legislation. A complementary study of care requirements in homes for the aged and nursing homes will also be undertaken. Another key aspect of this strategy will be to ensure that the quality of care in rest homes is regulated.

The *fifth* strategy is the introduction of comprehensive planning and management of health and social services for the elderly at both the provincial and local level.

At the local level there is a parallel requirement to ensure comprehensive planning and management of health and social services. Accordingly, the Minister plans to explore the feasibility of assigning responsibility for planning and management of community services to appropriate local authorities.

Before producing the White Paper, the Minister held consultation meetings across the province with senior citizens' organizations and those who provide them with services. This method of gathering information has proven to be very popular with those involved and has provided the Minister with a considerable amount of information.

A second, larger tour was conducted following the release of "A New Agenda" to receive feedback on the White paper. The most recent tour, concerning "One-Stop Shopping," met with similar reaction. Given these results, it is likely that local consultation meetings will be employed in the future.

# Section 7
# GENERAL GOVERNMENT MINISTRIES

The General Government Ministries support the activities of the government and coordinate overall government fiscal, economic, management, and public policy. The five General Government Ministries are the Management Board of Cabinet; the Ministries of Government Services; Intergovernmental Affairs; Revenue; and Treasury and Economics. The Ontario Women's Directorate, the Native Affairs Directorate, and the Office of Francophone Affairs are also described in this section.

# MANAGEMENT BOARD OF CABINET

## INTRODUCTION

For many years, the responsibilities now fulfilled by the Management Board of Cabinet were part of the mandate of the Treasury Board, a committee of the Executive Council. The Treasury Board was first established in 1886 under the *Audit Act*, and continued from 1954 under the *Financial Administration Act*. Its members were drawn from the Executive Council, with the Treasurer of Ontario assuming the role of Chairman. The Board was the overseer of all matters relating to government finance, revenues, estimates, expenditures, and financial commitments.

In 1956 and later years, amending legislation progressively authorized the Treasury Board to include a Secretary supported by staff. Ultimately, a Treasury Board Secretariat was created to operate as a government ministry. When the Management Board of Cabinet was formally established in 1971 under the *Management Board of Cabinet Act,* it assumed responsibilities of the former Treasury Board for coordinating the government's resource-allocation process, and, in addition, it was assigned responsibility for coordinating the government's administrative operations.

## ROLES AND FUNCTIONS

Management Board is a Cabinet committee consisting of six to eight Cabinet ministers headed by a chairman and vice-chairman appointed by the Lieutenant Governor in Council. The chairman is also a member of the Policy and Priorities Board, which advises the Cabinet on overall government priorities.

The Management Board of Cabinet serves as the general manager of the Ontario Government on behalf of the Cabinet. It also fulfills the role of employer for the government. Only Cabinet Minutes supersede the Board's decisions.

Typically, the Management Board meets weekly to consider matters concerning the efficient implementation of government programs, including the effective deployment of the government's financial and other resources. It also develops, analyzes, and reviews all government-wide management, technological, and administrative policies. It has a further responsibility to evaluate the results achieved by each ministry (e.g. work-process outputs, benefits to clients, broader consequences) in relation to the ministry's programs that have already been approved.

MANAGEMENT BOARD SECRETARIAT

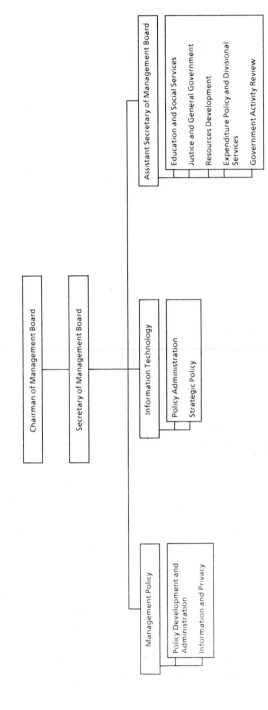

Chairman of Management Board

Secretary of Management Board

Management Policy
- Policy Development and Administration
- Information and Privacy

Information Technology
- Policy Administration
- Strategic Policy

Assistant Secretary of Management Board
- Education and Social Services
- Justice and General Government
- Resources Development
- Expenditure Policy and Divisional Services
- Government Activity Review

The functions of the Management Board as set out in the *Management Board of Cabinet Act* are:

1. To coordinate the implementation of programs sanctioned or provided for by the Legislature;

2. To direct the preparation and review of forecasts, estimates, and analyses of revenues, expenditures, commitments, and other data pertaining to authorized or proposed programs and to assess the results thereof;

3. To control expenditures of public money within the amounts appropriated or otherwise provided for by the Legislature;

4. To approve organization and staff establishments in the public service;

5. To establish, prescribe, or regulate such administrative policies and procedures as the Board considers necessary for the efficient and effective operation of the public service generally;

6. To initiate and supervise the development of management practices and systems for the efficient operation of the public service; and

7. To report to the Executive Council on any other matter concerning general administrative policy in the public service that is referred to it by the Executive Council or on which the Board considers it desirable to report to the Executive Council.

Management Board of Cabinet is responsible for coordinating the implementation of programs sanctioned by the Legislature:

1. To maintain appropriate control over the expenditure of public funds;

2. To monitor performance to ensure that Cabinet decisions are being carried out by ministries and that the Management by Results (MBR) program of the government is being adhered to in the allocation and use of resources;

3. To balance political and management objectives;

4. To manage at the corporate level the government's programs and policies.

## ORGANIZATION

The Management Board of Cabinet is supported in its functions by Management Board Secretariat, the Human Resources Secretariat, and a regulatory agency, the Civil Service Commission.

### Management Board Secretariat

The Secretariat is responsible for providing analytical and administrative support to the Management Board of Cabinet. The Secretariat:

1. Develops and distributes the Ontario Government's administrative and operating policies contained in the Management Board's Directives manual;

2. Develops guidelines for government-wide management and administrative practices;

3. Administers the annual allocation of resources through the preparation and monitoring of ministry expenditure estimates;

4. Coordinates the ministries' program implementation and monitors program results;

5. Provides advice to the Cabinet and its committees on a range of financial, program, and administrative matters.

The Secretariat is organized into three divisions: Information Technology, Management Policy, and Programs and Estimates (see organization chart).

*Information Technology Division*

The Information Technology Division develops and supports corporate strategies and policies to encourage the effective use of information technology in the Ontario Government. It advises the Management Board of Cabinet and other Cabinet Committees on the technological aspects of the program proposals of the ministries and also manages the Management Board Secretariat's information systems. One of its programs established an Information Technology Strategy Steering Committee to develop, in conjunction with government employees and technical specialists, a corporate strategy for the government-wide management of information technology. The Division is organized into four offices: Policy Administration, Policy Development, Corporate Strategy, and Systems Development.

*Management Policy Division*

The Management Policy Division is responsible for the development and administration of management policies other than those related to technology and personnel administration. For example, it is currently reviewing the management of government accommodation with a view to improving accountability and ensuring compatibility with the recently introduced Capital Expenditure Program. The Division advises the Management Board of Cabinet on the management-policy aspects of the program proposals of the ministries. It has one branch, Policy Development and Administration, which focuses specifically on the policies contained in the Management Board's Directives manual. There is also a Branch that works with the coordinators in each government ministry and agency covered by the *Freedom of Information and Protection of Privacy Act.*

*Programs and Estimates Division*

The Programs and Estimates Division is responsible for corporate expenditure control, the expenditure-estimates process, and the promotion of comprehensive, multi-year capital planning and management through its Capital Expenditure Program. It also participates in the annual resource-allocation process. The Division advises the Management Board of Cabinet and other Cabinet committees on the cost implications and results of each ministry's proposals and program changes. It has five branches, including Resources Development, Education and Social Services, Justice and General Government, Expenditure Policy and Divisional Services, and Government Activity Review. The first three branches generally correspond to the groupings of ministries in the Cabinet Committees on Economic Policy, Social Policy, and Justice and General Government ministries combined. The Expenditure Policy and Divisional Services Branch is responsible for developing overall expenditure policies for the government and for providing support services to the other branches of the Programs and Estimates Division. The chief aim of the Government Activity Review Branch is to ensure that program evaluations become a regular practice of government managers.

### Human Resources Secretariat

The Human Resources Secretariat (HRS) was established in March 1986, as a result of the Government's acceptance of the Moher report, *Managing Human Resources in the Ontario Public Service* (OPS). This report concluded that a new framework for human resources management was required to meet the needs of the public service and that the Civil Service Commission should be an organizational unit distinct from the staff group responsible for policy development and coordination. A separate deputy minister was appointed, who is responsible to the Chairman of Management Board of Cabinet. The authority for policy development and administration of human resources management was delegated by the CSC to the HRS. With this change, the staff of the CSC became the staff of the new secretariat.

The Human Resources Secretariat is the corporate advocate for promoting the best practices in human resources management and for providing advice and support to ministries. The Secretariat develops human resources management policies, programs, and initiatives in consultation with ministries and in support of the business of government. The secretariat provides advice to Management Board of Cabinet on the implications of ministry proposals for human resources management. It also acts on behalf of Management Board of Cabinet, the employer, in collective bargaining and employee relations matters, and on behalf of the CSC regarding most human resources functions set out in the *Public Service Act*. The human resources management principles of the secretariat are based on fundamental values which confirm that employees are a critical resource and that fairness and equity are the cornerstones of human resources management policies.

Seven operating principles guide the HRS. They state that the secretariat will:

1. Be service oriented;

2. Openly communicate and consult with client ministries;

3. Be action oriented and timely in developing and delivering its initiatives;

4. Be flexible and responsive to the changing workplace environment;

5. Demonstrate the best practices of human resources management through model programs;

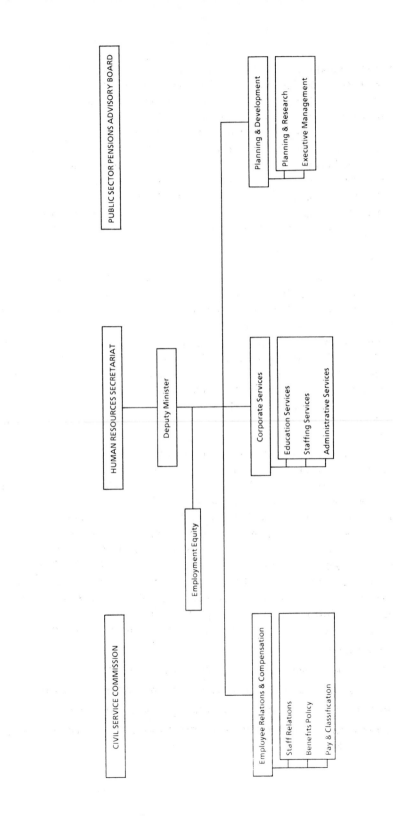

6. Support client ministries in the development and implementation of human resources management systems; and

7. Delegate to ministries the authority to implement personnel policies, wherever appropriate.

The Human Resources Secretariat is organized into three divisions: Corporate Services, Employee Relations and Compensation, and Planning and Development (see organization chart).

### Corporate Services Division

The Corporate Services Division provides corporate services and policy direction to ministries in staffing, education, and French language services, as well as financial, administrative, and personnel services to the HRS, the CSC, and the Public Sector Pensions Advisory Board. It also offers a corporate consultative service in human resources management. The division has three branches: Education Services, Staffing Services, and Administrative Services.

### Employee Relations and Compensation Division

The Employee Relations and Compensation Division acts on behalf of Management Board of Cabinet as the employer in all matters concerning collective bargaining and employee relations. It coordinates occupational health and safety across the Ontario Public Service. It develops, recommends, implements, and maintains policies and standards with respect to pay and position administration, and monitors pay and classification in the public service. The division also develops benefits and pensions policies for public servants and provides advice and guidance to ministries and government agencies on special compensation issues. The division has three branches: Staff Relations, Benefits Policy, and Pay and Classification.

### Planning and Development Division

The Planning and Development Division provides leadership in the development of plans and systems in the human resources field. It conducts research on the social, economic, and legislative environment, and on employment policies and practices in the private and public sectors. It also integrates various government initiatives to ensure that human resources management considerations are included in ministries' strategic plans. The Communications Section is also included in this division. The division assists in the development and training of executives and gives support to the Associate Secretary of Cabinet, Executive Resources.

Within the Human Resources Secretariat, staff develop policies on recruitment, including the attraction and selection of candidates, conditions of appointment, temporary leaves of absence, separation, lay-off, and recall; on training and development of staff, including performance appraisal and manpower and career planning;

on all aspects of compensation for public servants, including a classification system, pay, and benefits; discipline and other employee relations matters; on personnel administration relating to staffing, compensation, and development of executives; and on employment strategies which reflect private and public sector policies and which are consistent with the government's goals and strategic directions.

Secretariat Staff also operate the government's temporary employment services; develop service-wide classification standards; monitor ministry classification activities; develop pay proposals in line with market conditions and internal relations; negotiate with the Ontario Public Service Employees Union and the Ontario Provincial Police Association for salaries, employee benefits, and working conditions; maintain liaison with certain government agencies on collective bargaining and other employee relations matters; assist ministries in resolving grievances and other employee relations problems; train personnel officers and managers in specific aspects of the personnel process, such as selection and compensation; provide a central career counseling service; provide training courses of general interest; provide consulting services; provide French-language training services; publish *Topical* and *Job Mart*—the government's only service-wide editorial and personnel advertising publication; act as liaison between ministries and an advertising agency in order to advertise for personnel in external media; and provide other corporate services, such as publication of Volume 2 of the Manual of Administration, and the coordination of blood donor clinics and the Quarter Century Club.

The Management Board of Cabinet is located in Toronto. Management Board Secretariat employs 100 public servants, while the Human Resources Secretariat employs approximately 240 public servants.

## EXPENDITURE ESTIMATES

*Estimated Expenditures 1987–88*:

| | |
|---|---|
| Ministry Administration | $175,957,632 |
| Finance and Administrative Policy | 10,778,400 |
| Administration | 4,139,206 |
| Human Resources | 16,206,000 |
| Public Services | 1,573,100 |
| **Management Board total:** | **$208,654,338** |

## AGENCIES, BOARDS, AND COMMISSIONS

The following ABCs report to the Legislative Assembly through the Chairman of Management Board:

### Civil Service Commission

The Civil Service Commission, which has a long and distinguished history, can be traced back to the Office of the Civil Service Commissioner for Ontario, established by the *Public Service Act, 1918.* In 1947, the *Public Service Act* was amended to provide for the establishment of a Civil Service Commission, consisting of three persons appointed by the Lieutenant Governor in Council. In 1961–62 the *Public Service Act* was amended to make the Commission a Department. This provision was clarified in a 1965 amendment which stated that the staff of the Commission constituted the Department of Civil Service. Between 1961–62 and 1969, the Chairman of the Commission was also the Deputy Minister of the Department of Civil Service. From 1969 until 1972, the position of Chairman of the Commission was separated from that of Deputy Minister and the two positions were filled by different persons. In 1972, on the recommendation of the Committee on Government Productivity the *Public Service Act* was amended again to return CSC to the status of a Commission, and the reference to the staff of the commission constituting a department was repealed. The CSC has continued to function in this guise since that date, but recent organizational changes have resulted in a major delegation of its powers under the *Public Service Act* to another body.

The Commission is responsible to a member of the Executive Council designated by the Lieutenant Governor in Council for the administration of the *Public Service Act.* The current designated Minister is the Chairman, Management Board of Cabinet. Until March 1986, the Commission provided its own direct support staff. For convenience, the budgeting and estimates processes for the Management Board of Cabinet Secretariat, the Human Resources Secretariat, and the Civil Service Commission have been combined and are reviewed by the Legislature as the estimates of Management Board of Cabinet. Generally, administrative support for the Commission is provided by the Ministry of Treasury and Economics.

In 1986, when the Commission delegated to the Deputy Minister of the Human Resources Secretariat all of its corporate personnel policy and program responsibilities, the staff of the Civil Service Commission became the staff of the Secretariat. The Commission retained only those powers and duties which it could not legally delegate under the *Public Service Act* as it is presently constituted. The Commission also remained responsible for reporting on compliance with the merit principle and the *Public Service Act.*

The Civil Service Commission currently consists of the Chairman, Donald Crosbie, the Secretary of Management Board, the Deputy Minister of Consumer and Commercial Relations, and the Assistant Deputy Ministers of the Corporate Services and Planning and Development Divisions--Human Resources Secretariat, for the purpose of carrying out the Commission's legislative and adjudicative functions. This is an interim arrangement pending the revision of the *Public Service Act.*

*Programs*

Under the *Public Service Act,* the Civil Service Commission is directly responsible for evaluating, classifying, and determining the qualifications for each position in the classified service; for recruiting qualified persons for the civil service and establishing lists of those eligible; for assigning persons to positions in the classified service and specifying the salaries payable; for determining perquisite charges for civil servants; and for providing and assisting in or coordinating staff development programs. In practice, however, the first three functions have been delegated to deputy ministers of ministries subject to corporate policies, practices, and standards.

The Commission is also responsible under the Act for recommending to the Lieutenant Governor in Council the salary range for each classification, except those established through collective bargaining pursuant to the *Crown Employees Collective Bargaining Act.* Subject to the approval of the Lieutenant Governor in Council, the Commission may make regulations with respect to a wide range of specified personnel management functions including terms and conditions of employment, employee benefits, employee conduct and discipline.

### Other Agencies, Boards, and Commissions

*Ontario Provincial Police Grievance Board:* Has sole responsibility for adjudicating grievances and disputes concerning those working conditions and terms of employment covered by the Memorandum of Understanding between the Province of Ontario and the Ontario Provincial Police Association, the regulations under the *Public Service Act,* and the Ontario Manual of Administration, Vol.2.

*Ontario Provincial Police Negotiating Committee:* Has sole responsibility for negotiations between the Ontario Provincial Police Association and the Management Board of Cabinet on matters relating to terms and conditions of employment, including rates of remuneration, hours of work, overtime and other premium allowances for work performed, benefits, insurance plans, leaves of absence, and methods of effecting promotions, demotions, transfers, layoffs, and reappointments.

*Public Service Classification Rating Committee:* Classification rating committees are periodically appointed to adjudicate the grievances concerning the position classification of employees not covered by the *Crown Employees Collective Bargaining Act.* Such employees for the most part include those who have been employed in a managerial or confidential capacity.

*Public Service Grievance Board:* Adjudicates the grievances concerning employees who are not members of a bargaining unit on matters related to dismissal, suspension, other forms of discipline, merit increases, promotions, and transfers.

*Public Sector Pensions Advisory Board:* Informs and advises the Chairman of the Management Board on all matters pertaining to employee pensions in Ontario's public sector. The Advisory Board also receives submissions on these issues from interested parties, including public employers, employees, unions, pensioners and pension-plan administrators, and trustees.

*Public Service Superannuation Board:* Recommends payments of annuities, pensions, and disability benefits to the employees of the Ontario Public Service.

The Superannuation Board rules on the application of these payments under the *Public Service Superannuation Act.*

## LEGISLATION

The Management Board of Cabinet is responsible for the following Acts:

*Freedom of Information and Protection of Privacy Act:* Gives individuals a legal right of access to information held by the government and its agencies, with certain exceptions such as Cabinet documents, police records, or personal information of others. The Act also gives individuals a right of access to their personal information and establishes standards to ensure that this information is protected. Two directories have been published listing information available under the Act, the *Directory of General Records* and the *Directory of Personal Information Banks.* These may be obtained at the Ontario Government Bookstore or consulted in libraries, and ministry and agency offices. Also, a Freedom of Information Coordinator has been appointed in each ministry and agency covered by the Act to assist individuals in locating records and personal information maintained by Ontario Government ministries and agencies.

*Management Board of Cabinet Act:* The purpose of this Act is to promote and encourage effective and efficient management and administrative practices within the Government of Ontario and to ensure, on behalf of Cabinet, that programs ad policies are being implemented effectively.

*Public Service Act:* Within the Ontario Government service, the primary statutory authority governing the operation of the personnel function is the Public Service Act. This Act:

(1.) Establishes the Civil Service Commission and defines its powers and duties;

(2.) Authorizes the Commission, subject to the approval of the Lieutenant Governor in Council, to make regulations respecting any matter necessary or desirable to carry out the intent and purpose of the Act;

(3.) Specifies rules regarding: deputy minister's authority and responsibility, appointments of public servants, assignment of public servants to positions, oath of office and secrecy and oath of allegiance, political activities of Crown employees, discipline and dismissal, and retirement and resignation.

*Public Service Superannuation Act:* The purpose of this Act is to provide pensions for public servants and members of such agencies as specified in the Act.

*Successor Rights (Crown Transfers) Act, 1977:* This Act establishes the framework for representation when units are transferred into or out of provincial jurisdiction.

*Superannuation Adjustments Benefits Act:* The purpose of this Act is to provide superannuation adjustment benefits to persons in receipt of pensions that are paid out of a pension fund to which contributions are paid directly or indirectly out of the Consolidated Revenue Fund.

## INNOVATIONS

The following innovations have had a positive impact on the operations of Management Board:

*Revision of Ontario Manual of Administration*

In 1985, the Management Board Secretariat launched a revision of the Ontario Manual of Administration in line with the recommendations of the Study of Management and Accountability in the Government of Ontario that had been presented in January of that year. The Study advised that the 10-year manual should be streamlined, updated, and redesigned to better serve ministry managers. It also called for the development of training material on the use of the manual that could be included in the government's management-development program.

The new manual, known as the Management Board Directives, was published in the autumn of 1986 after extensive consultations with ministries and manual designers, with the recommended training sessions beginning a few weeks later. In addition, supplementary Guidelines, developed to explain and interpret particular directives, were published in a separate binder. The revised Directives binder, multi-coloured by section for easy reference and about half the size of the old manual, has been praised for being flexible, readable, usable, and in keeping with good management practices.

*Other Innovations*

Other innovations introduced by the Ontario Government in which the Management Board Secretariat is assisting ministries include:

1. Budgeting so that all increases are offset from within current allocations;

2. Relocation of some government facilities to northern Ontario;

3. Manpower control;

4. Expenditure pressures for 86/87 and beyond;

5. Determining future candidates for government activity reviews.

*The Human Resources Secretariat*

The Human Resources Secretariat is responding to the changing workplace and workforce. It recognizes that for the Ontario Government to remain a competitive employer in the 1990s, the Ontario Public Service needs reshaping, revitalizing, and redeployment. The secretariat has developed a new human resources management program called Planning for People. The first in a series of initiatives under this program, Strategies for Renewal, was announced recently.

The government has made three major strategic statements including corporate objectives and recommendations to achieve that renewal of the workforce: the composition of the Ontario Public Service shall reflect more closely the diversity of Ontario society; the organization shall exemplify the best management styles and be responsive to changes in the working environment; and recruitment in the Ontario Public Service shall change to planned staffing initiatives that provide equality of access.

Highlights of the renewal initiative include: a new emphasis on human resources planning; more open recruiting; increased use of secondment, job rotations, developmental positions and exchanges; improved use of staff training and career development programs; designing flexible workplaces and innovative jobs; increasing the number of employees under age 25; re-establishing trainee positions in selected occupations; employment equity programs for women, minorities, natives, francophones, and people with disabilities; and increasing the number of appointments from the public sector.

To provide a catalyst for implementing these initiatives, a voluntary exit options program took effect in April 1987. Other proposed initiatives in the Planning for People program include succession planning, performance pay, and performance appraisal.

## Civil Service Commission

Within the Civil Service Commission, the principal innovations in corporate personnel management during most of the 1970s and the first half of the 1980s related primarily to what may be described as "personnel administration" (position classification and employee benefits), and more urgently, to adapting to a lengthy period of financial constraint, staff reduction, and severe inflation. The establishment of the Human Resources Secretariat in 1986, and the changing role of the Civil Service Commission, were the initial steps in creating and maintaining a predominant emphasis on pro-active "human resources management" (in contrast to "personnel administration") in the Ontario Public Service. Further steps, which are now underway involve the revision of the *Public Service Act.*

# MINISTRY OF GOVERNMENT SERVICES

## ROLES AND FUNCTIONS

The Ministry of Government Services (MGS) is concerned with virtually every aspect of the working environment in the Government of Ontario, from building design and management to office equipment, computers, telecommunications, human resource services, corporate services, purchasing, and employee benefits. Ministry activities include centralized services as diverse as collective purchasing, assets disposal, translation, and government mail. MGS recently assumed responsibility for the marketing of provincial lands not required by ministries for their program needs.

The bulk of the Ministry's budget and staff is committed to providing physical facilities for the Ontario Government. Services include construction, renovation, maintenance, and leasing of buildings which house government operations. The Ministry provides information technology services and products, including computers, telephones, data transmission facilities, and audio and visual technology. The Ministry's three computer centres, with 6,500 terminals, handle approximately 80 percent of the government's computing.

MGS is also responsible for the coordination of the Northern Ontario Relocation Program, which is a key component of the government's northern economic diversification initiatives. Under this program, MGS is coordinating the relocation of various head office programs of several ministries to selected northern Ontario communities (e.g. the head office of the Ministry of Northern Development and Mines to Sudbury).

## BACKGROUND HISTORY

The Ministry of Government Services was created in 1972, to combine the functions of former departments, including the Department of Public Works. The first Commissioner of Public Works and Agriculture was appointed in 1867. Since that time, the functions associated with MGS have been the responsibility of a variety of Cabinet Ministers, including the Minister of Public Works, the Minister of Public Works and Highways, the Minister of Public Works and Labour, the Minister of Public Works and Public Welfare, the Provincial Treasurer, and finally the Minister of Government Services. As the size of the Ontario Government increased through the 1960s and into the early 1970s, the mandate of MGS broadened extensively, particularly in the areas of personnel administration and property management.

## ORGANIZATION

The Ministry of Government Services is organized into four divisions (see organization chart):

1. *Computer and Telecommunications Services:* Assists Ontario Government ministries to provide more effective service to the people of Ontario through the application of information technology.

2. *Finance and Administration:* Provides the Ministry with financial and administrative services, such as operational review, analysis, and planning, information systems, audit and legal services. The Division also provides administrative support to the Office of the Lieutenant Governor, and the Offices responsible for Women's Issues, Senior Citizen Affairs, and Disabled Persons. It performs some accounting functions for the Office of the Legislative Assembly and the Ombudsman's Office.

3. *Supply and Services:* Provides a variety of support services to ministries and agencies of the government and the public by promoting access to government information, coordinating government purchasing activities, and delivering common services. Also, Supply and Services coordinates government efforts and services to provide an integrated and effective approach to human resources management in the public service. Ministry services are provided by the Personnel Services Branch and Employment Equity for Women Program, while corporate (government-wide) services are provided by the Employee Benefits and Data Services Branch and the Employee Services Branch.

4. *Realty Group:* This diverse group comprises three divisions:

   *(a.) Program Development and Management Division:* Includes the Client Services, Corporate Services, Land Development, Land Management, Land Marketing, Mortgages Administration, and Portfolio Management Branches.

   *(b.) Property Management Division:* Represents the Ministry province-wide through regional and district offices, providing operational maintenance, repair, alterations, and construction services to Ontario Government-owned buildings.

   *(c.) Design and Construction Division:* Includes the Design Services, Contract Management, and Project Management Branches.

In addition, the Public Service Superannuation Board reports to the Legislative Assembly through the Minister of Government Services (see Agencies, Boards, and Commissions).

MINISTRY OF GOVERNMENT SERVICES

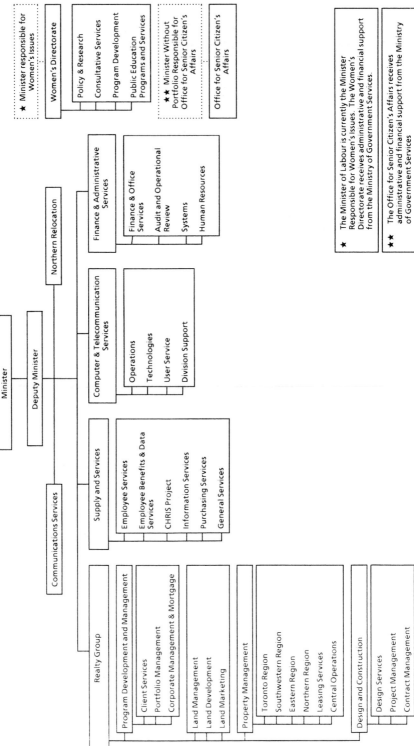

Minister

Deputy Minister

Communications Services

Northern Relocation

**Supply and Services**
- Employee Services
- Employee Benefits & Data Services
- CHRIS Project
- Information Services
- Purchasing Services
- General Services

**Computer & Telecommunication Services**
- Operations
- Technologies
- User Service
- Division Support

**Finance & Administrative Services**
- Finance & Office Services
- Audit and Operational Review
- Systems
- Human Resources

**Realty Group**

**Program Development and Management**
- Client Services
- Portfolio Management
- Corporate Management & Mortgage
- Land Management
- Land Development
- Land Marketing

**Property Management**
- Toronto Region
- Southwestern Region
- Eastern Region
- Northern Region
- Leasing Services
- Central Operations

**Design and Construction**
- Design Services
- Project Management
- Contract Management

★ Minister responsible for Women's Issues

**Women's Directorate**
- Policy & Research
- Consultative Services
- Program Development
- Public Education Programs and Services

★★ Minister Without Portfolio Responsible for Office for Senior Citizen's Affairs

**Office for Senior Citizen's Affairs**

★ The Minister of Labour is currently the Minister Responsible for Women's Issues. The Women's Directorate receives administrative and financial support from the Ministry of Government Services.

★★ The Office for Senior Citizen's Affairs receives administrative and financial support from the Ministry of Government Services

The head office of the Ministry of Government Services is located in Toronto; branches of the Ministry are located throughout the city. The Ministry also operates three regional and fourteen district offices, providing MGS services to client ministries and agencies and to the public throughout the province. The Ministry of Government Services employs approximately 2900 public servants.

## PROGRAMS

### Realty Group

The Realty Group consists of three divisions: Program Development and Management, Property Management, and Design and Construction.

*Program Development and Management Division*

The Program Development and Management Division has seven branches:

*Corporate Management:* Provides policy and program direction in the finance and technology areas of the Realty Group, and administers the Accommodation Management Information System, which provides information to ministries on government-owned and leased premises.

*Portfolio Management:* Administers the government's real estate portfolio of land and buildings.

*Client Services:* Assists clients in developing short- and long-term accommodation requirements and develops accommodation programs.

*Land Management:* Performs appraisals, surveys, negotiations, and expropriations for the acquisition of real estate, and assists OPS employees transferred to other locations in Ontario through the Home Owner Relocation Plan.

*Land Marketing:* Responsible for the marketing and sale of all provincial lands no longer required for program purposes for residential, industrial, and commercial development.

*Land Development:* Responsible for the planning and development of land where title is held by MGS.

*Mortgage Administration:* Provides administrative support for repayment of mortgages and leases committed under various government lending programs, such as Renterprise and Convert-to-Rent (under Ministry of Housing).

*Property Management Division*

The Property Management Division provides maintenance, repair, alteration, and construction services province-wide through a network of three regional and fourteen district offices.

*Leasing Services Branch:* Arranges appraisals, negotiations, acquisition, and payment of rental and adjustment claims for leased real estate accommodation from the private sector and municipalities.

*Central Operations Branch:* Renders divisional administration and support.

*Regional and District Staff:* Responsible for the operation, maintenance, and repair of building structures, heating, ventilating, air-conditioning, and electrical systems, and provide housekeeping, security, groundskeeping, and common administrative services within their geographical area. They also administer tendering and supervision of construction, and respond to emergency situations requiring protection of staff, public, and government owned property.

## Design and Construction Division

The Design and Construction Division includes the Design Services, the Contract Management and the Project Management Branches.

*Design Services Branch:* Provides advisory and design accommodation-alteration projects, and commissions works of art for government buildings. The government art collection has been valued at $10 million.

*Contract Management Branch:* Supplies contractual, construction, and financial control on capital projects in the provision of buildings, accommodation, and other facilities for government ministries and agencies.

*Project Management Branch:* Provides project management services for designated projects to ensure adherence to deadlines and budget, and effective overall project accountability through a single government branch.

## Computer and Telecommunications Services Division

The Computer and Telecommunications Services Division provides computer services to ministries and agencies of the Government offering service to the public. For example, MGS computers process OHIP payments for the Ministry of Health, provide on-line information to police departments, and support Ministry of Transportation and Communications driver and vehicle licensing offices around the province. Telecommunications services such as video and audio teleconferencing facilities, teletype and facsimile services, radio communications, and computerized telephone systems are also made available. Expertise in office automation, computer hardware and software, and information security is offered. Mainframe computer processing and printing is provided at three large computer centres. These facilities and thousands of individual computer terminals in Government offices around the province are linked through the Division's data network. The Division's Ontario Communications Network is a telecommunications link between government offices and provides low-cost calling for government business.

## Supply and Services Division

### Information Services Branch

The Information Services Branch provides essential information services to client ministries and agencies, and the general public.

*Government Mail Service:* Provides collection and distribution of regular Canada Post and inter-ministry mail and bulk mail, a courier and messenger service, and a mail service operation (addressing, labelling, folding, and inserting mail.) The Branch operates the 24-hour Queen's Park switchboard and the Citizens Inquiry Bureau, a government information and referral service, including a TTY/TDD service for the hearing impaired.

*Access Databases and Directories:* Assembles public information from all ministries and structures it for use by the government and public. This section publishes the *Ontario Government Telephone Directory* and the *KWIC Index to Services*, and offers the online GUIDE service for locating government offices and the KWICplus service, which gives a description of government services.

*Records Centre:* Provides storage and retrieval of inactive government records, hard copy, computer tape, and microfilm.

*Translation Service:* Provides translation to government and the public.

*Publication Services:* Maintains an inventory of Ontario Government publications, including *Hansard, Ontario Gazette*, and all *Annual Reports* of ministries, agencies, boards, and commissions, which are marketed and distributed through Ontario Government Bookstores and a province-wide library depository system.

## General Services Branch

The General Services Branch provides Ontario Government ministries with operational support services.

*Food Services Section:* Provides a policy review and advisory role in support of the delivery of food service in most government buildings. (Property Management Division is responsible for the operation of food services.)

*Government Payments Services:* Responsible for printing cheques drawn on the Consolidated Revenue fund for most major programs in the government, upon authorization from the ministry concerned.

*Central Collection Service:* Collects debts owing to the government.

*Insurance and Risk Management Section:* Purchases insurance for the government, and advises all Ontario ministries and agencies on insurance coverage (excluding employee benefits.)

*Official Documents Section:* Prepares, records, microfilms, searches, and makes copies of Ontario official documents such as land patents, affidavits, congratulatory scrolls, and Commission Certificates of appointment under the Great Seal of the Province of Ontario and the Privy Seal of the Lieutenant Governor.

## Purchasing Services Branch

*Sourcing Information Service:* Maintains an automated vendor sourcing service for goods and services purchased by MGS, where vendors wishing to do business with the Ministry may register.

*Collective Purchasing Section:* Operates the Public Tenders Office to receive tenders for government supply contracts, and establishes government-wide standing agreements and offers for the purchase of commodities and services commonly used by various government ministries and agencies.

*Government Stationery Service:* Operates a retail outlet by purchasing common stationery, office supplies, and souvenir products and supplying them on a charge-back basis to government offices throughout the province.

*Printing Services:* Handles contracting for all printing of legislation (bills and regulations), offers a graphic design service, and purchases printing services from the private sector.

*Vehicle Repair and Trucking Section:* Maintains and repairs government vehicles and provides a province-wide trucking service.

*Assets Disposal Service:* Receives, warehouses, and arranges (through public auction or donations to charitable organizations) for the re-use or disposal of surplus furniture and equipment.

### Employee Benefits and Data Services Branch

The Employee Benefits and Data Services Branch administers benefit plans for Ontario Public Service (OPS) employees in accordance with the *Public Service Superannuation Act.* This branch also administers the Integrated Payroll and Employee Benefits System and the Central Attendance Recording System for OPS employees, which includes pay lists, cheques, work history data, ministry organization structures, status changes of employees, pension contribution data, life insurance, OHIP information, T-4 income tax forms, and salary structure information.

### Employee Services Branch

The Employee Services Branch provides client ministries and agencies with a number of employee services.

*Employee Counselling:* Offers confidential counselling for OPS employees and rehabilitation services for employees experiencing long-term illness and/or disability; assists employees in making day care arrangements for children; and provides consultation to managers and personnel administrators in dealing with work performance problems.

*Employee Health Services:* Provides health surveillance programs for OPS employees exposed to dangerous substances; health promotion and education programs; and direct health care services through twelve health centres in Ontario government buildings in the Toronto area.

*Safety Services:* Provides occupational safety services to government ministries, conducts fire safety and building air quality inspections, and develops evacuation plans for government workers.

*Employee Volunteer Programs:* Organizes the Employee United Way campaigns throughout the province, and coordinates the Employee Blood Donor Clinics.

## EXPENDITURE ESTIMATES

*Estimated Expenditures 1987–88*:

| | |
|---|---|
| Ministry Administration | $ 17,450,038 |
| Realty Services | 382,282,500 |
| Corporate Services | 17,728,800 |
| Human Resource Services | 89,688,100 |
| Computer and Telecommunications Services | 13,348,700 |
| **Ministry total:** | **$520,498,138** |

## AGENCIES, BOARDS, AND COMMISSIONS

The *Public Service Superannuation Board* reports to the Legislative Assembly through the Minister of Government Services. The Board recommends payment of annuities, pensions, and disability benefits to employees of the Ontario Public Service. It rules on applications in respect of past service credits and pension credit transfers under the *Public Service Superannuation Act.* The Board hears appeals from contributors, pensioners, or dependents against administrative decisions made by the Employee Benefits and Data Services Branch.

It should be noted that the functions associated with the former *Ontario Land Corporation* and its subsidiary, the *Ontario Mortgage Corporation* were merged with the Property Management Division of the Ministry of Government Services. The merger was approved by Cabinet in April 1986, and completed in April 1987.

## LEGISLATION

The Ministry of Government Services is responsible for the following Acts:

*Flag Act:* Provides for the designation of the official flag of the Province of Ontario.

*Floral Emblem Act:* Provides for the designation of the trillium as the official floral emblem of the Province of Ontario.

*Ministry of Government Services Act:* Establishes and continues the Ministry of Government Services.

*Official Notices Publication Act:* Provides for the publication of official notices in the *Ontario Gazette.*

*Public Service Superannuation Act:* Establishes and continues the Public Service Superannuation Board to hear complaints and to resolve disputes arising over Ontario Public Service employees and the Government.

## INNOVATIONS

The following innovations have had a positive impact on the operations of the Ministry of Government Services:

*Accommodation:* The Realty Group of the Ministry represents the largest segment of the Ministry's resources. It is responsible for planning, developing, and managing corporate accommodation and real property. In 1986, an entirely new strategic approach to land management in the Government of Ontario was initiated. The strategy, called the Portfolio Management Strategy, is designed to streamline and coordinate the approach to the government's land and building inventory. A database on 3 1/2 million acres of land and 9,000 buildings is being established.

The Ministry is continuing to focus strongly on the correlation between the work environment and productivity. Over the past several years, a new direction was taken in office design. Emphasis is now placed on flexible space, equipment automation, adaptable furniture, improved ventilation, and high energy conservation standards. Finally, Ontario government buildings are now as accessible as possible for disabled persons, through the provision of ramps, washroom facilities, and other modifications.

*Corporate Service:* By buying bulk through collective purchasing arrangements, certain efficiencies are reflected in the cost of goods to clients. When it comes to purchasing, MGS buys Canadian-produced commodities and services wherever possible. Two procurement studies, on inventory management and supplier lists, were initiated by Management Board in 1985, in order to "open up" the business of government. The studies recommend cost saving measures and techniques that will open up and simplify the process of securing government contracts. Pilot projects are now underway in the Ministry, based upon the recommendations of these studies. When finalized, these measures will save taxpayers' dollars and help to ensure equal access for all potential suppliers.

*Human Resources:* New and improved methods of developing the skills and future potential of MGS staff has become a very high priority. Development of the Corporate Human Resource Information System (CHRIS) began in 1984–85, and is a priority project within the Ministry. A new concept in personnel and payroll management, CHRIS provides a single integrated source of information on the human resources of the Ontario Public Service, and will be extended to all provincial ministries and agencies. Staff development at all levels will continue through job rotation, secondments, and formal training. Existing payroll, personnel, employee benefits, and attendance information systems are being overhauled. A new database is being developed to provide a comprehensive range of human resource information services. Finally, the efforts of the ongoing Affirmative Action Program continue to increase the number of women in underrepresented areas of MGS.

*Technology:* One of the biggest challenges for MGS was, and will continue to be, to provide improved service by implementing the latest methods of information technology. By committing itself to leadership in videotext, data processing, and minicomputers, the Ministry can help increase productivity throughout government. In 1985, the Ministry's Computer and Telecommunications Services Division developed a five-year strategic plan for coherence and consistency in the use of technology throughout the government.

# MINISTRY OF
# INTERGOVERNMENTAL AFFAIRS

## ROLES AND FUNCTIONS

The mandate of the Ministry of Intergovernmental Affairs (MIGA) is to identify and advance Ontario's interests and to conduct relations with the Government of Canada, the other provinces and territories of Canada, and governments abroad and their representatives in Ontario. Given the nature of intergovernmental affairs, and because it is a policy advisory ministry, the Premier plays a more active role than in other ministries. The Premier has held the Intergovernmental Affairs portfolio since 1985.

## BACKGROUND HISTORY

The Ontario Ministry of Intergovernmental Affairs has existed only since 1978, but the functions which are administered by the Ministry have had their separate existence since at least the 1960s. Some—such as intergovernmental relations—have roots in the division of responsibility between the two levels of government at the time of Confederation. But the emergence of specialized agencies to handle intergovernmental affairs is a recent phenomenon in Canada, rooted in the growth of governments and the increasing complexity of political life in the post-World War II era. Against a background of expanding intergovernmental activity in the 1960s—such as First Ministers' and Premiers' Conferences—and a need for concerted efforts in social service and fiscal policy development, governments recognized the need to view and manage their encounters in a more distinctive, specialized fashion.

In 1962, Ontario Premier Leslie Frost decided that closer attention should be given to intergovernmental affairs, and changed the Department of Economics to the Department of Economics and Intergovernmental Affairs, so that the preparation for and conduct of negotiations with other governments on policy issues could be facilitated. In 1965, in response to growing concern about federal fiscal initiatives and the implications of Quebec nationalism, Premier John Robarts created the Department of Economics and Development, headed by Chief Economist Ian Mac-Donald. One of the four branches of the Department was the Federal-Provincial Affairs Secretariat. The Department merged with the Department of Treasury in 1966 to become the Department of Treasury and Economics under the Honourable Charles McNaughton as Minister. The early activities of the Federal-Provincial Affairs Secretariat focused on non-fiscal issues, especially constitutional reform. Increasing interaction within the Department in policy planning and analysis of major federal-provincial fiscal and economic issues allowed the secretariat to extend its involvement into non-constitutional matters by 1972.

There is also a long history of relations between Ontario and governments abroad. The Office of the Agent-General of Ontario in London, England, dates from the pre-Confederation era and continues to represent the province today. After 1945 the Ontario Government became increasingly aware of the importance of events abroad and the impact of close ties with the American economy and culture. In the 1960s trade offices were developed in the United States and Europe and trade missions were sent abroad to sell Ontario products. The province became involved in international aid in agricultural projects and began to participate in "La Francophonie" as well as in Commonwealth Conferences. Such participation was coordinated through the Premier's Office.

In 1972, in response to the findings of the Committee on Government Productivity (which stated that there was a need "to ensure that the municipal, regional, provincial, federal, and international programs and activities of the government are properly related, coordinated, and consistent with government policy"), Premier William Davis established the Ministry of Treasury, Economics and Intergovernmental Affairs, under the Honourable Darcy McKeough as Minister, and Ian MacDonald as Deputy Minister. The new Ministry was organized into four main divisions; the Economic Policy and Intergovernmental Affairs Division, under Don Stevenson, was responsible for intergovernmental relations.

One of the main features of the new organization was its broadened perspective on intergovernmental matters, including relations with the federal government in Ottawa, with other provinces, governments abroad, and Ontario's municipalities. The Office of Intergovernmental Affairs within the Economic Policy and Intergovernmental Affairs Division was divided into three secretariats: Federal-Provincial and Interprovincial Affairs, External Activities Coordination, and Provincial-Municipal Affairs. The latter secretariat was relocated in the Local Government Division of TEIGA in 1974, to consolidate the Ministry's dealings with municipalities.

The Federal-Provincial and Interprovincial Affairs Secretariat focused all of its attention on non-constitutional matters in the mid-1970s, in response to Quebec's ongoing pressure for increased responsibility in social and cultural policy and the new aggressiveness of the Western Provinces in the resource field. The Secretariat began to prepare an analysis of the significance of these developments for Ontario, and to provide information in an advisory capacty in support of the intergovernmental activities of line ministries. The External Activities Coordination Secretariat maintained liaison with the Federal Department of External Affairs in Ottawa, and ensured a coordinated approach to the international activities of Ontario ministries.

Meanwhile, other aspects which were later to become part of the Ministry's mandate were developed in other ministries in the 1970s. The Office of Protocol, which handled arrangements for royal visits, visits of heads of governments, and liaison with the consular corps in Toronto, grew in size under the Ministry of Government Services. The office of the Government Coordinator of French Language Services was also created, to promote the development of government French language services to meet the needs of the Franco-Ontarian community.

In 1978, in response to Darcy McKeough's resignation, Premier Davis split TEIGA into two separate ministries. Thomas Wells was named Minister, and Don Stevenson, Deputy Minister, of the new Ministry of Intergovernmental Affairs. In so doing, the Ontario Government was following the lead of other governments, where separate units (with a Ministerial head) had been established to provide a different set of perspectives on intergovernmental relations, in addition to the views of the line ministries. Given the increasing number and complexity of intergovernmental economic and constitutional issues in Canada in the late 1970s, this approach enabled the government to have a Cabinet level focus on such activities.

When the Ministry was established, it was decided that support services such as personnel, purchasing, accounting, and audit would continue to be provided by Treasury and Economics. However, a small Planning and Management Group was established to provide advice on corporate planning and resource allocation. A separate Information Services Section also became an integral component of the Ministry in 1980.

The Office of the Coordinator of French Language Services was administratively attached to MIGA in 1978, when the Ministry was created. It was enlarged in 1982 in response to an in-depth review of bilingualism in the public service. The Protocol Office joined MIGA from the Ministry of Government Services in 1979.

In 1981 the Local Government Division was separated from the Ministry and merged with the Ministry of Housing to form the Ministry of Municipal Affairs and Housing. The Office of Intergovernmental Affairs was reorganized to form the present Federal-Provincial Relations Branch and the International Relations Branch. The former was restructured in 1982 into a Policy Development Section responsible for analysis and research into intergovernmental relations and constitutional issues in Ontario ministries, the federal government, and other provinces.

In 1983 the Cabinet Committee on Federal-Provincial Relations was created, with the Premier as Chairman and the Minister of Intergovernmental Affairs as Vice-Chairman, allowing MIGA to raise matters of intergovernmental importance in Cabinet. In January 1984, Gary Posen was appointed Deputy Minister and the former Deputy Minister, Don Stevenson, was appointed Senior Representative of the Government of Ontario to the Federal Government and the Government of Quebec, reporting directly to the Minister in his liaison capacity. Stevenson now works from an Ontario corporate office in Ottawa and a new office in Quebec City.

The Ministry underwent some fundamental changes after the resignation of Premier William Davis. The Minister, Thomas Wells, was appointed as Ontario's Agent-General in London. The new Premier, Frank Miller, retained for himself the portfolio of Minister of Intergovernmental Affairs. This was the first time in Ontario history that a Premier formally assigned this important responsibility to himself, although it has always been recognized that the ultimate responsibility for the external relations of the province rested with the Premier. Following the provincial election of 1985 and the Liberal-NDP accord, Premier David Peterson also decided to retain the ministerial responsibility for intergovernmental affairs.

In February 1985, the responsibility for French Language Services was transferred administratively to the Ministry of Health. The Office of Francophone Affairs is now attached to Cabinet Office.

Following the 1987 election, Premier David Peterson retained the Intergovernmental Affairs portfolio.

## ORGANIZATION

The Ministry of Intergovernmental Affairs is organized into two major divisions: General Management and Intergovernmental Relations (see organization chart).

*General Management:* Includes four organizational units:

1. *Minister's Office and Office of Senior Representative of Government of Ontario.*

2. *Deputy Minister's Office.*

3. *Information Services Branch:* Provides a central media service to the government for major public events and supports the Minister and Ministry in the development and dissemination of speeches, statements, reports, publications, news releases, and communications planning.

4. *Planning and Management Group:* Coordinates the planning and allocation of Ministry resources and provides the corporate management and corporate secretariat function for the Ministry.

*Intergovernmental Relations:* Has three organizational units:

1. *Federal-Provincial Relations Branch:* Focuses upon the Government of Canada and the other provinces and territories in Canada.

2. *International Relations Branch:* Focuses on the broad aspects of Ontario's relationships with governments outside Canada.

3. *Office of Protocol Services:* Provides hospitality to official visitors; organizational assistance; services and advice on protocol matters for special events and ceremonial occasions; and strengthens the province's relationship with foreign representatives tativestativestativestativestativestativestativestativesin Ontario.

The Ministry of Intergovernmental Affairs is located in Toronto. The Ministry employs approximately 70 public servants.

MINISTRY OF INTERGOVERNMENTAL AFFAIRS

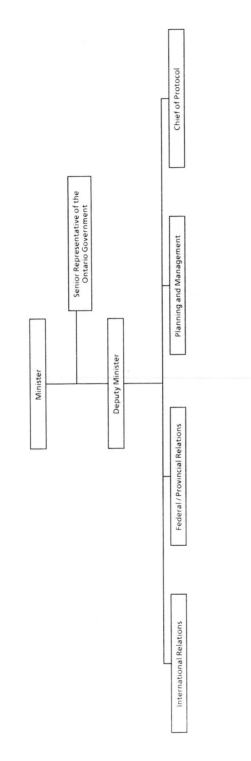

Minister

Senior Representative of the
Ontario Government

Deputy Minister

International Relations

Federal / Provincial Relations

Planning and Management

Chief of Protocol

## PROGRAMS

The activities of the Ministry of Intergovernmental Affairs are designed to provide advice, information, services, and programs to the Premier, the Cabinet, senior personnel of all ministries, all offices of the Government of Ontario outside Canada, and to other jurisdictions for the purpose of ensuring that Ontario's interests are furthered through all external relations. Under the Act that defines the Ministry, and from Cabinet decisions, directives, and expectations of the government, the Ministry has been given the responsibility for Federal-Provincial and Interprovincial Relations, International Relations, Protocol Services, and Information Services.

*Federal-Provincial and Interprovincial Relations:* Includes developing government policy on constitutional and institutional reform and intergovernmental procedures; monitoring federal government policy; assisting ministries in the conduct of their federal-provincial relations and negotiations; managing Ontario's participation in major intergovernmental forums (i.e. First Ministers' and Premiers' Conferences); monitoring and analyzing intergovernmental implications of major sectoral issues; reviewing and analyzing major federal studies for their impact on Ontario (e.g. MacDonald Commission, Nielsen Task Force); and identifying intergovernmental implications of social and political indicators.

The Federal-Provincial and Interprovincial Relations Branch is also responsible for assisting ministries in the conduct of interprovincial relations and negotiations, monitoring the overall policies of the Quebec Government and the general mood of Quebec, managing Ontario corporate offices in Ottawa and Quebec City, and coordinating the activities of the Ontario-Quebec Permanent Commission.

*International Relations:* Includes maintaining links with the federal Department of External Affairs, in order to inform them of Ontario's interests and activities abroad and of international travel by ministers and senior personnel; informing the Ontario Government and its ministries about Canadian foreign policy; assisting ministries in their involvement with External Affairs; monitoring international events likely to impact on Ontario; monitoring overall activities of the U.S. Government; and advising on trans-border issues likely to affect Ontario. The International Relations Branch is also responsible for nominating Ontario representatives to be part of Canadian delegations at international meetings, briefing the Premier and Ministers on travel abroad and on important visitors to Ontario, managing Ontario's participation in disaster relief activities, and taking a leading role in setting goals, objectives, and priorities of Ontario Houses and Government of Ontario offices abroad (a MIGA officer acts as a policy advisor to Agents General).

*Protocol Services:* Provides operational, management, and advisory services in the organization of visits of dignitaries, ceremonials, and public events, government conferences and hospitality functions; supplies information and advice on the correct usage of state symbols, etiquette, and protocol; makes resources available to organizations hosting national or international events in Ontario; maintains liaison with representatives of foreign governments in Ontario; and manages Ontario's participation in royal visits.

*Information Services:* Provides general publications and programs to the Minister, and coordinates media services on major intergovernmental events on behalf of the government.

In addition to broad advisory, information, and service functions, the Ministry of Intergovernmental Affairs has several specific program responsibilities allocated to it by the Government of Ontario. These involve coordinating and managing the corporate intergovernment agenda, including the preparation of briefing materials for First Ministers' and Premiers' Conferences; analyzing and preparing policy and program proposals in all areas involving Ontario's broad corporate intergovernmental relations and concerns; providing annual review of Ontario's federal-provincial and international relations; coordinating the participation by the Government of Ontario and its individual ministries in the exchange programs of the Ontario-Quebec Permanent Commission; directing and managing the programs and activities in Ontario Houses abroad; assisting individual ministries in the conduct of their relations with other jurisdictions; managing Ontario's assistance to the Canadian Intergovernmental Conference Secretariat and the Institute of Intergovernmental Relations; supporting and coordinating activities related to the twinning relationship between the Province of Ontario and the Province of Jiangsu, China; and providing government and government-assisted hospitality.

## EXPENDITURE ESTIMATES

*Estimated Expenditures 1987–88:*

| | |
|---|---|
| Ministry Administration | $1,555,300 |
| Intergovernmental Relations | 5,915,800 |
| *including federal-provincial relations, international relations, protocol services* | |
| **Ministry total:** | **$7,471,100** |

## AGENCIES, BOARDS, AND COMMISSIONS

The following advisory agencies report to the Legislative Assembly through the Ministry of Intergovernmental Affairs' Awards and Medals Secretariat in the Office of Protocol:

1. *Advisory Council to the Order of Ontario*
2. *Advisory Council to the Ontario Medal for Good Citizenship*
3. *Advisory Council to the Ontario Medal for Firefighter Bravery*

4. *Advisory Council to the Ontario Medal for Police Bravery.*

In each case, it is the purpose of the Council to select nominees who, in its opinion, have the greatest merit for each award.

5. *Ontario-Quebec Permanent Commission* (OQPC):Promotes cultural and educational exchanges between governments, individuals, groups, schools, and organizations in Ontario and Quebec to foster understanding and cooperation between residents of the two provinces. The OQPC does not fund or operate programs directly, but encourages Ontario and Quebec ministries responsible for such areas as education and cultural affairs to provide joint program funding and grants. It also coordinates exchanges between Ontario and Quebec civil servants to permit sharing of views and experiences on common problems of public administration.

## LEGISLATION

The only legislation administered by the Ministry of Intergovernmental Affairs is the Act that created the Ministry.

*The Ministry of Intergovernmental Affairs Act, (1980):* Defines intergovernmental affairs as "any relationship between the Government of Ontario and Government of Canada or a minister, agency, or official thereof, the government of another province or territory of Canada or any minister, agency,or official thereof, or the government of a foreign country or state of any agency thereof" (section 1b).

The Act sets out the responsibilities of the Minister as "making recommendations to the Executive Council on the programs and activities of the Government of Ontario and its agencies in relation to federal-provincial, interprovincial and international affairs" (section 5).

## INNOVATIONS

The following innovations have had a positive impact on the Ministry's operations:

*Management Improvement Project:* Innovative use of the Minister's staff to develop various management improvement initiatives and policies has resulted in greater understanding among the staff of the Minister's missions; it has contributed toward the creation of a desirable corporate culture; and it has ensured the acceptance and use of the resulting management policies by all staff.

*Application of Computer Technology:* The development of the Ministry's financial management information system was carried out without the input of consultants, systems analysis, or programmers, at a significant saving to the Ministry. The Ministry has developed a small network of microcomputers to produce the financial information needed to manage its programs and operational projects effectively. In the area of wordprocessing, the Ministry had made an investment in wordprocessing equipment to improve the efficiency of producing finished documents. At present all support staff and 25 percent of the professional staff have access to the equipment.

*Support Services:* Although the Ministry of Intergovernmental Affairs is a separate legal entity, in an effort to control costs and increase efficiency, it continues to participate in the sharing of most administrative services with the Ministry of Treasury and Economics, which provides routine services such as finance, audit, and purchasing.

*Human Resource Development:* The relatively small size of the Ministry of Intergovernmental Affairs has allowed for a management development program, through assistance in career planning, the opportunity to gain first-hand experience in a wide range of activities, and secondment to other ministries.

# MINISTRY OF REVENUE

## ROLES AND FUNCTIONS

The chief functions of the Ministry of Revenue are to collect taxes by administering the provinces major taxing statutes, to assess real property in order to provide a tax base for Ontario municipalities, to administer a number of income redistribution programs, and to operate the Province of Ontario Savings Office.

## BACKGROUND HISTORY

The Department of Revenue was created in July 1968 when the Revenue Division, the Province of Ontario Savings Office, and the Deputy Provincial Treasurer (Revenue) were separated from the Department of Treasury and Economics. In April 1972, as a result of a general provincial government reorganization following the recommendations of the Committee on Government Productivity, the Department of Revenue was enlarged to include municipal property assessment (transferred from Municipal Affairs) and was renamed the Ministry of Revenue.

The Ministry was reorganized in 1980, as the Tax System Operations and Design Division was created to provide a customer service program through the Tax Payer Services Branch. Further, the Property Assessment Division was created to meet the sophisticated demands of property assessment brought on by a rapidly expanding population.

The Ministry of Revenue was one of the first provincial ministries to be relocated away from the downtown Toronto core. As part of a government initiative to stimulate employment and economic development east of Toronto, the Ministry's head office was moved to Oshawa in 1983. The Minister and Deputy Minister have maintained offices at Queen's Park.

A 1986 reorganization created the Information Technology Division. This division applies new technology in the operations of the Ministry, the programs of which were seen to be highly conducive to computerization, office automation, information/word/data processing, and the electronic transfer of information. The application of technology has provided a coordinated and integrated approach to planning and implementation that stands as a model for the rest of government.

As a result, the Ministry of Revenue has converted its head office in Oshawa into a "showcase" of information technology, where Ministry personnel perform computer demonstrations for visiting public service managers, and operate a technology

MINISTRY OF REVENUE

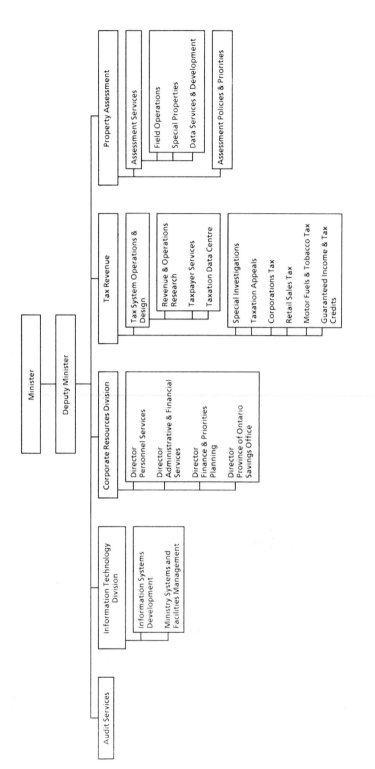

Minister

Deputy Minister

**Audit Services**

**Information Technology Division**
- Information Systems Development
- Ministry Systems and Facilities Management

**Corporate Resources Division**
- Director Personnel Services
- Director Administrative & Financial Services
- Director Finance & Priorities Planning
- Director Province of Ontario Savings Office

**Tax Revenue**
- Tax System Operations & Design
- Revenue & Operations Research
- Taxpayer Services
- Taxation Data Centre
- Special Investigations
- Taxation Appeals
- Corporations Tax
- Retail Sales Tax
- Motor Fuels & Tobacco Tax
- Guaranteed Income & Tax Credits

**Property Assessment**
- Assessment Services
- Field Operations
- Special Properties
- Data Services & Development
- Assessment Policies & Priorities

training centre for the government.

## ORGANIZATION

The Ministry of Revenue is organized into four major divisions (see organization chart):

1. *Corporate Resources Division:* Provides support services to the Ministry and coordinates the Province of Ontario Savings Office.

2. *Information Technology Division:* Coordinates the Ministry's use of information technology.

3. *Property Assessment:* Assesses all real property for the purposes of municipal and school taxation, and undertakes municipal enumeration for voters lists, jury lists, and demographic statistics.

4. *Tax Revenue and Grants Division:* Administers many of the province's tax statutes and coordinates the Ministry's tax grants programs.

The head office of the Ministry of Revenue is located in Oshawa, Ontario. The Ministry also delivers its programs through 78 regional and field offices located throughout Ontario. The Ministry employs approximately 3,900 public servants.

## PROGRAMS

*Municipal Property Assessment:* Operating through 31 regional assessment offices, this program assesses the value of all land and buildings in Ontario. These assessments form the basis of residential, commercial, and school taxes levied by municipalities. The Ministry of Revenue provides property valuations to all municipalities on an annual basis. The municipalities use these figures to collect taxes on their own. The program also conducts a triennial municipal enumeration, to determine voter and jury lists, and school support.

*Province of Ontario Savings Office* (POSO): Established in 1921 to provide loans to farmers, POSO is a savings office that functions much like a bank. POSO operates 21 branches in 15 Ontario communities, many of which are still in rural farming areas, and provides banking services to the public. Deposits received by POSO from the public are held in individual accounts, which pay competitive interest rates, with free-chequing privileges. Other financial services such as safety deposit boxes, traveller's cheques, money orders, and the purchase and sale of securities are available. POSO no longer grants loans. Locations of POSO offices include:

| | | | | |
|---|---|---|---|---|
| Aylmer | Hamilton (2) | Owen Sound | St. Catherines | Walkerton |
| Brantford | London | Pembroke | St. Mary's | Windsor |
| Guelph | Ottawa | Seaforth | Toronto (6) | Woodstock |

*Small Business Development Corporations Program:* Encourages private sector venture capital investment in small business in Ontario and provides business and managerial expertise. Individual investors who buy new equity shares in an SBDC receive a grant of 30 percent of their investment (and corporations receive a 30 percent credit against their Ontario corporations income tax) when the investment is in a small business in northern or eastern Ontario. Otherwise the grant or tax credit is 25 percent of the investment.

*Tax Collection:* The Tax Revenue and Grants Division administers many of Ontario's major tax statutes. Taxes are collected through head office in Oshawa and 13 retail sales tax district offices throughout Ontario, and remitted to the Consolidated Revenue Fund. There are ten main tax statutes in the province, with the Retail Sales Tax and the Corporations Tax accounting for most of the revenue. The Ministry of Revenue does not collect provincial income tax. This is done by Revenue Canada on Ontario's behalf through a tax-sharing agreement, with Ontario's share remitted to the Ministry of Treasury and Economics. Other ministries are responsible for the collection of some taxes (e.g. Alcohol Tax--Ministry of Consumers and Commercial Relations). The Ministry of Revenue collects $7 billion a year in taxes, or $20 million a day.

*Tax Grants:* The Tax Revenue and Grants Division also administers:

1. *Guaranteed Annual Income System* (GAINS): Ensures a minimum income for seniors through payments determined from Federal Guaranteed Income Supplement rates.

2. *Ontario Tax Grants for Seniors* (OTG): Provides property and sales tax grants for seniors.

3. *Ontario Tax Credits* (OTC): For sales and property tax, and political contributions, administered through the federal income tax system and claimed by those under 65.

## EXPENDITURE ESTIMATES

*Estimated Expenditures 1987–88*:

| | |
|---|---|
| Ministry Administration | $ 22,308,406 |
| Property Assessment | 89,299,800 |
| Province of Ontario Savings Office | 8,044,000 |
| Tax Grants and Revenue | 616,496,400 |
| **Ministry total:** | **$736,148,606** |

## AGENCIES, BOARDS, AND COMMISSIONS

No agencies, boards, or commissions report to the Legislative Assembly through the Minister of Revenue. It should be noted, however, the Province of Ontario Savings Office (POSO), while a branch of the Ministry, is self-financing, and in this respect operates as a quasi-agency of the Government.

## LEGISLATION

The Ministry of Revenue is responsible for the following Acts:

*Agricultural Development Finance Act:* In 1921, created the Province of Ontario Savings Office, with a mandate to make loans to farmers.

*Assessment Act:* Transferred responsibility for all municipal assessment to the provincial government.

*City of Toronto 1981 Assessment Complaints Act:* All owners of residential properties reassessed in the City of Toronto in 1981 were deemed to have appealed their reassessments.

*Corporations Tax Act:* Corporate income tax and capital tax is levied on every corporation with a permanent office in Ontario.

*Fuel Tax Act:* The tax on diesel fuel is collected from wholesalers.

*Gasoline Tax Act:* Taxes on gasoline and aviation fuel are collected from wholesalers.

*Income Tax Act:* Provincial income tax is levied on Ontario taxpayers.

*Land Transfer Tax Act:* A tax is collected on the sale of real property.

*Mining Tax Act:* A tax is collected on mining operations in Ontario.

*Ministry of Revenue Act:* This statute created the Ministry and enables it to operate.

*Ontario Guaranteed Annual Income Act:* Provides for a guaranteed income for seniors.

*Ontario Pensioners Property Tax Assistance Act:* Provides for property and sales tax grants for seniors.

*Provincial Land Tax Act:* Enables the collection of taxes in unorganized territories in Ontario.

*Race Tracks Tax Act:* A tax is collected on all pari-mutuel bets placed at Ontario race tracks.

*Retail Sales Tax Act:* A tax is collected at the retail level on most goods and services sold in Ontario, as well as on prices of admission.

*Small Business Development Corporations Act:* Encourages investment in Ontario small businesses through grants to small business owners and tax credits to investors.

*Tobacco Tax Act:* Taxes are collected from wholesalers on tobacco, cigarettes, and cigars.

## INNOVATIONS

The following innovations have had a positive impact on the operations of the Ministry of Revenue:

1. The creation of a telephone enquiry centre which answers questions from across the Province, in eighteen languages.

2. The establishment of a walk-in tax enquiry centre at Queen's Park, Toronto. Tax payments may also be made at this office.

3. The creation of a tax banking arrangement, where tax payments can be made at chartered banks.

4. A continuing and significant program of tax simplification and deregulation. Highlights include the abolition of several out-dated tax statutes; the streamlining of tax payment and refund processes; and a significant expansion of the public enquiry function, both at head office and at field offices.

5. Continued and new major investment in new technology and high-speed electronic processing to improve efficiency, turn-around times, etc. These have significant implications for improving customer services and generating productivity gains.

6. The consolidation of all revenue tax appeals under one branch to add objectivity and to streamline the process.

7. The creation of a Head Office building in Oshawa specifically designed for present and future needs and conducive to new technology.

# MINISTRY OF TREASURY AND ECONOMICS

## ROLES AND FUNCTIONS

The Ministry of Treasury and Economics recommends fiscal, economic, and regional policies to the government; provides advice to ensure consistency among these policies and other government programs; develops and monitors the provincial Budget; and manages the Province's finances. The Treasurer influences government policy as a member of the Cabinet's Policy and Priorities Board and Management Board, and as chairman of the Cabinet Committee on Economic Policy.

## BACKGROUND HISTORY

Ontario's Treasury Department was established in 1867. The Province's first Treasurer tabled a Budget in that year with projected revenues of $1.8 million and expenditures of $1.3 million. The department had a staff of five plus a one-man audit branch.

Almost immediately, Treasury began what proved to be a long tradition of involvement, direct and indirect, in various government functions and projects, including education (1867–77), the Queen's Printer (1867–1926), the Censor Board (1911–58), the Motion Picture Bureau (1917–34), the Bureau of Archives (1923–33), the Bureau of Statistics and Research (1943–54), the Travel and Publicity Bureau (1944–46), the Athletics Commission (1947–49), the Ontario Racing Commission (1954–71), and the Fuel Board (1955–58).

Notwithstanding these diverse activities, Treasury remained essentially the custodian and manager of the government's finances. Through the decades, the Ontario Government's fiscal framework--cash management, borrowing, tax policy, and revenue structure--became firmly anchored in the department. Borrowing was confined for the most part to specific capital improvements; there was little emphasis on using fiscal policy as a tool for shaping Ontario's growth and development. This attention to financial management was honed during the 1920s and '30s, an era of judicious cost-cutting and reduced spending.

The 1940s and '50s marked the beginning of professionalization in government and a greater awareness of the world beyond Ontario's boundaries. Post-war programs included new financial protection for farmers, increased spending on highways and education, and early moves towards expanded social assistance. By the early 1960s, the Province's first billion-dollar Budget had been tabled.

The late 1960s brought a period of unparalleled economic expansion. Ontario now perceived a need for extensive development that could take place only through government action. Over the next several years, successive Treasurers took the initiative in instituting a broad sweep of innovation and change affecting tax policies, borrowing, provincial-municipal finance, municipal and regional government, federal-provincial relations (notably taxation and revenue sharing), regional planning, education (notably the development of community colleges), transportation (highway development), and health (medicare).

Treasury underwent a series of organizational changes during this period. In 1967, it was set up with two divisions, Finance and Economics, and Revenue, each with a deputy minister. In the following year, the Department of Treasury and Economics was formed, and Revenue became a separate department.

The most sweeping organizational reform occurred in 1972 on the recommendation of the Committee on Government Productivity (COGP). Government departments were redesignated as ministries and, in an effort to improve policy coordination, most ministries were grouped into one or another of three policy fields. As the senior ministry accountable for fiscal and economic policy, Treasury and Economics was not included in any one policy field. It was, however, merged with the Department of Municipal Affairs to become the Ministry of Treasury, Economics and Intergovernmental Affairs, and assumed some functions from the Office of the Provincial Secretary.

In this new organization, Treasury's duties were expanded to cover not only taxation and fiscal matters--other than revenue collection--but also federal, provincial, and municipal relations, and regional planning. Its mandate was carried out by a skilled staff of primarily young economists, urban planners, and other specialists recruited, mainly in the late '60s, to raise the level of professionalism in government administration and modernize its operations.

The world-wide economic slowdown of the mid '70s produced a gradual change in the emphasis of government from that of reform to restraint. In 1978, the Ministry of Treasury, Economics and Intergovernmental Affairs, the municipal functions of which had recently been reassigned to the Ministry of Housing, was split into two ministries--Treasury and Economics, and Intergovernmental Affairs.

The first half of the 1980s was marked by a conscious effort by the Province to achieve a new equilibrium between the private and public sectors. The private sector was seen as the engine of economic development, and government as the facilitator, aiding the economy through the transition into the post-industrial age. Government initiatives affecting the economy took on a new character, with line ministries such as Transportation and Communications, Natural Resources and Industry, Trade and Technology at the forefront in their respective fields, and Treasury and Economics functioning as a policy formulator and coordinator.

In 1987, the Treasurer tabled a Budget projecting revenues of approximately $34 billion and expenditures of approximately $35 billion.

## ORGANIZATION

The Ministry of Treasury and Economics is organized into four major divisions (see organization chart):

1. *The Office of the Budget and Intergovernmental Finance Policy,*
2. *The Office of Economic Policy,*
3. *The Office of the Treasury,* and
4. *Administration.*

### Office of the Budget and Intergovernmental Finance Policy

The Office of the Budget and Intergovernmental Finance Policy provides the Treasurer with analysis, technical support, and policy advice in preparing the Ontario Budget, is responsible for the production of Budget documents, and monitors and reports on Budget performance. It assists the Treasurer in establishing, implementing, and monitoring expenditure priorities, taxation and revenue policies, and the overall Provincial fiscal framework. It also provides the Treasurer with analysis and advice on federal-provincial policy (including Established Programs Financing), provincial-local finance policy (including transfers to local governments), and public- and private-sector pension policy and income support issues. This division is composed of the Fiscal Planning Policy, the Taxation Policy, and the Intergovernmental Finance Policy branches.

*Fiscal Planning Policy:* Responsible for the coordination and preparation of the Province's fiscal plan, which is published annually in the Budget and updated quarterly in Ontario Finances.

*Taxation Policy:* Monitors the Ontario tax system, analyzes alternative tax options, and provides liaison where required with the Ministry of Revenue, which administers Ontario's major tax programs. It also makes recommendations as to the appropriate level and mix of taxation in the Province.

*Intergovernmental Finance Policy:* Responsible for the negotiation of some major federal-provincial financial agreements, such as Established Programs Financing; provides advice to other ministries on appropriate financial terms for federal-provincial cost-sharing agreements; and monitors the general trends in this area. It coordinates the level and distribution of grants to municipalities and school boards and advises on specific grant issues. It also advises on intergovernmental pension and income support issues.

### Office of Economic Policy

The Office of Economic Policy assists the Treasurer in his or her capacity as Minister of Economics. It provides the government with forecasts, research, and advice on issues and events affecting the Ontario economy. It initiates research into macroeconomic policies, intergovernmental economic issues, the design and implementation of sectoral and structural studies of the economy, and the design and

MINISTRY OF TREASURY AND ECONOMICS

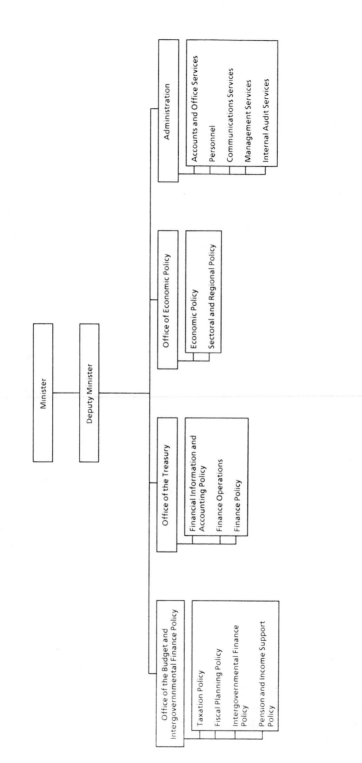

coordination of development policies aimed at enhancing the economy of the province. It also coordinates statistical activities and data dissemination with other government ministries. The division provides briefing, background papers, and statements for the Premier at First Ministers' Conferences on the economy. This division is composed of the Economic Policy and the Sectoral and Regional Policy branches.

*Economic Policy Branch*

The Economic Policy Branch conducts research in the following areas: employment and income stabilization policy; anti-inflation policy; social policy; industrial and business policy; international and inter-provincial trade policy; competition policy; human resources policy; and short- and medium-term economic forecasts.

*Sectoral and Regional Policy Branch*

The Sectoral and Regional Policy Branch provides research, policy options, and support for provincial economic development policy, with particular emphasis on the development of regional and specific sectors of the Ontario economy. It researches policy options in the manufacturing, energy, resource, and transportation sectors. It administers the Community Economic Transformation Agreements (CETA) program. It coordinates negotiations with the federal government and with other Ontario ministries on cost-shared agreements for economic development of the Province; and advises the Province on statistical policy, administers the *Ontario Statistics Act*, and maintains close relations with Statistics Canada. The branch also provides Treasury and other ministries with statistical information and demographic projections for policy development.

**Office of the Treasury**

The Office of the Treasury develops and directs the systems of financial information and control and the accounting policies for the Province; reports to the Legislature, investors, and the public on the Province's financial position; provides recommendations to the Treasurer on the management and direction of the borrowing and investment activities of the Province; and is the custodian and fiscal agent for the securities of the Province and of certain of its agencies.

This division has three branches: Financial Information and Accounting Policy, Finance Management, and Securities.

*Financial Information and Accounting Policy Branch*

The Financial Information and Accounting Policy Branch manages Ontario's requirements in overall government accounting, control, and consolidated public and internal financial reporting. It maintains records of all revenue and expenditure transactions and prepares reports for use by the Treasurer before the Legislature, the public, and the financial community, e.g., *Public Accounts* and the annual *Financial Report*. The branch operates central financial information systems by analyzing and consolidating data on revenues, expenditures, budgets, and forecasts. It provides all ministries and agencies with direction on financial transactions to ensure quality and understanding of accounting and financial management policies; coordinates inter-ministry efforts on in-house systems to ensure compatibility with central financial information systems; and provides expertise on all accounting and financial matters as referred by Management Board and all ministries and agencies. It also provides liaison with the banking community.

*Finance Management Branch*

The Finance Management Branch provides policy recommendations, implementation, and research in public finance to ensure sound strategy and to maintain Ontario's status in capital markets; controls and manages the government's cash flows to ensure that obligations are met without default and that surplus funds are fully invested; provides direction for the Province's centralized financing policy and government debt management requirements, including the issuance and retirement of Ontario debt securities (debentures and treasury bills); and coordinates overall debt policy for the public and non-public financing of the Province, Ontario Hydro, and all boards, commissions, and agencies utilizing the provincial guarantee.

*Securities Branch*

The Securities Branch acts as registrar and transfer agent of the provincial public debt issues, both domestic and foreign. The branch is responsible for the prompt payment of interest on the public debt; supplies investors with information on transfer requirements; and arranges for complete service of debentures from issue to maturity. It also provides support for the programs of the Finance Management Branch in the investments of the Province and holds in safekeeping securities deposited with the Province by the public in accordance with the regulations of provincial legislation.

**Administration**

Administration includes the Administration Division, the Ministry Office, and the Legal Services Branch.

*The Administration Division*

The Administration Division consists of six branches and one program:

1. *Accounts and Offices Services Branch:* Provides a full range of administrative services, including accounting, financial analysis, data processing services, purchasing, accommodation, and records and forms management. The branch coordinates the acquisition and operation of equipment for office automation.

2. *Communications Services Branch:* Informs the public, client groups, and the media about the ministry's activities. It establishes the ministry's communications policy, advises its branches on communications problems, and

provides communications support to the Treasurer and the Deputy. Its activities includes media monitoring and liaison, answering public inquiries, and producing and distributing news releases, statements, and publications.

3. *Internal Audit Services Branch:* Through independent and systematic comprehensive audits, reviews and appraises the ministry's operations and advises senior management on the efficiency, effectiveness, and economy of the financial controls and management practices.

4. *Library Services Branch:* Provides a full range of library services to the Ministry.

5. *Management Services Branch:* Develops, coordinates, and monitors the ministry's system for the allocation and utilization of resources and for its system of managing by results. It monitors the ministry's organization and provides staff to the ministry's chief administration officer. The branch also coordinates the ministry's administrative relationship with Management Board of Cabinet.

6. *Personnel Branch:* Develops and administers human resource management policies and procedures, including classification and compensation levels, recruitment, labour relations, staff development, and employee counseling. It also maintains personnel records and processes payroll data.

7. *Employment Equity Program:* Aims to improve women's participation in staff development opportunities in the Ministry, increase their representation in all occupational groups, and expand the number of women in senior management.

### The Ministry Office

The Ministry Office provides an overall liaison function between the Minister's and Deputy Minister's offices and staff in the ministry. It coordinates the preparation of briefing material for the Treasurer for Cabinet meetings, pre-Budget discussions, and other meetings. It also handles the correspondence for the Treasurer and Deputy. The manager of the Ministry Office reports to the Deputy Treasurer.

### Legal Services Branch

The Legal Services Branch prepares legislation and Orders-in-Council and provides legal interpretation on matters affecting ministry operations. The director of this branch reports to the Deputy Treasurer; the branch is responsible to the Attorney-General's Office.

It should also be noted that the Ministry of Treasury and Economics provides the following administrative services to the Ministry of Intergovernmental Affairs, the Ministry of Energy, and the Niagara Escarpment Commission:

1. Audit Services (Internal Audit);

2. Financial Services (Accounts);

3. Library Services (excluding the Ministry of Energy);

4. Personnel Services; and

5. Supply and Office Services.

The Ministry also provides the above services, with the exception of Personnel Services, to Management Board Secretariat, and the Human Resources Secretariat. Since October, 1985, Personnel Services, Management Services, Financial Services, Supply and Office Services, and Internal Audit Services have been provided to the Office of the Premier and Cabinet Office.

The Ministry of Treasury and Economics is located in Toronto. The Ministry employs approximately 400 public servants.

## PROGRAMS

As a central agency responsible for fiscal and economic policy, the Ministry of Treasury and Economics is not typically involved in the implementation of economic development programs. However, in response to a growing need to assist communities in responding to local economic problems, and based on the Ministry's capacity to coordinate the efforts of a number of supporting ministries, Treasury developed and began administering the *Community Economic Transformation Agreements* (CETA) program following the 1984 Ontario Budget. The program is administered by the Sectoral and Regional Policy Branch in the Office of Economic Policy.

The CETA program was renewed and expanded in the 1986 Budget. It is currently a two-year, $25-million program designed to provide special assistance to communities experiencing substantial economic dislocation. Funding is available for a variety of municipal or private-sector projects that lead to long-term job creation, private-sector investment, and economic diversification. For municipally-sponsored projects, the CETA program will normally provide up to 50 percent of total project costs. For private-sector projects, assistance will take the form of incentive loans, which may include interest subsidies or forgiveness features.

## EXPENDITURE ESTIMATES

*Estimated Expenditures 1987–88*:

| | |
|---|---|
| Ministry Administration | $ 7,553,932 |
| Budget & Intergovernmental Finance Policy | 6,913,200 |
| Economic Policy | 175,231,000 |
| Treasury | 4,158,235,000 |
| *(includes interest on provincial debt, and Public Service Superannuation)* | |
| **Ministry total:** | **$4,347,933,132** |

## AGENCIES, BOARDS, AND COMMISSIONS

The following ABCs report to the Legislative Assembly through the Treasurer and Minister of Economics:

*Ontario Municipal Employees Retirement Board:* Administers the *Ontario Municipal Employees Retirement System Act* (OMERS), which is designed to provide pensions for employees of municipalities and local boards in Ontario. The Board reports to the Treasurer, who is the Minister responsible under the legislation. The Lieutenant Governor in Council appoints the eleven-person Board: eight are members of employees' association; two are members of municipal or local boards; one is a representative of the Province.

*Ontario Municipal Improvement Corporation* (OMIC): Established in 1950, the Corporation purchases debentures from smaller municipalities (under 20,000 population) or school boards on a last-resort basis in the event of their being unable to sell to advantage elsewhere. The Corporation also provides advice to potential borrowers on public markets and the expectations of private investors. OMIC's lending rate varies periodically with market fluctuations; contemporary rates are available on request.

*Stadium Corporation of Ontario Limited:* A Crown Corporation set up in 1984 to arrange financing and construction and to oversee the operation of a retractable-roof, multi-purpose domed stadium. The Corporation's board currently consists of eleven members and two honorary members appointed by the Treasurer, the sole shareholder of the Corporation.

*Teachers' Superannuation Commission:* Provides pensions under the *Teachers' Superannuation Act, 1983* for teachers in elementary and secondary schools who hold a valid Ontario Certificate. These pensions are provided upon retirement or early retirement. The Commission is composed of five persons appointed by the Treasurer and five persons elected by teachers' organizations. As of April 1, 1984, the Treasurer assumed responsibility for administration of the Act. Contact is coordinated through the Intergovernmental Finance Policy Branch of the Ministry of Treasury and Economics.

## LEGISLATION

The Ministry of Treasury and Economics is responsible for the following Acts:

*Audit Act:* Establishes the Office of the Provincial Auditor and prescribes his or her powers and duties.

*Farm Loans Act:* Authorizes the formation of farm loan associations. The purpose of the associations is to promote individual prosperity and agricultural development by securing for their members short-term loans for current expenditures.

*Farm Loans Adjustment Act:* Allows a person who has received a loan under the Farm Loans Act to apply to a judge to obtain a reduction in the amount of the principal or interest of the loan or an extension of time for payment of the loan.

*Financial Administration Act:* Concerns the management of public money and the Consolidated Revenue Fund, the disbursement of public money, and the issue of securities by the Province of Ontario.

*Ministry of Treasury and Economics Act:* Establishes and continues the Ministry of Treasury and Economics and prescribes the powers and duties of the Treasurer of Ontario.

*Ontario Loan Act:* Authorizes, on an annual basis, the borrowing of monies for the Consolidated Revenue Fund.

*Ontario Municipal Employees Retirement System Act:* Establishes the Ontario Municipal Employees Retirement Fund and provides for the payment of pension benefits to members of the Fund and their widows, widowers, and children, in accordance with regulations made under the Act.

*Ontario Municipal Improvement Corporation Act:* Continues the Ontario Municipal Improvement Corporation and authorizes the corporation to purchase from municipalities debentures issued for specified municipal purposes.

*Public Sector Prices and Compensation Review Act, 1983:* Provides for the assessment and review of compensation and prices in the public sector of Ontario's economy and for an orderly transition to the resumption in the public sector of full collective bargaining following the final year in which increases in compensation were controlled by the *Inflation Restraint Act, 1982.*

*Statistics Act:* Authorizes the collection of statistical information by the Government of Ontario and allows the Government of Ontario to enter into agreements with the federal government and other provincial governments providing for the exchange or joint collection of statistical information.

*Supply Act:* Authorizes payment out of the Consolidated Revenue Fund of the charges and expenses of the public service for a particular fiscal year, or portion thereof, and ensures that the sums are applied in accordance with the votes and items of the estimates and supplementary estimates.

*Teachers' Superannuation Act, 1983:* Continues the Teachers' Superannuation Commission and Teachers' Superannuation Fund and provides for the payment of pension benefits to teachers.

## INNOVATIONS

The Office of the Treasury has been challenged to create new ways of adapting to modern market forces. During the past decade, for example, high inflation and real interest rates have produced dynamic changes in the functioning of capital and money markets. The Province has made extensive use of internally designed computer modelling and systems in its cash management and investment operations to stay on the leading edge of technological advances in this area. Software programs are utilized to help assess the suitability of investment alternatives, to forecast both monthly and daily cash requirements, and to provide trading and market intelligence quickly and regularly to Treasury's trading and management staffs.

The Office of Economic Policy was among the first in government to adopt new office automation hardware and software. Extensive use is now made of microcomputers for an array of econometric modelling exercises. The Office has also vastly increased its monitoring of the U.S. economy in response to the increasing dependence of the Ontario economy on the U.S. economy and U.S. economic policy. The Office of Economic Policy has also been involved in developing and utilizing new sources of economic and social data. A number of in-house data bases have been compiled and a complex automated system of input, storage, and retrieval has been established to handle these data, as well as information from traditional sources such as Statistics Canada. These data are used extensively by Treasury staff, as well as by other ministries, in analyzing Ontario's economy and in developing economic policy at both the macro and micro levels.

The Office of the Budget and Intergovernmental Finance Policy has also utilized innovations in the "high tech" area in order to refine policy analysis. For example, as the tax system has expanded in both scope and complexity, tax policy analysis has evolved.

Complex simulation and modelling techniques, first developed internally during the early '70s, were initially used only in such areas as personal income taxation, and income security, due to their high costs, data limitations, and the specialized computer skills they entailed. Today, personal computers and a broad range of off-the-shelf software provide the basis for low-cost tax data management and modelling and forecasting capabilities in virtually all tax fields.

## PUBLICATIONS PRODUCED BY TREASURY AND ECONOMICS

*Census Data:* Parts I and II produced by Statistics Section of Sectoral and Regional Policy Branch as census data becomes available from Statistics Canada. Circulation in 1987: 1,000 of each volume.

*Demographic Bulletin:* Produced intermittently (about three times a year) by Sectoral and Regional Policy Branch. Available (free) at Ontario Government Bookstores. Current circulation (approx.): 1,000.

*Ontario Budget:* Produced annually by Office of the Budget. Circulation in 1987 (approx.): English, 25,000; French, 5,000.

*Ontario Budget Highlights:* Produced annually by Office of the Budget. Circulation in 1987 (approx.): English, 30,000; French, 5,000.

*Ontario Budget Paper(s):* Produced annually by Office of the Budget (two were produced in 1986). Circulation in 1987 for each volume (approx.): English, 20,000; French, 5,000.

*Ontario Economic Accounts:* Produced quarterly by Economic Policy Branch. Distributed (free) by the Economic Policy Branch to Ontario ministries as well as to selected libraries, federal government departments, universities, chartered banks, and several industry associations. Current circulation (approx.): 200.

*Ontario Finances:* Produced quarterly by Fiscal Planning Policy Branch. Projected 1987 circulation: English, 3,500; French, 500.

*Ontario Financial Report:* Produced annually (August) by the Office of the Treasury. 1987 circulation: English, 4,000; French, 1,500.

*Ontario Statistics:* Produced every two years by the Sectoral and Regional Policy Branch. Available to the public at Ontario Government Bookstores. Complimentary copies are distributed to the Ministry, libraries, and high schools. Projected 1987 circulation: English, 3,500; French, 1,500.

*Public Accounts--Three Volumes:* Produced annually by Financial Information and Accounting Policy Branch. Projected 1987 circulation for each volume: English 2,400; French, 1,200.

# OFFICE OF FRANCOPHONE AFFAIRS

## ROLES AND FUNCTIONS

The mandate of the Office of Francophone Affairs is to provide the Minister Responsible for Francophone Affairs with the support and resources necessary to fulfill the responsibilities conferred on the Minister by the *French Language Services Act*; to advise the government, its ministries, and agencies on matters concerning the francophone population and the provision of French language services by developing appropriate policies and formulating appropriate programs; to coordinate, monitor, and oversee the implementation of government programs concerning French language services and make recommendations concerning their financing; to ensure the dissemination of government policies and decisions concerning French language services; and to maintain ties with the francophone community and encourage its development.

## BACKGROUND HISTORY

Ontario's French language services policy was first enunciated by Premier John Robarts in 1968. It was a commitment to make the government's services available in French in areas of the province with a large concentration of French-speaking Ontarians.

In 1970, the Office of the Coordinator of Bilingualism was established with a mandate to promote the development of government French language services to serve the needs of the Franco-Ontarian population. The Secretary to Management Board and Co-President of the Ontario-Quebec Permanent Commission became the first Coordinator.

In September 1974, Cabinet approved the creation of an "Advisory Council on Franco-Ontarian Affairs," whose mandate would be to advise the Minister of Colleges and Universities on educational matters, specifically on post-secondary education. The Council for Franco-Ontarian Affairs was established as an Advisory Committee under an Order-in-Council dated January 22, 1975, pursuant to the provisions of the Ministry of Culture and Recreation Act, 1974.

In 1975, the Government of Ontario agreed to expand the Council's mandate, giving it responsibility for advising the Minister of Culture and Recreation on any subject related to the Franco-Ontarian community. Three years later, on February 1,

1978, the Order-in-Council was amended in order to change the name of the advisory committee to Conseil des Affaires franco-ontariennes (CAFO). By that time, the Council's responsibility was extended to include all Government of Ontario ministries if and when each asked for advice.

In 1977, an Assistant Deputy Minister within the then Ministry of Treasury, Economics and Intergovernmental Affairs, assumed the responsibilities of Coordinator. His title was changed to Government Coordinator of French Language Services, and the office was appropriately renamed the Office of the Government Coordinator of French Language Services. At the same time the mandate of the Office was redefined to include the coordination of the development and the implementation of the government's French language services policy.

In 1978, the Provincial Secretary for Resources Development, became the first Minister explicitly named as responsible for French language services. The Office of the Government Coordinator of French Language Services was transferred to the Ministry of Intergovernmental Affairs in 1978, when that Ministry was created and the position of Government Coordinator of French Language Services continued to be filled by the same senior official in addition to his appointment as Deputy Minister of Intergovernmental Affairs.

In March 1979, Cabinet approved a recommendation that allowed the Conseil des Affaires franco-ontariennes to act on its own initiative, without waiting to be called on for advice. It could now, according to its own judgement and requirements, provide the Government with its observations, analyses, and criticisms relating to all matters under the jurisdiction of a ministry or government agency and of interest to Franco-Ontarians.

By 1981, the heavy and diversified area of education was officially entrusted to the Council for Franco-Ontarian Education (CAFO). CAFO could now devote its entire attention to all other areas of concern to the Franco-Ontarian community. These included arts and culture, telecommunications, human resources planning, literacy, youth and women's issues, business, health and social services, and sports and physical activity. Also, in 1981, the administration and control of the Council was transferred from the then Ministry of Culture and Recreation to the Ministry of Intergovernmental Affairs.

In 1982, following an in-depth review of French language services within the Government of Ontario, it was recommended that the Office of the Government Coordinator be strengthened and provided with more staff. A position of Deputy Coordinator was created in 1983 to provide day-to-day direction to the Office. Two sections were established within the Office, a Corporate Programs and Community Liaison section and a Projects section, later renamed Research and Inter-Ministry Relations section.

In December 1983, the position of Government Coordinator of French Language Services was assumed by an official of the Cabinet Secretariat, who was also Secretary to the Policy and Priorities Board of Cabinet.

In February 1985, the Council was transferred from the Ministry of Intergovernmental Affairs to the Ministry of Health. The Minister of Health, became the

Minister responsible for French-Language Services. At that time, the Coordinator left his position with the Policy and Priorities Board to assume the full-time role of Government Coordinator in the Ministry of Health, where he was assistant deputy minister.

In May 1985, the government made possible an administrative reorganization whereby CAFO was attached directly to Cabinet Office. It remained, nonetheless, under the authority of the Minister Responsible for Francophone Affairs. At the same time, the Office of the Government Coordinator of French Language Services came under the administration of Cabinet Office. In June 1985, the Office was renamed the Office of Francophone Affairs, and the Government Coordinator became the Associate Secretary of Cabinet for Francophone Affairs.

Also in June 1985, following the change in government, the appointment as the Minister Responsible for Francophone Affairs was assigned to the Minister of Municipal Affairs, and an Executive Director of the Office of Francophone Affairs was appointed. In September 1987, when the incumbent minister was transferred to the Ministry of Revenue, he retained the appointment of Minister Responsible for Francophone Affairs.

In May 1986, the Government tabled the *French Language Services Bill,* which received Royal Assent on November 18, 1986. The Act stipulated the functions of the Office of Francophone Affairs as set out above. Also, as a result of this Act, CAFO was abolished in December 1986.

Under the Act, the Office of Francophone Affairs was re-organized. A new Ministry Services section was created to advise and assist ministries on the implementation of their French language services according to the Act. The section, Corporate Programs and Community Liaison, became Communications and Community Relations, and the third section, Research and Inter-ministry Relations, became Research and Policy.

## ORGANIZATION

The Office of Francophone Affairs is administratively attached to Cabinet Office. The Office comprises three branches: Communications and Community Relations, Ministry Services, and Research and Policy. (See the Cabinet Office Organizational Chart in Part One.)

## PROGRAMS

### Communications and Community Relations Branch

The Communications and Community Relations Branch:

1. Provides internal and external communications services for the activities of the Minister and the Office;

2. Coordinates the preparation, and distribution of documents and reports of the Minister, and the Office;

3. Informs, advises, and assists communications branches in other ministries;

4. Maintains liaison with the English and French language media;

5. Maintains close contacts with francophone community organizations;

6. Administers the *Community Support Fund* which assists in the development and improvement of community services and activities aimed at the province's francophone population in accordance with the priorities of the Government of Ontario. The objectives of the program are to increase the number of services available, to improve the quality of existing services, and to meet specific needs of the francophone population. A committee of representatives from several ministries recommends to the Minister the allocation of available grants, through the Office of Francophone Affairs.

7. Ensures the adequate distribution of government information in French, directly or in cooperation with ministries. The goal of the *Renseignements Ontario* program is to facilitate contact between Ontario's francophone residents and the provincial government. A toll-free telephone service has been set up for this purpose. The main objectives of the program are to provide information in French on government programs to Ontario's francophone population and to maintain a high level of quality of information regarding government programs. In addition, *Renseignements Ontario* participates in numerous meetings, conferences, and exhibits throughout the province to offer information directly to the francophone community.

### Ministry Services Branch

The Ministry Services Branch:

1. Advises and aids ministries, agencies, and commissions to implement French language services according to the Act;

2. Evaluates ministries' implementation programs, and makes recommendations on financing and on time frames for implementation;

3. Coordinates with the senior management committees of ministries, their finance and personnel branches, Management Board, and other central agencies the full range of government activities related to the implementation of services;

4. Prepares criteria for the designation of public service agencies and evaluates proposals for designation; and

5. Prepares the implementation reports required of the Office by the French Language Services Commission.

## Research and Policy Branch

The Research and Policy Branch:

1. Performs research projects related to the activities of the Office;

2. Identifies and develops policies to be adopted concerning the provision of services to francophones;

3. Ensures policy liaison with Cabinet committees, and the policy branches of other ministries;

4. Prepares reports on policy for the French Language Services Commission;

5. Analyzes and evaluates acts, policies, and government programs to ensure that they meet the needs of francophones;

6. Supports the Minister Responsible for Francophone Affairs in his activities in the Legislature Assembly and in Cabinet;

7. Supports the Minister and the Executive Director in their activities with other governments;

8. Receives complaints addressed to the Minister and assures their analysis and resolution; and

9. Maintains adequate documentation concerning francophone affairs.

## EXPENDITURE ESTIMATES

*Estimated Expenditures 1987–88*:

Office of Francophone Affairs            $3,475,600
*Note: This amount is included in the Estimates
of Cabinet Office.*

## AGENCIES, BOARDS, AND COMMISSIONS

*The Ontario French-Language Services Commission* was established under article 15 of the French-Language Services Act, 1986. Its mandate is to review the availability and quality of French language services and make recommendations for their improvement; recommend the designation of public service agencies and the addition of designated areas to the Schedule; require non-profit corporations and similar entities, facilities, homes, and colleges referred to in the definition of "government agency" to furnish to the Commission information that may be relevant in the formulation of recommendations respecting their designation as public service agencies; recommend changes in the plans of government agencies for the provision of French-Language services and make the plans and recommendations public; make recommendations in respect of an exemption or proposed exemption of services and make the recommendations public; and perform any other function assigned by the Minister responsible for Francophone Affairs, the Executive Council, or the Legislative Assembly. The functions of the Chairman of the Commission are to liaise with the Minister Responsible for Francophone Affairs, the Office of Francophone Affairs, and the francophone community; to ensure that at the close of each fiscal year the report of the Commission is submitted to the Speaker of the Legislative Assembly; to determine the agenda for the meetings of the Commission, to chair them, and to ensure the recommendations made therein are transmitted to the appropriate interested parties; and to ensure that the mandate of the Commission is carried out in an effective and timely manner.

## LEGISLATION

The Office of Francophone Affairs is responsible for:

*French Language Services Act, 1986:* The Act gives any person the right to receive services from and communicate with the Government of Ontario in French in designated areas of the province where large numbers of French-speaking residents live. This right also applies to corporate entities, in addition to individuals. The Act includes a three-year period before the legal guarantees come into effect. The Act establishes that the Office of Francophone Affairs is responsible for the administration of the functions of the Minister responsible for Francophone Affairs, as defined under the Act. The Act also establishes the Ontario French Language Services Commission. The Commission is responsible to the Minister responsible for Francophone Affairs. Upon the dissolution of the Commission, three years after its creation, its functions shall be performed by the Office of Francophone Affairs. The senior official of the Office of Francophone Affairs, is a member of the Ontario French Language Services Commission by virtue of the Office, but does not have a vote.

## INNOVATIONS

The major innovation of the Office is the adoption of the *French Language Services Act, 1986,* which gives a legislative framework to the provision of delivery of French language services. An implementation procedure manual has been distributed by the office to all managers in the government. Guidelines and directives will be issued by the Office as required during the implementation phase.

# ONTARIO NATIVE AFFAIRS DIRECTORATE

## INTRODUCTION

The Ontario Native Affairs Directorate is a small, central agency of the Ontario government. It carries out the mandate of the Minister Responsible for Native Affairs. Currently, this portfolio is assigned as an additional responsibility of the Minister who is Attorney General, but the Native Affairs Directorate is a distinct and separate agency from the Ministry of the Attorney General. The Minister Responsible for Native Affairs is Ontario's representative on the Tripartite Council. The Ontario Native Affairs Directorate coordinates and manages the province's participation on the Tripartite Council.

The Office employs approximately 15 public servants.

## BACKGROUND HISTORY

The history of the current Directorate dates to 1976. Prior to that date, Ontario provided programs and services to native peoples in the province in a decentralized manner. These programs were developed and delivered by as many as a dozen major ministries. It became apparent that proper coordination of Native programs was essential.

In 1976, a Minister without Portfolio was assigned the responsibility for the coordination of policy development for Native Affairs and the coordination of communications between the Government of Ontario and Native organizations. The Minister's new responsibilities were assigned by Order in Council.

Initially, the Minister was supported by a single policy advisor and an advisory committee, made up of the senior official in each policy field and the ministries with major responsibilities, programs, and services, affecting the lives of Native people. In 1977, when the Minister was appointed Provincial Secretary for Resources Development, he retained his Native Affairs responsibilities.

The *Ontario Tripartite Council* was set up in 1978 to address issues of common concern to the Federal Government, the Government of Ontario, and the representatives of Status Indian associations in Ontario. The three parties on the council are assisted by the Indian Commission of Ontario. When requested, it acts as a mediator to help the three council parties examine and resolve any issues of common concern.

In 1979, it was felt that many of the Native Affairs issues identified for response by the Ontario government, or line Ministries, required consideration by Cabinet. As a result, the Cabinet Committee on Native Affairs (CCNA) was established, with the Provincial Secretary for Resources Development as chairman. CCNA is made up of the Cabinet members whose ministries are responsible for major programs and policies affecting Native people. The committee serves as a forum for discussion and review of Native Affairs issues and initiatives with government-wide implications. It meets every two weeks. Native delegations often meet with CCNA to discuss matters of concern to their members.

The following Ministers make up the CCNA: the Minister Responsible for Native Affairs (Chairman); the Solicitor General; the Ministers of Correctional Services; Citizenship; Colleges and Universities; Community and Social Services; Culture and Communications; Education; Health; Housing; Natural Resources; Northern Development and Mines; Skills Development; and Tourism and Recreation. Other Ministers are invited to CCNA to consider specific Native Affairs issues related to their responsibilities.

In 1981, corporate responsibilities for Native Affairs were assigned to the new Provincial Secretary for Resources Development. The mandate was expanded to include the development of government-wide Native Affairs policy and the staff resources were increased. Six new positions were added to the Native Affairs area in 1981, but the office did not have an official name. Some of the work carried out by the Office included negotiations with the Islington and Grassy Narrows Indian Bands and management of Ontario's participation on the Ontario Tripartite Council. The Directorate still did not have an official name, but was called "the office of native affairs".

In June 1985, when the Liberal government was elected, the Attorney General was appointed Minister Responsible for Native Affairs, and the staff of the ad hoc office was transferred to his direction. The Minister's responsibilities were defined by an Order-in-Council on July 1985, which reads as follows:

"The Attorney General shall be designated as the Minister responsible for Native Affairs. The responsibilities of the Minister related to Native Affairs shall be defined as follows:

1. To develop Ontario corporate policy;

2. To coordinate policy development, program delivery, and special corporate projects among ministries;

3. To coordinate corporate communications, negotiations, including tripartite negotiations, and mediation processes with Native organizations, Indian Bands, Federal and other Provincial Governments, and personal and corporate entities;

4. And to monitor line Ministry policy development and program delivery."

As of 1986, the mandate of the Minister was augmented, through Cabinet Minutes, to include negotiation of Native issues including land claims, aboriginal constitutional matters, and aboriginal self-government agreements. On January 1, 1987, the staff agency officially became the Ontario Native Affairs Directorate. Its role is to carry out the mandate of the Minister Responsible for Native Affairs. The Directorate now has a total staff of 13, including support staff. Similarly, the mandate of the Directorate and its predecessor has developed according to the evolution of the mandate of the Minister Responsible for Native Affairs.

Within the Government, the staff of the various line ministries are kept informed through the *Interministerial Committee on Native Affairs,* which is a forum in which staff with major responsibilities affecting Native people identify, discuss, and clarify Native Affairs issues, to be addressed by the Cabinet Committee on Native Affairs, or by the senior management of individual Ministries. The interministerial Committee regularly receives presentations from Native and non-native organizations on specific Native issues.

## EXPENDITURE ESTIMATES

*Estimated Expenditures 1987–88*:

Ontario Native Affairs Directorate     $4,379,800

# OFFICE RESPONSIBLE FOR WOMEN'S ISSUES
## (ONTARIO WOMEN'S DIRECTORATE)

### ROLES AND FUNCTIONS

The Ontario Women's Directorate fosters the economic, social, and legal equality of women in Ontario. Policy staff within the Ontario Women's Directorate (OWD) work with their counterparts in other ministries and agencies to identify gaps in existing programs, to point out policies and practices which may inadvertently disadvantage women, and to develop programs which actively assist women in achieving economic, social, and legal equality. Recommendations are made by directorate staff through the Minister Responsible for Women's Issues. In addition, the Minister, as a member of key Cabinet committees, brings forward views and recommendations affecting women.

The Women's Directorate also maintains links with the Ontario Advisory Council on Women's Issues, women's organizations, and individual women on a variety of issues.

The *goals* of the Directorate are: to advise the Ontario Government on women's issues; to coordinate the development of provincial policies in employment equity for women, pay equity, and wife assault; and to foster the development and delivery of programs and services to benefit women through partnerships with business, labour, government and community. In order to further these goals, the Directorate informs and educates internal and external audiences on women's issues; monitors and comments on public and private sector progress in achieving equality for Ontario women on key strategic issues; and strives to achieve greater support for programs and policies fostering the equality of Ontario women in Ontario.

### BACKGROUND HISTORY

The first Ontario Minister Responsible for Women's Issues was appointed in May 1983. In June 1983, the Ontario Women's Directorate was established as a central agency to coordinate the development, delivery, and communication of programs and policies to enhance equal opportunity for women in Ontario. It incorporated the Women's Bureau, which had been established in 1963 to deal with women in the labour force outside the provincial government, and the Women

Crown Employees Office, which was created in 1974 to coordinate affirmative action initiatives for the Ontario Public Service.

## ORGANIZATION

The Ontario Women's Directorate, with a staff of approximately 50 public servants, is located in Toronto. It is structured into four major branches:

1. *Consultative Services Branch:* Provides a consulting service to the public.
2. *Policy and Research Branch:* Engages in research and analysis of women's issues.
3. *Program Development Branch:* Responsible for developing women's issue programs.
4. *Public Education Programs and Services Branch:* Responsible for delivering OWD programs to the public.

In addition, the Ontario Advisory Council on Women's Issues reports to the Legislative Assembly through the Minister Responsible for Women's Issues.

## PROGRAMS

*Policy and Research Branch:* Analyzes and monitors existing and proposed legislation, policies, and programs for their impact on women. This branch coordinates the Ontario Government's response to specific problems facing victims of family violence; develops and coordinates policies which will enhance the status of women; and maintains a liaison with line ministries and central agencies to focus and coordinate the government's efforts to identify gaps in policies which may discriminate against women. This branch also provides comprehensive research and data as required for the Directorate, monitors developments in Ontario and other jurisdictions, and prepares policy material for use at federal-provincial forums.

*Public Education Programs and Services Branch:* Communicates the programs, policies, and issues of OWD to the public, governments, business, labour, and women; provides a communications consulting service to the Minister, Assistant Deputy Minister, and the Directorate; and develops and manages public education programs on women's issues in general, and about pay equity, employment equity, and family violence in particular. This branch also develops and manages programs to identify emerging strategic issues requiring action on the part of the OWD, and provides education services, including a public inquiries service, regional exhibitions, and special projects.

*Program Development Branch:* Develops program and project initiatives relating specifically to women's issues, and coordinates and administers the Community Grants Program which funds projects by community groups, and other appropriate bodies.

*Consultative Services Branch:* Provides consulting services to public and private sector organizations and institutions on the subject of employment equity, increases employer awareness of Employment Equity, and provides leadership and motivation to implement Employment Equity programs. This branch also recommends programs, initiatives, and policies to develop and ensure responsiveness to government policy on women's issues.

## EXPENDITURE ESTIMATES

*Estimated Expenditures 1987–88*:

| | |
|---|---|
| Ontario Women's Directorate | $17,495,800 |
| Ontario Advisory Council on | |
| Women's Issues | 447,000 |
| **Office total:** | **$17,942,800** |

## AGENCIES, BOARDS, AND COMMISSIONS

*Ontario Advisory Council on Women's Issues:* The Council advises the Ontario government on matters pertaining to the status of women in Ontario. Appointed by Order in Council, the Council has sixteen members. The Council evaluates and monitors existing legislation, policies, and programs related to the needs and status of women. It identifies specific areas requiring government attention; recommends legislation and program changes; consults with public groups in regions throughout Ontario; and responds to requests from the Minister for advice and consultation on matters pertaining to women.

# INDEX